ACCESS

CALIFORNIA WINE COUNTRY

D0049946

ORIENTATION

Many people, even some San Franciscans, don't realize how close the wine country is to the City by the Bay. The town of **Sonoma**, where California's wine-making history began in the mid-19th century, is only about an hour's drive away, and the entire **Sonoma County** is close enough for an easy day trip. **St. Helena** and the heart of **Napa Valley** are less than 1.5 hours from San Francisco by car, and if the traffic gods smile upon you,

you may make it from one end of the valley to the other in about a half hour. Not that you should—there's so much to see and do along the way. The wine country of **Mendocino** and **Lake Counties** lies farther north—about a 2.5- to 3-hour drive from San Francisco. While you're visiting wineries in Sonoma and Mendocino, take time to explore the nearby coast, which is rugged, sparsely populated, and extraordinarily beautiful.

You'll need a car to visit the wineries; another option is to look into an organized guided bus tour to squire you around (see "Tours" on page 12). Once you're in the wine country, it's easy to get around and almost impossible to get lost, except when searching for small wineries off the beaten track or for those that require an appointment and don't have a sign out front.

When planning a trip, remember that this region, especially Napa Valley, is popular. The best time to visit is during the less crowded off-season (November through May), although it's exciting to see the grape crush (generally in August through October), when the normally serene landscape is animated with grape pickers moving along the vineyard rows, the streets are lined with trucks loaded with grapes, and the scent of fermenting juices suffuses the air. It's almost worth enduring the throngs to feel a part of the wine-making experience.

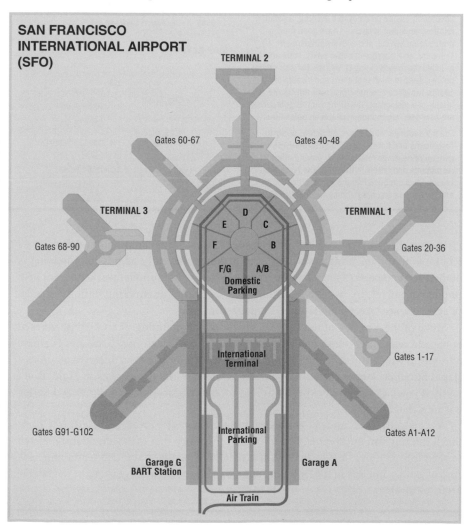

SAN FRANCISCO INTERNATIONAL AIRPORT (SFO)

TERMINAL 2

Gates 60-67

Gates 40-48

TERMINAL 3

Gates 68-90

D
E   C
F   B
F/G   A/B
Domestic Parking

TERMINAL 1

Gates 20-36

International Terminal

Gates 1-17

Gates G91-G102

International Parking

Gates A1-A12

Garage G
BART Station

Garage A

Air Train

How to Read This Guide

Access® California Wine Country is arranged so you can see at a glance where you are and what is around you. The numbers next to the entries in the following chapters correspond to the numbers on the maps. The text is color-coded according to the kind of place described:

Restaurants/Clubs: Red

Hotels: Purple | Shops: Orange

🅟 Outdoors: Green | Sights/Culture: Blue

WHEELCHAIR ACCESSIBILITY

California law mandates wheelchair accessibility in all commercial establishments.

RATING THE RESTAURANTS AND HOTELS

The restaurant ratings take into account the quality, service, atmosphere, and uniqueness of the restaurant. An expensive restaurant doesn't necessarily ensure an enjoyable evening; a small, relatively unknown spot could have good food, professional service, and a lovely atmosphere. Therefore, on a purely subjective basis, stars are used to judge the overall dining value (see the star ratings below). Keep in mind that chefs and owners often change, which sometimes drastically affects the quality of a restaurant. The ratings in this guidebook are based on information available at press time.

The price ratings, as categorized below, apply to restaurants and hotels. These figures describe general price-range relationships among other restaurants and hotels in the area. The restaurant price ratings are based on the average cost of an entrée for one person, excluding tax and tip. Hotel price ratings reflect the base price of a standard room for two people for one night during the peak season.

RESTAURANTS

★	Good
★★	Very Good
★★★	Excellent
★★★★	An Extraordinary Experience
$	The Price Is Right (less than $10)
$$	Reasonable ($10–$15)
$$$	Expensive ($15–$28)
$$$$	Big Bucks ($28 and up)

HOTELS

$	The Price Is Right (less than $100)
$$	Reasonable ($100–$200)
$$$	Expensive ($200–$300)
$$$$	Big Bucks ($300 and up)

MAP KEY

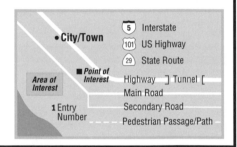

During the peak season and on weekends, most hotels and bed-and-breakfasts require a minimum 2-night stay. Be sure to reserve as early as possible; lodging is limited and can be extremely hard to find on holidays and summer weekends. For help finding vacancies, try using a referral service by calling or checking online (for a list of agencies, see "Accommodations" on page 14).

Much of the pleasure of this type of trip lies in the planning. Start tasting wines at home and read about those you like. Check the winery's web site. Taste and compare one type of wine from different producers within a region and from different counties—**Napa, Sonoma, Mendocino,** and **Lake**—to appreciate the differences in style. Don't worry if you lack the proper vocabulary; even vintners struggle to accurately describe a wine's characteristics.

As you swirl, sniff, and sip your way through the region, travel at a leisurely pace. Smell the fragrant eucalyptus, lavender, and rosemary that grow abundantly. Listen to the birdsong, and take in the colorful palette of plants, mountains, and blue sky. And of course, indulge in the fine wine and gourmet food that have brought worldwide fame to the area.

Area code 707 unless otherwise noted.

Getting to the Wine Country

Airports

The closest airports to the wine country with commercial flights are **San Francisco International Airport (SFO)**, **Oakland International Airport (OAK)**, **San Jose International Airport (SJC)**, and **Sonoma County Airport (OQ3)** in **Santa Rosa**. No commercial flights are available to Mendocino and Lake Counties; both have airports for small private and charter planes only.

San Francisco International Airport (SFO)

SFO, located south of San Francisco (approximately 1.5 hours from Napa and Sonoma Counties and 2.5 to 3 hours from Mendocino and Lake Counties), is the fifth-busiest airport in the US. The airport can be reached from **Highway 101** or **Interstates 280** and **380**, which connect with Highway 101 and the airport exits. Long-term airport parking is available off Highway 101 at the **San Bruno Avenue East** exit. The AirTrain blue line travels between the parking lots and the airport 24 hours a day. The AirTrain red line on the upper level of the airport provides transportation between terminals every 5 minutes between 5:30AM and 1AM.

AIRPORT SERVICES

Web site	www.flysfo.com
Airport Emergencies	650/876.2323
Airport Police	650/821.7111
Business Services	650/877.0421
Currency Exchange	650/877.0264
Customs	650/624.7200
Ground Transportation Information	650/876.2377
Immigration	650/837.2800
Interpreters	lower-level information booths
Lost and Found	650/821.7014
Parking	650/821.7900
Traveler's Aid	650/821.2735
Airport Information and Paging	650/821.8211

AIRLINES

Air Canada	Terminal 1	
888/247.2262	www.aircanada.ca	
Alaska Airlines	Terminal 1	
800/426.0333	www.alaskaair.com	
Alaska Airlines (Mexico Flights)	International	
800/426.0333	www.alaskaair.com	
America West Airlines	Terminal 1	
800/235.9292	www.americawest.com	
American Airlines	Terminal 3	
800/433.7300	www.aa.com	

Continental Airlines	Terminal 1	
800/525.0280	www.continental.com	
Delta Airlines	Terminal 1	
800/221.1212	www.delta.com	
Frontier Airlines	Terminal 1	
800/432.1359	www.flyfrontier.com	
Hawaiian Airlines	Terminal 1	
800/367.5320	www.hawaiianair.com	
Horizon	Terminal 1	
800/547.9308	www.horizonair.com	
Japan Airlines	International	
800/525.3663	www.japanair.com	
KLM Airlines	International	
800/447.4747	www.klm.com	
Korean Air	International	
800/438.5000	www.koreanair.com	
LACSA	International	
800/225.2272	www.grupotaca.com	
Lufthansa	International	
800/645.3880	www.lufthansa.com	
Mexicana	International	
800/531.7921	www.mexicana.com	
Midwest Express	Terminal 1	
800/452.2022	www.midwestexpress.com	
Northwest (domestic)	Terminal 1	
800/225.2525	www.nwa.com	
United Airlines (domestic)	Terminal 3	
800/241.6522	www.ual.com	
United Airlines (international)	International	
800/241.6522	www.ual.com	
United Express	Terminal 3	
800/241.6522	www.ual.com	
US Airways	Terminal 1	
800/428.4322	www.usairways.com	
Virgin Atlantic	International	
800/862.8621	www.virgin-atlantic.com	

Getting to and from San Francisco International Airport (SFO)

BY BUS/SHUTTLE

Airporters, privately operated scheduled bus services, provide service between SFO and Napa and Santa Rosa. **Evans Airport Service** departs nine times daily for the 2-hour ride to Napa. **Sonoma Airporter** makes six runs a day to Santa Rosa, and the **Sonoma County Airport Express** makes 26 runs. All three companies depart from the Center Island transportation zones on the lower ground level of Domestic Terminals 1 and 3 and outside the baggage claim area of the International Terminal. For more information, call **Ground Transportation** information (650/876.2377). Contact each company for pickup times or check online.

Napa County

Evans Airport Service 707/255.1559

THE MAIN EVENTS: WINE COUNTRY FESTIVALS

Between winery visits, you may want to take in one of the many fairs, festivals, and other special events that are held each year in wine country. Some are 1- or 2-day affairs, whereas others can last as long as a month, but all of the special celebrations offer visitors the opportunity to mix with local residents and get the feel of the area. Visitor information centers also post schedules on their web sites under special events. Here is a selection of events:

January

Winter Wineland   As many as 64 wineries in the **Russian River** region pull out those special bottles of wine that you don't see at their regular tastings and pair them with foods during this extravaganza, which also features wine sold at discounted prices. 800/723.6336

Mendocino Crab & Wine Days   Crab season inspires this weeklong celebration up and down the Mendocino coast. Restaurant menus, winemaker dinners, and all-day crab cruises all enhance one's knowledge and appreciation of Dungeness crab. Call for a Winery & Brewery Passport. 866/466.3636. www.goMendo.com

February

Calistoga Jazz Festival   A single ticket buys admission to performances by area and San Francisco musicians. Venues include local restaurants, art galleries, and the community center. 942.6333

Napa Valley Mustard Festival   Celebrate the yellow blossoms that are the first and most beloved sign of spring in wine country. The celebration continues through the end of March, with individual Napa Valley towns hosting a variety of festivities. 944.1133

March

Mendocino Whale Festival   Whales and their recently born calves head up the California coast on their northward migration in March, and people in Mendocino celebrate on the first full weekend of the month. In addition to guided whale viewings on boats and hiking on the headlands, there are tastings of wine, microbrews, and seafood chowders. 961.6300, 800/778.5252

Russian River Wine Road Barrel Tasting   In this free event, people can go from winery to winery in the Russian River region tasting wine right out of the barrel, before it is bottled. 800/723.6336

April

April in Carneros   Fourteen Carneros-area wineries hold open houses in mid-April. Highlights include tastings of new and rare releases, wine-country home cooking, discount wine sales, and (at **Schug Winery**) a mustard tasting. 939.9363. www.carneroswineries.org

Heron Days   At midmonth, go out and see these magnificent birds on pontoon boat trips through the **Anderson Marsh State Historic Park** in **Lower Lake**. Horseback tours, nature walks, and children's activities are also featured. 994.0688, 800/525.3743

Apple Blossom Festival   In honor of the blossoming of the area's apple trees, **Sebastopol** holds a parade and other festivities on the last weekend of April. There are wine tastings and dancing, and arts, crafts, and food are sold. 823.3032

May

Red Hot & Rollin'   A car and motorcycle show is held the first week of May on the **Lake County Fairgrounds**, **Lakeport**, along with a chili cookoff and beer tasting. 800/525.3743

Living History Day   For a day in midmonth, **Petaluma Adobe State Park** re-creates some of the sounds and sights of the park's historic adobe home as it was when General Mariano Vallejo lived here in the 1840s. 769.0429, 762.4871

Luther Burbank Rose Parade and Festival   Honoring the great botanist who lived and worked in **Santa Rosa**, this event has been held annually since 1894 and features a parade, a rose competition, and an open house at the **Burbank House and Gardens**. 544.ROSE

June

Plaza Art & Artisan Show   The Valley of the Moon Art Association invites 100 local arts-and-crafts professionals to set up booths in the **Sonoma Plaza**, **Sonoma**, on the first full weekend of the month. Saturday features live music, and on Sunday a marathon race is followed by an ox roast. 996.1090

Napa Valley Wine Auction   For 3 days on the first weekend of the month in Napa, consumers get to participate in an auction, just like the big *négociants*. There are lot previews and barrel tastings, hospitality events, and the annual Vintners' Ball. Participation is limited; call well in advance to request an invitation. Auction Napa Valley is the world's most successful charity wine auction, with over $52 million raised for local nonprofit agencies since its inception in 1981. 963.3388, 800/982.1371. www.napavintners.com

Wild West Days   In early June, **Upper Lake** puts on a community celebration with a parade, firefighters' competition, barbecue, and entertainment. 800/525.3743

Duncans Mills Festival of the Arts   The historic Russian River town of Duncans Mills hosts a large arts-and-crafts show on the weekend closest to the summer solstice. There are art competitions, wine and microbrew tastings, food booths, and music on two stages. 869.9212

Red & White Ball   In late June, wine lovers converge on Sonoma's city hall plaza for an evening of wine tastings, hors d'oeuvres, live music, and dancing. 996.1090

Sonoma Valley Shakespeare Festival   Between two and four theater companies, each with a repertory of two or three Shakespeare plays, are in residence each summer at various Sonoma wineries and rural locations like the **Dunbar Meadows**. 996.1090

July

Sonoma County Showcase of Wine and Food   More than 70 vintners and 40 chefs participate in this 3-day benefit event. Activities include appellation tours, a golf tournament, a barrel auction, and the **San Francisco Symphony** in an outdoor performance followed by fireworks. Tickets: 800/937.7666. www.showcase@sonomawine.com

Lake County Independence Day Celebrations   Lake County lights up for the glorious Fourth with parades, a street fair in Lakeport, and a lakeside fireworks display. Don't miss the Worm Races in **Clearlake**. 800/525.3743

Cabernet Sauvignon

Pinot Noir

Merlot

Chenin Blanc

Zinfandel

Chardonnay

DRAWINGS BY PATRICIA KEELIN

THE MAIN EVENTS: WINE COUNTRY FESTIVALS

Napa County Silverado Fourth of July Parade   A slam-bang traditional Fourth of July parade down Calistoga's **Lincoln Avenue** is the culminating event of the **Napa County Fair**. 942.6333

Willits Frontier Days and Rodeo   A carnival, parade, gunfighting performances, lots of music and dancing, and 3 days of rodeo enliven the Mendocino County town of Willits at the beginning of the month. 459.7910

August

Redwood Empire Fair   During the first weekend in August, Ukiah puts on a good ol' country fair—featuring carnival rides, arts-and-crafts exhibits, a livestock auction, truck pulls, and lots of homemade and typical fair fare. 462.4705

Salute to the Arts   For 2 days at the beginning of the month, on the beautiful Sonoma Plaza, paintings and sculptures are on show, local writers sign books, actors perform scenes, music of all genres is performed, chefs prepare regional dishes on the spot, and Sonoma County vintages are tasted. 938.1133

Big Time at Petaluma Adobe State Historic Park   A weekend early in the month is devoted to California Indian artists and craftspeople. There are demonstrations, exhibits, and arts-and-crafts sales. Traditional dances are a highlight. 769.0429, 762.4871

Gravenstein Apple Fair   In midmonth, when the great red-yellow Gravensteins are harvested, the Sonoma County Farm Trails Association celebrates the apple in style. The fair, held in **Ragel Ranch Park**, Sebastopol, features crafts, country music, international food, a petting zoo, and the requisite Gravenstein pies, turnovers, and strudels. Sonoma County Farm Trails, 571.8288

Napa County Fair   Five days of events and entertainment at the **Napa County Fairgrounds**—including a demolition derby and rodeo, plus the more traditional displays of produce, livestock, and domestic crafts such as home baking and canning—are climaxed by tastings from almost every Napa winery. 35 Oak Street, Calistoga. 942.5111. www.napacountyfair.com

Bodega Bay Seafood Art and Wine Festival   The weekend before Labor Day, an art festival benefiting the **Chancellor Wetlands Wildlife Sanctuary** is held on a working horse ranch overlooking the sanctuary itself. There's wine tasting and a recycled art competition. 875.3866

Art in the Redwoods Festival Gualala Arts sponsors exhibits, concerts, classes, and lectures at its center on 11 acres in the redwoods. Third weekend. www.gualala.org

September

Sonoma Valley Harvest Wine Auction   This offbeat live auction at the **Sonoma Mission Inn & Spa** is the highlight of a weekend of Labor Day events also including picnics, dinners, and dancing—all charity fund-raisers sponsored by the Sonoma Valley Vintners & Growers Alliance. Call to request an invitation. Also see page 103. 996.1090

Russian River Jazz Festival   Name performers show up for this event on **Johnson's Beach**, **Guerneville**, on the first weekend after Labor Day. 869.3940, 869.9000

Winesong!   Around midmonth, this festive charity auction draws visitors from all over the country who come to sample California's best vintages and superb cuisine at the **Mendocino Coast Botanical Gardens**. There's also live music, from French and Irish folk to jazz and classical. 961.4688

Fabulous Flashback Car Show   Classics dating back to the 1920s draw vintage-car lovers to **Ukiah** in mid-September. 463.6729

The Great Calistoga Ice Cream Festival   The little community of **Calistoga** draws thousands each September for its homemade ice-cream competition and all-day festival, complete with free tastings and live music. 942.6333

Celtic Festival   Toward the end of the month, a hugely expanded version of Santa Rosa's old **Caledonian Festival** takes place in Sebastopol. There's piping, fiddling, and plenty of food and drink. 826.3032

Kelseyville Pear Festival   At the end of the month, the harvest of the fabled Lake County Bartletts is over and the growers take time out to celebrate with a parade, quilt show, barbecue, and the sale of pear products from booths in downtown Kelseyville. 800/525.3743

Valley of the Moon Vintage Festival   Usually held during the last weekend of September, this century-old celebration brings together Sonoma County vintners, artists, musicians, food vendors, and visitors on the plaza. 996.1090

October

Sonoma County Harvest Fair   On the county fairgrounds in Santa Rosa at the beginning of the month, there are tastings of current vintages from local wineries and locally produced food products, plus a grape stomp. 545.4203

Calistoga Beer and Sausage Festival   It's as simple as its name: An entrance fee gives you a tasting glass so you can sample the wares of 35 microbreweries, and a number of local sausage companies provide something to wash down. There is also a chili competition. 943.6333

Old Mill Days, Bale Grist Mill State Historic Park   On the third weekend of the month, a living history event takes place here—the mill runs all day, storytellers entertain the kids, and local artisans, including coopers and candlemakers, demonstrate the crafts of the 19th century. 942.4575

Ukiah Pumpkin Fest   On the weekend closest to Halloween, Ukiah holds a 2-day street fair with music, dancing, a barbecue, and a parade. 462.4705

November

Mendocino Wine & Mushroom Fest   November brings the annual mushroom festival to the Mendocino coast. Mushroom foragers teach you how to stalk the wild mushroom and chefs show you dishes prepared with porcini, Portobello, chanterelles, and other varieties. Mushroom lovers won't want to miss the winemaker dinners held throughout Mendocino County during this event, held early November. Call 866/466.3636. www.goMendo.com

Carols in the Caves   Throughout November and December, master musician David Auerbach plays on a hundred or so different instruments to accompany his stories of the holiday season, presented in caves or barrel rooms of Napa Valley wineries. Call ahead to find out where he's working on a given weekend and book well in advance. 226.7459

Festival of Harps   Early in November, the **Spreckels Center** in the town of **Rohnert Park** features a special matinee and evening performance of harpists, whose style could range from classical, jazz, or Celtic to South American, Chinese, or African. 588.3434

Santa's Steamboat Arrival and Antique Wagon Procession   Petaluma welcomes Old St. Nick with this old-fashioned parade on the last Saturday of the month. Decorated horse teams and costumed fairy-tale characters escort Santa to the town's Victorian center, where music, storytelling, crafts, and entertainers take over. 769.0429

Yountville Festival of Lights   On the day after Thanksgiving, a tree-lighting ceremony along **Main Street** kicks off a month of festivities—including mini-concerts, carriage rides, pictures with Santa, and a jazz festival. 944.0904

December

Calistoga Christmas Bazaar and Tractor Parade   This event honors the working part of the vineyards with an all-day open house in downtown shops, a tree-lighting ceremony, and a parade of illuminated tractors with drivers wearing lighted vests. 942.6333

Victorian Holiday Candlelight Tour   On the second Saturday of the month, several historic homes dress up in their holiday best and open their doors to visitors. The tour also features an antique car collection, choral performance, and wine-tasting reception in Petaluma. 769.0429

Russian Heritage Christmas Celebration   The week before Christmas, Guerneville celebrates the holiday with a Russian accent, with open house in the downtown shops, lights, and a parade featuring Father Christmas and his wife. 869.9000

Sonoma and Mendocino Counties

Sonoma Airporter ....707/938.4246, 800/611.4246, www.sonomaairporter.com

Sonoma County Airport Express ....707/837.8700, 800/327.2024, www.AirportExpress.com

Connecting service to Mendocino County:
Mendocino Transit Authority (MTA) 800/696.4MTA

BY CAR

You will need a car to visit the wineries. It is better to rent a car at the airport and then drive to the wine country than to take a bus to your destination and rent a car once you get there.

The following rental-car companies have 24-hour counters located at the Rental Car Center. The AirTrain blue line delivers customers there.

Avis..............................650/877.3156, 800/331.1212

Budget 650/877.0998, 800/800.4000

Dollar 650/244.4131, 800/800.4000

Enterprise 650/697.9200, 800/736.8222

Hertz 650/624.6600, 800/654.3131

National 650/616.3000, 800/227.7368

Thrifty 650/259.1313, 800/847.4389

Oakland International Airport (OAK)

Located 6 miles southeast of downtown **Oakland** on **Interstate 880**, off the Hegenburger Road exit, and an hour from Napa and Sonoma Counties via **Interstate 80** and **Route 29**, **OAK** is smaller and easier to navigate than **SFO**. Less expensive fares are sometimes available as well. Long-term parking is available in the **economy lot** on the airport grounds, with free shuttle service to passenger terminals every 5 minutes, 24 hours a day.

AIRPORT SERVICES

Web site ....www.oaklandairport.com

Airport Information 888/IFLYOAK, 510/563.3300

Police 510/563.2900

Business Services 510/577.4000

Customs 510/563.3300

Ground Transportation 888/IFLYOAK, 510/577.4000

Immigration 415/782.9210

Interpreters 510/577.4000

Lost and Found 510/563.3982

Parking 510/577.4409

Traveler's Aid 510/444.6834

AIRLINES

Alaska 510/577.5812,

....800/426.0333

Aloha 800/367.5250

American...800/443.7300

America West 800/235.9292

Continental 800/525.0280

Delta 800/221.1212

Jet Blue 800/538.2583

Mexicana 800/531.7921

Southwest 800/435.9792

United/United Express...........................800/241.6522

Getting to and from Oakland International Airport (OAK)

BY BUS/SHUTTLE

Ground transportation stops are in front of each terminal. **Evans Airport Service** (255.1559) also has direct bus service between Napa and the airport. And **Sonoma County Airport Express** (707/837.8700, 800/327.2024) serves Sonoma.

BY CAR

Rental-car companies have counters in **Terminals 1** and **2**. The following companies have 24-hour counters at the airport:

Avis..............................510/577.6370, 800/331.1212

Budget 510/568.6150, 800/527.0700

Dollar 510/638.2750, 800/800.4000

Enterprise 510/567.1760, 800/736.8222

Hertz 510/639.0200, 800/654.3131

National 510/632.2225, 800/227.7368

BY PRIVATE PLANE

Napa County Airport (APC)

Only small private and charter planes can use Napa County's airport (2030 Airport Rd, west of Rte 29, Napa, 224.0887, 644.1658).

Sonoma County Airport (OQ3)

Sonoma County's airport (2200 Airport Blvd, just west of Laughlin Rd, 524.7240), is 6 miles north of Santa Rosa. **Avis** and **Hertz** offer car rentals at the airport, but their fleets are small, so be sure to make reservations in advance.

Mendocino (ENI) and Lake County Airports

No commercial flights are available to Mendocino County. Small private and charter planes can fly into **Boonville Airport** (Q17) (895.2949), Anderson Valley Airport (837.8700, www.andersonvalley.org/Airport.htm), **Little River Airport** (048) (937.5129), or **Ukiah Municipal Airport** (UKI) (467.2855). In Lake County, **Lampson Field Airport** (LOP) (www.airnav.com/airport/102). **Air Royale International**, headquartered in Los Angeles, provides private air charter on Lear jets and Hawker aircraft. Contact them for a written quote on several options for your itinerary (800/7.ROYALE, www.airroyale.com).

Bus Stations

Tickets for **Greyhound** by mail may be purchased through the Ticket Center on www.Greyhound.com or by calling the Telephone Information Center at 800/229.9424. Tickets are not sold at the location in Willits. Bus depots are located at:

San Francisco
425 Mission St (between Fremont and First Sts) 415/495.1575

Napa County
Although there is no bus station in Napa County, **Greyhound** does make flag stops in Napa, **Yountville**, and **Oakville**. Travelers can also take **Napa Transit** buses from the **Greyhound** station (1500 Lemon St at Curtola Pkwy, 643.7661) in Vallejo, 30 minutes south of Napa.

Sonoma County
435 Santa Rosa Ave, Santa Rosa 545.6495

Mendocino County
1488 Main St (at McDonald's), Willits 800/229.9424

Lake County
14642A Lakeshore Dr (between Emory and Mullen Aves), Clearlake 995.0610

Train Station

Northern California's main **Amtrak** station is in **Emeryville** at 5885 Horton St, just north of Powell St (510/450.1080, 800/872.7245, www.amtrak.com).

Getting Around the Wine Country

BUSES/SHUTTLES

NAPA COUNTY
American Canyon 556.8221, 648.7275

Calistoga Handyvan 963.4229

Napa Downtown Trolley ......251.2800, 800/696.6443, www.nctpa.net/trolley

Napa Valley Transit .... 225.7631, 800/696.6443, www.nctpa.net

St. Helena VINE Shuttle 963.3007

Up Valley 963.4222

Valley Intracity Neighborhood Express (The Vine) 225.7631, 800/696.6443

Yountville Shuttle 944.1234

SONOMA COUNTY
Clover Transit 894.1743

Golden Gate Transit 541.2000

Healdsburg Municipal Transit 431.3309

MTA Coast Bus (Santa Rosa to Point Arena) ..884.3723

Santa Rosa CityBus 543.3333

Sonoma County Transit .... 576.7433, 800/345.7433, www.sctransit.com

MENDOCINO COUNTY
Fort Bragg 964.1800

Gualala to Point Arena Information 884.3723

Mendocino Stage 964.0167

Mendocino Transit Authority (MTA) intercity buses 800/696.4MTA, www.4mta.org

MTA Dial-a-Ride, door-to-door transportation ..462.1422

Ukiah 462.3881

Willits 459.9038

LAKE COUNTY
Clearlake Dial-a-Ride 994.3334

Lake County Transit 263.3334, 994.3334

Lakeport Dial-a-Ride 263.3334

DRIVING

Many roads in the regions included in this book are quite narrow, making the mix of tourist vehicles and locals trying to go about their business a frustrating combination. Keep an eye on your rearview mirror, and if you have one or two cars following closely behind, clearly wanting to go faster, pull over to let them pass. This is especially important on roads such as **Route 128** to the **Anderson Valley** or anywhere along the coast, where many of the roads have only one lane of traffic on either side. Also, the shoulder is not very wide, so watch for bicyclists, particularly when approaching a blind curve. Driving tours online at www.gomendo.com make it easy to explore Mendocino County by car.

If you're following a heavy schedule of wine tasting, don't drink too much before getting behind the wheel of a car. Either conscientiously spit the wines out after you taste them, as the professionals do (see "Making the Most of Your Winery Visits" on page 21), or appoint a designated driver. Bear in mind that summer heat intensifies the effects of alcohol. Wearing a seat belt is required by law.

PARKING

In general, parking meters allow for either 30-minute, 1-hour, or 2-hour parking and operate Monday through Saturday between 9AM and 6PM. There are exceptions to this rule, so watch for the occasional meter that is monitored on Sunday. Certain parking zones may not have meters but are marked as 20-minute, 1-hour, or 2-hour zones.

Fortunately, there are few places in the wine country where you have to worry about a lack of parking spaces. Most wineries offer ample parking (with designated spaces for people with disabilities) and often have special areas reserved for buses and RVs.

TAXIS

NAPA COUNTY

Taxi Cabernet (and tours) ....963.2620, www.taxicabernet.com

Black Tie Taxi Co, LLC 259.1000, 888/544.8294

Napa Valley Cab 257.6444

SONOMA COUNTY

A-C. Taxi 526.4888

Bear Flag Taxi 938.1516

Yellow Cab/George's Taxi................................546.3322

MENDOCINO COUNTY

Hey Taxi Inc 962.0800

Mendocino Limousine 964.8294

LAKE COUNTY

Clear Lake Cab Company................................994.8294

Sightseeing Options

BIKING

The wine country is crisscrossed with quiet back roads that are ideal for recreational bicycling. Some tour companies not only rent bicycles, helmets, and gloves but also provide van support along the way for those needing a break from pedaling. **Getaway Wine Country Bicycle Tours and Rentals** has locations throughout the region (568.3040, 800/499.BIKE, www.getawayadventures.com). There are numerous other bike tour and rental outfits. In Napa, try **Napa Valley Bike Tours and Rentals** (255.3377, 800/707.BIKE); in Mendocino, **Catch a Canoe & Bicycles, Too!** (937.0273) and **Mendocino Mountain Bike Tours/Guides** (937.3069); in Fort Bragg, **Ocean Trail Bikes & Rental** (964.1260) and **Fort Bragg Cyclery** (964.3509); in Sonoma, **Good Time Bicycle Co.** (938.0453) and **Sonoma Valley Cyclery** (935.3377, www.bikeroute.com/SonomaCyclery); and in Ukiah, **Fetzer Cycles** (462.4419). To enjoy hassle-free biking, book a wine country trip with **Backroads** (800/GO-ACTIVE, www.backroads.com). They offer 6-day luxury vacations with 50 departures from March through December. Bike part of the day on a custom touring bike, then spend afternoons at the spa or tasting rooms. **Andiamo Adventours** (800/549.2363, www.andiamoadventours.com) are hiking and biking pros offering 5-day bike tours April through October on easy terrain and luxury B&B accommodations. **Napa Valley Bike Tours** (251.8687, 800/707.BIKE [2453], www.napavalleybiketours.com) offers bicycle, van, limousine, kayak, horse, and balloon adventures in a single or multisport itinerary.

BOATS AND CRUISES

The *Petaluma Queen* features brunch, lunch, and dinner cruises, plus poker and blackjack (762.2100); the *Clear Lake Queen* (see page 220) offers dining and sightseeing on Clear Lake in Lake County (994.5432).

Clear Lake is renowned among fisherfolk as the Bass Capital of the West. Let Sandie Hager (263.8300, e-mail: bassnclearlake@juno.com), George Hawley (279.9269, www.biggeorgesguide.com), or Bob Thein (994.4886, www.bobtheinguide.com) guide you to the best fishing spots. Sportfishing and whale-watching expeditions are offered by charter companies along the Mendocino Coast. Noyo Harbor in Fort Bragg is your starting point for a day out on the ocean, where several operators provide fishing trips, whale watching, and sunset cruises. Try **All Aboard Adventures on the Sea Hawk** (964.1881, www.allaboardadventures.com), **Anchor Charter Boats** (964.4550, 964.3854, www.anchorcharterboats.com), and **Noyo Fishing Center** (964.3000, www.fortbraggfishing.com). Paddle through Big River's forested canyon in a handcrafted outrigger redwood canoe, tandem canoe, or sit-on-top kayak with **Catch a Canoe & Bicycles, Too!** (937.0273). In the **Russian River Valley**, kayak tours can be booked at **California Rivers** (579.2209, www.calrivers.com); canoe trips along the **Russian River** can be arranged through **W.C. "Bob" Trowbridge Canoe Trips** (433.7247, 800/640.1386, www.trowbridge canoe.com) in Healdsburg or Konocti Harbor Marina (279.6628, 800/660.LAKE, www.konoctiharbor.com). Fishing boats, water skis, and Jet Skis for exploring **Clear Lake** can be rented at Lakeport's **On the Waterfront** (263.6789). **American Safari Cruises** (888/862.8881, www.amsafari.com) offers 3- and 4-night cruises from September through December. At the height of the annual crush, passengers have a riverside view of the activity. You explore towns and tour vineyards and art studios in the live-aboard comfort of a deluxe 22-passenger yacht. Hop aboard an electric, luxury riverboat for a 2-hour cruise on the Napa River. **Napa River Adventures** (224.9080, www.napariveradventures.com) also has birdwatching tours and harvest evening cruises.

TOURS, LIMOUSINES

You can't beat the freedom of touring the wine country by car on your own schedule, making brief stops at some wineries, lingering at others, putting together an impromptu picnic with supplies from a country store. But organized tours for individuals or small groups are available too.

Stop by or call any of the visitors' bureaus listed on page 16 for information on tour companies, including **Napa Valley Holidays Winery Tours** (255.1050), which offers Bay Area pickup for groups of 10 or more (and will also customize tours for two or more). The **Napa Valley Shuttle** (800/258.8226), 257.1950, www.wineshuttle.com) picks up at selected Napa hotels and wineries and offers 1- and 2-day tours of 15 wineries. In Sonoma and Napa, **Wine Country Jeep Tours** (800/539.5337, www.jeeptours.com) offers the adventurous guided back-road and off-road tours of the wine country in four-wheel-drive open-air vehicles (see page 63). In Sonoma, **Pure Luxury Limousine & Transportation** (755.2929, 800/626.5466, www.pureluxury.com) and **California Wine Tours** (800/294.6386, 586.1568, www.californiawinetours.com) provide luxury wine country tours, as do some other limousine companies in Sonoma and Napa. See "Ballooning" (page 25), and

Phone Book

EMERGENCIES
Ambulance/Fire/Police 911
AAA Emergency Road Service...............800/222.4357
Dental Referral (Mendocino and Lake Counties) ....
....546.7275
Handicapped Crisis Line (24 hours) 800/426.HAND

HIGHWAY PATROL WWW.CHP.CA.GOV
Lake County...279.0103
Napa...253.4906
Rohnert Park 588.1400
Ukiah...467.4040

HOSPITALS
Clearlake: Adventist Health Redbud Community Hospital
....994.6486
Ft. Bragg: Mendocino Coast District Hospital Emergency
....961.1234
Lakeport: Sutter Lakeside Hospital.................262.5000
Napa: Queen of the Valley Hospital Emergency ....
....257.4044
Deer Park: St. Helena Hospital 963.6475
Santa Rosa: Memorial Hospital 546.3210
Ukiah: Ukiah Valley Medical Center Emergency ....
....462.3111

LOCKSMITHS
AAA 800/222.4357

MEDICAL REFERRAL
Mendocino and Lake Counties 462.1694
Napa County 255.3622
Sonoma County 544.2010

PHARMACIES
Napa: Lucky Prescriptions 255.7767
Santa Rosa: Rite-Aid Prescriptions 544.8875,
....546.8207

POISON CONTROL CENTER (24 HOURS)
Hotline 800/222.1222
Sonoma, Napa, and Mendocino Counties ....
....800/523.2222
Lake County 800/876.4766

POLICE (NONEMERGENCY)
Napa County
  Calistoga 942.2810
  Napa 257.9223
  St. Helena 967.2850
Sonoma County
  Healdsburg...431.3377
  Santa Rosa...543.3600
  Sonoma 996.3602
Mendocino County
  Ft. Bragg...961.2800
  Ukiah 463.6242
Lake County
  Clearlake 994.8251
  Lakeport..263.5491

VISITORS' INFORMATION
American Youth Hostels
Marin County 415/331.2777
San Francisco.......................................415/771.7277
Amtrak..800/872.7245
Better Business Bureau 510/238.1000,
....415/243.9999
Greyhound Bus 800/229.9424
Metro Transit ....See "Buses/Shuttles" on page 11.
Road Conditions 800/427.7623
Time ....POP.CORN (or 767 and any four digits)
US Customs (San Francisco) 415/782.9210
Weather ....www.weather.com

"Biking" (page 12), "Boats and Cruises" (page 12), and "Trains" (below) in this chapter for more touring options.

TRAINS
The **Napa Valley Wine Train** (253.2111, 800/427.4124, www.winetrain.com) chugs through the valley on 3-hour excursions several times a day. The train departs from Napa, traveling to St. Helena and back (see page 31). Another scenic route can be enjoyed on the narrow-gauge **Skunk Train** (964.6371, www.skunktrain.com), which takes passengers through 40 miles of redwood forests and mountain passes, between **Ft. Bragg** and **Willits** (see page 188).

WALKING
Charming small towns with old-fashioned main streets or squares ideal for exploring on foot can be found throughout the region (Here's where you find cooperative tasting rooms.): **Napa, Yountville, St. Helena,** and **Calistoga** in Napa County; **Petaluma, Sonoma,** and **Healdsburg** in Sonoma County; **Mendocino** and **Ft. Bragg** in Mendocino County; and **Lakeport** and **Kelseyville** in Lake County. Combine wine-tasting and hiking around **Beauty Ranch**, Jack London's former estate, and hiking up **Mount St. Helena** on a 5-night getaway with **Tahoe Trips & Trails** (800/581.HIKE, www.tahoetrips.com). For more serious walking, trust

13

The Wayfarers (174 Bellevue Ave, Newport, RI 02840. 800/249.4620, www.thewayfarers.com) to know the wine trails better than anyone. The best-known name in walking holidays, Wayfarers offers 6-day tours in spring and fall.

FYI

ACCOMMODATIONS

The **Sonoma Valley Visitors' Bureau** (996.1090, www.sonomavalley.com) can help to arrange accommodations. In addition, the following agencies provide free assistance in finding a bed-and-breakfast in the wine country. Inquire about age restrictions. Also ask about midweek discounts, usually on Tuesday and Wednesday from December through February.

NAPA COUNTY

Bed-and-Breakfast Inns of Napa Valley ....944.4444, ...800/793.7959

Napa Valley Reservations Unlimited ......800/251.NAPA, www.napavalley.winecountry.com

SONOMA COUNTY

www.bedandbreakfast.com/sonoma

www.russianriverrentals.com

www.sonomacounty.com

www.sonoma.com/lodging

www.sonomavalley.com

www.sonoma.winecountry.com

MENDOCINO COUNTY

www.gomendo.com

www.mendocino.org

LAKE COUNTY

www.lakeportchamber.com

CLIMATE

Weather in the wine country is generally mild but varies from region to region. A warm summer day in Napa or Sonoma might turn to chilly fog over on the coast, making the "layered look" the most practical option for dressing. The rainy season is generally between December and February. Temperatures range from an average winter low of 61 degrees to a summer high of 92 inland and between 40 and 65 degrees in coastal areas.

DRINKING

The legal age for drinking in California is 21. Liquor is sold in a wide variety of venues, from supermarkets and gourmet food markets to all-night convenience stores and specialized liquor stores and wineshops.

HOURS AND ADMISSION CHARGES

Opening and closing times for shops, attractions, wineries, coffeehouses, tearooms, and so on, are listed by day(s) only if normal hours apply (between 8 and 11AM and between 4 and 7PM). In all other cases, specific hours will be given (e.g., 6AM-2PM, daily 24 hours, noon-5PM). The majority of wineries charge a $3 to $6 tasting fee.

To comply with the use-permit restrictions, many new tasting rooms admit visitors by appointment only, so bring your cell phone and call from the car.

MONEY

The major banks in Napa County include Bank of America, Citibank, Security Pacific, and Wells Fargo; in Sonoma County, look for Bank of America, California First, Security Pacific, Wells Fargo, and West America Bank; and in Mendocino and Lake Counties, American Savings Bank, Bank of America, and Wells Fargo.

Because the wine country is limited when it comes to exchanging money, it is advisable to change it at the point of embarkation—that is, at the airport or in San Francisco. In an emergency, **Thomas Cook Foreign Exchange** has an office in **Corte Madera** (The Village Shopping Center, 1554 Redwood Hwy, at Tamalpais Dr, 415/924.6009), about a 40-minute drive from the town of Napa; it's open Monday through Saturday. The San Francisco offices of **American Express** (455 Market St at First St, 415/536.2600) and **Thomas Cook Foreign Exchange** (75 Geary St at Grant Ave, 415/362.3452, www.travelex.com) are open Monday through Saturday.

PUBLICATIONS, WEB SITES

For serious coverage of wines and wine regions around the world, consult *The Wine Spectator*, a bimonthly magazine available at newsstands and wineshops. A subscription is $49.95 per year. Call 800/395.3364 or subscribe online at www.winespectator.com.

Read the latest on wines from columnists James Laube and Matt Kramer.

The Wine Advocate, a bimonthly guide to wine, is based on research by one of the most influential wine critics and writers in the business, Robert M. Parker Jr. This publication is available only by subscription and costs $60 per year (second-class mail). Subscribe online at www.erobertparker.com or call 410/329.6477.

Other good sources for up-to-date information on wine and wineries are Gerald Asher's well-written column in *Gourmet* magazine and Anthony Dias Blue's lively column in *Bon Appétit* magazine, online at www.epicurious.com. A good local newspaper to read is the *Press Democrat*, online at www.pressdemocrat.com. *The Vine*, online at www.vinemag.com, is an award-winning publication with in-depth feature articles.

RESTAURANTS

Fine food and wine go together in the wine country, thanks to an abundance of excellent local produce in the hands of top chefs. "California" or "Wine Country" cuisine typically leans toward Mediterranean in influence, prepared in creative ways with the region's bounty of produce, from Hog Island oysters and Petaluma duck to Sonoma rabbit, lamb, or foie gras and local artisan cheeses, with lots of fresh vegetables and herbs as sides or in the sauces. Be sure to make reservations in advance where recommended. Most dining spots accept credit cards.

DECIPHERING A WINE LABEL IN NINE EASY STEPS

1 This title is usually either the **brand name** or the name of the wine producer. (Some producers bottle wines under several different brand names.)

2 The term **estate bottled** indicates that the wine was made entirely from grapes grown or supervised by the producer and was created and bottled by the producer.

3 The **vintage** is the year that at least 95% of the grapes used to make the wine were grown and harvested. Not all wines have a vintage date, in which case the wine inside the bottle is a blend of wines from different vintages (a typical practice for making Champagne and port). Wine without a vintage date is not necessarily an inferior wine.

4 When the grapes come from a special vineyard or section of a vineyard that consistently yields a particularly high quality of grape, the producer will sometimes, but not always, indicate that fact by placing the name of the vineyard on the label. By law, 95% of the grapes must come from the named vineyard.

5 The **appellation** (place of origin) specifies the geographic area where the grapes were grown. If the appellation is a state (California), 100% of the grapes must come from that state, and the wine must be made there or in a contiguous state (you can actually make an Oregon wine in California, if the grapes are from Oregon, but not a Washington wine). For a county designation, 75% of the grapes must be from that county. To have a more specific viticultural appellation, such as Stag's Leap or Guenoc Valley, 85% of the grapes must come from the area indicated.

6 The wine type in California is most often the **grape varietal**, such as Chardonnay, Merlot, or Zinfandel, and 75% of the grapes used to make the wine must be the stated varietal. If the wine is made from a blend of grapes, the label may bear a generic name, such as *Table Wine* or the more old-fashioned terms *Chablis* or *Burgundy*, which were borrowed from wine regions in France and bear little resemblance to wines produced in those two regions.

7 What is listed on this section of the wine label varies from bottle to bottle, but generally it provides information about the wine **producer** and **bottler**. When this line says "produced and bottled by," the winery made the wine and watched over the wine until it was bottled, but a large percentage of the grapes were purchased from other vineyards. If it only says "bottled by," the winery probably bought the finished wines and blended them at their cellar before bottling. "Grown, produced, and bottled by" is essentially the same as "estate bottled."

8 This is the **trade name** and address of the wine bottler.

9 The **alcohol content** of the wine is listed here (plus or minus 1.5%), and it may not exceed 14% for most wines. Dessert wines may not be more than 21% alcohol by volume.

The terms **reserve, special reserve,** and **private reserve** may be added to a wine label by the producer to indicate a special wine, such as one that comes from a particular cask or that has been aged a little longer.

Sulfites (sulfur dioxide) are a natural product of fermentation. Some sulfite is also added in the processing of wine. Because 1% of the population is sensitive to sulfites, the government has mandated the sulfite warning on the back label. Asthmatics can suffer severe reactions to sulfite.

Terroir is a French word reflecting the conditions of soil, climate, and terrain in the finished wine. The terroir of the vineyard dictates the selection of varietals and the wine styles the estate produces.

SHOPPING

Though there are some snazzy shopping centers in the wine country, and even a number of fabulous discount shopping outlets, happily, it is the small shops that still dominate the marketplace. For that treasured one-of-a-kind souvenir, there are antiques, handcrafted items by local artisans, and food-related products, such as locally made olive oils, herb vinegars, mustards, salsas, and more. Some wineries have their own retail shops stocked with wine-related goods, including wine-spiked food products and wine soaps. Shipping is often available too. Some of the smaller mom-and-pop establishments do not take credit cards; it's always a good idea to check before taking a purchase to the checkout line.

SMOKING

More and more Californians are becoming nonsmokers, and the sensitivity to smoking is acute. Ask permission before you smoke anywhere indoors. Smoking is prohibited in restaurants and bars (although some are trying to repeal the bar legislation) and also in some inns and bed-and-breakfast establishments. When smoking is allowed, it's generally restricted to certain rooms of the hotel. If you smoke, be sure to inquire about the establishment's policy when you make your reservation.

SPAS

The wine country is blessed not only with an ideal grape-growing climate but also with a number of natural hot springs to add to the sybaritic experience. Mud baths, mineral baths, facials, and massages are offered at spas throughout the wine country. Many offer overnight accommodations but allow nonguests to use the spa facilities during specific hours.

TAXES

All hotels and overnight lodging (including bed-and-breakfast establishments) are subject to a county- and/or city-imposed tax. The taxes in the wine country range from 6% to 12%. Sales tax in Sonoma County is 7.5% and in Napa County, 7.75%.

TELEPHONE

Local calls from pay phones start at 55 cents but may vary (the rates are posted on the front of the phones); and because the 707 area code encompasses all of Napa, Sonoma, Mendocino, and Lake Counties, many calls within that area code cost more. Find out what is considered a local call before holding any lengthy phone conversations.

THEME VACATIONS

If you want to include cooking classes in your wine-country getaway, Food & Wine Trails (800/367.5348, www.foodandwinetrails.com) combines educational and culinary experiences in a five-day Sonoma tour. Under the tutelage of a master chef, you learn how to make cheese at Bellwether Farms, bake artisan bread at Downtown Bakery, and blend Zinfandel at St. Francis Winery.

Harmony Ranch Yoga Retreat offers classes, day-long retreats, and meditation sessions at its remodeled ranch. Owners Dr. Nehrad Nazari and Michele Hebert have an extensive background in yoga (Spa Spirit, P.O. Box 1565, Glen Ellen, CA 95442; 939.8887, www.spaspirit.com).

Many artists live in creative communities throughout the wine country, many of whom give demonstrations and workshops. Gerald Huth offers classes at his fine art studio and gallery in Forestville (5895 Anderson Rd, off Covey Rd, 887.9540, www.geraldhuthart.com).

Hand-spinners invite visitors to their farms and ranches and lively menagerie of angora rabbits, angora goats, llamas, alpacas, and prized herds of sheep. The spinners work year-round creating clothing and gifts. You can buy raw and carded fleece, yarn, dyes, and gifts. Open by appointment. No dogs. For a list of farms, contact Sonoma County Fiber Trails (874.3374, www.saxelrod.com/FiberTrails).

TIME ZONE

The wine country is in the Pacific time zone, 3 hours behind New York City.

TIPPING

In Northern California, it is customary to tip 15% to 20% of your restaurant bill including the tax, depending on your satisfaction with the service. Some restaurants automatically tack on a 15% gratuity for parties of five or more. A taxi driver is usually tipped about 15%, whereas whoever carries your bags at a hotel might expect $1 to $2 per bag. Whether you tip the housekeeper at your hotel is up to you, but a few dollars per day is typical.

VISITORS' INFORMATION CENTERS

Wherever you are in wine country, tourist information is always close at hand. In Napa County, visitors' information centers include the **Calistoga Chamber of Commerce** (Calistoga Depot Railroad Station, 1458 Lincoln Ave, between Washington and Brannan Sts, 942.6333, www.calistogafun.com), the **Napa Valley Conference & Visitors' Bureau** (1310 Napa Town Center Mall, off First St, between Coombs and Franklin Sts, Napa, 226.7459, www.napavalley.org), the **St. Helena Chamber of Commerce** (1080 Main St, between Charter Oak Ave and Pope St, 963.4456, 800/767.8528, www.sthelena.com), and the **Yountville Chamber of Commerce & Visitors' Information** (6516 Yount St, at Washington St, 944.0904, 800/959.3604, www.yountville.com). All are open daily year-round except for the St. Helena Chamber of Commerce, which is open Monday through Friday, and the **Yountville Chamber of Commerce & Visitors' Information**, which is open Monday through Saturday.

In Sonoma County, tourist information is available at the following centers, most open daily year-round: the **Healdsburg Chamber of Commerce** (217 Healdsburg Ave, between Mill and W Matheson Sts, 433.6935, www.healdsburg.org), the **Russian River Chamber of Commerce and Visitor Center** (16209 First St, Guerneville, 869.9212, 877/644.9001, www.russian

river.com; see also page 160); the **Sonoma Valley Visitors' Bureau** (453 First St E, between E Napa and E Spain Sts, Sonoma, 996.1090), and, in Santa Rosa, the **Convention & Visitors' Bureau** (9 Fourth St, west of Wilson St, 577.8674). Call 996.1090 (or visit www.sonomavalley.com) for a free colorful, comprehensive visitors' guide. **The Sonoma Valley Visitors' Bureau** (see page 105) offers information and wine tastings.

Mendocino County visitors' centers include the **Ft. Bragg–Mendocino Coast Chamber of Commerce** (332 N Main St, between E Redwood and E Laurel Sts, Ft. Bragg, 961.6300, 800/726.2780, www.mendocinocoast.com), which is open Monday through Saturday; the **Ukiah Chamber of Commerce** (**Ukiah Valley**) (200 S School St at W Church St, Ukiah, 462.4705, www.ukiahchamber.com) which is open Monday through Friday; and the **Willits Chamber of Commerce** (239 S Main St, between E Valley St and E Mendocino Ave, 459.7910, www.willits.org), also open Monday through Friday. Visit Mendocino County Alliance online (www.goMendo.com) or call toll-free (866/goMENDO).

In Lake County, visitors' information is available at the **Lake County Visitors' Information Center** (875 Lakeport Blvd, just east of Rte 29, Lakeport, 263.9544, 800/LAKESIDE, www.lakecnty.com), which is open Monday through Saturday June through September and Tuesday through Saturday October through May, and at the **Lakeport Chamber of Commerce** (560 Lakeport Blvd, near Parkway Blvd, Lakeport, 263.5092, www.lakeportchamber.com), which is open Monday through Friday.

Vintner Associations

The very knowledgeable and friendly staff at the **Wine Institute** provides information on the wine industry, including referrals to classes on related subjects. Free wine-country booklets and maps are also available. The Wine Institute (425 Market St, Suite 1000, San Francisco, CA 94105, 415/512.0151, www.wineinstitute.org) is open Monday through Friday between 9AM and 5PM.

Other associations to contact include Alexander Valley Winegrowers (707/431.2894, www.alexandervalley.org); Napa Valley Vintners Association (707/963.3388, www.napavintners.com); and Sonoma Valley Vintners and Growers Alliance (707/935.0803, www.sonomavalleywine.com).

Napa Valley, which was in-habited by six Indian tribes before white settlers arrived in the 1830s, derives its name from an Indian word meaning "plenty." Less than an hour and a half northeast of San Francisco, this world-renowned wine-growing region—an American Viticultural District—is bounded by the **Mayacamas Mountains** to the west and the **Vaca** range to the east. It extends some 30 miles from **San Pablo Bay** to the foot of the extinct volcano **Mount St. Helena** to the north. Within the Napa Valley are the wine-growing areas of **Los Carneros, Wild Horse Valley,**

and **Atlas Peak** in the south, **Mount Veeder, Stag's Leap District,** and **Oakville** in the central sector, and **Howell Mountain, Rutherford,** and **Spring Mountain** district in the north. Napa Valley is an agricultural paradise, with a ravishing landscape of gently rolling hills and an assortment of wineries that consistently surpass their European counterparts in international competitions. Add to that a wealth of fine restaurants, intriguing shops, sites of literary and historic interest, and recreational opportunities galore, and you've got "plenty" indeed. The tradition of wine-making in Napa Valley goes back more than a century and a half—early in American history, but a mere blink of the eye by European standards. In 1838 the trapper, explorer, and Napa Valley pioneer George C. Yount planted vines obtained from General Mariano Vallejo's estate in Sonoma on part of the huge land grant he had received from the Mexican government. Yount produced his first wine in 1841; the grape was not the Chardonnay or the Cabernet Sauvignon the valley is known for today, but the Mission grape brought to Northern California by Franciscan fathers in 1823 and used primarily for sacramental wines.

Others quickly followed Yount's lead. By 1880 the wine business was booming. Napa Valley wines were served in the best restaurants in San Francisco and New York. More than 10,000 acres were planted with vines, and the number of wineries had rapidly grown to an astonishing 175—with a combined output the equivalent of one million cases of wine a year. The valley's pioneering winemakers, from France, Italy, and Germany, had laid the foundations for today's thriving wine industry, using grape varieties and skills borrowed from their homelands.

Today Napa's wines, particularly Chardonnay and Cabernet Sauvignon, are known and respected all over the world. The vineyards cover over 34,000 acres, and the valley boasts more than 250 wineries, ranging from tiny mom-and-pop establishments where the cellar is practically part of the house to immense operations owned by corporations and holding companies. The international presence in Napa Valley has increased in

THE BEST

Gary Andrus

Managing General Partner and Winemaker, Pine Ridge Winery

Fishing for steelhead on the **Russian River**.

A candlelight dinner with my wife, Nancy, on the balcony of **Auberge du Soleil** overlooking vineyards while we enjoy a bottle of Andrus Reserve at sunset.

Hiking **Pine Ridge** just as the sun comes up and hearing wind rustle the Monterey pines.

The mud baths at **Golden Haven Hot Springs** in **Calistoga**, followed by dinner at the **Wappo Bar Bistro**.

Spending 2 hours at **di Rosa Preserve** learning about contemporary art and observing a car hanging from a tree and a desk filled with water—I still have a lot to learn about art!

Visiting the **Culinary Institute of America at Greystone** in **St. Helena** and enjoying appetizers on the patio.

Tasting my favorite poached salmon dish at **Terra** restaurant in **St. Helena**, my favorite dessert at the **French Laundry**.

Recommending the wine-tasting courses at University Extension, **University of California, Davis,** for great educational weekends.

Encouraging my children to mountain-bike Oat Hill Trail below the **Palisades** or hike **Mount St. Helena** and wander the **Robert Louis Stevenson State Park**.

recent years. Some wineries are owned outright by European families or companies, whereas others are joint ventures with European wineries.

As celebrated as it is, Napa Valley accounts for only 10% of the wine grapes harvested in California. The valley's wineries have, for the most part, made every effort to concentrate on quality over quantity. This trend seems likely to persist. As a new generation of winemakers takes the helm, many of them trained at the prestigious **School of Enology** at the **University of California, Davis,** they continue to learn from one another, making improvements in both wine production techniques and viticulture.

Since the 1950s Napa County has grown from a sleepy country outpost, a paradise enjoyed by the privileged few residents of the valley, to a prime vacation destination that attracts nearly five million visitors each year. Driving down either of the county's two main arteries, Route 29 or the **Silverado Trail** (one of California's most beautiful drives), you will pass tractors chugging along at their own pace and trucks stacked with oak barrels from the forests of Burgundy or with premium wines on their way to fine shops and restaurants. Sleek sports cars race past pickups, but bicyclists cling to the edge of the road.

Wineries vie with one another to attract visitors by creating lavishly appointed tasting rooms, special tastings, award-winning architecture, informative tours, displays on Napa Valley history, and world-class art collections. If premium and reserve wines are on the menu, they are well worth the higher tasting fee. These wines are usually vineyard-designated. An estate vineyard owned by Sterling Vineyards, for example, is Diamond Mountain Ranch, high above the valley floor on a steep northern face of the Mayacamas Mountains near Calistoga. At elevations between 1,500 and 1,700 feet, Cabernet Sauvignon has to struggle in the warmer microclimate and thin, deep, well-drained volcanic soils. The austere soils and lack of water stress the vines. The result is small, intensely concentrated fruit that lends a deep pigment and rich body and tannins to the wine.

Restaurants vie with one another to match the wineries' premium output. Chefs here have developed a distinctive wine-country fare based on premium local ingredients and dishes carefully designed to showcase the wines. Elegant establishments such as

Domaine Chandon Restaurant, Auberge du Soleil Restaurant, and The Restaurant at Meadowood are right at home next to such sassy bistros as **Mustards Grill, Tra Vigne,** and La Toque. And you can still find intimate restaurants where specially created personal cuisine is the rule, such as **The French Laundry** in Yountville, **La Toque** in Rutherford, **Trilogy** in St. Helena, and **Catahoula** in **Calistoga**, along with an exotic locale like **Brix** with fusion cuisine, in Yountville.

On many weekends, especially in the summer, Route 29 is one big traffic jam. But most visitors make it to only a few dozen of the prominent wineries along this road; some never manage to get off the main drag, and the majority never make it to what the locals call the up-valley (the section of the valley located north of St. Helena). To avoid the crowds, a good strategy is to head north first and work your way south, cutting over to the parallel (and much more scenic) Silverado Trail whenever possible. If you want to visit the most popular wineries, such as **Robert Mondavi, Beringer**, and **Niebaum-Coppola,** plan to make your trip early in the day.

Many visitors try a different method of exploration and map out an itinerary by bicycle. It takes longer to cover the territory this way, of course, but you'll experience the tranquil landscape up close, stopping along the way for winery visits and tastings. And then there is the **Napa Valley Wine Train** that carries passengers in luxurious Pullman lounge cars; during the three-hour tour, riders sip Napa Valley wines, enjoy an elegantly presented meal, and view the region from the train windows.

A Napa County ordinance designed to control development and tourism in the valley limits drop-in public tours and tastings primarily to those wineries that were already offering them before 1991. All other wineries may allow tours and tastings *by appointment only.* But don't let this requirement dissuade you from visiting. "By appointment" simply means calling ahead. More than a hundred small wineries offer intimate, leisurely tours and tastings. Your tour guide may well be the winery owner or winemaker, and often the tour may be custom-tailored to your interests, perhaps including a vineyard walk or a barrel tasting of the latest vintage. Wineries use a variety of distribution channels: wholesale sales, retail sales at wineries, Wine Club sales, and Internet sales, which are limited to legal ship-to states.

In case you're hunting for Napa's cult Cabernets, the wineries that produce Oakville's $150-to-$250 Cabs, such as Araujo, Harlan Estates, and Screaming Eagle, are not open for sales or tasting nor are their mailing lists open.

MAKING THE MOST OF YOUR WINERY VISITS

The number of wineries in **Napa** and **Sonoma** can be daunting to the first-time visitor. From the highway, the names of famous wineries whiz by, and it's natural to want to stop at all of them. But too many visits in one day can leave you exhausted and ready to head for the nearest beer. The following tips should make your wine country visit as enjoyable as possible.

First of all, there's no need take the tour at every winery you visit. One or two tours will give you the gist of how wine is made—after that, the rows of stainless-steel fermentation tanks, presses, and bottling lines quickly become redundant.

In choosing an itinerary, keep in mind that some wineries present information better than others. For example, **Robert Mondavi**'s tours always include well-thought-out educational components, and the winery offers several different types of tours, depending on visitors' interests. **St. Supéry** has a good self-guided tour that presents information on soil types and pruning methods. Also be sure to visit a historic winery, such as **Beringer** or **Buena Vista**, for a look at 19th-century wine-making practices. The focus of most winery visits, however, should be tasting the wines. The general procedure is to start with the simplest white wines (such as Chenin Blanc and Colombard) and move up the ladder through the more complex Sauvignon Blanc and Chardonnay to the red wines, finishing with a dessert wine. Most wineries do not offer food along with their wines, although some provide crackers to clear the palate. However, many are now stocking cheese, crackers, packaged cold cuts, and more, so visitors can put together a picnic lunch without having to drive back to town.

Sampling all of the offered vintages may be too much for one set of taste buds; your palate can quickly become fatigued and unable to distinguish the differences among the various wines. Tasting too many wines also poses a potential hazard if you're driving. The best strategy is to limit your winery visits to only a few per day and choose the wines you'd like to taste rather than opting to sample the winery's entire lineup. Another essential is to spit out the wine after you've had a chance to let it register on your palate, or pour out the remaining sample after you've taken a sip (special buckets are usually provided for this purpose). These are practices the professionals engage in all the time—no one will be offended by such actions.

If you're hoping to find bargain prices at the wineries, you'll most likely be disappointed. Wineries don't want to compete against the shops that sell their products, so prices at the wineries are generally higher than in the stores. The only time it's worth buying wines from the source is if the winery is offering selections from its "library"—that is, older vintages that are no longer available in wineshops—or if the wines are made in such limited quantities that they are sold only at the tasting room.

There is absolutely no obligation to buy a bottle of wine when you visit a tasting room. The rooms are there to promote brand recognition, not push bottles. This is evident from the number of non-wine-related objects bearing the name and logo of the winery that are for sale in many tasting rooms: T-shirts, baseball hats, umbrellas, refrigerator magnets, pasta sauces—you name it.

A good tactic for visiting the wine country is to include a mix of large and small wineries in your itinerary and set an easy pace. (You're here to relax, remember?) If you like Chardonnay, for example, you might want to organize your itinerary around top Chardonnay estates. Your hotel concierge or innkeeper should be able to advise you, but you'll have to carefully assess any suggestions because not everybody living in the wine country is well informed about wine. Before you begin planning your trip, ask a wine merchant you know and trust which wineries and estates he or she suggests visiting. Read up on the latest new wineries in wine magazines such as *The Wine Spectator*, study the wine column in your local newspaper, and start buying the Wednesday edition of *The New York Times* for Frank J. Prial's informative column, written with the layperson in mind.

If you really have a strong interest in wine, a visit to a small premium winery that requires an appointment may be the highlight of your tour, because you'll get the winery's story straight from the source, often from the winemaker who has created the wine. Understandably, small wineries that have no tasting-room staff or even formal tasting rooms have a limited amount of time to receive visitors, but it doesn't hurt to ask.

Finally, keep in mind that you don't have to do all your tastings at the wineries. You can take a bottle on a picnic or visit one of the local restaurants to try a fine wine with food—which, after all, is the way wine is supposed to be enjoyed.

NAPA

The town of Napa was founded by Nathan Coombs, a member of the infamous Bear Flag Party that declared the Republic of California independent from Mexico in 1846. Two years later Coombs surveyed Napa's original town site. The first building went up in 1848, but its owner rushed off to the gold fields to seek his fortune, returning disillusioned a year later to open the Empire Saloon. By the mid-19th century, the valley's wine business was flourishing and a steamship line carried its products from Napa to San Francisco. Because of its location at the head of navigation of the **Napa River**, the city of Napa controlled the local wine trade for almost a century. Today it is a riverfront city of about 64,000 people, with a rich heritage of Victorian domestic architecture. Stroll through the restored downtown district and you'll pass Victorian mansions, a Gothic-style church, historic bridges, and 19th-century commercial buildings. Self-guided walking tours of Napa's historic structures are available for a nominal fee at **Napa Valley Conference and Visitors' Bureau** (see page 35) and **Napa County Landmarks** (see page

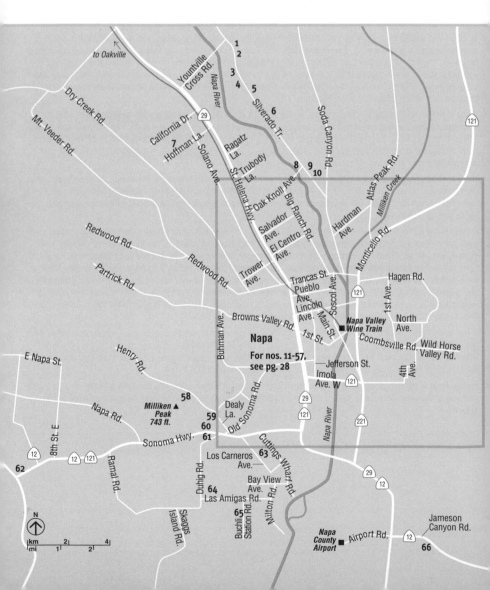

33). Napa's redevelopment of the Napa River includes public docks, inlets, walking paths, restaurants overlooking the riverbanks, and the 70,000-square-foot **Copia: American Center for Wine, Food and the Arts**, which chronicles the role of wine in the great civilizations of the world.

1 ROBERT SINSKEY VINEYARDS

Robert Sinskey founded his Stags Leap District winery in 1986 and has been garnering a fine reputation for his well-crafted Pinot Noir, Merlot, and Chardonnay. The wine-maker is proud that his wines, which he creates to accompany cuisine, are served in the nation's finest restaurants. Famed San Francisco chef Maria Helm-Sinskey is a new member of the team, directing RSV's wine and food programs. Visit the culinary garden, which is used in the cooking classes and culinary events. The modern stone-and-redwood winery, with a 35-foot-high cathedral ceiling and columns twined with wisteria, was designed by Oscar Leidenfrost. It's nice to stop and sit on the edge of the koi pond or walk around the small rose garden before heading inside for some serious tasting. A deck to one side offers picnic tables and a view of the valley. ♦ Fee. Tasting and sales daily; tours by appointment only. 6320 Silverado Tr (just south of Yountville Cross Rd). 944.9090; fax 944.9092

2 SHAFER VINEYARDS

John Shafer, former corporate executive-turned vintner, and his son Doug, a UC-Davis enology and viticulture grad, make an effective team in this small family winery. Shafer winemaker Elias Fernandez turns out excellent Cabernet, Merlot, Chardonnay, and Sangiovese from hillside vineyards in the Stags Leap, Carneros, and Oak Knoll Districts. The top wine here is the Stags Leap District Hillside Select Cabernet Sauvignon. Firebreak is a Tuscan-inspired proprietary blend of Sangiovese and Cabernet Sauvignon. ♦ Tours M-F by appointment only. 6154 Silverado Tr (south of Yountville Cross Rd). 944.2877; fax 944.9454

3 SILVERADO VINEYARDS

Set high on a knoll west of the Silverado Trail, this Spanish-style fieldstone winery with a tiled fountain and an entrancing view of the valley is known for its Cabernet and Chardonnay, notably the limited reserves produced only in outstanding vintages. The winery also makes Sauvignon Blanc, Sangiovese, and Merlot. The regular Cabernet is a great value. The winery is owned by the Walt Disney family, who sold grapes from their vineyards before constructing the current building in 1981. ♦ Tasting and sales daily. 6121 Silverado Tr (between Oak Knoll Ave and Yountville Cross Rd). 257.1770

4 PINE RIDGE WINERY

Sample Cabernet Sauvignon, Merlot, Chardonnay, and a crisp Chenin Blanc in the small, rustic tasting room on the western edge of the Stags Leap area. If you have time, tour the aging cellars dug into the terraced hillside. There also is a shady picnic area and swings for the kids. A trail leads up to the ridge that gives the winery its name. ♦ Fee. Tasting and sales daily; tours 10:15AM, 1PM, and 3PM by appointment only. 5901 Silverado Tr (between Oak Knoll Ave and Yountville Cross Rd). 252.9777; fax 253.1493; 800/486.0503. www.pineridgewinery.com

5 STAG'S LEAP WINE CELLARS

In the now-famous Paris tasting of 1976, California wines competed with top French vintages in a blind taste test. Much to the chagrin of French producers and tasters alike, the best Cabernet Sauvignon was not a pedigreed Bordeaux but a California wine—the 1973 Cabernet Sauvignon from this winery, which had been founded only the year before. Vintners Warren and Barbara Winiarski have continued to produce consistently world-class Cabernets; their Cask 23 is among the most coveted and expensive California wines. They also make Chardonnay, White Riesling, Sauvignon Blanc, Petite Sirah, and Merlot. The lovely winery is set in a terraced hillside sheltered by trees. ♦ Fee. Tasting and sales daily; tours by appointment only. 5766 Silverado Tr (north of Oak Knoll Ave). 944.2020; fax 255.7501

6 CLOS DU VAL WINERY

Known for its Cabernet Sauvignon (especially the reserve), velvety Merlot, and graceful Zinfandel, this winery has had a French winemaker, Bernard Portet, at the helm since its founding in 1972. Portet grew up at Château Lafite-Rothschild in Bordeaux, where his father was cellar master, and successfully combines Bordeaux tradition with California technological innovation. The tasting-room staff is friendly and personable. An added attraction is the series of witty wine-related postcards and posters on wine themes by artist Ronald Searle. Relax at the picnic tables under old oak trees. ♦ Tasting and sales daily; tours by appointment only. 5330 Silverado Tr (north of Oak Knoll Ave). 259.629.2200; fax 259.6125

6 CHIMNEY ROCK WINERY

In 1980, after decades in the international soft drink and hotel business, Hack and Stella Wilson decided to become vintners. Nestled in a grove of poplar trees, the distinctive Cape Dutch architecture of the hospitality center and winery features steep roofs and gables with gracefully curving arches. Adorning the cellars is a frieze of Ganymede, cupbearer to Zeus; sculpted by Michael Casey, the resident artist for the California State Capitol restoration in Sacramento, it is a copy of a work by 18th-century German sculptor Antón Anreith. The winery produces a supple Bordeaux-style Cabernet and a barrel-fermented Chardonnay, as well as a Fumé Blanc. ♦ Fee. Tasting and sales daily; tours by appointment only. 5350 Silverado Tr (north of Oak Knoll Ave). 257.2641; fax 257.2036

7 CHÂTEAU CHÈVRE WINERY

The name means "goat castle," after the herds that once roamed the property. The concrete winery building used to be the barn, and the bottling line has taken over the milk room. Best known for its Cabernet Franc and Merlot, it also produces Chardonnay. ♦ Tasting and sales by appointment only. 2030 Hoffman La (west of Solano Ave). 944.2184

8 OAK KNOLL INN

$$$$ This luxurious, well-run bed-and-breakfast is set amid 600 acres of Chardonnay vines. Built of fieldstone collected from nearby vineyards, the impressive French country-style inn has four spacious guest rooms. Each has high wooden ceilings, lush carpeting, a king-size bed, a full fireplace with a comfortable sofa set in front, and a private bath tiled in granite. Tall French doors open onto a broad wooden veranda with a view of the vineyards and the mountainous Stags Leap District beyond. To make this wine-country retreat even more appealing, there is a large outdoor pool, an outdoor Jacuzzi, and a gazebo for poolside picnics. Another nice touch is the croquet setup on the front lawn. Innkeeper Barbara Passino will serve the full breakfast either in the dining room in front of the fireplace, on the veranda, or in your room. ♦ 2200 Oak Knoll Ave (between Silverado Tr and Big Ranch Rd). 255.2200; fax 255.2296

9 SIGNORELLO VINEYARDS

Owned by San Francisco native Raymond Signorello Jr., this small winery in the Stags Leap District produces much-praised

Chardonnay and Cabernet Sauvignon, as well as nicely crafted Zinfandel, Pinot Noir, Sémillon, and the white Rhône variety Viognier. ♦ Tastings and tours M-Th by appointment; tastings only F-Su, 10AM-5PM. 4500 Silverado Tr (just south of Oak Knoll Ave). 255.5990; fax 255.5990

10 DARIOUSH WINERY

Owners Darioush and Shahpar Khaledi cut the ribbon on their Persian palace visitors' center in 2004. Constructed over five years, the entry features 18-foot-high freestanding columns and an enormous building clad in yellow travertine stone from a quarry near Persepolis. The architects included many historic references to Persia's sixth-century BC capital city. Inside, the visitors' center is a rolling wall of water with abundant pre-cast moldings, furniture, fireplaces, and ironwork. Darioush crafts its Bordeaux-style wines from vineyards in Mt. Veeder, Oak Knoll, Atlas Peak, Oakville, and Carneros appellations. Visitors have a one-on-one tasting experience with a Darioush concierge. ♦ Fee. Daily tours and tasting. 4240 Silverado Tr (at Hardman Ave), Napa. 257.2345. www.darioush.com

11 KOVES-NEWLAN VINEYARDS & WINERY

Award-winning reds keep on coming from this small winery founded by the Newlan family in 1980. Owners Bruce and Jonette Newlan and winemaker Glen Newlan produce Cabernet Sauvignon, Pinot Noir, and Zinfandel, along with two whites: Chardonnay and a late-harvest Johannesburg Riesling. The beautiful carved door that leads to the tasting rooms once graced the entrance of an old church. ♦ Tasting and sales daily; tours by appointment only. 5225 Solano Ave (between Orchard Ave and Darms La). 257.2399. www.kovesnewlanwine.com

12 RED HEN ANTIQUES

Don't miss this 50-year-old red barn with the eponymous red hen perched on top; inside, 70 antiques dealers display their wares. ♦ Daily. 5091 St. Helena Hwy (between Orchard Ave and Washington St). 257.0822; fax 257.0345

12 THE RED HEN

★$ After splurging on antiques, walk over to this cantina for a Mex fix and a mean margarita. ♦ Mexican ♦ Daily. 5091 St. Helena Hwy (between Orchard Ave and Washington St). 255.8125

13 TREFETHEN VINEYARDS

Built in 1886, the tall, rust-colored winery building, shaded by centuries-old oak trees, is the last example of a three-level gravity-flow

Up, Up, and Away: Where to See Napa from the Air

Whether you drift in a hot-air balloon or soar in a glider or small plane, there's nothing like an aerial view of one of the world's most scenic wine regions. Here's where you can get that high in the sky:

Hot-Air Balloons

One-hour flights in Napa Valley cost about $200 to $250 per person.

ABOVE THE WEST HOT-AIR BALLOONING   Balloon flights over **Napa Valley** followed by a champagne breakfast. Transportation from San Francisco can be arranged. ♦ Daily by reservation. 944.8638, 800/627.2759

ADVENTURES ALOFT   Balloon trips topped off with a champagne brunch. ♦ Daily by reservation. 944.4408, www.napavalleyaloft.com

BALLOON AVIATION OF NAPA VALLEY   Trips over Napa Valley, with a continental breakfast before and a champagne brunch afterward. ♦ Daily by reservation. 944.4408, www.napavalleyaloft.com

BALLOONS ABOVE THE VALLEY   Flights from **Domaine Chandon** followed by a champagne brunch. ♦ Daily by reservation. Box 3838, Napa, CA 94558. 253.2222, 800/464.2224

BONAVENTURA BALLOON COMPANY   Rides from the St. Helena area followed by a champagne toast. Options include a full breakfast at the **Meadowood Resort**, a continental breakfast, or a picnic. ♦ Daily by reservation. 133 Wall Rd, Napa, CA 94558. 944.2822, 800/FLY.NAPA

CALISTOGA BALLOON ADVENTURES   www.bonaventuraballoons.com

HOT AIR BALLOON EXCURSIONS   Flights land in an open field where you will be taken to a European café for lunch. 800/456.4711, www.airflambuoyant.com

NAPA VALLEY BALLOONS, INC.   Trips from **Domaine Chandon** winery, with a continental breakfast before the flight and a full champagne breakfast afterward. Complimentary color photo of you in the balloon. ♦ Daily by reservation. 800/253.2224, www.napavalleyballoons.com

winery in California built entirely of wood. The Trefethen family, who restored the vineyards and winery in the early 1970s, have set up an outdoor exhibition of antique farm equipment near the building. All the wines, including a fine oaky Chardonnay and well-made Cabernet, Pinot Noir, and Riesling, are produced from grapes grown exclusively on this 600-acre estate at the cool southern end of Napa Valley. Special Library Selections of Chardonnay and Reserve Cabernet are available. For everyday drinking, the Eschol Cabernet Sauvignon and Eschol Chardonnay are always good values. ♦ Tasting daily; tours by appointment only. 1160 Oak Knoll Ave (between Big Ranch Rd and St. Helena Hwy). 255.7700; fax 255.0793

14 MONTICELLO VINEYARDS

Virginian Jay Corley pays tribute to Thomas Jefferson, a great wine connoisseur, at this brick replica of his famous estate. Jefferson certainly would have appreciated the wines, especially the distinguished Cabernet Sauvignon and Corley Reserve. An excellent Chardonnay is also made here, as are highly praised Merlot and Pinot Noir. The 1997 Jefferson Cuvée Cabernet Sauvignon is a winner, as is the 1999 Monticello Vineyards Viognier. The tasting room sells books about Jefferson, Monticello, and the former president's travels through the French wine country. Visitors may picnic at several tables set up on the lawn. ♦ Fee. Tasting, sales, and tours daily. 4242 Big Ranch Rd (south of Oak Knoll Ave). 253.2802; fax 253.1019; 800/743.6668

15 VAN DER HEYDEN VINEYARDS

Andre and Sande Van der Heyden have the right to boast, having produced what is perhaps a one-of-a-kind wine: a late-harvest Cabernet. And they've done it not once, but twice—with 1990 and 1994 vintages. The wine was awarded a gold medal from the International Wine Tasters Guild in a competition against wines from 19 other countries. Van der Heyden's production is mainly Chardonnay, both varietal and barrel-fermented reserve wines, and smaller lots of Cabernet Sauvignon and Zinfandel. ♦ Tastings and sales daily; call for appointment. 4057 Silverado Tr (between Trancas St and Oak Knoll Ave). 257.0130, 800/948.WINE; fax 257.3311

Restaurants/Clubs: Red | Hotels: Purple | Shops: Orange | Outdoors/Parks: Green | Sights/Culture: Blue

16 WILLIAM HILL WINERY

Founded in 1974, this Napa winery makes consistently well-crafted wines and produces regular Merlot and both regular and reserve bottlings of Chardonnay and Cabernet Sauvignon. Food and wine tastings and wine pairings are offered on weekends. ♦ Sales daily; tastings and tours by appointment only. 1761 Atlas Peak Rd (north of Hardman Ave). 224.4477; fax 224.4484

17 SILVERADO COUNTRY CLUB & RESORT

$$$$ An extensive luxury resort complex and country club occupies the 1,200-acre estate purchased in 1869 by Civil War general and US senator John Miller. His imposing mansion (built around an adobe house) has become the resort's clubhouse, with views of huge oak trees, palms, and the surrounding hills and mountains from the back terrace.

Clusters of junior suites and one-, two-, and three-bedroom condominium suites (280 total) are grouped around eight swimming pools and garden areas. The most popular units are on the clubhouse side and are an easy walk to the tennis courts, clubhouse, and golf courses, whereas **Oak Creek East**, one of the newer areas, is the most secluded. The presidential suite (with four bedrooms) is a good choice for those who want accommodations as large as a house. The rental units are individually owned by members but furnished according to club guidelines, with contemporary furniture, private baths, deck furniture, and full kitchens.

The club is a paradise for golf and tennis buffs—that's the real reason people come here. Its two challenging 18-hole championship golf courses, designed by Robert Trent Jones Jr., are among the best in the country, and the 20 plexipaved tennis courts—more than anywhere else in Northern California—make it one of the nation's top 10 tennis facilities. An added bonus: Head concierge Laurie Gordon is a native and knows the area as only an insider can. ♦ 1600 Atlas Peak Rd (between Monticello Rd and Westgate Dr). 257.0200, 800/532.0500 (reservations only); fax 257.5425

Within the Silverado Country Club:

SPA AT SILVERADO

Nothing at Silverado is done on a small scale, so let yourself revel in the resort's palatial 16,000-square-foot spa. It has 16 treatment rooms, a full-service beauty salon, fitness center, and lap pool, all of which are included with a spa treatment. If you are wont to unblock your vital energy, or qi, try the vigorous and energetic Tui-Na massage, which combines acupressure and stretching. Hot

stone therapy is also good for releasing tension. Estheticians are well trained in the latest skin-care products. They recently introduced the Epicurien enzyme facial, and the boutique carries the full line of Epicurien products, including the best lip balm on the market. ♦ Daily. 257.0200, 800/532.0500. craquelée www.silveradoresort.com

ROYAL OAK RESTAURANT

★$$$$ Standard fare simply prepared is par for the course here. The list of entrées might include a 2-pound broiled or steamed Maine lobster, double-cut lamb chops, and farm-raised young chicken with fresh herbs, among others. Start with a jumbo prawn cocktail, smoked salmon with potato salad, or onion soup gratinée. Dessert highlights include a warm Granny Smith apple tart with cinnamon-flavored ice cream, and a crème brûlée duo—classic vanilla and praline. ♦ American ♦ Daily, dinner. Reservations recommended. 257.5427

SILVERADO GRILLE

★$$ The **Silverado Country Club**'s casual restaurant serves well-prepared traditional dishes for breakfast and lunch. Start the day with eggs, pancakes, and such. If you want a light lunch, try the soup and salad bar selection, and for a trip down Memory Lane, there's tuna melt. ♦ American ♦ Daily, breakfast and lunch. 257.0200, ext 5380

18 ALTAMURA VINEYARDS AND WINERY

This tiny winery specializes in Cabernet Sauvignon and Sangiovese from its property 600 feet up in the rather remote Wooden Bowl. Vintner Frank Altamura honed his skills at **Caymus Winery** in Rutherford before he and his wife, Karen, founded Altamura in 1985. The property—housing the only winery located in these southeast foothills—has been in the family since 1852. ♦ Tasting by appointment only; call far in advance. 1700 Wooden Valley Rd (east of Monticello Rd; ask for directions when you call). 253.2000

19 LA RESIDENCE COUNTRY INN

$$$ This country inn features 20 guest rooms on a 2-acre estate just off Route 29. The 1870 Gothic Revival mansion has eight rooms, all with private baths. All are furnished with period American antiques, graceful plantation shutters, and queen-size beds. Most rooms have fireplaces, and two of the larger rooms have entrances onto the second-floor veranda. The remainder of the rooms—all of which are spacious, with private baths and fireplaces—are in **Cabernet Hall**, a building fashioned after a French barn. The large swimming pool between the two buildings is flanked by an arbor and a gazebo twined with

wisteria. Guests sit down to breakfast in the inn's French country–style dining room. ♦ 4066 St. Helena Hwy (just north of Salvador Ave). 253.0337; fax 253.0382

19 BISTRO DON GIOVANNI

★★★$$ Owner and executive chef Donna Scala and her husband and co-owner, Giovanni Scala, were previously partners in the very popular **Piatti** restaurant up the road in Yountville before opening this bistro. The menu may feature such tasty main courses as orecchietti pasta with broccoli rabe, pan-seared scallops, seared fillet of salmon, grilled double-cut pork chop, or rack of lamb. Medjool dates and shaved Parmesan—though it may sound strange—is an intriguing pairing of flavors for dessert. The large bar, although sometimes noisy, is a great hangout for sipping wines and unwinding from a day of sightseeing. ♦ Italian ♦ Daily, lunch and dinner. Reservations recommended. 4110 St. Helena Hwy (just north of Salvador Ave). 224.3300; fax 224.3395

20 LUNA VINEYARDS

If you love Italian varietals, stop at Silverado Trail's newest winery. Winemaker John Kongsgaard has been applying the best of Italian wine-making techniques to California-grown Sangiovese, Merlot, and Pinot Grigio, the grape planted at Luna's 42-acre estate vineyard and 7-acre home vineyard. The hospitality center has a Tuscany-inspired design, tile roof, and large patio. The current release of Pinot Grigio received a 90-point rating in the *Wine Advocate*. ♦ Fee. Daily. 2921 Silverado Tr (1.5 mile north of Trancas St). 255.5862. www.lunavineyards.com

21 NAPA VALLEY BIKE TOURS AND RENTALS

Rent your wheels here: 12-speed road touring bikes, 21-speed hybrid bikes (a cross between a mountain and a road bike), tandems, and Burley trailers (hold two children and additional gear). Delivery and one-way rentals are available too. The shop also offers tours that cater to beginning and recreational riders, as well as to experienced cyclists. ♦ Daily. Reservations recommended. 4080 Byway East (between Trower and El Centro Aves). 255.3377, 800/707.BIKE; fax 255.3380

22 JOHN MUIR INN

$$ Located at a busy crossroads on Route 29 at the south end of Napa Valley, this contemporary inn has 59 guest rooms with modern décor, cable TV, and private baths (some with whirlpool spas). Relax in the swimming pool and hot tub after the day's excursion. A continental breakfast is served. ♦ 1998 Trower Ave (at Byway East). 257.7220, 800/522.8999; fax 258.0943

23 NAPA VALLEY CHRISTMAS TREE FARM

Here are Christmas trees to cut yourself: Douglas fir, Scotch pine, Monterey pine, precut Noble fir, Silver Tip fir, and White fir. ♦ Daily from the day after Thanksgiving to 24 Dec; tours by appointment only. 2130 Big Ranch Rd (north of Trancas St). 252.1000

24 JOHN'S ROSE GARDEN

Allow at least an hour to stroll through John Dallas's garden and nursery, with its more than 500 kinds of roses, including many old-fashioned varieties. The best time to visit the garden is the end of April through June, when most roses are in full bloom. ♦ Daily by appointment only. 1020 Mount George Ave (off Olive Hill La). 224.8002

25 HESS COLLECTION WINERY

This restored, historic stone winery is not to be missed, despite the 15-minute drive from the main road. In 1978 Swiss mineral-water magnate Donald Hess took a long lease on the old **Christian Brothers Mont LaSalle Cellars** on Mount Veeder and produced a spectacular 1983 Reserve Cabernet Sauvignon. His elegant estate-bottled Chardonnay is just as impressive. A passionate art collector, Hess stored much of his extensive collection of European and American art at his headquarters in Bern, Switzerland, until he decided to showcase his wines and art under one roof. The old stone building has been renovated to house both the winery and a museum of contemporary art. The 130-piece collection is devoted to the work of 29 artists, including Francis Bacon, Robert Motherwell, Frank Stella, Theodoros Stamos, and Magdalena Akabanowitz. A self-guided tour takes you through the museum and includes glimpses of the cellars where Hess's Chardonnays and Cabernets ferment and age, ending in the handsome tasting room, where wines and mineral water are served. Highly recommended. ♦ Fee. Tasting, sales, and tours daily. 4411 Redwood Rd (west of Browns Valley Rd). 255.1144

25 CALAFIA CELLARS

Named for an Amazonian queen, this winery produces small quantities of Reserve Cabernet. ♦ Sales and tastings by appointment only. 1800 Mount Veeder Rd (north of Redwood Rd). 963.0114

Restaurants/Clubs: Red | Hotels: Purple | Shops: Orange | Outdoors/Parks: Green | Sights/Culture: Blue

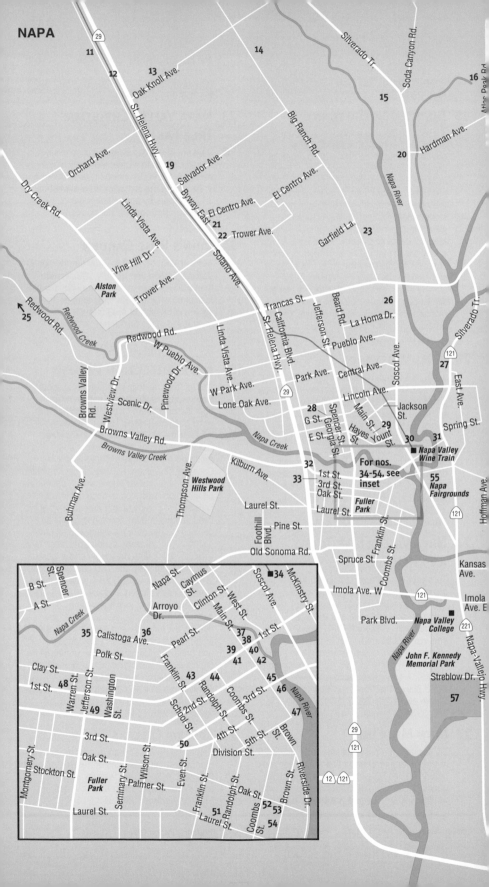

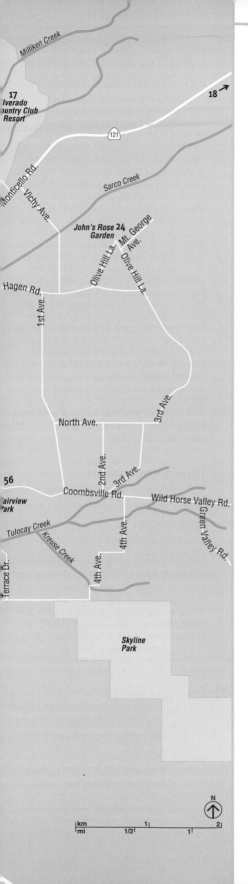

26 VON UHLIT RANCH

Harvest your own apples, pears, plums, pumpkins, almonds, and walnuts in season. Grapevine wreaths and fresh and dried flowers are sold in the barn here. ◆ Daily, noon-4PM. 3011 Soscol Ave (between La Homa Dr and Trancas St). 226.2844

27 MILLIKEN CREEK INN

★★★★$$$$ Just across the Milliken Creek bridge, this former stagecoach stop appeals to worldly travelers on the Silverado Trail. In restoring and landscaping the property, owners Lisa Holt and David Shapiro created the quintessential riverside estate. Paths meander among redwoods and California oaks, over a footbridge and out to a riverside dock. Always in sight, the Napa River flows gently past a gravel courtyard and fountain where guests often linger over coffee, fruit, quiche, and scones on sunny mornings. In choosing among the 12 rooms, you can indulge your preference for balconies, river views, or a muslin-draped canopy bed. Two premium rooms have couple spa tubs and duo-showers. All rooms have king-size beds, fireplaces, hydrotherapy spa tubs, Frette linens, robes, and Bulgari amenities. The British Raj décor rules with Balinese fans, Buddha heads, and leather chairs. Spa treatments also take place on-site including "four-hands massage" given by two massage therapists and Thai massage combining yoga, reflexology, and acupressure. Rates include breakfast and evening wine and hors d'oeuvres. The only thing you won't like about this riverside retreat is checking out. Book early, especially for weekends from April to November. ◆ 1815 Silverado Tr (between Lincoln Ave and Trancas St). 255.1197 or 888/622.5775. www.millikencreekinn.com

28 ARBOR GUEST HOUSE

$$ This white-frame structure built in 1906 makes a charming bed-and-breakfast, with three guest rooms in the main house and two in the restored carriage house out back. All have private baths and graceful period furnishings, including queen-size beds with handmade quilts; three rooms also have fireplaces. Enjoy breakfast in the garden, where a walkway edged with lavender trumpet vines leads from the main house to the carriage house. No smoking is allowed. ◆ 1436 G St (between Spencer and Georgia Sts). 252.8144

29 HENNESSEY HOUSE BED & BREAKFAST

$$ Formerly the residence of a local physician, this Eastlake Queen Anne Victorian is on the National Register of Historic Places. Today it is a gracious bed-and-breakfast run by Gilda and

Alex Feit. The inn has ten guest rooms, all with private baths. Five rooms have queen-size featherbeds; the other five have canopies and king, queen, or standard mattresses with old-fashioned quilts, period antiques, and many other elegant Victorian details; one has a fireplace. The four large rooms in the carriage house also feature whirlpool tubs; two have fireplaces, and two have private patios. A hearty breakfast is served in the dining room, with its rare, hand-painted, stamped-tin ceiling. **Napa Valley Wine Train** packages are available. No smoking is allowed. ♦ 1727 Main St (between Yount and Jackson Sts). 226.3774; fax 226.2975

30 RESTAURANT BUDO

*** $$$ Restaurant Budo has been packed with food lovers and connoisseurs since opening in fall 2004. Much like a Japanese country home, the restaurant has five dining rooms, decorated in earth tones and natural shades of green, centered around an Asian courtyard and garden. Budo, the Japanese word for grape, hints at the restaurant's emphasis on fine wine and its location in the heart of wine country. But it's the menu that makes Budo worth the drive up from San Francisco. Award-winning chef James McDevitt's primary love is Asian-accented cuisine. Make a grand beginning with the seafood tasting, which changes daily but may include bluefin toro tartare. There's also sturgeon caviar, big-eye tuna with summer truffle, and truffle ponzu. McDevitt has given a fresh twist to old favorites such as bison tenderloin with roasted chanterelle mushrooms and sticky-rice risotto. The squab is served with roasted sweet potato purée, dates, and pearl onions. The Hawaiian onaga snapper comes with charred scallion purée, taro root, and lotus root chips. A tasting menu is available in the bar and lounge until midnight. Located adjacent to River Terrace Inn ♦ Californian/Asian ♦ M-Sa, lunch and dinner. Reservations recommended. 1650 Soscol Ave (at Randean Way), Napa. 224.2330. www.restaurantbudo.com

30 RIVER TERRACE INN

$$ This modern inn offers 78 spacious rooms, with choice views reserved for 28 junior suites. Most rooms have sofas, handcrafted desks, and armoires. The beds are heavenly, with ergonomically designed pillow-top mattresses. Ask for a Napa River–view room or junior suite with a balcony and oversize whirlpool tub. **River Terrace Café** serves a complimentary full breakfast each morning, as well as lunch and dinner. **The Wine Bar** specializes in local boutique wines with tasting-size pours (2 oz.) so you can sample new wines. ♦ 1600 Soscol Ave (at Randean Way), Napa. 320.9000, 866-NAPA-FUN. www.riverterraceinn.com

31 COPIA: THE AMERICAN CENTER FOR WINE, FOOD & THE ARTS

"The good life is a religion in Northern California. Now it finally has a temple," writes a journalist after visiting Copia. Named for the goddess of abundance, the 80,000-square-foot center celebrates wine, food, and the arts like nowhere else in the US. The museum displays witty culinary-related exhibits and the Food Forum hosts cooking demonstrations and food tastings. At the Wine Spectator tasting bar you can sample more than 40 domestic and international wines. The selections reflect a theme, such as late-harvest wines, Rhône varietals, sparkling wine, Italian wines, or New York wines. Outside the center lie 13 acres of vegetable and ornamental gardens. A tour with garden curator Jeff Dawson is a horticultural adventure. You could happily wander for hours among the orchards, vineyard, and seasonal plantings of vegetables, fruits, herbs, and flowers. Entertainment extends to movies with a food theme shown Friday evenings, and concerts on Monday evenings. ♦ From Hwy 29, exit First St and follow the signs. Admission; plus an additional fee for some programs. W-M. Closed Tu, 16 May to Sept 30; closed Tu and W, 1 Oct to 15 May. 500 First St (near Soscol Ave). 259.1600 or 888/51.COPIA. www.copia.org

Within Copia:

JULIA'S KITCHEN

★★★$$ Dungeness crab consommé with Meyer lemon confit and seared scallops with pancetta not only show off Victor Scogle's skill but his devotion to local products. He reinvents his menu weekly from the seasonal products at local farmers' markets. Entrées may include olive-oil poached Alaskan halibut with roasted eggplant purée, and braised veal short ribs served with roasted celery root and wild mushrooms. Scogle writes inventive menus around any wine grouping selected for Copia's lively winemaker-hosted dinners. ♦ French-Californian. W-M, lunch; Th-Su, dinner. In winter, closed Tu and W and open Th-M, lunch only. Reservations recommended. 265.5700 or 888/51.COPIA

32 EMBASSY SUITES

$$$ Visitors' first reaction here is one of surprise—it's a member of a national commercial hotel chain with a courtyard garden and a mill pond with black-and-white swans floating serenely. More than just another part of the average cookie-cutter chain, this branch also boasts a plant-filled atrium where you can enjoy a complimentary breakfast; a bar with big chairs, glass tables, and ceiling fans; a restaurant (see page 31); and indoor and outdoor pools. A spa and sauna provide

THE BEST

Dan Berger

Wine Columnist, *Los Angeles Times*

Sipping a bottle of chilled Navarro Gewürztraminer before a fire in a cabin at **Bear Wallow**, hidden in the hills between **Anderson Valley** and the coast of **Mendocino**. Bear Wallow is a nearly unknown respite from the world: no phones, no TVs, no radio. But it has a one-match fireplace, windows to the trees, fresh air, and a bottle of sherry in every cabin.

Four miles east is **Boonville**, a lost-in-time town of ultimate charm that has one of the best restaurants in Northern California (the **Boonville Hotel Restaurant & Bar**), as well as some of the best locally grown apples (at **Gowan's Oak Tree**), and real people at the **Horn of Zeese Coffee Shop**. The wines of this region are among the best in the US.

A walk through **Armstrong Redwoods State Reserve** near **Guerneville** on a spring morning with espresso in a thermos and a sticky bun from the **Downtown Bakery & Creamery** in **Healdsburg**. An early-morning drive from **Santa Rosa** west over **Coleman Valley Road** in January, with the wind raking the leaves and newborn lambs frolicking on unsure legs. On the way home, stop at **Kozlowski Farms** near **Forestville** to buy a basket of fresh blueberries—which will never make it back to town untouched.

Dinner at **Tra Vigne** in St. Helena preceded by their homemade sardines, house-cured olives, fresh-baked olive bread dipped in olive oil, and sips of Spottswoode Sauvignon Blanc. Its sister restaurant, **Mustards Grill**, located down the road, may be tho best example of California cuisine in the state, but for intensity of flavor Tuscan style, Tra Vigne has it, with an amazing array of pastas, plus chicken, seafood, and a waitstaff both efficient and full of fun. I could eat here three times a week and never get bored.

A night at the modern-eclectic **Stevenswood Lodge** on the **Mendocino Coast**.

An important impromptu picnic lunch on the lawn in the **Sonoma** town square with all the accoutrements: a bottle of wine from a local winery, a loaf of sourdough bread still warm from the oven from the **Sonoma French Bakery** across the square, and a block of Ig Vella's hard, dry Sonoma Jack cheese from the cheese shop around the corner.

A Saturday art tour of **Napa Valley**, starting with the amazingly diverse **Hess Collection** at the southern end of the valley, followed by an afternoon seminar in the caves at **Clos Pegase**, listening to the enthusiastic Jan Shrem give his slide presentation on wine as an art form and art in the world of wine.

Taking a loaf of bread, a hunk of cheese, and a glass of a local red to **Jack London State Historic Park** in **Sonoma County**'s **Valley of the Moon** in September.

---

further pampering. The 203 suites with Mission-inspired décor have amenities galore, from a galley with wet bar and coffeemaker to two-line phones, modem, and two remote-control color TVs. A complimentary manager's reception offers beverages of your choice and, so that guests may stay buff, the hotel hands out passes to a local health and fitness center. ♦ 1075 California Blvd (at First St). 253.9540, 800/433.4600; fax 224.7708

Within the Embassy Suites:

RING'S

★★$$$ Most pleasing here is the seasonal menu that features a dozen or so interesting entrées with recommended wines. Selections include meat, fish, or poultry that's been cooked over oak and fruitwoods for an appealing enjoyable smoky flavor. You might start with a prawn cocktail with a tongue-tingling wasabi sauce and end with the dessert sampler—eaten while promising to start your diet tomorrow. The items on the wine list are decently priced and thoughtfully selected to complement the foods. ♦ California ♦ Daily, lunch and dinner; Su, brunch. 253.9540; fax 224.7708

33 BEST WESTERN ELM HOUSE INN

$$ Shaded by three old elm trees, this cedar-wood shingled inn blends comfortably into a quiet residential street. Each of the 16 rooms (several have Italian marble fireplaces) is decorated in pine and cheerful textiles and has a king- or queen-size bed and a private bath; stocked room refrigerators, hair dryers, and irons are among the amenities. A deluxe continental breakfast awaits guests each morning. All rooms are nonsmoking. ♦ 800 California Blvd (at Third St). 255.1831, 800/528.1234 (reservations only); fax 255.8609

34 NAPA VALLEY WINE TRAIN

This is Napa Valley's answer to the Orient Express. During the 3-hour, 36-mile ride, passengers relax in luxurious Pullman lounge cars and dining cars replete with etched glass, fine fabrics, shiny brass, and mahogany. You can board for a champagne brunch, lunch, or dinner run, with both fixed-price menus and à la carte items. A good selection of Napa Valley wines is available during the trip. Call for timetables, rates, and reservations. No smoking on board. Back at

---

Restaurants/Clubs: Red | Hotels: Purple | Shops: Orange | Outdoors/Parks: Green | Sights/Culture: Blue

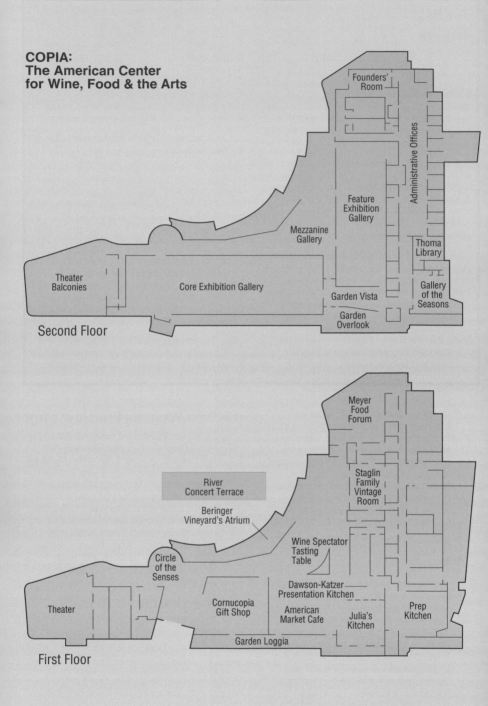

**COPIA:
The American Center
for Wine, Food & the Arts**

Second Floor

First Floor

the station, a shop stocks more than 200 Napa Valley wines, which the operators will gladly ship anywhere in the US. ♦ Daily excursions. Reservations and deposit required. 1275 McKinstry St (at Soscol Ave). 253.2111, 800/427.4124; fax 253.9264. www.winetrain.com

35 OLD WORLD INN

$$ This exquisitely preserved 1906 Napa residence is now a 10-room bed-and-breakfast run by Sam Van Hoeve. The building's exterior reflects a mixture of architectural styles, from its Colonial Revival porch columns to the two-story Queen Anne corner tower. Inside the inn is lavishly adorned with pastel colors, draped fabrics, and the kind of stuff Grandma would never let you touch. Each individually decorated room features a private bath (most with a claw-foot tub and shower), and some have either full or quarter-canopied queen-size beds. One room has its own Jacuzzi, and a large Jacuzzi outside awaits all guests who want to soak after a long day of wine tasting. A full breakfast is served, as is wine and cheese in the afternoon, a late-afternoon tea, and a popular self-serve late-night dessert buffet. No smoking is allowed. ♦1301 Jefferson St (between Clay St and Napa Creek). 257.0112, 800/966.6624

36 LA BELLE EPOQUE

$$ In the heart of Napa's historic Old Town, this bed-and-breakfast, spanning two homes, is one of the wine country's finest examples of Victorian architecture. The Queen Anne house of many gables has a high-hipped roof and stained-glass windows. The six bedrooms and three suites—each themed to a different wine type—have either queen- or king-size beds and private baths; several have working fireplaces. Period furnishings and antiques fill the interiors. Other touches are equally impressive: A garden sun porch displays blooming orchids and African violets; a fire cheers the dining room if there's a chill when the innkeeper serves her gourmet breakfast. Wine and appetizers in the wine-tasting room also rate raves. The guest book is full of love letters from guests—to La Belle Epoque. Smoking outdoors only. ♦ 1386 Calistoga Ave (at Seminary St). 257.2161, 800/238.8070

37 NAPA VALLEY OPERA HOUSE

This Italianate late-19th-century opera house, designed by architects **Joseph** and **Samuel Newson**, is one of the last surviving second-story theaters in California. A City of Napa Landmark, it is listed on the National Register of Historic Places. Built in 1879, it opened in 1880 with a performance of *HMS Pinafore*, but because *opera house* at that time was synonymous with *vaudeville hall*, performances also included minstrel shows, political rallies, and dog-and-pony shows. Today, the opera house hosts jazz concerts, comedy shows, touring orchestras, American dance troupes, and Grammy Award–winning singers and bands. ♦ 1030 Main St (between First and Pearl Sts). 226.7372. www.nvoh.org

38 COLE'S CHOP HOUSE

★★★$$$ A popular dining spot in historic downtown Napa, Cole's Chop House is chef Greg Cole's revitalized American steak house. He serves classic dry, aged steaks (New York strip steak, porterhouse), fresh seafood, and hard-to-beat martinis. No one can top his veal chop, lamb chops, and center-cut pork chop with side orders of creamed spinach, grilled asparagus or broccoli with hollandaise, baked potato, and hash browns. You dine amid the rich ambiance of an 1890s exhibition hall. Desserts are a return to yesteryear too, with bananas Foster, Scotch whisky bread pudding, and all-American pecan pie. ♦ American ♦ Dinner, Tu-Su. Reservations accepted. 1122 Main St (between First and Pearl Sts). 224.6328

39 NAPA COUNTY LANDMARKS

The city of Napa has a rich heritage of carefully restored historic buildings. Self-guided Landmark Walks explore **City Hall**, the **Old Courthouse**, and well-preserved Victorian neighborhoods. Maps for these self-guided tours in Napa, as well as walks in Yountville, St. Helena, and Calistoga, are available here and at the **Napa Valley Conference and Visitors' Bureau** for a nominal fee. The organization offers guided walks through Napa neighborhoods for a small charge on Saturday between 10AM and 11:30AM, May through September; refreshments are served afterward. ♦ M-F. 1026 First St (between Main and Coombs Sts), or write to Box 702, Napa, CA 94559. 255.1836

40 NAPA VALLEY COFFEE ROASTING COMPANY

★$ Owned by partners Denise Fox and Leon Sange, this coffee emporium is housed in a beautifully restored brick building in downtown Napa. The cozy space is decorated with marble bistro tables, old-fashioned coffee tins, signs, and other memorabilia. Faithful patrons drop in to enjoy an espresso or a cappuccino made from green coffee beans that have been imported from plantations all over the world and roasted right in the store. In addition to espresso drinks and the house coffee, you'll find a stash of freshly

---

Restaurants/Clubs: Red | Hotels: Purple | Shops: Orange | Outdoors/Parks: Green | Sights/Culture: Blue

THE SCOOP ON SAMPLING HIGH-END WINES AT DOWNTOWN NAPA'S TASTING ROOMS

Victorian mansions, riverside retreats, and a world-famous culinary center are not the only attractions in downtown Napa. Adding to the river town's vitality is a crop of tasting rooms. Some are wine bars with wines by the taste or glass, while others are small retail stores with a tasting area. But all are devoted to the small, out-of-the-way wineries that were denied permits in the interests of controlling tourism in Napa Valley. So the small wineries have banded together for your benefit. At these tasting-room collectives, prices range from $5 to sample three to four wines to $5 to $8 by the glass.

Napa General Store

Napa General Store in the Hatt Building has a tasting bar offering a rotating selection of premium Napa Valley and California wines. You can also order pizzas, sandwiches, and salads to accompany your wine. The patio overlooks the river. M-Sa, lunch, wine tasting. 540 Main St. 259.0762.

Bayview Cellars

Inside the Napa Treasures gift store is the Bayview Cellars tasting bar, which features the winery's current releases. Bayview Cellars is known for a Cabernet and Merlot blend called Tradition, Sauvignon Blanc, and Gewürztraminer. Daily wine tasting. 1202 Main St. 226.2044, 800/627.2044.

Napa Wine Merchants

Napa Wine Merchants represent 11 boutique Napa Valley wineries. The tasting bar, run by Gustavo Thrace Winery, also features Liparita, Rocca Family, Treppaux, Young Ridge, Astrale e Terra, Hendry, Benessere, Michael-Scott, St. Barthelemy, Bacio Divino, and Crichton Hall. Wine expert Norma Poole holds wine classes on Tuesday evenings. Tu-Su, wine tasting; Tu, wine class, 6PM. 1146 First St (Coombs St). 257.6796.

Robert Craig Winery

Robert Craig Winery from Howell Mountain is the only winery downtown with a tasting room, and is upgrading its facility to be attractive to visitors. M, Th, F, Sa, noon-5 PM for tasting, and by appointment. 880 Vallejo St, 265.9631.

The Vintner's Collective

Vintner's Collective in the historic stone Pfeiffer Building, a former saloon and brothel, provides a handsome tasting room. Among the wineries it represents are the highly prized wines from Judd's Hill, Clark-Claudon Vineyards, Strata Vineyards, Cafaro Cellars, Elan Vineyards, Mason Cellars, Melka Wines, Mi Sueño Cellars, Patz & Hall, and Vinoce Vineyards. W-M, tasting. 1245 Main St at Clinton.

Back Room Wines

Back Room Wines is primarily a retail store that sells wines, many imported. It also offers tastes of wine and sells cheese and other snacks to match with the wine. It holds Friday-night tastings twice a month from 5PM to 9PM. M-Sa. For tasting, 974 Franklin St. 226.1378, 877/322.2576.

baked goodies from local bakeries. ♦ Café ♦ Daily, 7AM-6PM. 948 Main St (at First St). 224.2233; fax 224.9276. Also at 1400 Oak Ave (at Adams St), St. Helena. 963.4491

41 TUSCANY

★★★$$ Located in a renovated 1855 building, **Tuscany** has just the sort of menu to appeal to day-trippers checking out downtown Napa's mini-renaissance. A wood-burning pizza oven, grill, and rotisserie turn out satisfying meals in a warm room of antique brick and original hardwood floors. A meal might begin with one of the traditional antipasti selections: fried Dungeness crab filled with romaine leaves and served with a tomato coulis, thinly sliced veal in a caper-tuna sauce, or Tuscan grilled bread with various toppings. From the rotisserie you can choose rabbit in pancetta, leg of lamb, pork loin, or chicken. For dessert, try the tiramisù with espresso and rum, chocolate truffle cake, or cannoli with cream and candied orange topped with a warm peach compote. The wine list favors Napa Valley and Italy, with some very good Orvieto, Pinot Grigio, and Chianti Classico. ♦ California/Italian ♦ Daily, lunch and dinner. Reservations recommended. 1005 First St (at Main St). 258.1000

42 DOWNTOWN JOE'S BREWERY & RESTAURANT

★$$ After a day of wine tasting, a cool glass of Tail Waggin' Ale, Past Due Dark Ale, or Lickity Split Lager at this riverfront pub is a refreshing change, particularly if imbibed at an outdoor table overlooking the Napa River. The ginger ale and root beer served here are brewed on the premises. The menu features salads, burgers, sandwiches, pasta, and a fish of the day. ♦ American ♦ Daily, breakfast, lunch, and dinner. 902 Main St (at Second St). 258.2337; fax 258.8740

43 NAPA VALLEY CONFERENCE AND VISITORS' BUREAU

Information on restaurants, wineries, lodging, attractions, and activities, plus hints about travel in Napa Valley, are provided at this office. You may also pick up free information on a self-guided walking tour of Napa's historic buildings here. ♦ Daily. 1310 Napa Town Center Mall (off First St, between Coombs and Franklin Sts). 226.7459 (no calls taken on weekends; only walk-in visitors); fax 255.2066

44 NAPA COUNTY HISTORICAL SOCIETY

Conceived during a pioneer picnic at the Old Bale Mill in 1948, the historical society has a library of books on Napa Valley history, manuscripts, and hundreds of old photographs of early settlers and historic sites, plus an archive of historical newspaper clippings. Housed in the **Goodman Library Building**, designed by local architect **Luther M. Turton** at the turn of the 19th century, it also includes a small museum of Napa Valley artifacts. Pick up the inexpensive short guide *California Historic Landmarks of Napa County*, along with notecards and posters of noteworthy sites. ♦ Tu, Th, noon-4PM. Tours by appointment. 1219 First St (between Coombs and Randolph Sts). 224.1739

45 VETERANS MEMORIAL PARK

This grassy slope overlooking the Napa River at the Third Street Bridge makes a good impromptu city picnic spot. ♦ Main St (between Third and Second Sts)

46 NAPA RIVER ADVENTURES

Bring your own picnic hamper and enjoy a leisurely cruise of the Napa River aboard an 11-passenger electric launch. The guide points out sights usually hidden from view. Sunset is a good time to be on the river, but the local birdwatchers love the heightened activity during the winter migration. When you cruise by the restored marsh 2.5 miles south of downtown Napa you may spot woodpeckers, golden eagles, snow geese, and blue herons. You can also rent canoes and kayaks. Call for reservations one day in advance. ♦ All cruises depart Main Street Dock (at Main and Third Sts). 224.9080. www.napariveradventures.com

47 THE HATT BUILDING houses the following businesses:

NAPA RIVER INN

$$$ This boutique riverfront hotel offers 66 rooms among three different buildings in a 2.5-acre riverside site that orginally housed the 1884 Napa Mill. The Embarcadero Building has 26 rooms, all with a nautical theme and cherry-wood paneling; the Hatt Building houses one suite and seven deluxe rooms with sitting areas, slipper tubs, and historic art. The Plaza Building has 34 contemporary rooms with oak furniture and California landscape art. All rooms have the modern conveniences of televisions, refrigerators, terry robes, and climate control systems. It's worth a splurge to book the historic Hatt Suite, which has a king-size bed with a draped cornice, tufted lounge chairs, and velvet ottomans by the fireplace and a slipper tub in the bathroom. Dogs are also welcome to stay with you. Continental breakfast is included. ♦ 500 Main St (at Fifth St). 251.8500 or 877/251.8500. www.napariverinn.com

NAPA GENERAL STORE

At this specialty market and café, you can fill a picnic hamper, or your pantry, with tapenade, antipasto, pâté, and cheese. The deli prepares made-to-order sandwiches, salads, and rotisserie chicken, and a brick oven pumps out pizza all day. Daily. 259.0762. www.napageneralstore.com

DOWNTOWN NAPA TROLLEY

To leisurely sample the downtown sights, board the historic trolley at any of 14 stops posted along the river, Fuller Park, and Highway 29 at the Napa Premium Outlets mall. The trolley stops every 20 minutes and operates 11AM to 7PM on weekdays, and 11AM to 10PM on weekends. No service on Tuesday. The trolley connects to the VINE transit system to take you to other destinations. 255.7631. www.napavalleyVINE.net/trolley

---

Restaurants/Clubs: Red | Hotels: Purple | Shops: Orange | Outdoors/Parks: Green | Sights/Culture: Blue

Gondola Servizio

Sounds of Venetian love songs and the sight of elegant gondolas plying the Napa River may lead you to the Gondola Servizio shop to make a reservation. Inside the shop, which carries glass, festival masks, and other Venetian crafts, you can book a 30- to 60-minute ride under the bridge and out into the countryside. Music, wine, and professional portraits are a few of the added frills. The gondolas are imported from Venice. (Note: Closed during the winter, but private viewings of Venetian glass collection can be arranged by reservation.) 540 Main St. 257.8495 or 866/737.8494. www.gondolaservizio.com

Celadon

★★★$$$ A charming 40-seat creekside restaurant in the historic Hatt Building, Celadon has a loyal following. Chef Greg Cole's trademark, a love-at-first-sight menu, will also win you over. Entrées include Hawaiian escolar with fingerling potatoes and broccolini with roasted fennel; braised Moroccan lamb shank with couscous; and roasted chicken breast with Mongolian barbecue sauce. Vegetarians can tuck into grilled polenta Napoleon with garden vegetables, fresh mozzarella, and balsamic glaze. For lunch or a smaller portion, try the Thai steak salad or pan-roasted mussels. Chef Cole, a local celebrity, also owns Cole's Chop House in downtown Napa. ◆ American ◆ Daily, lunch and dinner. Reservations recommended. 254.9690. www.celadonnapa.com

48 Beazley House

$$$ In the heart of a fine old neighborhood of dignified houses and tree-lined streets, this Colonial Revival building has changed owners only a few times since its 1902 construction, which has helped it to retain its original character. On a half acre of land, the inn boasts 11 large guest rooms with high ceilings, comfortable period furnishings, handmade

---

---

quilts, and private baths. The **West Loft**, a favorite with many guests, boasts a 15-foot cathedral ceiling and a stained-glass window over the king-size bed. Innkeepers Jim and Carol Beazley will sit down with guests to map out an itinerary of the best that Napa Valley has to offer. Breakfast here includes fresh fruits, homemade muffins, and a special **Beazley House** coffee blend sold at the **Napa Valley Coffee Roasting Company** (see page 33). Smoking is not allowed. ◆ 1910 First St (at Warren St). 257.1649, 800/559.1649. www.beazleyluxuryinns.com

49 La Boucane

★★$$$ In a 19th-century house painted white with blue awnings, Jacques Mokrani offers classic French dinners. Specialties range from prawns Provençal (sautéed with cognac, tomatoes, lemon, and garlic) and salmon poached in champagne and cream to rack of lamb accented with herbs and a dynamite duck à l'orange. For dessert, try the Grand Marnier or chocolate soufflés. This feels like a romantic French country restaurant transplanted to California wine country! The wine list has some rare vintages. ◆ French ◆ M-Sa, dinner; closed the first 2 weeks in January. 1778 Second St (at Jefferson St). 253.1177

50 ABC/Alexis Baking Company and Café

★$ The friendly staff at this casual café offers a limited menu of pizzas, hamburgers, roasted chicken, salads, soups, and good homemade breads and desserts, along with a short wine list. Counter service is available too. Don't miss the bathrooms, which local artists have painted with whimsical designs of flying pizzas, angels, and hamburgers. No smoking is allowed. ◆ Eclectic/Takeout ◆ Daily, breakfast and lunch, and takeout. 1517 Third St (between School and Fourth Sts). 258.1827; fax 258.1916

51 Inn on Randolph

$$ This gabled Gothic Revival structure, circa 1860, set on a half acre of landscaped grounds, has five guest rooms and three additional rooms housed in two delightful 1930s garden cottages. The décor bears echoes of the past while also showcasing local artists' work. The inn serves its southern-style breakfast to guests in the main house and also delivers it to the cottages. Aside from relaxing in the cozy main building, guests can enjoy outdoor serenity on the deck or in the gazebo or engage in hammock eavesdropping on the garden's feathered guests. ◆ 411 Randolph St (between Laurel and Oak Sts). 257.2886; 800/670.6886

52 CEDAR GABLES INN

$$ This cozy old mansion was designed by English architect **Ernest Coxhead** in 1892 in a style reminiscent of Shakespearean days. Happily, today 21st-century amenities abound. The **Churchill Chamber** (named for original owners Edward Wilder and Alice Ames Churchill) boasts a queen-size bed with cascading draperies, wood-burning fireplace, and curtained four-poster, two-person whirlpool tub. Proprietors Margaret and Craig Snasdell serve a substantial morning repast in the light and airy breakfast room, plus wine and cheese in the early evening in the wood-paneled parlor. No smoking allowed. ♦ 486 Coombs St (at Oak St). 224.7969, 800/309.7969

53 CHURCHILL MANOR

$$ Built in 1889 for Napa banker Edward S. Churchill, this spectacular Colonial Revival mansion with stately columns and a spacious veranda is listed on the National Register of Historic Places. Now an elegant bed-and-breakfast run by Joanna Guidotti, the three-story house boasts 10 guest rooms, all with private baths. Full breakfast and afternoon tastings of Napa Valley wines are offered in the solarium. Bicycles, including two tandems, and croquet equipment are available for guests. ♦ 485 Brown St (at Oak St). 253.7733; fax 253.8836

54 BLUE VIOLET MANSION

$$$ For Old World charm in elegant surroundings, consider this 1866 Queen Anne with a lush, 1-acre garden. Stunning stained glass, hand-painted murals, two Victorian parlors, plus a swimming pool and gazebo add to the ambiance. Breakfast consists of fruits and juices from the gardens; pancakes, waffles, and pastries; and coffee and tea. Wine or tea are offered later in the day. Guests may request champagne breakfast or dinner for two or schedule a massage in their rooms. The inn also will prepare picnic lunches. ♦ 443 Brown St (between Laurel and Oak Sts). 253.2583; 800/592.2983

55 NAPA FAIRGROUNDS

The Napa Town & Country Fair, held here for 5 days every August, ranks among the best in the country, with a demolition derby, a rodeo, live entertainment, and plenty of country-style exhibits, including displays of flowers, crafts, baked goods, homemade jams, and livestock. The highlight of the fair is the wine tasting, where you may sample the wares of almost every Napa Valley producer. Numerous other activities and events are held here year-round. ♦ Call for the current schedule. 575 Third St (between Silverado Tr and Soscol Ave). 253.4900

56 TULOCAY WINERY

Chardonnay, Pinot Noir, Zinfandel, and a rich, intense Cabernet Sauvignon are produced here. The winery, adjacent to the family home, is so small that the telephone number is the same for both. ♦ Tasting, sales, and tours by appointment only. 1426 Coombsville Rd (between First Ave and Silverado Tr). 255.4064

57 NAPA MUNICIPAL GOLF COURSE

ⓟ A public 18-hole championship golf course (6,506 yards, par 72, rated 70.5), driving range, pro shop, and rental clubs and carts are available here, as well as a coffee shop and snack bar. Reservations may be made a week in advance or on the morning of the day of play. (You also can come without a reservation, but you may have to wait for an open spot.) No spectators are permitted. ♦ Daily. 2295 Streblow Dr (just west of Napa-Vallejo Hwy). 255.4333

58 ARTESA

This Napa Valley winery fits snugly into its site at the foot of Milliken Peak, where an outstanding staff is expanding and transforming the output. From a distance, it's hard to make out the modernistic structure; the architect built the ecologically sound winery right into the hillside and covered the top with an earthen berm planted with drought-resistant California grasses to create the cool, stable conditions ideal for producing and storing high-quality wine. A series of terraces leads into the winery past columns and reflecting pools, and the view from inside is a stunning panorama of the Carneros District. The dramatic, $22 million facility opened as Codorníu, named in honor of the Spanish owner, the House of Codorníu, which has been making wines in the Catalonian region of Spain for more than 400 years. Artesa, the new name, means "craftsman" or "artisan" in Catalan. Winemaker Don Van Staaveren creates intense, ripe, fruit-forward wines. Tours of the winery, designed to give an overview of *méthode champenoise* wine-making, are followed by a tasting of Chardonnay, Pinot Noir, and Sauvignon Blanc. ♦ Fee. Tasting and tours daily. 1345 Henry Rd (west of Dealy La). 224.1668

59 CARNEROS CREEK WINERY

A barnlike building just off Old Sonoma Road marks this small Carneros District producer. The emphasis here is on Chardonnay and Pinot Noir, though the winery also makes

---

Restaurants/Clubs: Red | Hotels: Purple | Shops: Orange | Outdoors/Parks: Green | Sights/Culture: Blue

Cabernet Sauvignon and Merlot. A few picnic tables sit under a lovely pergola (overhead trellis), and there's also a tasting room. ◆ Fee. Tasting and sales daily. 1285 Dealy La (between Old Sonoma and Henry Rds). 253.9463

60 DI ROSA PRESERVE

Lace up your sneakers for a walking tour of the vast outdoor-indoor art collection of avid patron of the arts Rene di Rosa. Indoor displays—an assembly of styles done by artists in the greater San Francisco area during the latter part of the 20th century—are housed in a 100-year-old winery that later became a residence; the 200-acre grounds, an exhibit in themselves, boast vibrant gardens, undulating meadows, and a 35-acre lake. ◆ Admission. M-F, June-Sept; M-F, Oct-May; Sa till 1PM year-round. Guided tours available; call in advance for reservations. 5200 Sonoma Hwy (west of Old Sonoma Rd). 226.5991; fax 255.8934

61 DOMAINE CARNEROS

Founded in 1987 by the French Champagne house Taittinger, this winery is devoted to making sparkling wines by the traditional *méthode champenoise*. Managing director and winemaker Eileen Crane has extensive experience making sparkling wine in California. Designed by **Thomas Faherty & Associates** of St. Helena, the massive winery was inspired by the Château de la Marquetterie, a historic 18th-century residence owned by the Taittinger family in Champagne. A grand cement staircase leads from the parking lot to the elegant reception and tasting room, where visitors can relax at tables with a glass of Domaine Carneros Brut. The downstairs gallery offers views of the bottling line and fermentation stages, along with historical photos of the harvest in Champagne. ◆ Fee. Tasting, sales, and tours daily. 1240 Duhig Rd (just south of Sonoma Hwy). 257.0101; fax 257.3020

62 THE CARNEROS INN

$$$ At first sight, you feel that the clock has turned back to 1950 and you feel like Dorothy

In the late 19th century, peregrine falcons nested on Mount St. Helena. But by the 1950s the bird of prey's numbers had been reduced to just 10 breeding pairs in all of California, primarily due, it is believed, to the widespread use of the insecticide DDT. In 1977 a pair settled on Mount St. Helena, and peregrine falcons have been doing well on the mountain ever since. Watch them dive through the skies above the extinct volcano; they can reach speeds of 180 to 217 miles per hour and are considered the fastest animals in the world.

returning to her Midwest farming community. The Inn is not really an inn but 8 to 10 vacation cottages arranged in 10 separate compounds. Each cottage has an old-fashioned porch and a front door facing a common lawn and watering trough. Inside, the 21st-century side of the resort is abundantly evident with plasma TVs and Frette towels and the cherry-wood floors and wood-burning fireplaces are warm and welcoming. The bathrooms in the larger cottages are a marvel of slate and limestone, with soaking tubs and connecting indoor and outdoor showers. The cottage deck spans the length of the cottage and has teak furniture and high walls for privacy. Ask for a cottage with the back deck facing the hillside vineyards or the apple orchard, which grows the same apple varieties that Carneros farmers once harvested. A pleasant stroll along connecting gravel pathways lined with lavender bring you to the hilltop pool, spa, dining room, and lobby living room, all with panoramic views of this idyllic setting. ◆ 4048 Sonoma Hwy (across from Cuttings Wharf Rd). 299.4900. ⅃ www.thecarnerosinn.com

Within the Carneros Inn:

BOON FLY CAFÉ

★★ $$ The bright red barn, porch swings, and simple menu of tasty fare are just what the locals ordered when chef Philip Wang consulted them before opening the Boon Fly Café. Inside, under a 25-foot-high ceiling, is a cheerful dining room, with cozy banquettes, wooden tables, cherry-wood floors, and a large community table beneath a farmstead-style candle chandelier. Roll up your sleeves and dig into farm-fresh, organic soup, salad, vegetable side dishes, and entrées. The roasted organic chicken comes with bacon, potatoes, roasted garlic, and sautéed mushrooms. The wild king salmon is grilled to order and comes with mashed potatoes. The wine list features lusty Carneros wines that pair well with the flatbreads and wine-country toppings such as coastal field mushrooms, chicken sausage, mozzarella di bufala, and fresh basil. The namesake dessert, boon fly pie, is a gooey-sweet confection of pecan-pie filling on a graham-cracker crust, topped with chocolate-marshmallow fluff. ◆ American ◆ Daily, breakfast, lunch, and dinner. Reservations recommended. 299.4900 ⅃

SPA AT CARNEROS INN

A destination spa in the true sense, the Carneros Inn becomes your personal playground as a day-spa guest. Included in the price of two spa treatments is a spacious cottage and full use of the inn, hilltop pool, and private dining room. After checking into your cottage, have a massage on your private deck. At the pool you can order a hair and

THE BEST

Paul Franson

Franson writes about wine, food, and travel from Napa Valley, including a weekly column on what's new in the *Napa Valley Register*.

A perfect day in Napa Valley

A balloon ride. There's no better way to appreciate the Valley from above, especially from the quiet of a balloon. A number of companies offer similar trips, all starting at Domaine Chandon, then drifting slowly south.

Tasting wine at Frank Family Vineyards. There are more than a hundred places to taste wine in Napa Valley, but none is more fun than Frank Family Vineyards, the old Kornell Larkmead Cellars. Start with sparkling wine, and they may invite you into the back room for some of the richest wines made in the Valley.

A picnic at Rutherford Hill Winery. High above the Valley, you can enjoy a picnic with one of the re-energized winery's excellent wines.

A wasted afternoon on the patio at Tra Vigne. Buy a $15 rosé or a $250 cult classic from the Cantinetta's Wine Bar and sit under an umbrella, imagining you're in Italy.

A glass of sparkling wine on the deck at Auberge du Soleil. Even if you've seen the view from Rutherford Hill above, the deck at sunset gives a completely new view of the Valley. Prices are reasonable at the bar, too; the house sparkler is from Schramsberg.

Dinner at Bistro Jeanty. Deciding where to eat in Napa Valley is tough; there are too many great choices. Jeanty offers authentic superb French bistro food and atmosphere, and it even has a communal table for those without reservations.

A suite at Napa River Inn. The new Inn in an old mill offers luxury right on the Napa River in the heart of the new Napa and within walking distance of new restaurants and wine bars, plus the Opera House and Copia.

scalp treatment. The farmstead theme appears in spa treatments such as the mustard-seed massage and the warm goat-butter massage. Check-out time for spa guests is 6 PM. ♦ Daily.

63 SAINTSBURY

Named in honor of the 19th-century wine connoisseur and writer George Saintsbury, best known as the author of *Notes on a Cellar Book*, this Carneros District winery is housed in a weathered redwood building. Partners Richard Ward and David Graves are dedicated to making Burgundian-style Pinot Noir and Chardonnay. The Chardonnay is fermented and aged in barrels coopered in France. The partners make three styles of Pinot Noir: the fresh and lively Garnet, the more classic Carneros Pinot Noir, and the richest and most full-flavored, Reserve. All their wines are first rate and are sold at excellent prices. ♦ Limited tours M-F by appointment only. 1500 Los Carneros Ave (between Middle Ave and Sonoma Hwy). 252.0592; fax 252.0595

64 ACACIA WINERY

Not only does winemaker Dave Lattin turn out highly acclaimed Chardonnay and Pinot Noir but he also has been earning a well-deserved reputation for a notable Zinfandel and vintage-dated *méthode champenoise* Brut sparkling wine. The sleek modern winery was

established in 1979 and became part of the Chalone group in 1986. ♦ Daily by appointment. 2750 Las Amigas Rd (between Milton Rd and Duhig Rd). 226.9991; fax 226.1685

65 BOUCHAINE VINEYARDS

Perched on a hillside overlooking San Pablo Bay, Gerret Copeland's small, modernized winery tucked into an existing older building specializes in Carneros-grown Pinot Noir and Chardonnay made by traditional Burgundian methods. It also has started to produce a small amount of Alsatian-style Gewürztraminer. The original wine estate at this site dates from 1887. ♦ Tasting, sales, and tours by appointment only. 1075 Buchli Station Rd (just south of Las Amigas Rd). 800/654.WINE; fax 252.0401

66 CHARDONNAY CLUB

This championship 18-hole golf course (5,983-6,816 yards, par 71, rated 71.7) regularly appears on *California Golf* magazine's list of the 25 best courses in the state. Golf shops, a clubhouse with a grill and restaurant, a snack bar, and a practice range are available. There's an 18-hole private course, too. ♦ Daily. Reservations must be made at least 2 weeks in advance. 2555 Jameson Canyon Rd (east of N Kelly Rd). 257.1900; fax 257.0613

Restaurants/Clubs: Red | Hotels: Purple | Shops: Orange | Outdoors/Parks: Green | Sights/Culture: Blue

YOUNTVILLE/OAKVILLE/ RUTHERFORD

Founded by George Calvert Yount, a pioneer and adventurer who traveled to California from North Carolina, Yountville, with a population of 3,000, is the first town along the 26-mile route from Napa to Calistoga. After visiting Mexican general Mariano Vallejo at his Sonoma ranch, Yount became the first American to settle in **Napa Valley** and the first to receive a land grant from the Mexican government—12,000 acres in the heart of the valley called **Rancho Caymus**. With the help of local Indians, he also planted the first grapevines in Napa Valley with cuttings he obtained from General Vallejo. By 1855, a town had grown up on the southern borders of Rancho Caymus, which Yount dubbed Sebastopol (not to be confused with the Sebastopol in Sonoma County). In 1867, 2 years after Yount's death at age 71, the town's name was changed to Yountville in his honor. The Yountville appellation covers 3,500 acres, 2,200 of which are planted in vines by 43 growers and six wineries. **Domaine Chandon** and **Dominus Estate** are widely known, the former for its sparkling wines and the latter for Christian Moueix's Bordeaux-style red wine. One of Napa Valley's modern architectural landmarks, **Dominus Estate Winery**, at 2570 Napanook Road, has a façade of dark green basalt covered in stone wickerwork of galvanized wire baskets filled with local stones. Its architects, **Jacques Herzog** and **Pierre de Meuron**, won the acclaimed Pritzker Prize for the building in 2001. Yountville is also home to Thomas Keller's famous **French Laundry** restaurant.

A short jaunt from Yountville up Route 29 are the twin towns of Oakville and Rutherford, where some of the world's best Cabernet Sauvignon vines thrive in a microclimate similar to France's Bordeaux region. Some of the most sought-after wine in the United States comes from Oakville, from wineries such as **Harlan Estates, Screaming Eagle, Silver Oak,** and **Paradigm.** Some great wineries to visit are **Robert**

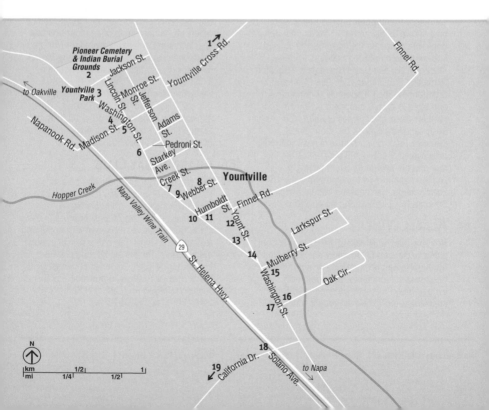

Mondavi, **Opus One**, Niebaum–Coppola, and Beaulieu. Summer and harvesttime (August through October) are the busiest times to visit.

1 NAPA RIVER ECOLOGICAL RESERVE

Shady picnic spots under a grove of oak and sycamore trees beside the Napa River can be found here. ◆ Off Yountville Cross Rd (at the Napa River), Yountville

2 PIONEER CEMETERY AND INDIAN BURIAL GROUNDS

The early history of the valley can be traced in the tombstones here, which include a monument to town founder George C. Yount. Part of this 1848 cemetery still serves as the burial grounds for the local Wappo Indian tribe. ◆ Jackson St (between Yount and Washington Sts), Yountville

3 YOUNTVILLE PARK

This small park has shaded picnic tables, barbecue grills, and a children's playground. ◆ Bounded by Lincoln, Washington, and Jackson Sts

4 NAPA VALLEY LODGE

$$$ Tucked into the quiet north end of Yountville, this pleasant, well-run 55-room inn was built in Spanish-hacienda style, with wooden balconies, private baths, and a terra-cotta roof. Small two-room suites are available for families, and a helpful staff will arrange bicycle rentals and other wine-country activities. Many rooms have vineyard views. A large pool, sauna, and small fitness room help keep guests in shape. ◆ 2230 Madison St (at Washington St), Yountville. 944.2468; fax 944.9362

5 WASHINGTON SQUARE

A dozen shops and a few restaurants fill this small shopping center. ◆ Daily. 6795 Washington St (at Madison St), Yountville. 944.0637; fax 944.0941

Within Washington Square:

NAPA VALLEY GRILLE

NAPA VALLEY GRILLE

★$$$ Executive chef Thad Lymen is at the helm of this pleasant restaurant offering a lunch and dinner menu that includes good salad and pasta dishes. Grilled chicken on focaccia, burgers, and grilled eggplant make up some of the midday fare. Main courses at dinner may include pepper-crusted rack of pork, grilled Atlantic salmon, and grilled game hen. Or try the tender medallions of ostrich with huckleberry sauce. Be sure to leave room for the lavender crème brûlée for dessert. Equally engaging is the Sunday brunch menu, which features such tempting dishes as Dungeness crab cakes with poached eggs, *huevos rancheros*, and fresh berry blintzes topped with crème fraiche. The outdoor patio is a popular seating area in good weather. There's an award-winning wine list, and wine-maker dinners are scheduled throughout the year. ◆ California ◆ M-Sa, lunch and dinner; Su, brunch and dinner. Reservations recommended. 6595 Washington St. 944.8686. www.tavistockrestaurants.com

VERANDA CLUB SPA

Calling itself "Napa Valley's smallest and finest spa," this recently expanded club—formerly **Massage Werkes**—was founded by Wil Anderson and is still under his direction. This is the place to indulge in an hour-long body massage, enjoy an herbal facial, or have a body wrap. Fitness packages are available. ◆ Daily, by appointment only. 944.1906; 877/912.5068. www.verandaclubspa.com

6 PÈRE JEANTY

★★★$$$ Paris's bistros are famous for their veal chops, *tournedos au poivre*, and porterhouse steak with Béarnaise sauce. Jeanty's steak house is a bit of steak heaven this side

Temperature for wine (in°F)	
Champagne	50 degrees
White wines	55 degrees
Dessert wines	60 degrees
Reds	60 degrees

Restaurants/Clubs: Red | Hotels: Purple | Shops: Orange | Outdoors/Parks: Green | Sights/Culture: Blue

TO YOUR HEALTH!

At the start of the 21st century, scientists are just getting around to confirming what doctors believed centuries ago. Wine, it seems, really is an elixir of good health.

Wine was widely used as medicine in the earliest days of civilization; among other things, it served as a dressing for wounds and a treatment for digestive ailments. Americans stopped using wine for medicinal purposes during Prohibition. Afterward, antibiotics and other "miracle" drugs led to other ways of treating ills. And until the release of several recent scientific studies, there was no substantive proof that wine had beneficial powers.

What reengaged the public's interest in the health benefits of wine in recent years was a 1991 *60 Minutes* report on a study by the French National Institute of Health. The study found that although the French consume large amounts of milk fat (i.e., cheese), the rate of heart disease is lower in France than in other industrialized countries such as the US and Great Britain. The study's by-now familiar conclusion: People in France are protected from heart disease by the chemical properties of wine, especially red wine. In 1992, the year after the *60 Minutes* report, sales of red wine in the US soared.

Since then, additional data on the health benefits of wine and other forms of alcohol have been published in a variety of respected medical journals and have been key topics at medical conferences. In fact, the US government's *Dietary Guidelines for Americans* now states that drinking moderate amounts of alcohol (one drink a day for women and two a day for men) can help prevent heart disease, especially when combined with a healthy lifestyle that includes exercise and a sensible diet. (Of course, individuals with some health-related issues should not consume any alcohol.)

Of all alcoholic beverages, wine is thought to have the most heart-protective properties. Studies show that people's levels of high-density lipoproteins (HDLs)—which remove damaging fats that can build up inside artery walls and narrow the blood vessels—increase with the consumption of moderate amounts of wine. Studies also cite polyphenals (color pigments and tannins) found in wine as helpful in reducing levels of the so-called bad cholesterol (low-density lipoprotein, or LDL, cholesterol). Wine is also thought to play a role in strengthening arterial walls and preventing cardiac arrest.

All of which may explain why the traditional toast in many countries means "To your health!"

of the Seine. Whether you sit by the fireplace or outdoors in the garden under a canvas umbrella, the ambiance of a private home in the French countryside surrounds you. Money is no object in obtaining the highest-grade US meat: The Kobe beef short ribs are from Snake River Ranch and the lamb rack is from Colorado. Jeanty roasts the veal chops, then grills them over mesquite. Along with your chops and steaks, choose a side dish of au gratin potatoes, fresh green beans, and silky rich mushroom sauce, Béarnaise sauce, or fresh horseradish cream. ♦ Steak house ♦ Daily, dinner. 6725 Washington St (between Pedroni and Madison Sts), Yountville. 945.1000. & www.perejeanty.com

7 FRENCH LAUNDRY

★★★★$$$$ Situated in a historic stone building that was once a laundry, this intimate but unfussy restaurant has long been a favorite among the world's food connoisseurs. Thomas Keller, former chef and owner of the popular restaurant Rakel, in New York City, prepares critically acclaimed, superb French haute cuisine. A meal here is a leisurely affair;

the table is yours for the evening, or for lunch. The prix-fixe menu, which changes daily, is generally four, five, or nine courses. Among the intriguing appetizers are "oysters and pearls," a sabayon of pearl tapioca and oysters topped with caviar, and risotto with white truffles. Main courses might include butter-braised Maine lobster or quail stuffed with sweetbreads. For dessert, try the Shirley Temple, a pomegranate juice–and–champagne sorbet with gingered gelée; milk chocolate–and–lemon mousse with citrus custard sauce; or Maui pineapple sorbet. The fine wines from France and California have been carefully selected to complement the cuisine. ♦ French ♦ Daily, dinner; F-Su, lunch. Reservations (required) are accepted 2 months in advance. 6640 Washington St (at Creek St), Yountville. 944.2380

8 LAVENDER

$$$ One of the Four Sisters Inns collection, as is **Maison Fleurie**, and just as charming. Lavender reflects Early American simplicity in design and décor. An herb and flower garden surrounds the property, and the scent of lavender wafts through open windows. In the main house, there is a two-room suite downstairs and two rooms upstairs with dormer windows, hand-stitched quilts, and tiled bathrooms. For guests who seek luxury and

privacy, there are six guest rooms in three cottages; each has a king-size bed, fireplace, enclosed patio, and private hot tub. A full gourmet breakfast is served on the veranda and a wine hour with hors d'oeuvres in the garden. In warm weather, guests often team up for a game of boules. ♦ 2020 Webber St (between Yount and Jefferson Sts), Yountville. 944.1388; fax 944.9342, 800/522.4140. www.foursisters.com

9 BORDEAUX HOUSE

$$ Designed in the 1980s by architect **Robert Keenan**, this unusual redbrick inn faces a quiet residential street. The eight guest rooms feature queen-and king-size beds, fireplaces, and private baths; the best is the **Chablis Room** upstairs, which has its own balcony. Innkeeper Jean Lunney serves a continental breakfast each morning in the common room, with muffins or other pastries, granola, yogurt, juice, and coffee. ♦ 6600 Washington St (at Webber St), Yountville. 944.2855; fax 945.0471. www.bordeauxhouse.com

10 VINTAGE INN

$$$ Designed by **Kipp Stewart**, who also created the sybaritic Ventana Inn in Big Sur, this French country–inspired inn has 80 guest rooms and four villas interspersed with gardens. Fireplaces, pine armoires, private baths, ceiling fans, refrigerators with a complimentary bottle of wine, and private patios or verandas for every room make this a comfortable base for exploring the wine country. Other amenities include a 60-foot lap pool and spa heated year-round, two tennis courts, and bikes for rent. The concierge will arrange for private tours of wineries, mud baths and other spa services, and hot-air balloon rides. A champagne buffet breakfast is included in the room rate. ♦ 6541 Washington St. 944.1112, 800/351.1133, 800/982.5539. www.vintageinn.com

11 MOSSWOOD

Relocated from St. Helena, this shop has top-of-the-line garden tools imported from England, plus French galvanized watering cans, gardening gloves, and other essentials for the upscale gardener. There's also an array of birdbaths, fountains, and statues in various materials and sizes, plus handcrafted accessories for home and garden. ♦ Daily. 6550 Washington St (at Humboldt St), Yountville. 944.8151

12 MAISON FLEURIE

$$$ The balcony of this cozy brick building, which has been operating as a hotel since 1873, once graced the old French Hospital in San Francisco. Now a French-style country inn owned by Four Sisters Inns, the property boasts 13 rooms in the main building and two newer annexes, all with private baths and furnished with antiques. There is also a large swimming pool and a Jacuzzi for hotel guests. Innkeeper Roger Asbill serves a full breakfast in the dining room. No smoking is permitted. ♦ 6529 Yount St (between Washington and Humboldt Sts), Yountville. 944.2056. www.foursisters.com

13 GROEZINGER WINE COMPANY

A good selection of current Napa Valley releases, along with selected older wines, is offered in this shop. Employees are helpful and knowledgeable. They'll ship wines almost anywhere in the US too. ♦ Daily. 6528 Washington St (between Yount and Humboldt Sts), Yountville. 800/356.3970; fax 944.1111

13 BOUCHON

★★★$$$ Thomas Keller and his brother Joseph own the 72-seat brasserie but Jeffrey Cerciello presides over the kitchen. The menu is true to the original bouchons of Paris and Provence. The 1800s brick building was once a Wells Fargo stagecoach stop. You will want to linger over Bouchon's impressive oyster and seafood platter or a classic charcuterie platter. Don't miss dessert: the profiteroles come with a pitcher of warm chocolate sauce, and many other chocolate goodies come from **Bouchon Bakery** (944.BAKE). ♦ Daily, lunch and dinner ♦ 6534 Washington St. 944.8037

14 VINTAGE 1870

When Gottlieb Groezinger's Yountville winery was built in 1870, it was hailed as the largest and best equipped in the valley. Today the brick winery and the old train station next to it are a handsome shopping complex, with more than 45 specialty stores, gift shops, and boutiques (which seem to change every few months). Muzak is piped inside and outside the building, and many shops concentrate on silly souvenirs, so it takes determination to find the few interesting places inside. And the overpowering scent of popcorn and cheap snacks doesn't add to the complex's appeal. On either side of the property are two attractive luxury inns. ♦ Daily. 6525 Washington St (between Mulberry and Humboldt Sts), Yountville. 944.2451; fax 944.2453

Within Vintage 1870:

ADVENTURES ALOFT

This company offers balloon flights above Napa Valley with a catered light brunch and champagne. ♦ Reservations required (preferably 2 weeks in advance). 800.944.4408; www.napavalleyaloft.com

A LITTLE ROMANCE

Victoriana lovers will swoon over the Battenberg-lace duvet covers, flowered chintz coverlets, antique quilts, old-fashioned hatboxes, profusion of pillows, reproductions of Victorian tea sets, and books on country houses and the like in this boutique. ♦ Daily. 944.1350

BLUE HERON GALLERY

Located in the complex's courtyard, this shop features a mélange of art—pottery, sculpture, oil and watercolor paintings (many of Napa Valley scenes), prints, and even handmade clocks. ♦ M, W-Su. 944.2044

THE TOY CELLAR

Interesting toys and books for kids of all ages fill this shop; the wonderfully helpful salesperson will assist you in finding that special something and gift wrap it with a smile. ♦ Daily. 944.2144

VINTAGE 1870 WINE CELLAR

This well-stocked wine shop and tasting bar has a stock that includes about 500 California wines. They'll also ship worldwide. ♦ Daily. 944.9070, 800.WINE.4.US; fax 944.9073

PACIFIC BLUES CAFÉ

★$ Burgers, ribs, black beans, chili, steak, pasta, salads, and sandwiches are served in a restored railroad depot with a pleasant outdoor wooden deck that's entwined with wisteria. For breakfast, the kitchen turns out classic egg dishes, as well as burritos and a wicked vanilla-cinnamon French toast. There's also a good selection of microbrew beers and ales, including Mt. St. Helena Pale Ale, and wines by the glass. ♦ American ♦ Daily, breakfast, lunch, and dinner. 944.4455

CUCINA À LA CARTE

Like the marketplaces throughout France and Italy, this store holds a cornucopia of goods, complete with a wine bar and espresso counter. Before heading out on country roads, stock up on homemade sandwiches, pizza, pasta, or gourmet take-out meals. Fill your picnic hamper to the rim or enjoy your feast in the garden patio. 944.1600. www.cucinaalacarte.com

14 WHISTLE STOP CENTER

The old **Southern Pacific** train station, built in 1889, has been restored as a shopping center that houses several stores. ♦ 6505 Washington St (at Yount St), Yountville. 944.9624

Within the Whistle Stop Center:

OVERLAND SHEEPSKIN COMPANY

This shop sells superb sheepskin rugs, coats, hats, mittens, and slippers, all made in Taos, New Mexico. Coats are made from *entre fino*—the finest European sheepskin—in a variety of styles but come in only one price range: high. The prices of the shearling gloves and the beautifully crafted shearling-lined booties are more down-to-earth. You'll also find authentic Panama hats (which aficionados know actually come from Ecuador), oilskin raincoats from Australia, and handsome leather luggage for world-class adventurers. And don't miss the unusual all-leather animals (including hippos, tigers, and horses) made in India. ♦ Daily. 944.0778; fax 944.9644

IMAGES SOUTH

This gallery is chock-full of original contemporary artworks. Custom framing is available for your selection. ♦ Daily. 944.0606. Also at 6540 Washington St (between Yount and Humboldt Sts). 944.0404

14 HURLEY'S RESTAURANT & BAR

★★★$$ Like many chefs creating magic in California's bountiful wine country, Bob Hurley receives at his kitchen door the freshest ingredients from local farmers and food artisans. After apprenticeships with the late Masa Kobayashi and Jeremiah Tower and executive-chef posts at **Domaine Chandon** and **Napa Valley Grille,** Hurley opened his own place. His innovative style is unique and satisfying, on par with the best in the valley. For the diner, this means fine dining whether for lunch or dinner. Hurley is an ace at creating seafood dishes that pair well with red wine, especially from the Yountville appellation. Try the crayfish risotto or sea bass with mussels, fennel, and leeks in saffron broth. Other tasty offerings are rabbit stew, grilled pork chop with cranberry beans, and rib-eye steak with fine-herb buttermilk mashed potatoes, baby squash, and Cabernet-tarragon sauce. He serves the same menu all day, so sandwiches are extra special. Many locals come in just for the tuna sandwich, a house special of poached olive-oil tuna along with basil, tomato, baby lettuce, olives, sliced egg, and sweet peppers. Or try the fresh mozzarella on ciabatta bread with sun-dried tomatoes, olive tapenade, basil, and a side of orzo artichoke salad. ♦ Californian ♦ Daily, lunch and dinner. 6518 Washington St (at Yount St), Yountville. 944.2345. ᵹ www .hurleysrestaurant.com

15 BISTRO JEANTY

★★★$$$ A classic bistro in a handsome stone building with an arbor-covered patio, Bistro Jeanty is like a neighborhood open house, where Philippe Jeanty is cooking up food he loves. This is where the student-chefs from the Culinary Institute of America come in the evenings to dine on *terrine de lapin* (rabbit pâté), *rillettes de canard* (duck and goat cheese pâté with cornichons), and main courses of *moules au vin rouge* (mussels steamed in red wine) and cassoulet (baked beans, duck confit, sausage, bacon). Chef Jeanty describes this fare as "satisfying foods that change with the seasons and define regional homey French cuisine." ♦ French ♦ Daily, lunch and dinner. Reservations (required) are accepted 2 months in advance. 6510 Washington St (near Mulberry St), Yountville. 944.0103

15 ANTIQUE FAIR

If you fall in love with a beautiful hand-painted mirror or French armoire, George and Alice Rothwell will ship it to you. The New Jersey couple started out with weekend garage sales, gradually moving into hard-to-find European antiques. ♦ Daily. 6512 Washington St (at Mulberry St), Yountville. 944.8440. ᵹ www.antiquefair.com

16 YOUNTVILLE CHAMBER OF COMMERCE & VISITOR INFORMATION

You'll find free maps of Yountville here, as well as brochures on wineries and activities in the area. Information on wedding packages is also available. ♦ M-Su. 6484 Washington St. (at Oak Cir), Yountville. 944.6540. www.yountville.com

17 VILLAGIO INN & SPA

$$$ This 86-room, 26-suite luxury inn has a full-service, European-style health and beauty spa—designed by architect **Adrian Martinez** of Sonoma. Rooms have balconies overlooking flower-filled gardens, streaming water, and faux ruins, much like a country village setting. Villagio offers the same posh amenities as the **Vintage Inn** (see page 43), including its own pool, Jacuzzi, and tennis courts, plus a wide range of sumptuous spa treatments and beauty and fitness services in a stylish spa environment. The spa is available to guests at both inns, and nonresidents are also permitted to enjoy its services. ♦ 6481 Washington St (at Oak Cir). 944.8877, 800/351.1133. www.villagio.com

18 DOMAINE CHANDON

The French Champagne house Moët et Chandon, with more than two centuries of experience, has been making sparkling wine in Napa Valley since 1977. In California, this winery has pioneered the use both of exclusively classic varietals in its sparkling wines and of certain production techniques. More than six million bottles of sparkling wine are produced here annually. The star of the line is the Etoile, composed of many reserve wines dating back several years and further aged 4 years "sur lie," on yeast sediments, to develop finesse, complexity, and a richer texture. The best value is the crisp Blanc de Noirs. Reserve Cuvée, produced by winemaker Dawnine Dyer and consulting enologist Richard Geoffroy from Moët et Chandon in France, is aged a minimum of 4 years. Their Brut Cuvée, made primarily of Pinot Noir and Chardonnay and aged 18 months, has an intensely fruity flavor. Tours explain how sparkling wine is made by the traditional *méthode champenoise* and include a visit to a museum

---

Restaurants/Clubs: Red | Hotels: Purple | Shops: Orange | Outdoors/Parks: Green | Sights/Culture: Blue

devoted to the history of Champagne. Come just to stroll around the extensive, beautifully landscaped gardens or enjoy the winery's informal bar, **Le Salon**, where Domaine Chandon sparkling wine is sold by the glass and by the bottle, along with sparkling-wine cocktails, mineral water, and juice. ♦ Fee. Tasting, sales, and tours daily, May-Oct; W-Su, Nov-Apr. 1 California Dr (just west of St. Helena Hwy), Yountville. 944.2280

Within Domaine Chandon:

DOMAINE CHANDON RESTAURANT

★★★$$$ With its candlelit tables and sweeping views of the vineyards, this restaurant remains one of the most romantic settings in Napa Valley; in warm weather you may also dine outdoors. Ron Boyd's menu focuses on seasonal foods; selections change frequently, and partnered perfectly with the appropriate wine, become special events. For example, try a glass of Brut with an appetizer of seared Sonoma foie gras with green papaya and tamarind or potato-and-truffle soufflé. Red-wine lovers will toast his poached filet mignon with onion confit. A French cheese plate for two is a grand way to finish off that fine bottle of Cabernet or Merlot. Seafood selections— lobster with cauliflower and curry lobster broth, or almond-crusted pike with green olives, endive, and preserved lemon—pair well with a fruity bubbly. If you can't decide, order the seven-course tasting menu and a parade of small dishes will arrive. The desserts are spectacular, especially the pear frangipane tart with orange and star anise. The service is attentive without being pretentious, and the extensive wine list offers a number of Napa Valley's best wines at good prices. ♦ Californian ♦ Th–M, lunch and dinner; M, Tu, lunch June-September. Closed, January. Reservations recommended; no jeans. 944.2892. www.chandon,com

19 NAPA VALLEY MUSEUM

This shrine to Napa history opened in January 1998 in a new $3.5 million, 10,000-square-foot home beautifully set in a mature redwood grove bordered by a creek. Designed by the Berkeley-based firm of **Fernau and Hartman Architects**, the sleek concrete, metal, and stucco structure is set amid outdoor gardens and landscaped exhibit terraces. The museum salutes the unique historical, artistic, and environmental heritage of the Napa region; its current collection boasts approximately 4,000 artifacts. For many visitors, the highlight of the museum is the $1.5 million permanent exhibit *California Wine: The Science of an Art*, donated by the California Science Center in Los Angeles, that takes viewers through a year

in wine-making, from soil to bottling. Included in the exhibit are a chronology of wine, its myths and realities, how to select the right wine, and what happens during the aging process. Located on the grounds of the Veterans Home. ♦ Fee. M, W-Su; till 8PM the first Thursday of each month. 55 President's Cir (off California Dr), Yountville. 944.0500. www.napavalley.com

20 PLUMPJACK WINERY

PlumpJack wines are crowd pleasers, from the Cabernet Oakville Cuvée to the Napa Syrah. Luckily, the winery holds back enough bottles to supply the tasting room. You'll also be enchanted by the tasting-room interior, chock-full of whimsical art. Take in the splendid views of the Mayacamas, the Vaca Mountains, and 50 acres of "cult" Cabernet Sauvignon vines. PlumpJack's reserve Cabernet Sauvignon Oakville is available for purchase only. ♦ Fee. Daily tasting. 620 Oakville Cross Rd (near Silverado Tr), Oakville. 945.1220. www.plumpjack.com/winery

21 NAPA WINE COMPANY

Stop at this tasting room located at a "custom crush" facility that produces some of Napa's most renowned wines. They rotate the wines you can taste, but among them may be La Sirena—the label of cult winemaker Heidi Peterson Barrett—Pahlmeyer, Oakford, and Showket, as well as the owners' own excellent Napa Wine Company wine. Also in the tasting room is the famous collectible Marilyn Merlot made by Nova Wines with a picture of Marilyn Monroe: the oldest vintages cost up to $3,000. The Cellar Door is open daily for tasting and sales. A $5-$10 fee includes tastings of four wines plus premium tasting of selected wines at additional cost. Check the web site for special events and winemaker dinners. ♦ 7830-40 St. Helena Hwy at Oakville Crossroad. 944.1710, 800/848.9630. www.napawineco.com

22 CARDINALE & PEPI WINERY AND VINEYARDS

In this contemporary winery, vintner Jess Jackson and winemaker Charles Thomas produce Cardinale's Cabernet Sauvignon and Merlot, while winemaker Marco DiGiulio continues the tradition of the Pepi vineyards with such wines as Classic Sangiovese, Sauvignon Blanc, and a Sangiovese blend *Due Baci* (Two Kisses). ♦ Tasting and sales daily. 7585 St. Helena Hwy (between Yount Mill and Oakville Grade Rds), Oakville. 945.1391; fax 944.8603

23 POETRY INN

$$$ The only B&B in the Stags Leap District, the Poetry Inn takes full advantage of its

WINE-COUNTRY FLICKS

Photogenic California wine country's verdant groves, terraced vineyards, quaint towns, and wild coast have long attracted filmmakers in search of evocative locations. The following are among the movies that have been filmed in this region:

American Graffiti (1973)   The George Lucas classic, shot in **Petaluma**, follows four guys through a night of painting their hometown red in a nostalgia-tinted 1962.

The Birds (1963)   In Alfred Hitchcock's virtuoso rendition of a Daphne du Maurier shocker, Tippi Hedren and Rod Taylor try to cope as great flocks of strangely vicious birds terrorize the folk of **Bodega Bay**.

The Candidate (1972)   Robert Redford, as a true believer in good causes—including preserving the Northern California environment—runs for the US Senate and wins, but he loses something more important in the process.

The Farmer's Daughter (1947)   Loretta Young got an Oscar for her performance as a **Sonoma County** Scandinavian farm girl who gets a job as a domestic for a Congressman and ends engaging in some inspiring politics herself.

Forever Young (1992)   Mel Gibson is a test pilot frozen in a cryogenics experiment just before World War II; he gets defrosted in 1992, just in time to fall in love with Jamie Lee Curtis in **Point Arena, Mendocino**.

Frenchman's Creek (1943)   Based on the Daphne du Maurier bodice ripper, this film features Joan Fontaine as a 17th-century lass fleeing corrupt London for her girlhood home in Cornwall, where she finds romance with a French pirate. Shot dramatically on the **Mendocino Coast**, it won an Oscar for its art direction.

Inventing the Abbotts (1997)   Billy Crudup and Joaquin Phoenix are two brothers seeking revenge for the injustices of the class system by pursuing the wealthy Abbott sisters (Jennifer Connelly, Joanna Going, Liv Tyler). The drama takes place in 1957, in a small Midwestern town discreetly played by **Santa Rosa** and **Healdsburg**.

Johnny Belinda (1948)   Jane Wyman won an Academy Award for her portrayal of a young rape victim who can't tell the townspeople who fathered her child because she's a deaf-mute. **Mendocino** is the town.

Lolita (1997)   This second movie version of Vladimir Nabokov's great but unfilmable novel, directed by Adrian Lyne and starring Jeremy Irons and Dominique Swain, tries harder than the cold-hearted 1962 version by Stanley Kubrick. In the end it doesn't succeed any better, but there is some fine acting and lovely footage of **Sonoma County**.

The Man Who Wasn't There (2001)   In this film noir homage to black-and-white films of of the 1940s and '50s, Billy Bob Thornton plays Ed Crane, a laconic barber in 1940s Santa Rosa. The plot twists and turns, as when Ed decides to blackmail his wife's boss with whom she (Frances McDormand) is having an affair.

Peggy Sue Got Married (1986)   Filmed in **Petaluma** and **Santa Rosa**, Francis Coppola's dark take on early-1960s nostalgia examines the era through the eyes of a woman (Kathleen Turner) working through complicated memories at her 25th high school reunion.

Racing with the Moon (1984)   Richard Benjamin directed Sean Penn, Elizabeth McGovern, and Nicolas Cage in an evocation of the wartime atmosphere of 1942, with two Marine recruits saying good-bye to their youth in a small town represented by locations in **Mendocino** and **Ft. Bragg**.

The Russians Are Coming! The Russians Are Coming! (1966)   Alan Arkin stars in the Cold War comedy about what happens when a Soviet submarine runs aground at an American seaside resort. The story was set on the Connecticut coast but filmed bicoastally, partly in Nantucket and partly in **Mendocino County**.

Same Time, Next Year (1978)   In this film version of Bernard Slade's Broadway hit, Ellen Burstyn and Alan Alda, married to others, carry on a secret affair for 25 years, meeting once a year at the same romantic inn in **Mendocino**.

A Walk in the Clouds (1995)   A young woman (Aitana Sanchez-Gijon) comes home from college to her family's **Napa County** winery, accompanied by a returning World War II vet (Keanu Reeves). She's pregnant and he's pretending to be her husband to protect her from the wrath of her traditionalist California father (Giancarlo Giannini).

Sideways (2004) In this dark comedy, wine lover Miles (Paul Giamatti), a divorced middle-school English teacher, and his actor buddy, Jack (Thomas Haden Church), take a romp through Central Coast wineries. Their good qualities overwhelm the bad in scenes of life's little comedies. Sampling rosé, Miles urges Jack to stick his nose into the wineglass. He demonstrates by wedging half his face into his own·glass, detecting aromas of citrus and strawberry and notes of asparagus and an obscure cheese.

Restaurants/Clubs: Red | Hotels: Purple | Shops: Orange | Outdoors/Parks: Green | Sights/Culture: Blue

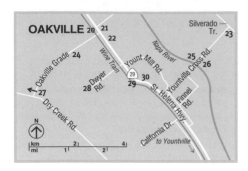

ment only. 1119 State La (between Yountville Cross Rd and Silverado Tr), Yountville. 944.1986; fax 944.9551

26 CLIFF LEDE VINEYARDS

Founded in 1971, this small, family-owned winery reminiscent of a one-room schoolhouse specializes in Chardonnay and sparkling wines made by the traditional *méthode champenoise*. A spectacular 7,000-square-foot aging cave has been tunneled out of a volcanic-rock hillside overlooking the estate's vineyards. Owners Cliff and Cheryl Lede reserve the best fruit from select vineyards for their flagship Poetry label. ♦ Fee. Tasting and sales daily; tours daily, 10:30AM and 2:30PM. 1473 Yountville Cross Rd (between Finnel Rd and Silverado Tr), Yountville. 944.8642, 800/428.2259. www.cliffledevineyards.com

location. Spacious suites have wood-burning fireplaces and French patio doors that open onto stunning vistas of green hills and vineyards, which you'll appreciate all the more over a gourmet breakfast delivered to your suite. There are also soaking tubs, indoor-outdoor showers, luxurious bath amenities, and Frette robes. Poetry Inn is part of the **Cliff Lede Vineyards** estate and is named for its flagship Poetry wine label. ♦ 6380 Silverado Tr (at Yountville Cross Rd), Napa. 944.0646. ♿ www.poetryinn.com

24 LA FAMIGLIA DI MONDAVI

This Spanish Colonial–style winery, owned by the Robert Mondavi family, sits high on a hill with a stunning view of the vineyards. This establishment used to focus on California wines—Chardonnay, Cabernet, and the like—but now Italian vintages have taken center stage. Winemaker Heather Pyle tempts your taste buds with wines from several regions of Italy, but more important, with even rarer finds in California: the dry aromatic, fruity Tocai Friulano; lush, citrusy, floral-scented Moscato Bianco; Rosato, here as a dry rosé; and delicately sweet, exotic floral and fruity Malvasia Bianca. There are tables in a small, shady picnic grove (you have to buy a bottle of wine to picnic here) and a boccie court for visitors. ♦ Fee for tasting without a tour. Tasting, sales, and tours daily. 1595 Oakville Grade (between St. Helena Hwy and Dry Creek Rd), Napa. 944.2811; fax 944.9224

27 MAYACAMAS VINEYARDS

A formidable road takes you to this historic property with terraced vineyards high on the slopes of the extinct volcano Mount Veeder. The three-story stone building, set in the volcano's crater, was built in 1889 for John Henry Fisher, a native of Stuttgart, Germany. The winery was reestablished in 1941 when the British chemist Jack Taylor restored it and replanted the vineyards. It has been owned by banker-turned-vintner Bob Travers and his wife, Nonie, since 1968. The winery is known for its rugged, intense Cabernet and rich, oaky Chardonnay, both of which age remarkably well. The vineyard also produces Pinot Noir and Sauvignon Blanc. ♦ Tasting and tours M-F, by appointment only. 1155 Lokoya Rd (just west of Mount Veeder Rd), Napa. 224.4030; fax 224.3979

Goosecross Cellars

25 GOOSECROSS CELLARS

Napa Valley Chardonnay is the specialty of this small winery overlooking 10.5 acres of grapes and a rose garden. Cabernet Sauvignon is also available. At the free Wine Basics class held every Saturday at 11AM, you can taste rare signature wines in the barrel room. Guests are welcome to stroll through the vineyards after visiting the cellar. ♦ Tasting and sales daily; tours by appoint-

27 CHÂTEAU POTELLE

This winery located on scenic Mount Veeder produces Chardonnay, Sauvignon Blanc, Cabernet, and Zinfandel from grapes grown on its mountain vineyards. French proprietors Jean-Noël and Marketta Fourmeaux du Sartel named the winery after their family's 11th-century castle in France. Customers can avail

WHO INVENTED THE WINE BOTTLE?

Throughout the Roman Empire, the wine bottle and the cork enjoyed widespread use. Cork was forgotten after the fall of the Roman Empire, then brought back in the 16th century. The Roman bottle remained in use, unchanged until a 17th-century edict.

At that time, King James I wished to halt the destruction of England's forests. Demand for windows, drinking glasses, and expensive, fragile bottles caused a rise in glass production and an increase in the number of glass furnaces. The alarmed monarch forbade the use of wood-burning furnaces for glass-making. That prompted Sir Kenelm Digby—courtier, author, alchemist, and pirate—to use coal to fire glass into thick, heavy, dark, cheap bottles. At first the bottles were globular in shape, much like a bubble with a tall narrow neck ending in a rim where the stopper was tied. As it became known that wine ages more gracefully if the bottle lay on its side, the bubble shape gradually became the shape we use today.

themselves of the winery's picnic area with its lovely panoramic view of mountains and vineyards. ◆ Tasting and sales M, Th-Su; call in advance Dec-Feb. 3876 Mount Veeder Rd (between Lokoya and Dry Creek Rds), Napa. 255.9440; fax 255.9444

28 PARADIGM WINERY

Out stalking Oakville's "cult" Cabs? Renowned winemaker Heidi Peterson Barrett makes the wines at the Paradigm vineyard that was laid out by her father, Dick Peterson. Ren and Marilyn Harris purchased the property in 1976 but replanted it with red Bordeaux varietals—Cabernet Sauvignon, Merlot, Cabernet Franc, and Zinfandel—that do so well in the Oakville district. All Paradigm wines are aged in French oak barrels for 20 months, with additional bottle aging—20 months for the Cabernet Sauvignon, 14 months for other reds. Paradigm's annual production is limited to 5,000 cases. Afternoon tours and tasting by appointment only, so call a day or more in advance. The winery is located 2 miles north of Yountville at the end of Dwyer Road, just beyond a sign reading NO WINERIES ON THIS ROAD. ◆ Fee. Dwyer Rd (off Hwy 29), Oakville. 944.1683. www.ParadigmWinery.com

29 BRIX

★★★★$$$$ For a memorable dining experience worth splurging on, this elegant place provides every table with a view of the distant Napa hills, vineyards, and the organic gardens that serve the kitchen. Inside, quiet colors, wood beams, and soft lighting complement the innovative, beautifully presented cuisine. The exquisitely presented dishes are the expression of executive chef Ryan Jackson's marriage of Asian and traditional French cuisines. And true to its surroundings, Brix's extensive wine list features top wines from many California, Washington, and Oregon wineries. The ahi tuna sashimi, marinated cucumber salad appetizer goes just right with a glass of Sauvignon Blanc. The Dungeness crab and artichoke beignets with roasted red pepper remoulade is another favorite, and a glass of good bubbly stands up to it. Main dishes—including grilled filet mignon sandwich with caper aioli, Gruyère, and grilled onions—pair well with a Pinot Noir or Sangiovese. For dessert, try the Meyer lemon soufflé tart with brown sugar meringue and huckleberry sauce with a glass of a late-harvest Riesling. The restaurant also has a wine shop specializing in California wines, among them many hard-to-find and rare selections. ◆ Fusion ◆ Daily, lunch and dinner. Reservations required. 7377 St. Helena Hwy (between Madison St and Dwyer Rd), Yountville. 944.2749. www.brix.com

29 MUSTARDS GRILL

★★★$$ The quintessential wine-country restaurant, this ever-popular establishment is the brainchild of Cindy Pawlcyn (who devises all the menus), Bill Upson, and Bill Higgins. Its major assets are a carefully chosen, well-priced wine list and a menu that always induces you to order far more than you had intended. The menu changes frequently, but you can count on a superlative burger and heavenly onion rings (order them with homemade ketchup). Consider starting with crispy calamari with curry slaw or grilled pasilla pepper with tamale stuffing and salsa ranchera. Lovers of complex flavors will savor such entrées as tea-smoked Peking duck; calves' liver with caramelized apples; or braised veal shank with vodka risotto. Those with more traditional appetites can tuck into a huge portion of steak and potatoes. The side dishes are terrific—don't overlook the mashed potatoes or griddled goat cheese polenta with tomato–onion chutney. And if you have room, go for the desserts, which may include a fresh deep-dish apple pie with maple ice cream. There also are microbrews, wines, an extensive selection of brandies, fortified wines, and a nifty martini made with vintage-dated, organic sourmash vodka. You might sip it at the bar while watching the game on TV. ♦ California ♦ Daily, lunch and dinner. Reservations recommended. 7399 St. Helena Hwy (between Madison St and Dwyer Rd), Yountville. 944.2424 www.mustardsgrill.com

29 OLEANDER HOUSE

$$ The five rooms at this bed-and-breakfast in a contemporary French country–style home just off Route 29 are furnished with Laura Ashley fabrics and antiques. Each has a queen-size bed, private bath, fireplace, and balcony. A bonus: It's virtually next door to **Mustards Grill**, so you can stroll home to bed after a filling dinner and wine. There's a full breakfast of fresh orange juice, fruit, and homemade pastries, plus such delicious starts of the day as an herb omelette or French toast with raspberries. Smoking is not allowed. ♦ 7433 St. Helena Hwy (between Madison St and Dwyer Rd), Yountville. 944.8315; fax 252.2804

30 MCALLISTER WATER GARDENS

Re-create scenes from Monet's paintings in your own backyard with the help of this nursery, which specializes in water lilies and pond plants. ♦ Th-Su, Mar-Sept. 7420 St. Helena Hwy (between Washington St and Yount Mill Rd), Yountville. 944.0921

30 CASTLE IN THE CLOUDS BED & BREAKFAST

$$$ Four hundred feet above the valley floor crowning a knoll is a pink mansion. Of the inn's four rooms, the valley-view room offers a spectacular panorama of vineyards and a four-poster king-size bed, a hand-carved Renaissance masterpiece. Innkeepers Larry and Jean Grunewald furnished each room with 19th-century European antiques. View the rooms online before making your selection. The Grunewalds were smart in planting Cabernet Sauvignon on their estate, which lies in the highly sought Oakville appellation. Room rates include a three-course breakfast served in the dining room or adjacent patio. ♦ The driveway is on Hwy 29, one mile north of Yountville opposite Mustards Grill. Ring at the call box and the gate will open. Follow the long drive past the vineyards. Mailing address: 7400 St. Helena Hwy, Napa, CA 94558. 944.2785. www.castleintheclouds.com

31 AUBERGE DU SOLEIL

$$$$ Without question this French country–style inn is the wine country's best resort—and certainly one of its most expensive. Despite the high price tag and magnificent appointments, however, the atmosphere is engagingly casual. And because of the privacy it affords, Auberge has become a honeymoon haven. The breathtaking setting is a 33-acre hillside olive grove overlooking Napa Valley. Architect **Sandy Walker** and the late designer Michael Taylor built the original 48 villas and included two rooms in the main house (recently two villas have been added, making a total of 52 one- and two-room accommodations), each named after a region of France; indeed, once inside one of these very private and romantic *maisons*, you'll feel as if you've been transported to a hill town in southern France. Every suite or room has its own entrance, fireplace, and French doors that open onto a completely private veranda overlooking the wine country. Windows are set deep into earth-toned stucco walls, much like a Provençal farmhouse. Hand-glazed terra-cotta tiles cover the floors, frame the fireplaces and bathtubs, and even top the bureaus and counters, and couches with soft, large cushions and leather chairs fill the high-ceilinged rooms. The deluxe **Auberge King** rooms are a third larger than the standard rooms and feature whirlpool baths,

but otherwise there's not much difference between the two types of rooms. The suites are the most romantic accommodations, although they don't include whirlpool tubs. The extensive grounds are planted with a profusion of flowers as well as a vegetable garden that provides ingredients for the restaurant's chef. A half-mile sculpture trail winds around the western end of the resort and features a variety of works by Northern California artists. There's a swimming pool and a tiny exercise room, both with stunning views, a basic spa with two steam rooms, showers, lockers, and a massage room (massages may be given in your room too), and a full-service beauty salon. The property also features picnic tables and three tennis courts. Don't miss sitting outside on the bar's terrace when the weather is mild—it's the best place in the valley to linger over a glass of wine at sunset. This "Inn of the Sun" is a member of the prestigious international Relais & Châteaux hotel association. Concierge and 24-hour room service are available. No children under 16 are allowed. ♦ 180 Rutherford Hill Rd (east of Silverado Tr), Rutherford. 963.1211, 800/348.5406; fax 963.0283. www.aubergedusoleil.com

Within Auberge du Soleil:

AUBERGE DU SOLEIL RESTAURANT

★★★★$$$$ Chef Joseph Humphrey continues to win high praise at this romantic dining room, one of the wine country's finest. His menu changes with the seasons and incorporates vegetables and herbs. Dinner might begin with pan-seared foie gras with caramelized sunchokes and dried cherry vinaigrette or spicy shrimp Indochine, complemented by Thai grilled eggplant, and a cooling cucumber herb salad, followed by such main courses as rosemary bacon-wrapped swordfish with shrimp-chive stuffing or chorizo-stuffed pork loin with bourbon demiglaze. One of the restaurant's signature dishes is rack of lamb encrusted with hazelnuts served with ragout of apple and bacon. Be sure to leave room for pastry chef Paul Lemieux's Meyer-lemon soufflé cake served with black currant coulis, or try the three-apple consommé with deep-fried cinnamon ice cream. Lunch often includes a pizza and pasta and soup of the day. The bar menu offers such interesting sandwiches as "California rock-n-roll," chilled rock shrimp in a tortilla wrap. The dining room, with its bouquets of seasonal flowers, comfortable banquettes, and seemingly endless views of the valley, has always been one of the most romantic in the area—weather permitting, however, the best seats in the house are at the tables on the terrace. ♦ California ♦ Daily,

breakfast, lunch, and dinner. Reservations recommended

31 RUTHERFORD HILL WINERY

Take an informative tour through this contemporary wood winery, including a walk through the extensive aging caves carved a half mile into the cliffs behind the winery. Tunnel specialist Alf Burtleson spent 13 months on the job, using an English drilling machine to burrow into the hard-packed earth and rock. Winemakers Kevin Robinson and Kent Barthman focus on Merlot, Chardonnay, Cabernet Sauvignon, and a Zinfandel Port. The picnic grounds, under the oaks and in an olive grove, share a panoramic view with **Auberge du Soleil**. ♦ Tasting and sales daily; tours M-F, 11:30AM, 1:30PM, and 3:30PM; Sa, Su, 11:30AM, 12:30PM, 2:30PM, and 3:30PM. 200 Rutherford Hill Rd (east of Silverado Tr), Rutherford. 963.7194; fax 963.4231

32 LAKE HENNESSEY PICNIC GROUNDS

If the lake has been stocked with trout, as it generally is each spring, you could catch a fish and fry it up right here in the barbecue pits in the picnic area. This is a reservoir for local drinking water, so no swimming is allowed; however, you can take a dip in the creek that runs alongside the picnic grounds. ♦ Sa, Su; holidays, Memorial Day through Labor Day weekend. Sage Canyon Rd (east of Silverado Tr). 257.9529

33 LONG VINEYARDS

This tiny family winery on Pritchard Hill east of the Silverado Trail was founded in 1978 by Zelma Long, one of California's most prominent winemakers and president of **Simi Winery** in Sonoma County, and her former husband, Bob Long. Zelma is now a consultant at the winery, and Bob, the owner, and winemaker Sandi S. Belcher continue to produce first-class Chardonnay, Riesling, Cabernet Sauvignon, Sauvignon Blanc, and Pinot Grigio, all of which are hard to find because quantities are so limited and sought after by connoisseurs. Another bottle to covet is the opulent late-harvest Johannisberg Riesling, produced only in years when conditions are right. ♦ Tours by appointment only. 1535 Sage Canyon Rd (east of Silverado Tr). 963.2496; fax 963.2907

33 CHAPELLET VINEYARD

Donn and Molly Chapellet's pyramid-shaped winery, founded in 1967 and

---

Restaurants/Clubs: **Red** | Hotels: **Purple** | Shops: **Orange** | Outdoors/Parks: **Green** | Sights/Culture: **Blue**

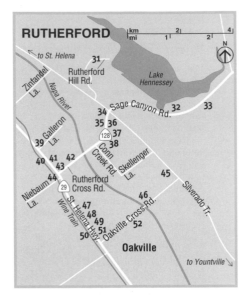

RUTHERFORD

to St. Helena
31
Rutherford Hill Rd.
Lake Hennessey
Zinfandel La.
Napa River
Galleron La.
Sage Canyon Rd.
34
32
33
35 36
128 37
39
38
40 41 42
43
Conn Creek Rd.
Skellenger La.
45
44 Rutherford Cross Rd.
29
46
Silverado Tr.
Niebaum La.
St. Helena Hwy.
Wine Train
47
48
49
51
50
52
Oakville Cross Rd.

Oakville

to Yountville

located on a spectacular site on Pritchard Hill, is devoted to five wines: one of California's best Chenin Blancs, a crisp straightforward Chardonnay, and a very good Cabernet, Merlot, and Sangiovese, all from the terraced vineyards. ♦ Tours by appointment only. 1581 Sage Canyon Rd (east of Silverado Tr). 963.7136; fax 963.7445

34 QUINTESSA

Built into a hill, this winery offers a contemporary low-key setting in which to sample Quintessa's Meritage wine. Grapes are crushed on the roof, then flow down into the fermentation room and ultimately into French oak barrels in the caves below. Owners Agustin and Valeria Huneeus use biodynamic techniques to farm the 170-acre vineyard. In spring, workers spray the vines with homeopathic "teas" of silica, chamomile, oak bark, stinging nettle, valerian, and other herbs. Winemaker Aaron Pott specializes in the Bordeaux grape varieties—Cabernet Sauvignon, and smaller blocks of Merlot, Cabernet Franc, Petit Verdot, and Carmenère—planted on the estate. To fully appreciate the care that goes into producing these dense, full-bodied wines, tour the caves and vineyards. ♦ Fee. Tours and tasting daily by

"Women can spin very well, but they can't write a good book of cookery."

—Samuel Johnson,
quoted in *The Delectable Past* by Esther Aretsy (Simon & Schuster, 1964)

appointment. 1601 Silverado Tr (between Conn Creek Rd and Zinfandel La), Rutherford. 967.1601. ♦ www.quintessa.com

FROG'S LEAP

35 FROG'S LEAP

Founded in 1981 on the site of an old frog-raising farm (hence the name) in St. Helena, this winery moved south to new quarters in 1994. Owners John and Julie Williams have restored the historic red barn to its original condition and continue to use the organic farming methods for which they are well known. Their best wines are the Cabernet Sauvignon and Sauvignon Blanc, but the Chardonnay is not far behind. They also make a spicy Zinfandel and a fruity Merlot. The Williamses' wine labels are notable as well: artist Charles House's labels have won national graphic-design awards and are now part of the Smithsonian Institution's permanent collection, bringing fame to both House and the wines. The winery provides a great tour. ♦ Sales M-Sa; tastings and tours by appointment only. 8815 Conn Creek Rd (between Rutherford Cross Rd and Silverado Tr), Rutherford. 963.4704

36 VILLA MOUNT EDEN–CONN CREEK WINERIES

Owned by Stimson Lane, which also owns Château Ste. Michelle and Columbia Crest in Washington, this winery—under winemaker Mike McGrath—concentrates on limited-production wines: Chardonnay ('94 Reserve award-winner at Vin Expo in Bordeaux, France); sumptuous Pinot Blanc; an excellent Cabernet Sauvignon; impressive Pinot Noir (especially Napa Valley Grand); nicely balanced Merlot; distinctive Syrah; pleasant Zinfandel; and slightly carbonated Orange Muscat dessert wine. **Conn Creek**'s Cabernet Sauvignon also is available here. ♦ Tasting and sales daily; tours by appointment only. 8711 Silverado Tr (between Skellenger La and Sage Canyon Rd), Rutherford. 944.2414; fax 963.7840

36 MUMM NAPA VALLEY

This joint venture between French Champagne producer G.H. Mumm and the Seagram wine company produces several pleasant sparkling wines made by the traditional *méthode champenoise*. The winery building, with its steep-pitched roof and redwood siding, is

THE BEST

Susan Karakasevic

Owner, Domaine Charbay Winery & Distillery, Napa Valley

My favorites around Napa Valley:

Morning walks to the end of Spring Street in **St. Helena**, which becomes a country lane weaving through redwoods, a resort, and along a creek.

Coffee in **St. Helena** at the **Model Bakery** or the **Napa Valley Coffee Roasting Company**.

Stroll through **St. Helena** for creative energy. Peek through **St. Helena Antiques**. Check the used-book store for autographed books. Across the street is tiny **Trilogy** restaurant, a romantic little find we like.

Head north—check out **Hurd Beeswax Candles** at **Freemark Abbey**, unique candles, made right there. They carry locally crafted Wolford lamps. Ask to see where the bees are making their honeycomb.

To get out of town, drive to **Calistoga**—park and walk. Visit the **Artful Eye** for some outrageous gifts. Walk to **All Seasons Café** or **Catahoula Restaurant & Saloon**

for a fun lunch or dinner; cruise through **Palisades Market** to see the colorful array of foods, wines, and more.

An afternoon stop at the **Culinary Institute of America at Greystone** is a relaxing pause. Take a tour; walk through the students' cookware and food shop; make a lunch or dinner reservation. As you leave, look up—catch the panoramic view.

Lunch or dinner at **Ristorante Tra Vigne** is a must. Outside is our favorite. If you get Walt or Murph, let him take away the menus and call the shots! You'll walk away feeling as if the whole valley loves you! Watch the way Joël delivers a bottle of wine—like a baby! Ahh, a little French touch!

Domaine Chandon gives a super tour on Champagne-making.

If you have to head south, **Bistro Don Giovanni** will wow all your senses. It's where we celebrated the end of harvest this year. Very delicious.

Plan to keep coming back. The B&Bs are perfect for that dreamy state of being away in a beautiful land. We still feel lucky meeting folks from around the world. They drive up soooo relaxed. It's contagious.

---

reminiscent of the traditional Napa Valley barn. You may taste the Brut Prestige, Blanc de Noirs, and other selections in the salon overlooking the vineyard, where many quality gifts are also available. There is a photography gallery and large porch open to the vineyards with views of the Mayacamas Mountains, and, in warm weather, a patio area is set with shaded tables. The winery produces a Prestige Cuvée DVX, and, in certain years, a vintage-dated reserve—a blend of Chardonnay and Pinot Noir—that's aged 2 years on the yeast. ◆ Fee. Tasting, sales, and tours daily; private tours and tastings are available by appointment only. 8445 Silverado Tr (between Skellenger La and Sage Canyon Rd), Rutherford. 942.3400; visitors' center 934.3434, 800/686.6271; fax (toll free) 888/231.5028. www.mumm.com

37 ZD WINES

Former aerospace engineers Gino Zepponi and Norman deLeuze took the first letters of their last names to form their logo when they started making wine in Sonoma in 1969. They moved their operation to the Silverado Trail in 1979. Now run by deLeuze and his wife, Rosa Lee, with their three children, Robert, Julie, and Brett, the winery's star continues to be Robert's opulent barrel-fermented Chardonnay. Also look for its Pinot Noir,

powerful Cabernet Sauvignon, and the newest addition, an intense Merlot with delightful aromas of cinnamon, oak, and rich fruit. ◆ Fee. Tasting and sales daily; tours by appointment only. 8383 Silverado Tr (between Skellenger La and Sage Canyon Rd), Rutherford. 963.5188; fax 963.2640

38 CAYMUS VINEYARDS

Charlie and Lorna Wagner and their son Chuck, second- and third-generation winemakers, run a no-nonsense operation that just happens to have a reputation for some of Napa Valley's best Cabernet Sauvignons (the Special Selection is one of California's greatest). Their knowledge of vineyards and wine-making consistently yield wines rich in character and complexity. Drive past the ranch-style house to the small tasting room. In addition to Cabernet Sauvignon, the winery also makes a very good Sauvignon Blanc as well as Conundrum (a rich, spicy,

---

distinctive blend of Chardonnay, Sauvignon Blanc, and Muscat). ◆ Fee. Tastings and sales by appointment. 8700 Conn Creek Rd (between Skellenger La and Sage Canyon Rd), Rutherford. 963.4204

39 FRANCISCAN VINEYARDS

This state-of-the-art building is the headquarters of four California properties where you can stop and taste wines from Franciscan Vineyards and **Mount Veeder** wineries. Franciscan's flagship wines are the Franciscan Oakville Estate Meritage, a blend of red Bordeaux varietals, and Cuvée Sauvage, a Chardonnay fermented in French oak barrels by the naturally occurring wild yeast present in the vineyard. The winery is owned by the Eckes family, which has been involved in wine-making and brandy distilling in Germany for five generations, and by Agustin Huneeus, president of Franciscan. ◆ Fee. Tasting and sales daily. 1178 Galleron La (at St. Helena Hwy), Rutherford. 963.7111; fax 963.7867

39 NAPA VALLEY GRAPEVINE WREATH COMPANY

This is a great spot to find unique handmade items made from Cabernet Sauvignon grapevine cuttings in many shapes (hearts, or at Christmas, reindeer) and sizes (up to 36 inches across, or even larger by special order); there's also an assortment of vine-woven baskets. ◆ M, W-Su. 8901 Conn Creek Rd (between Rutherford Cross Rd and Silverado Tr), Rutherford. 963.8893; fax 963.3325

40 GRGICH HILLS CELLAR

A dapper émigré vintner from Yugoslavia, Miljenko (Mike) Grgich is among the pioneers who established the reputation of Napa Valley wines in the early 1970s. He began his career at **Château Montelena** (he made the 1973 Chardonnay that won the famous Paris tasting

of 1976) and then opened his own winery with partner Austin Hills (of the Hills Bros. Coffee family) in 1977 in a functional Spanish Colonial building along Route 29. Grgich is an undisputed master of Chardonnay and has priced his wines accordingly. He also makes a distinguished Fumé Blanc, a full-bodied Cabernet, and a Zinfandel from old vines. On weekends you may taste older library wines, and selected older vintages are for sale. This should be a mandatory stop on your wine itinerary. ◆ Fee for tasting older wines. Tasting and sales daily; tours by appointment only. 1829 St. Helena Hwy (between Niebaum and Whitehall Las), Rutherford. 963.2784; fax 963.8725

41 BEAULIEU VINEYARD

Don't miss this historic Rutherford estate prominently located on St. Helena Highway. Founded in 1900 by the French émigré Georges de Latour, who gave it a French name (meaning "beautiful place"), the winery is now known for its Chardonnay, Sauvignon Blanc, and especially its Cabernet Sauvignon. The Rutherford and Georges de Latour Private Reserve are the benchmark California Cabernets, which have a long track record for their aging potential. In addition, Merlot, Pinot Noir, and a sweet Muscat de Beaulieu are made here. A small tasting room next door showcases the reserve wines: older and current vintages of the Georges de Latour Private Reserve and Carneros Reserve Chardonnay and Pinot Noir. ◆ Wine tasting in the main room is free, but there is a small charge for the reserve wines. Tasting, sales, and tours daily. 1960 St. Helena Hwy (between Rutherford Cross Rd and Mees La), Rutherford. 963.2411, 967.5200; fax 967.9149

42 RANCHO CAYMUS INN

$$ Sculptor Mary Tilden Morton (whose family founded the Morton Salt Company) built this rustic 26-unit Spanish Colonial–style hotel, where **Flora Springs** winery proprietor John Komes is the owner and son Otto Komes is the innkeeper. The two-story building, with its wisteria-covered balconies, is constructed around a central courtyard with a fountain. To decorate her inn, Morton hired local carpenters and craftspeople skilled at creating stained glass, wrought iron, and ceramics. She designed and built the adobe fireplaces and collected crafts from Ecuador, Peru, and Mexico to adorn the rooms and suites (all with private baths). The four master suites, each named for a local historical figure, feature Jacuzzis, full kitchens, and large balconies and are ideal for long stays. ◆ 1140 Rutherford

Cross Rd (east of St. Helena Hwy), Rutherford. 963.1777, 800/845.1777; fax 963.5387

Within Rancho Caymus Inn:

La Toque™

LA TOQUE

★★★★$$$$ Sharing the Rancho Caymus Inn's romantic courtyard is a culinary hot spot popular with the movers and shakers of the local wine industry. La Toque chef Ken Frank combines French haute cuisine with California wine-country cuisine. To sample four courses of perfectly matched food and wine, order the wine pairing menu, created by Scott Tracy, which often showcases small boutique wines unavailable to consumers. A 1997 T Vine Meritage, Napa Valley, is paired with rib roast with fried potatoes, Cabernet foie gras sauce, and lima and cranberry bean ragout with pesto. A 1997 Crocker Starr, Stone Place Cuvée, St. Helena, Napa Valley, enhances the Maine lobster with orzo. You can follow dinner with a cheese course or dessert course. The raspberry tart with roasted figs and buttermilk ice cream is a perfect way to end the evening. ♦ California/French ♦ W-Su, dinner. Reservations recommended 2 weeks in advance in winter, 4 to 6 weeks in advance in summer. 1140 Rutherford Cross Rd (at St. Helena Hwy), Rutherford. 963.9770. www.latoque.com

43 RUTHERFORD GRILL

★★$$ Right next door to the **Beaulieu** tasting room (see page 54), this large, casual restaurant with a handsome bar, burgundy leather booths, and a sleek open kitchen serves wood-fired, spit-roasted chicken, leg of lamb, ribs, steak, and a good seared tuna salad. Don't miss the blue-cheese potato chips. Wines from the well-selected list can be ordered by the glass or bottle. The whole wood-roasted chicken can be ordered to go— perfect for picnicking. ♦ American ♦ Daily, lunch and dinner. 1180 Rutherford Cross Rd (east of St. Helena Hwy), Rutherford. 963.1792; fax 963.1920

44 NIEBAUM-COPPOLA ESTATE WINERY

Having purchased the old **Inglenook** estate with his wife, Eleanor, Francis Ford Coppola turned his passion for wine to the goal of turning out wines to rival the great Inglenook Cask Cabernets of old—wines that age well over the long term. This remains the goal of winemaker Scott McLeod with the wines he produces from Coppola's 195-acre organic vineyards in Rutherford. The Coppola winery saga started, appropriate to an author-filmmaker, with a flashback: to Gustave Niebaum, a Finnish sea captain, who founded the famous Inglenook estate in Napa Valley in 1879. Niebaum wanted to produce wines that would rival those produced in France. In 1975, the Coppolas purchased part of the immense property and joined the Niebaum and Coppola names on the label. The first wine produced (1978) was Rubicon, a rich blend of Cabernet Sauvignon, Cabernet Franc, and Merlot; it continues to draw raves today. By 1995, the Coppolas had acquired the rest of the Inglenook estate. The purchase—from Heublein & Co., a wine and spirit company, for a reported $8 million to $10 million— included 120 acres of prime vineyard, a large barrel-aging facility, a fine collection of historic Inglenook wines, the Gustave Niebaum Collection label—and the 1879 château. Coppola's meticulous renovation of the 39,000-square-foot Victorian stone château returned the property to its former glory as a great Napa estate—no small undertaking. It took four master woodworkers more than a year to create the sweeping staircase of exotic hardwoods; a large stained-glass window, conceived by Coppola, dramatizes the estate's reunification. Exotic woods were also used in the tasting room, where the featured stars are reds with cameos by Chardonnay and Bianco. Visitors may sample old vintages of Rubicon plus Edizione Pennino (named for Coppola's maternal grandfather), Zinfandel, Francis Ford Coppola Family wines, and Niebaum-Coppola Claret wines. Wines, wine-related merchandise, and Francis Ford Coppola Selects specialty foods are for sale here. Visitors also like to linger in the museum of movie- and wine-making memorabilia, which includes (what else?) Don Corleone's desk and chair from *The Godfather*. ♦ Fee for tasting. Tasting, sales, self-guided tours daily. 1991 St. Helena Hwy (at Niebaum La), Rutherford. 963.9099; fax 963.9084

45 RUDD WINERY

One of California's best wineries (formerly **Girard Winery**), this family-owned property has supplied grapes to a number of top Napa Valley vintners and now, still under the Girard label, produces a rich, barrel-fermented Chardonnay, an impressive Cabernet Sauvignon, and a Chenin Blanc. The Rudd brand is a reserve-style Cabernet Sauvignon. ♦ Tasting and sales daily; tours M-F, by appointment only.

7717 Silverado Tr (between Oakville Cross Rd and Skellenger La), Oakville. 944.8577

46 GROTH VINEYARDS AND WINERY

The top-ranking Cabernet Sauvignon made here is produced by Atari computer maven Dennis Groth, his wife, Judith, and winemaker Michael Weiss. Their Cabernets are among the most sought after in California; Sauvignon Blanc and Chardonnay are also produced here. ♦ Tasting and tours M-Sa, by appointment only. 750 Oakville Cross Rd (between Silverado Tr and Money Rd), Oakville. 944.0290; fax 944.8932

47 ST. SUPÉRY VINEYARDS AND WINERY

Budding enologists will enjoy the walk-through display vineyard, where they can see different grape varieties and various examples of pruning and trellising. Inside the functional modern winery building, an informal exhibition is devoted to promoting the arts in Napa Valley. Shows change every month and range from exhibits by individual local artists to group shows with participating Napa Valley galleries; occasionally artisans may demonstrate fabric painting or a variety of other textile crafts. The Queen Anne Victorian farmhouse on the property has been restored in period furnishings as a living museum of 1880s viticultural life in Napa Valley. The self-guided tour includes exhibits on soil types, growing conditions, and climate, plus a lesson in wine jargon. Wines include Chardonnay, Sauvignon Blanc, and Cabernet Sauvignon. ♦ Tasting, sales, and tours daily. Reservations recommended for tours. 8440 St. Helena Hwy (between Oakville Cross and Rutherford Cross Rds), Rutherford. 963.4507; fax 963.4526

47 PEJU PROVINCE WINERY

Founded in 1983, this family-owned winery produces Cabernet Sauvignon, French Colombard, Chardonnay, and Sauvignon Blanc. Tour the charming garden with a goldfish pond and interesting statuary, beautifully planted with iceberg bells, salvia, Peruvian lilies, Canterbury bells, and large dahlias. ♦ Tasting, sales, and self-guided tours daily. 8466 St. Helena

Hwy (between Oakville Cross and Rutherford Cross Rds), Rutherford. 963.3600; fax 963.8680. peju.com

48 CAKEBREAD CELLARS

This small, family-owned winery housed in a simple redwood barn was designed and built in 1986 by San Francisco architect **William Turnbull**. Jack and Dolores Cakebread, with sons Bruce as winemaker and Dennis as business manager, specialize in regular and reserve Cabernet Sauvignon, Chardonnay, and Sauvignon Blanc. In 1999 the winery purchased 160 acres on Howell Mountain and the adjacent winery and introduced ultrapremium Benchland Select and Three Sisters Cabernet Sauvignon. ♦ Tasting, sales, and tours daily by appointment only. 8300 St. Helena Hwy (between Oakville Cross and Rutherford Cross Rds), Rutherford. 963.5221

48 SEQUOIA GROVE VINEYARDS

The James Allen family owns this small winery located in a 19th-century barn shaded by sequoia trees that are over 100 years old. Three generations of the family work the vineyards and the winery, producing Chardonnay, Cabernet Sauvignon, and Gewürztraminer. Old Chardonnay vines by the river provide grapes for the winery's estate bottlings. ♦ No tours given. Tasting and sales daily. 8338 St. Helena Hwy (between Oakville Cross and Rutherford Cross Rds), Rutherford. 944.2945; fax 963.9411

49 TURNBULL WINE CELLARS

This small winery is housed in an award-winning, barnlike structure. Current owner Patrick O'Dell concentrates his efforts on growing and producing premium reds on 160 acres in wide-ranging microclimates in the Oakville appellation. Winemaker Jon Engleskirger, formerly of Robert Pepi and Hanna, turns out well-made Cabernet Sauvignon, along with small lots of Merlot, Sangiovese, Syrah, and Zinfandel; plans are under way to add Sauvignon Blanc. ♦ Sales daily; tasting and tours by appointment only. 8210 St. Helena Hwy (between Oakville Cross and Rutherford Cross Rds), Oakville. 963.5839, 800/887.6285; fax 963.4407

50 ROBERT MONDAVI WINERY

If there's one person who has put California on the international wine map, it is the ebullient Robert Mondavi—he seems to have spread the gospel of Napa Valley wine to every country in the world. Even in the early years he believed that California was capable of making world-class wines, and his vision and tireless promotional efforts have cultivated much of the success of Napa Valley's image both in this country and abroad. In his own winery, Mondavi has been an innovator in technology, viticulture, and marketing. His greatest coup may have been the joint venture he formed with Baron Philippe de Rothschild of Château Mouton-Rothschild in Bordeaux to produce Opus One, a Bordeaux-style Cabernet blend with cachet to burn (see **Opus One** winery, opposite). The Mission-style winery building, designed in 1966 by **Cliff May**, graces the ubiquitous Mondavi label, and the firm turns out a vast array of benchmark Napa Valley wines, from straightforward varietals to exquisite reserves. This is the first stop on everyone's wine route—the tasting room and tours are packed with visitors year-round, but a reservation system for tours helps manage the crowds. In addition to the usual 1-hour tour given by knowledgeable guides, there's a 3- to 4-hour, in-depth tour and tasting several times a week (less often in winter). ♦ Tasting, sales, and tours daily. Reservations recommended for tours. 7801 St. Helena Hwy (between Oakville Grade and Manley La), Oakville. 259.WINE; 800/MONDAVIX

51 OAKVILLE GROCERY CO.

This is the place to shop for a sumptuous picnic. It's stocked with a vast array of gourmet goodies (with gourmet-level prices): wonderful pâtés, cold cuts, caviar, crusty country breads, crackers, and carefully tended cheeses, including local jack and goat. You may also opt for the prepared sandwiches, such as turkey and pesto or roast beef with blue cheese. (They usually sell out by about 1PM.) A tiny produce section stocks tender leaf lettuces, fresh herbs, and ripe summer fruit. Also note the top-quality olive oils and vinegars, and don't miss the desserts (truffles, tarts, cookies), which come from local bakeries. With 2 days' notice, the staff will put together anything from bicycle box lunches to lavish honeymoon picnics. There's also a small espresso bar tucked in the corner. This top-notch grocery store is the granddaddy of gourmet shops in the Bay Area; its mail-order catalog carries many delicacies, including those from **Katz & Company**, once a specialty food shop in Yountville.♦ Daily. 7856 St. Helena Hwy (just north of Oakville Cross Rd), Oakville. 944.8802, 800/736.6602; fax

944.1844. Also at 124 Matheson St (at Center St), Healdsburg. 433.3200; fax 433.2744

51 OPUS ONE WINERY

This is a successful—and expensive—$20 million collaboration between the late Baron Philippe de Rothschild of Château Mouton-Rothschild in Bordeaux and the Robert Mondavi family of Napa Valley. Its first vintage was 1979. Winemakers Timothy Mondavi and Patrick Léon produce only one wine: A rich, complex, consistently superb Cabernet Sauvignon, it's among Napa's most expensive. The winery is housed in one of the most architecturally impressive buildings in the valley—an 80,000-square-foot contemporary classical structure of Texas limestone and untreated redwood by renowned architect **Scott Johnson** of **Johnson Fain Partners** of Los Angeles. **The Salon** (where tour-goers wait) boasts custom-designed, contemporary bronze-and-glass furniture complemented by centuries-old French appointments; the 15,000-square-foot **Opus One Chai** (barrel room) is also worth viewing. Tours are given by well-informed guides. ♦ Fee for tasting. Daily; tasting and tours by appointment only. 7900 St. Helena Hwy (just north of Oakville Cross Rd), Oakville. 944.9442; fax 944.2753

52 SILVER OAK WINE CELLARS

This small winery specializes in the production of only one varietal—a rich, powerful Cabernet Sauvignon made in two sites: Napa Valley and Alexander Valley. The result: two knockout Cabernets, aged 3 years in oak and 2 years in the bottle before they're released. It's worth a special trip to taste these beauties. ♦ Fee. Tasting and sales M-Sa; tours M-Th, 1:30PM, by appointment only. 915 Oakville Cross Rd (at Money Rd), Oakville. 944.8808

Restaurants/Clubs: Red | **Hotels: Purple** | Shops: Orange | **Outdoors/Parks: Green** | Sights/Culture: Blue

ST. HELENA

This small town in the heart of **Napa Valley** got its start around 1846, when Edward Bale built a flour mill beside a creek 3 miles north of the present town. Bale was an impoverished British surgeon who sailed to California aboard a whaling vessel and later married into General Mariano Guadalupe Vallejo's family. The land was part of **Rancho Carne Humana**, an immense Spanish land grant covering about 20,000 prime acres—virtually all of northern Napa Valley—that Bale received in 1839. He later sold 100 acres

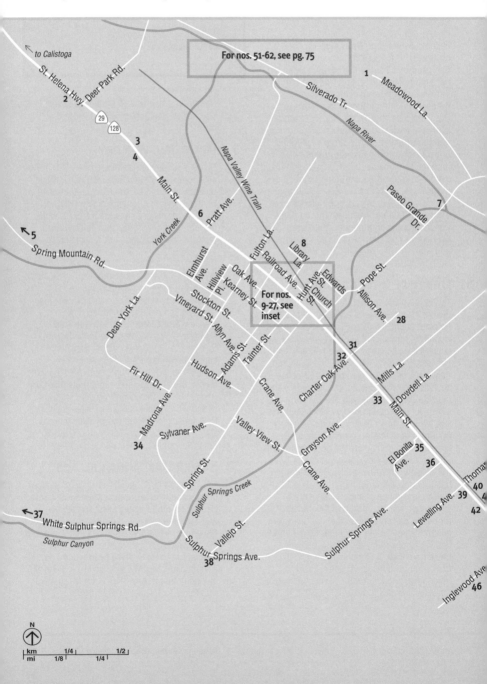

For nos. 51-62, see pg. 75

to Calistoga

St. Helena Hwy.

Deer Park Rd.

2

29

128

3

4

Main St.

York Creek

5

Spring Mountain Rd.

6

Pratt Ave.

Napa Valley Wine Train

Silverado Tr.

Napa River

1

Meadowood La.

Paseo Grande Dr.

7

8

Library La.

Fulton La.

Railroad Ave.

Ave. St.

Edwards

Hunt Church

St.

Pope St.

Elmhurst Ave.

Hillview Pl.

Oak Ave.

Kearney St.

For nos. 9-27, see inset

Allison Ave.

28

Dean York La.

Stockton St.

Vineyard St.

Allyn Ave St.

Adams St.

Tainter St.

31

32

Mills La.

Fir Hill Dr.

Hudson Ave.

Crane Ave.

Charter Oak Ave.

33

Main St.

Dowdell La.

Madrona Ave.

Sylvaner Ave.

34

Spring St.

Valley View St.

Grayson Ave.

Crane Ave.

El Bonita Ave.

35

36

Thomas

Lewelling Ave.

39

40

42

37

White Sulphur Springs Rd.

Sulphur Canyon

Sulphur Springs Creek

Sulphur Springs Ave.

Vallejo St.

38

Springs Ave.

Sulphur Springs Ave.

Inglewood Ave.

46

N

km
mi

1/8

1/4

1/4

1/2

to a fellow Englishman, J. H. Still, who promptly opened a general store. That became the nucleus of the town, which took its name from Mount St. Helena.

Main Street, with its stately, 19th-century stone buildings, is a stretch of the valley's main highway and has been a significant thoroughfare since the days of the horse and buggy. The infamous Black Bart, who taught school and wrote poetry when he wasn't busy robbing stagecoaches (he thoughtfully left bits of verse at the scenes of his crimes), passed through here before his capture in 1883. On a more romantic note, author Robert Louis Stevenson and his new bride, Fanny, also made their way through the town en route to nearby Calistoga, where they spent their honeymoon in the summer of 1880.

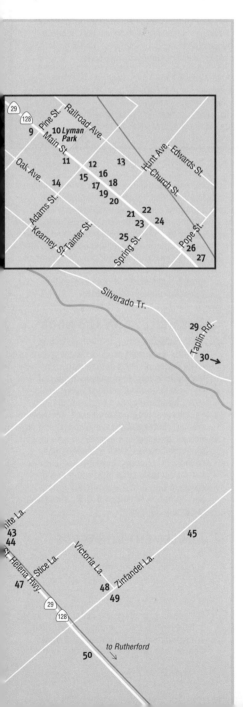

1 MEADOWOOD RESORT

$$$$ Originally a private country club for well-to-do Napa Valley families, this luxurious retreat has great charm and style. After a fire destroyed the old clubhouse, Sausalito architect **Kirk Hillman** rebuilt it, using elements of New England's grand turn-of-the-century cottages. Trimmed in white, with tiers of gabled windows and wraparound porches, the two main lodges and the 18 smaller lodges scattered over the 256-acre, wooded property evoke a feeling of old money and tradition and attract the likes of Danielle Steel and the Mondavi family. The staff's attention to detail imparts an Old World sense of service. The 99 rooms range from one-room studios to large four-bedroom suites (most with stone fireplaces); all have private baths, porches, beds covered in chintz and plump down comforters, thick terry robes, wet bars, coffeemakers, and toasters. The grounds include a perfectly maintained and challenging nine-hole golf course and two international-regulation croquet lawns, as well as seven championship tennis courts strung along the foot of the lush hillside. There are also two heated pools, including a 25-yard lap pool and a 102-degree whirlpool. The health spa features a well-stocked weight room, aerobics classes, steam rooms, saunas, and a spa boutique. The **Croquet Classic at Meadowood** is held here every July, and the resort is also the site of the elegant annual Napa Valley Wine Auction in June. In addition to golf, tennis, and croquet pros, the resort has John Thoreen, an unpretentious and down-to-earth wine

THE BEST

Kent Domogalla

Consultant, Internal Fiscal Controls and Financial Investigations

Make mine the *upper* **Napa Valley**, where you can:

Have a calamari, Caesar salad, and Red Ale lunch in the garden at **Calistoga Inn**'s **Napa Valley Brewing Company**.

Visit Calistoga's **Sharpsteen Museum** with its sweeping dioramas of early Calistoga created by Oscar-winning Disney studio producer Ben Sharpsteen (check it out at www.napanet.net/vi/sharpsteen).

Sit on the patio of **Cindy's Backstreet Kitchen** in **St. Helena** in the fall and have sweetbreads prepared with figs from the massive tree overhead.

Overindulge yourself at the annual Chocolate & Cabernet Fantasy at **Sterling Vineyards**.

Rebuild body tissue at the **Wappo Bar Bistro** after a **Calistoga Spa Hot Springs** mud bath and spa treatment (sounds disgusting, looks even worse, but boy, does it feel good).

Have a murder mystery at dinner—as you roll through the night on the **Napa Valley Wine Train**.

Test the range of your olfactory senses by walking the length of Calistoga's Lincoln Avenue: the **Calistoga Roastery** (coffee beans being roasted), **Wexford & Woods** (bath and body products), **Calistoga Inn** (oak and mesquite outdoor grill), and so on.

And where do you go to get away if you already live in paradise? Why, the **North Coast Wine Country**, of course, where you wine taste your way through **Sonoma** and **Mendocino Counties** to Mendocino to attend the annual Mendocino Music Festival.

---

expert, to advise guests on winery itineraries or to conduct tastings for groups. Book well ahead for summer stays and weekend getaways. The property is a member of the prestigious Relais & Châteaux hotel association, as well as of the Small Luxury Hotels of the World and the Preferred Hotels & Resorts Worldwide. ♦ 900 Meadowood La (north of Howell Mountain Rd). 963.3646, 800/458.8080; fax 963.3532

Within the Meadowood Resort:

Meadowood

Napa Valley

THE RESTAURANT AT MEADOWOOD

★★★$$$$ This grand, conservatively elegant dining room accented with shades of pink and burgundy overlooks **Meadowood**'s tree-lined property and pristine golf course. One intriguing choice on the menu is the four-course Vegetable Tasting, offered alone or partnered with wines. Appetizers might include sautéed foie gras with a pomegranate–white port sauce and house-smoked sturgeon with Osetra caviar. On a recent visit, innovative main courses included peppery halibut paired with potato purée and assorted citrus with basil; and sea scallops steamed in corn husks, with vanilla bean butter, corn, and shiitake mushroom ragout. For something less exotic, try the fillet of beef

with a Merlot sauce, accompanied by fingerling potatoes, mushrooms, and onions. Brunch is served on Sunday, and an afternoon tea is offered daily. Request a table on the terrace overlooking the property when weather permits. ♦ Californian ♦ M-Sa, afternoon tea and dinner; Su, brunch, afternoon tea, and dinner. Reservations recommended; jackets suggested but not required for weekend dinners. 963.6346

THE GRILL AT MEADOWOOD

★$$ In mild weather, the terrace of this informal restaurant overlooking the golf course is a glorious place to dine alfresco. The breakfast buffet offers an attractive display of croissants, muffins, cereals, yogurt, fresh fruits, and beverages, or you may order French toast, eggs, or omelettes. The lunch menu includes salads, sandwiches, and pizza and pasta selections. Dinner offers a range of traditional dishes, such as lamb chops, salmon, and roasted chicken. Spa cuisine—low-fat cooking using little butter, oil, or cream in preparation—is offered at both lunch and dinner. ♦ American ♦ Daily, breakfast, lunch, and dinner

2 ST. CLEMENT VINEYARDS

The elegant Gothic Victorian mansion that appears on this vineyard's label was built in 1878 by San Francisco glass merchant Fritz Rosenbaum, and its stone cellar became one of the earliest bonded wineries in the valley. After years of neglect, the cellar was restored in time for the 1975 vintage. In 1990 this lovely building, now used as the **Visitors' Center**, was opened to the public for the first time in 100 years. The Bordeaux-style blends of this landmark estate are rich in color, aroma, and flavor. Oroppas—a Meritage wine of Cabernet Sauvignon, Merlot, and Cabernet Franc—has bold flavors of smoke and spice and a long, luscious finish. ◆ Tasting and sales daily; tours by appointment only. 2867 St. Helena Hwy (between Elmhurst Ave and Rockland Rd). 967.3033, 800/331.8266; fax 963.9174. www.stclement.com

3 CHARLES KRUG WINERY

Pioneer winemaker Charles Krug founded this winery in 1861, though it's been run by a branch of the Mondavi family since 1943. It produces six different varietals, among them its benchmark Vintage Selection Cabernets and Carneros Reserve Chardonnays. There also are four varietal blends, including a Reserve Sangiovese and Reserve Merlot. ◆ Fee. Tasting and sales daily; tours daily; call for the schedule. 2800 Main St (between Pratt Ave and Deer Park Rd). 967.2201; fax 967.2291

4 CULINARY INSTITUTE OF AMERICA AT GREYSTONE

If you were able to tour this impressive and historic estate when it was **Christian Brothers-Greystone Cellars**, count your blessings. The last tour was given in the summer of 1993, when the new tenants were required by the city of St. Helena to shut the doors to the public. Heublein Inc. (owners of **Christian Brothers**) donated all but $1.68 million of this 282-acre estate's $14 million price tag to the **Culinary Institute of America (CIA)**, a nonprofit culinary arts school based in Hyde Park, New York. First opened in 1889, the 117,000-square-foot main building is the largest stone winery in the world. A $14 million renovation launched in summer 1994 was completed the following year. The renovation affected only the interior; because this site is on the National Register of Historic Places, the buildings' exteriors cannot be touched (some exterior walls are as thick as 22 inches). Reinforcement of the massive winery provided the foundation for the construction of 115,000-square-foot teaching kitchens, a public restaurant, a 125-seat demonstration auditorium, a retail store, and extensive organic gardens. This branch of the Culinary Institute of America is said to be the only center in the world dedicated exclusively to continuing education and career development for profes-

sionals in the food, wine, health, and hospitality fields. A guesthouse on campus is available for registered students. The north wing houses the school as well as the **Greystone** restaurant, led by CIA's chef Robert Curry and staffed with various professionals and externs and fellows from the Hyde Park campus; it's open to the public daily for lunch and dinner. The south end of the estate contains a small public museum of food and wine and the **Campus Store and Spice Islands Marketplace**. ◆ Cooking demonstrations in the DeBaun Theater by student chefs include tasting and recipe cards. 2555 Main St (between Elmhurst Ave and Rockland Rd). 967.1100; fax 967.1113. For information on demonstrations, call 967.2320. www.greystone-experience.com.

Within the Culinary Institute of America at Greystone:

GREYSTONE GARDENS

Terraced in front of the main building are organic gardens for herbs, garlic and onion beds, edible flowers, and plants used to make herbal teas. Nearby are organic gardens designed by Jeff Dawson, **Fetzer Vineyards'** garden director, with 148 varieties of fruits and vegetables, including heirloom strains, exotic greens used in European and Asian cuisines, and various chilies. These gardens serve as student learning labs and a source of some of the restaurant's ingredients. The school also has its own vineyard.

THE CAMPUS STORE AND SPICE ISLANDS MARKETPLACE

This 3,000-square-foot store is filled to overflowing with merchandise aimed to please both professional and at-home cooks. Its 1,500 cookbooks are mere appetizers to such essentials as cookware, cutlery, bakeware, kitchen accoutrements—including chef's toques and aprons, potholders, and trivets—plus whimsical culinary jewelry and gardening accessories. The store offers food ingredients reflecting the range of cuisines on the school curriculum. ◆ Daily. 967.2309

Television fans the world over will recognize the exterior of the Spring Mountain Winery (2805 Spring Mountain Road, off Madrona Avenue) as the fictional mansion featured on the once-popular network TV show *Falcon Crest*. Unfortunately, however, the winery is closed to the public.

Restaurants/Clubs: **Red** | Hotels: **Purple** | Shops: **Orange** | Outdoors/Parks: **Green** | Sights/Culture: **Blue**

WINE SPECTATOR GREYSTONE RESTAURANT

★★$$$ Named for prestigious wine magazine *Wine Spectator* and created by noted restaurant designer Adam Tihany, this attractive dining place is cleverly configured to offer every guest a view of the kitchen. Diners seated at the stone tapas bar or rustic wooden tables can watch parts of their meals being prepared at the open bakery, rotisserie-grill, or state-of-the-art cooking stations. The décor is equally appealing: copper trim, complemented by cool blues, greens, and warm earth tones and accents of wrought iron; sculptures by Michael Bondi; and paintings by Ruby Newman. Table settings boast napkins in bold colors, Christofle cutlery, lovely wineglasses, and bistro china. There's also an outdoor patio. The menu celebrates "California's bounty from the land and sea" with local, seasonal cuisine. Winter menus feature foraged mushrooms, Dungeness crab, Angus beef, oysters, and organic field greens. Try the seared Sonoma foie gras with Muscat grapes as a first course. Second courses include sautéed squab with polenta cake, creamed corn, and chanterelles; the breast of Sonoma duck is prepared on the rotisserie and served with Swiss chard, green pepper sauce, and potato and turnip gratin. Temptations from the pastry kitchen include chocolate cannoli with minted crunch mascarpone. The wine list travels California wine country and includes a good selection by the glass and 3-ounce samplers of sparkling, white, and red wines, so you can change wines with each course. ◆ California cuisine ◆ Daily, lunch and dinner. 967.1010

5 ROBERT KEENAN WINERY

Perched on Spring Mountain, where a 1904 winery used to be, this family-owned winery produces only varietals: Chardonnay, Merlot, and a sturdy and tannic Cabernet Sauvignon. There is a picnic area too. ◆ M-F, Su, tasting and sales by appointment only; Sa, 11AM-4PM, no appointment necessary. 3660 Spring Mountain Rd (west of Madrona Ave). 963.9177; fax 963.8209

5 PHILIP TOGNI VINEYARD

Renowned vintner Philip Togni (who has acted as winemaker and manager for many top estates, including **Mayacamas**, **Chalone**, **Chapellet**, and **Cuvaison**) now produces wine here under his own label. Most notable are a rich and intense Cabernet Sauvignon and a crisp, lean Sauvignon Blanc. He's also producing a dessert wine, Ca'Togni. ◆ Tours by appointment only. 3780 Spring Mountain Rd (west of Madrona Ave). 963.3731; fax 963.9186

5 DOMAINE CHARBAY WINERY & DISTILLERY

The Karakasevic family's winery and distillery has been in business since 1983. Yugoslavian-born and raised Miles Karakasevic, a 12th-generation distiller and winemaker, and his son, Marko (in training to be the next), have functioned as a wine-making team for the past few years. The winery has a penchant for the unusual: there's Charbay, a brandy liqueur blended with Chardonnay; flavored vodkas; plus apple brandy or grappa, and honey-peach–scented late-harvest Sauvignon Blanc, Full Botrytis. The cognac-style brandy double-distilled by hand in a classic alambic pot still is aging in oak and was released in late 2001. ◆ Tours and tastings by appointment only. 4001 Spring Mountain Rd (west of Madrona Ave). 963.9327, 800/634.7845; fax 093.3343

5 SMITH-MADRONE WINERY

Founded by brothers Charles and Stuart Smith in 1971, this winery on Spring Mountain produces Chardonnay, Cabernet Sauvignon, and Riesling. The 1977 Riesling won the top award at the French wine-and-food magazine *Gault-Millau*'s tasting in 1979. ◆ Sales and tours, M-Sa, by appointment only. 4022 Spring Mountain Rd (west of Madrona Ave). 963.2283; fax 963.2291

5 RITCHIE CREEK VINEYARDS

Located up a long, winding road at the very top of Spring Mountain, this tiny winery produces small quantities of Chardonnay and Cabernet Sauvignon from steeply terraced vineyards on the Sonoma border. ◆ Tasting and sales by appointment only. 4024 Spring Mountain Rd (west of Madrona Ave). 963.4661

6 BERINGER VINEYARDS

The oldest continuously operating winery in Napa Valley, this place received its bond in 1876. Founder Frederick Beringer built the landmark **Rhine House** as a tribute to his former home when he emigrated from Germany in the mid-19th century. A popular tour of the vineyards includes the house and the caves excavated by Chinese laborers a century ago. The winery is

A Wine Country Safari

Who says you need a car to see the California wine country? **Wine Country Jeep Tours** take two to six people on 3-hour adventures in four-wheel-drive, open-air vehicles. Led by driver-guides well versed in wines, wine-making, and local lore, the tours include VIP visits to wineries and drives on the back roads—and even off the roads—of the scenic countryside.

Participants may choose from several routes and a variety of wineries—16 Sonoma wineries and eight wineries in Napa. A Sonoma excursion, for example, might include a private tour at **Martini & Prati** (see page 132), one of America's most historic wineries; and a limited-release tasting at **Lambert Bridge Winery** (see page 143).

At times, the Jeeps turn off the roads and head over bumpy paths right into the vineyards, offering passengers a close-up view of wonderfully aromatic grape-laden vines. Tours might also include other local attractions: an eye-popping view of **Geyser Peak**, a stroll around charming **Healdsburg Plaza**, or an off-road ride in **Sugarloaf Ridge State Park**.

The driver-guides are exceptionally well trained, having completed a 16-hour orientation course on wineries, wines, and area history. But although the driver-guides provide information galore, the tours are relaxed, with enough quiet time for participants to contemplate the beauties of the countryside. Tours are offered year-round and include passenger pickup. Boxed lunches are available for an additional fee and must be ordered in advance. For information and reservations call **Wine Country Jeep Tours**, 800/539.5337.

largely owned by the two private investment partnerships. Since 1977, the winery has been known for its extraordinary private reserve Chardonnay and Cabernet. Winemaker Ed Sbragia also produces a roster of other well-made wines. ♦ Tasting, sales, and tours daily. 2000 Main St (just north of Pratt Ave). 963.4812

7 Stonebridge Park

♦ This small park on the banks of the Napa River is a good place to sit and enjoy a picnic lunch. ♦ Pope St (between Silverado Tr and Paseo Grande Dr)

8 Robert Louis Stevenson Silverado Museum

ILLUSTRATION REPRODUCED WITH THE PERMISSION OF ROBERT LOUIS STEVENSON SILVERADO MUSEUM

This museum is devoted to the beloved Robert Louis Stevenson, author of *A Child's Garden of Verses* and *Treasure Island* (among other works), who spent his honeymoon in an abandoned bunkhouse at the old Silverado Mine on Mount St. Helena in 1880. Founded by bibliophile Norman Strouse, it has a touching and quirky collection of more than 8,000 items acquired from heirs and friends of Stevenson: letters, manuscripts, first editions, paintings, sculpture, photographs, and memorabilia. You'll see the Parmesan-cheese case his father used (mentioned in *Treasure Island*); a set of toy soldiers and a miniature tea set he played with more than a century ago; and the name board from the ship *Equator*, which carried the Stevenson family from Hawaii to Samoa in 1889. Also on view are the gloves that fellow author Henry James left behind during a visit, which Stevenson's wife, Fanny, put in an envelope with the note: "Henry James's gloves left in my house and dishonestly confiscated by me. FS." ♦ Free. Tu-Su, noon-4PM. 1490 Library La (north of Adams St). 963.3757; fax 963.0917

8 Napa Valley Wine Library

For anyone interested in wine lore, this 6,000-volume collection of books, tapes, and reference materials on wine and viticulture is definitely worth a visit. Browsers and borrowers alike are welcome. ♦ M-Sa. 1492 Library La (north of Adams St). 963.5244; fax 963.5264

Associated with the Napa Valley Wine Library:

Napa Valley Wine Library Association

Benefits of the $25 annual membership fee include a subscription to a newsletter listing new wine books in the collection, and an invitation to the gala tasting in August—in itself well worth the price. ♦ Box 328, St. Helena, CA 94574. 963.5145

Restaurants/Clubs: Red | Hotels: Purple | Shops: Orange | Outdoors/Parks: Green | Sights/Culture: Blue

NAPA VALLEY WINE LIBRARY ASSOCIATION COURSES

Weekend courses are offered each spring, including an informal introduction to wine appreciation presented by wine professionals from Napa Valley wineries. Lectures, field trips, and tastings cover sensory evaluations of wines, grape varieties, and production. The fee includes a year's membership in the association. ♦ Box 207, St. Helena, CA 94574

9 AMBROSE BIERCE HOUSE

$$ The modest exterior of this 1872 Victorian home hides a hospitable, superbly restored inn, former home of the famous 19th-century writer Ambrose Bierce, poet, essayist, and cartoonist best known for *The Devil's Dictionary*. Bierce lived here from the 1880s until his mysterious disappearance in Mexico in 1913. The rooms are named for historical figures whose presence influenced both Bierce and Napa Valley, and each has special decorative accents that call them to mind. They are air-conditioned, furnished with queen-size brass beds and armoires, and have private baths with claw-foot tubs and showers. The largest and most comfortable—a suite named for Bierce—is also equipped with cable TV and a VCR. Innkeepers John and Lisa Runnells offer a sumptuous continental breakfast featuring freshly squeezed juice, fruit, and baked goods, and tips on how to make the most of your visits. ♦ 1515 Main St (between Pine St and Madrona Ave). 963.3003

10 LYMAN PARK

You'll find picnic tables, barbecue pits, rest rooms, and a playground for kids here, as well as a gazebo where live concerts are sometimes held in the summer. ♦ Main and Pine Sts

11 VANDERBILT AND COMPANY

For the stylish picnic, this housewares-and-garden shop has a great collection of paper

Mature redwood trees draw water up from their roots, releasing 500 gallons of water into the atmosphere each day, thus affecting the local microclimate. This is why the species is said to make its own weather.

plates and matching napkins in grape, flower, or lettuce patterns; nifty Italian plastic plates that mimic old majolica pottery; and plastic champagne flutes and wineglasses. If you really want to go whole hog, they have lovely jacquard linens, hand-painted tablecloths, rustic terra-cotta, plus handblown wineglasses and pottery from Italy. ♦ Daily. 1429 Main St (between Adams and Pine Sts). 963.1010

12 STEVE'S HARDWARE & HOUSEWARES

Since 1878 this old-fashioned hardware store has been a fixture in St. Helena, offering picnic supplies and inexpensive cooking equipment such as knives, Styrofoam coolers, enamel coffeepots, wineglasses (in plastic versions too), pocket corkscrews, and other handy necessities. ♦ Daily. 1370 Main St (between Hunt Ave and Adams St). 963.3423; fax 963.2258

13 CINDY'S BACKSTREET KITCHEN

★★★$$$ Cindy Pawlcyn's successful eatery in a historic 1860 building features an inventive menu that focuses on local ingredients and clean, uncomplicated flavors—and serves as a showcase for Pawlcyn's considerable talents as chef. Otherwise familiar entrées are presented with unusual twists, such as the half chicken with corn stew and roasted Anaheim relleno, stuffed pasilla chile with molé and black beans, and the grilled hanger steak served with salsa fresca. For lighter fare, try the Oaxacan pizza with roasted tomatoes, sweet corn, and housemade queso fresca. There's also oysters with garlic and spinach, and roasted artichokes with cilantro and caper dip. Desserts, which also have a Latin twist, include Peruvian sweet corn crème brûlée, chocolate coconut mousse, and summer fruit cobbler. A big attraction here is the patio shaded by a century-old fig tree. Seasonal menus celebrate figs in late summer and wild boar in November. ♦ Latin American ♦ Tu-Su, lunch and dinner. Reservations recommended. 1327 Railroad Ave (between Hunt Ave and Adams St). 963.1200. www.cindysbackstreetkitchen.com

13 TERRA

★★★★$$$ Lissa Doumani and her husband, Hiro Sone, a Japanese chef who worked with Wolfgang Puck at Spago in Los Angeles, have created one of the best restaurants in Napa Valley, long a favorite among locals. If you enjoy truly fine food and wine, this place is a *must* on your wine-country itinerary. Sone's cooking is subtle and marvelously flavorful, featuring well-crafted, intelligently conceived dishes such as tartare of tuna and salmon spiced with lemon-ginger vinaigrette; terrine of foie gras with pear and black currant chutney; broiled sake-marinated Chilean sea bass with shrimp dumplings in shiso broth; grilled lamb with anchovy-and-black-olive sauce; and duck with wild mushrooms *vol au vent* (in a puff pastry shell). The two dining rooms, set in a historic stone building, have an elegant, understated ambiance. Doumani is a warm and welcoming host; the service here, professional and unobtrusive. The restaurant's extensive California wine list features many hard-to-find selections from small estates. ◆ California ◆ M, W-Su, dinner. Reservations recommended. 1345 Railroad Ave (between Hunt Ave and Adams St). 963.8931

14 NAPA VALLEY COFFEE ROASTING COMPANY

★$ Light floods through the French windows at this attractive corner café, making it a great spot for breakfast or whiling away the afternoon. Settle in at one of the bistro tables for some of the best espresso drinks in the valley. Partners Denise Fox and Leon Sange roast the more than 20 varieties of coffee beans at their downtown Napa location. (Forget the Napa Valley T-shirts and take home a pound or two of great coffee for a souvenir or a gift for those back home.) They offer freshly squeezed orange juice, the cappuccino of your dreams, bagels with cream cheese, scones, Danishes, and bread from Berkeley's Acme Baking Company. And if that isn't enough, they have outdoor seating on the porch. ◆ Café ◆ Daily, breakfast and snacks. 1400 Oak Ave (at Adams St). 963.4491; fax 963.1183

15 MODEL BAKERY

The best bread in the valley comes from this bakery's old-fashioned brick oven. Look for *pain du vin* (half-wheat, half-white sourdough), sour rye, sweet or sourdough baguettes, plus terrific poppy- or sesame-seed sandwich rolls. If you're thinking of a picnic, owner Karen Mitchell offers croissants stuffed with ham and cheese or spinach and feta, brie by the slice, sandwiches, and several types of pizza—call for an individual pizza to go. For dessert, she has chocolate-chip and oatmeal-raisin cookies, almond-studded biscotti, and, as an extra-special treat in the summer, lovely fruit tarts. Seating is also available in the bakery. ◆ Tu-Su. 1357 Main St (between Spring and Adams Sts). 963.8192

15 ART ON MAIN

Tom and Nancy Brown concentrate on the works of local artists, especially wine-related art, in this Napa Valley gallery. ◆ Daily. 1359

Main St (between Spring and Adams Sts). 963.3350

16 CAMEO CINEMA

Though this cozy small town theater dates from 1918, the original façade and interior were remodeled in the 1950s. Today the theater, which seats 172, shows current releases and classic films in runs that range from 2 days to 1 or 2 weeks. It also features comfortable rocking lounge chairs, chairs for two, Dolby stereo sound, and popcorn with real butter. ◆ 1340 Main St (between Hunt Ave and Adams St). 963.3946

16 I.O.O.F. BUILDING

Built in 1885, this remains one of the largest stone buildings in town. The brick façade boasts details such as lions' heads, brackets, and rosettes. Part of the base is painted cast iron. The upstairs area still houses the Odd Fellows meeting hall. ◆ 1350 Main St (between Hunt Ave and Adams St)

17 ST. HELENA MASONIC LODGE

The most elaborate building on Main Street, this fancy Victorian structure was erected in 1892 by **M.G. Ritchie** and bought by the Masons in 1972. The influence of British architect **Charles Eastlake** is obvious in such repetitive motifs as turned spindles and concentric circles. The façade is brick over structural stone, the bays are wood, and the sides show the use of stone repeating some of the wood designs. ◆ 1327–1337 Main St (between Spring and Adams Sts)

17 1351 LOUNGE

This Gen-X sports bar located in an 1890 former bank building is a great place to mix and mingle with young locals. The antique bar comes from Sacramento and a back room—once the bank vault—is for billiards. ◆ Daily, 10AM-2AM. 1351 Main St (between Spring and Adams Sts). 963.4045

17 MARKET—AN AMERICAN RESTAURANT

★★★$$ Nick Peyton, former partner and maître d' of Restaurant Gary Danko, presides over this community gathering spot with amiable charm. In both food and ambiance, Market succeeds in being down-home as well as upscale. A rustic 120-year-old fieldstone wall runs the length of the dining room, where soft leather banquettes line walls adorned with photographs of bustling farmers' markets. While the Valley regulars gather around a century-old mahogany bar (from San Francisco's Palace Hotel), diners settle down

Restaurants/Clubs: Red | Hotels: Purple | Shops: Orange | Outdoors/Parks: Green | Sights/Culture: Blue

to plates of star-spangled American classics—dishes you may not have seen since childhood. Top favorites are the meat loaf with gravy and mashed potatoes, prime rib with fresh horseradish cream, and chopped vegetable salad with Point Reyes blue cheese. Even the soups and salads are a notch above typical home cooking. Flavor abounds in the sugar pie pumpkin soup and the seared ahi salad with arugula, fennel, tangerines, caper berries, and olives. The house-special BLT is made with thick-cut Hobb's bacon, heirloom tomatoes, and butter lettuce on pressed grilled ciabatta. Bobby Stuckey, who is responsible for the wine list at **French Laundry**, put together an affordable list of Napa Valley wines along with select French and South American wines. For dessert, try the butterscotch pudding or s'mores—served with a table-top "campfire" for roasting marshmallows. ◆ Daily, lunch and dinner. 1347 Main St. 963.3799. www.marketsthelena.com

18 ARMADILLO'S

★★$ Great California-Mexican cuisine is served in this popular restaurant owned by Michael Scott and Tony Velazquez. Scott is the talent behind the whimsical décor, from the colorful frescoes and brightly painted tables and chairs to the *rufugio* broom sculptures and booths covered with traditional Mexican blankets. Velazquez, originally from Jalisco, Mexico, takes over in the kitchen, using only fresh local ingredients to create his homemade sauces, tortilla chips, and refried beans. ◆ Mexican ◆ Daily, lunch and dinner. 1304 Main St (between Hunt Ave and Adams St). 963.8082

18 COOK

★$$ With its long green bar and vintage opera posters, this place feels like a trattoria somewhere in the Italian countryside. The day's specials are chalked on a blackboard and might include fried calamari, gnocchi in Gorgonzola sauce, or ravioli with meat and porcini mushroom sauce. Generous portions are the rule. ◆ Italian ◆ Tu-Sa, lunch and dinner. 1310 Main St (between Hunt Ave and Adams St). 963.7088

19 HOTEL ST. HELENA

$$ Built in 1881, this inn boasts 18 comfortable, old-fashioned guest rooms decorated with period wallpapers, fabrics, and accessories. Some rooms share large

> When drinking, never cross malt with grape. For instance, if you've been drinking beer, follow it with whiskey; wine, follow it with brandy.

bathrooms; others have private baths. A continental breakfast is included. ◆ 1309 Main St (between Hunt Ave and Adams St). 963.4388; fax 963.5402

19 MAIN STREET BOOKS

Looking for a kids' book? Look no further. This attractive shop specializes in all kinds of books for young readers of wide-ranging ages and interests. ◆ M-Sa. 1315 Main St (between Spring and Adams Sts). 963.1338

20 MY FAVORITE THINGS

Handwoven throws, hand-painted pottery, nostalgic picture frames, and needlepoint pillows are some of the treasures you'll find at this boutique. ◆ Daily. 1289 Main St (between Spring and Adams Sts). 963.0848

21 ST. HELENA ANTIQUES

Among the finds here are antique corkscrews, 19th-century bottle-drying racks and wine carriers, crystal decanters, old ice-cream and butter molds in the shape of a cluster of grapes, handmade English basketry wine carriers, and garden furniture. ◆ Daily. 1231 Main St (between Spring and Adams Sts). 963.5878

22 NOBLE BUILDING

The hipped roof and double dormers mark this 1903 landmark as an example of Dutch Colonial architecture. Designed by **Luther M. Turton**, who created over 50 buildings in the valley, it has housed a furniture store, an undertaking establishment, and a chicken hatchery at various times. Now it's home to several small businesses. ◆ 1200–1204 Main St (between Pope St and Hunt Ave)

22 CALLA LILY

Debra Caselli has special sources in Europe for her luxury table and bed linens. Among the treasures here are exquisite handwoven Italian table linens; silky Belgian cotton percale sheets (300–600 to thread count), which can be monogrammed; Egyptian cotton towels; goose-down duvets; wool-filled bed pads; and bedcoverings and pillow shams in jacquard cotton or subtle piqué. Caselli will make custom sheets and bedcoverings in her high-quality fabrics too. The store also carries select home accessories

SIPPING SUDS IN WINE COUNTRY

Palate fatigued after one too many wine tastings? Take a brew break for a change of pace. In the past several years, new microbreweries have been popping up regularly in wine country. Even leading winemakers like **Korbel**, **Beringer**, and **Domaine Chandon** have gotten into the specialty beer business. The following wine-country micro-breweries are excellent places to develop your beer-tasting skills.

Lake County

Mount St. Helena Brewing Company   Brewmaster Greg Gabriel produces six ales year-round and two seasonal ales at his 20-barrel brewhouse. The menu ranges from bar snacks and pizza to complete meals, and there's a nice outdoor deck too. (Also see page 224.) ♦ 21167 Calistoga St (between Douglas and Main Sts), Middletown. 987.2106

Mendocino

Buckhorn Saloon/Anderson Valley Brewing Company   The eight kinds of beer and ale on tap at this homey, funky saloon are all brewed down the road at the brewing company (ask about tours). The pub grub is prepared with California flair. (Also see page 213.) ♦ 14081 Hwy 128 (north of Ukiah Boonville Rd), Boonville. 895.BEER

Mendocino Brewing Company   Opened in 1983, this brew pub was the first to operate in California since Prohibition. Four microbrews and appetizers, burgers, and sandwiches are served. There's an outdoor beer garden and live music on Saturday nights. (Also see page 183.) ♦ 13351 S Hwy 101 (north of Rte 175), Hopland. 744.1361, 744.1015

North Coast Brewing Company   Set in a 1916 building, this place serves handcrafted beers and sophisticated bar fare (including Tex-Mex and Cajun dishes). The most popular brew on tap is Red Seal Ale. (Also see page 188.) ♦ 444 N Main St (at E Pine St), Ft. Bragg. 964.BREW

Napa

Downtown Joe's Brewery & Restaurant   Ginger ale and root beer, as well as a variety of lagers, ales, and stouts, are brewed at this riverfront pub. Outdoor tables overlook the Napa River. The menu features salads, sandwiches, pasta, and fish. (Also see page 35.) ♦ 902 Main St (at Second St), Napa. 258.2337

Napa Valley Brewing Company   This microbrewery is housed in an old water tower in back of the turn-of-the-century **Calistoga Inn**. The shady patio is an ideal place to enjoy the house brews and simple fare. (Also see page 90.) ♦ Calistoga Inn, 1250 Lincoln Ave (at Cedar St), Calistoga. 942.4101

Sonoma

Bear Republic Brewing Company   Locals hang out at this comfy brew pub, in Healdsburg's downtown clock-tower building. Snacks like hot chicken wings and Cajun fries complement handcrafted ales made from complex blends of American and Belgian malts and specialty grains. ♦ 345 Healdsburg Ave (between W Matheson and W North Sts), Healdsburg. 433.BEER

Dempsey's   There's a serious menu of dishes with Mexican and Asian influences and five ales (ranging from Petaluma Strong to Ugly Dog Stout) at this casual pub with a patio overlooking the river. ♦ Golden Eagle Center, 50 E Washington St (between Weller St and Petaluma Blvd N), Petaluma. 765.9694

The Lagunitas Brewing Company   This hospitable family brewery offers between six and nine beers at a given time. DogTown Pale Ale and Lagunitas India Pale Ale are always available, and if you're lucky you might find Hairy Eyeball Ale or Old Gnarly Wine on tap. During the week, walk in for a tour and tasting; on weekends, call in advance. ♦ 1322 Ross St (between Holm Rd and McDowell Blvd N), Petaluma. 769.4495

Powerhouse Brewing Company   Six ales are brewed in a historic landmark—a 1903 powerhouse for the old railroad line. The featured brew is the double-hopped Powerhouse Ale. Menu options include sandwiches and burgers, vegetarian dishes, and pastas. There's a patio too. ♦ 268 Petaluma Ave (between Main St and Sebastopol Rd), Sebastopol. 829.9171

Russian River Brewing Company   Located behind the historic brandy tower at **Korbel Champagne Cellars**, this brewery produces three ales and a porter. The brews can be sampled at the **Korbel Delicatessen and Market**, a restaurant-deli that's also on the winery grounds. Excellent tours cover both the winery and the brewery. (Also see page 161.) ♦ 13250 River Rd (just north of McPeak Rd), Guerneville. 824.7000

Restaurants/Clubs: Red | Hotels: Purple | Shops: Orange | Outdoors/Parks: Green | Sights/Culture: Blue

and a line of personal care items. ◆ Daily. 1222 Main St (between Pope St and Hunt Ave). 963.8188

23 VALLEY EXCHANGE

This store has a little bit of a lot of things—bird feeders, baskets, candles, glassware—but many people come here for the lavender-scented hand lotion. ◆ Daily. 1201 Main St (at Spring St). 963.7423

24 ST. HELENA CYCLERY

Rent hybrid bikes (a mountain–touring cross) with helmets, side bags, and locks. The store doesn't take reservations, so arrive early, especially on weekends. Colorful biking togs, accessories, and books on biking in the wine country are for sale, too. ◆ Daily. 1156 Main St (between Pope St and Hunt Ave). 963.7736; fax 963.5099

25 MARTINI HOUSE

★★★$$$ The celebrated chefs settling in the wine country have no trouble attracting food and wine lovers to their doors. Todd Humphries left Wine Spectator's Greystone and set up shop on a quiet residential street at the invitation of his friend Pat Kuleto. Walter Martini, a retired opera singer and wine bootlegger, built this Arts and Crafts bungalow in 1923. In fine weather you can dine in his fountain garden enclosed in vine-covered arbors and enjoy the polished wood interior by one of three fireplaces. Kuleto's light shades, which pick up an Indian basketry motif, enhance the home environ-ment, a suitable setting for Humphries's soul-satisfying food. Humphries steers the menu toward the seasonal bounty of forest, farm, ranch, and his own vegetable garden. A recent menu included roasted mushroom soup, butternut squash soup, romaine and parsley salad with local Ascolano olives, and Atlantic salmon with potato *rösti* and sautéed yellowfoot mushrooms. The grilled California swordfish with braised porcini and fried sage showed the chef's inventiveness with seasonal ingredients. If you are a coffee lover, try the espresso crème brûlée for dessert. Daily, lunch and dinner. 1245 Spring St (at Oak Ave) (off Main St/Hwy 29). 963.2233. www.martinihouse.com

26 ST. HELENA CHAMBER OF COMMERCE

Information on St. Helena and Napa Valley, including lodging, restaurants, wineries, and

In wine speak, "ampelotherapy" is the treatment of human or animal ailments with grapes that sup-posedly possess curative properties.

bike routes, is available here. ◆ M-F. 1010 Main St (between Charter Oak Ave and Pope St). 963.4456; fax 963.5396. www.sthelena.com

27 MERRYVALE VINEYARDS

Visit this winery in its historic stone building and try the award-winning, barrel-fermented Chardonnay. Profile is a blend of the Bordeaux varietals Cabernet Sauvignon, Cabernet Franc, and Merlot from vineyards in and around the Rutherford Bench area. Under winemaker Bob Levy, a special label has been established to designate premium varietal wines. The tasting room also sells Zinfandel pasta sauce and ketchup, a Dijon Chardonnay mayonnaise, and other goodies under the winery label. Premium olive oils are also on sale here. On Saturday and Sunday mornings the winery offers a component-tasting class in which participants learn to taste tannin, sugar, and tartaric acid in wines. ◆ Fee. Tasting and sales daily; tours and Sa and Su component-tasting classes by appointment only. 1000 Main St (between Charter Oak Ave and Pope St). 963.7777; fax 963.1949

27 THE INN AT SOUTHBRIDGE

$$$$ This contemporary inn, a sister property to **Meadowood** (see page 59), was designed by local architect **William Turnbull Jr.** The two buildings' multiwindowed façades recall the small shops typical of town squares in European villages. Palms flank the build-ings, a fountain splashes in front, the courtyard is ablaze with  flowers, and flowers are found in abundance throughout the inn. The 21 spacious rooms boast cathedral ceilings and window shutters that open out and upward. A study in serenity, the rooms are decorated in muted colors, light woods, and down comforters; all have wood-burning fireplaces, TV, well-appointed bathrooms, and French doors opening to private balconies. A conti-nental breakfast buffet is served in the living room off the lobby, where a fire warms guests after cold-weather wine tasting. In good weather, breakfast is served in the courtyard. ◆ 1020 Main St (between Charter Oak Ave and Pope St). 967.9400, 800/520.6800

Within The Inn at Southbridge:

PIZZERIA TRA VIGNE

★★$ On the main floor and opening onto the courtyard of the inn is this casual restaurant, which means vine in Italian. Offerings here include well-prepared pastas, salads, and tasty pizzas made from your choice of ingredients in a wood-burning oven. The Benito is topped with fennel sausage, salami, smoked pork, and mozzarella. There are also large burgundy booths, plasma TV, and a billiard table. Take-out service is available. ♦ Italian ♦ Daily, lunch and dinner. 967.9999; fax 967.0495

Adjacent to The Inn at Southbridge:

HEALTH SPA NAPA VALLEY

This spa offers such exotic experiences as treatments with Napa Valley grape seeds, crushed and combined with essential oils for a rejuvenating Grapeseed Body Polish (for silkier, younger skin); the seed is also used for mud wraps and oil massage. Other exotica include Pancha Karma, an ancient treatment from India which consists of two massage therapists giving a synchronized massage with identical pressure and touch while applying warm sesame oil. The spa offers more familiar treatments too: the latest skin care treatments, herbal wraps, Swedish and Shiatsu massage, and reflexology. French doors in each treatment room open onto the Spa Garden, filled with aromatic herbs of the Napa Valley, as well as medicinal flowers and plants; herbs from the garden are used in body wraps. There is a complete range of fitness services and exercise equipment, yoga classes, personal training sessions, body composition testing, and activities such as hikes, bicycle tours, and walks. In addition to inn guests, the spa accepts day visitors. ♦ 967.8800

28 NAPA VALLEY OLIVE OIL MFG.

This hole-in-the-wall shop is one of those off-the-beaten-path wine-country treasures. Osvaldo, Ray, and Leonora Particelli and Policarpo Lucchesi have been selling their golden-green California olive oil (regular and extra-virgin) at a very modest price since the 1930s. They also sell nuts, dried fruit (even dried strawberries and cherries), homemade antipasto, freshly grated imported Parmesan, sharp Pecorino Romano, imported pasta, and

dried porcini mushrooms. For picnics they have Sciambra bread from Napa, cheese, salami, prosciutto, and mortadella. The *grissini* (bread sticks) and focaccia come from Cuneo Bakery in San Francisco. Mozzarella drizzled with olive oil is a terrific first course. For dessert try the *torrone* (nougat), biscotti, amaretti cookies, or the Perugina chocolate *baci* (kisses). To find this hidden shop, look for the picnic tables with umbrellas next to the parking lot. ♦ Daily. 835 Charter Oak Ave (east of Main St). 963.4173

29 PHELPS VINEYARDS

In 1972, after building several wineries in the area, Joseph Phelps set about building the winery that bears his name. Over the years, the 600-acre ranch located in Spring Valley has become synonymous with high-quality wines. The winery is so cleverly designed that it is barely discernible on the hillside to the east of the Silverado Trail. Winemaker Craig Williams produces excellent vintages, including an outstanding late-harvest Riesling, a Bordeaux-style blend called Insignia, and vineyard-designated Cabernet Sauvignons. There's also a Vin du Mistral label for Rhône-style wines, including a Syrah, a rich and complex Viognier (white), a fruity Grenache Rosé, and an impressive red wine blend that's dubbed Le Mistral. ♦ Tasting and tours daily, by appointment only; sales, M-F, Su, 10AM-4PM. 200 Taplin Rd (east of Silverado Tr). 963.2745; fax 963.4831

30 MARIO PERELLI-MINETTI WINERY

This tiny family-owned winery produces only Cabernet Sauvignon and Chardonnay. Owner Mario Perelli-Minetti comes from one of California's oldest wine families. He was actually born in the Sonoma County winery built by his father, Antonio, who graduated from the Royal Academy of Viticulture and Enology at Conegliano, Italy. From 1902 until his death in 1976, Antonio was active in viticulture and wine-making in California and Mexico. ♦ Tasting room daily. 1443 Silverado Tr (just south of Zinfandel La). 963.8310; fax 963.0242

"If a wine is not good enough to drink, it is not fit to use in the kitchen. The poor flavor will be noticed and ruin any food in which it is used."

—James Beard,
The James Beard Cookbook
(Dell Publishing Co., 1959)

Restaurants/Clubs: Red | Hotels: Purple | Shops: Orange | Outdoors/Parks: Green | Sights/Culture: Blue

THE BEST

James Laube

Senior Editor, *Wine Spectator/*
Author, *Wine Spectator's California Wine*

For wine touring, get *Wine Spectator's Wine Country Guide* ($6.95) for ideas on places to visit, eat, hike, tour, or sleep.

There are 200-plus wineries in **Napa-Sonoma**—but don't miss the oldies: **Niebaum-Coppola**, **Sebastiani**, **Château Montelena**, or **Mayacamas**. Or the architectural beauty of **Ferrari-Carano**, **Robert Mondavi**, **Clos Pegase**, **Chateau St. Jean**, **Domaine Carneros**, **Opus One**, and **Jordan**. Art exhibits at **Hess Collection** and **Clos Pegase**.

In **Napa Valley**, drive north on **Highway 29** and follow your impulses: **Oakville Grocery Co.**, **Beaulieu Vineyard**, **Grgich Hills**. Hike through **St. Helena**. Then on to **Calistoga**—take a foot tour there and soak in a mud bath; then drive back down the valley on **Silverado Trail**. Beautiful sights for all seasons.

Ride a hot-air balloon over **Napa Valley** or climb **Mount St. Helena**. Biking trails are everywhere. Walk through the historic **Sonoma Plaza** for good eats, fresh breads and cheeses, books, and wines; then drive through **Sonoma Valley**. Visit **B. R. Cohn**, **Arrowood**, **Kenwood**, **Chateau St. Jean**, **Landmark**, and **St. Francis**. Hike through **Jack London State Historic Park** or **Annadel State Park**. Make an appointment to visit **Hanzell Vineyards**. Take your youngsters for a ride at **Traintown**.

In northern Sonoma, rent a canoe and paddle down the **Russian River** (summertime). In June, go to the Russian River Blues Festival; in September, the Russian River Jazz Festival, both on a sandy beach on the river. Hike through **Armstrong Redwoods State Reserve**.

Drive through **Dry Creek Valley** and visit **Dry Creek Vineyards**, **Ferrari-Carano**, **Quivira**, or **Rafanelli**. Then tour **Russian River Valley**, with stops at **J. Rochioli**, **Hop Kiln**, or **Korbel**. Visit **Bodega Bay** for a hike on the coast, fresh seafood, or world-class salmon fishing May to October—whale watching too.

Thomas Keller's **The French Laundry** in Yountville is the finest restaurant, but tough to get into. Best chef in America. Also: **Mustards Grill**, **Ristorante Tra Vigne**, **Bistro Don Giovanni**, **Kenwood Restaurant**, **Auberge du Soleil**, or **Rutherford Grill**.

31 TRA VIGNE

★★★★$$$ This place, whose name means "among the vines" in Italian, has been one of the hottest dining spots in the wine country since the day it opened. The beautiful brick building is actually situated among some grapevines (which often conceal the restaurant's sign), and the restaurant is spacious and lively with a stylish ambiance, popular with visitors and residents alike. For entrées, chef Michael Chiarello's gastronomic masterpieces might include grilled rabbit with Teleme layered potatoes, oven-dried tomatoes, and mustard pan sauce; pan-roasted Dungeness crab with warm orange sauce and basil vinaigrette and grilled focaccia; or one of the inventive vegetarian pastas or rustic pizzas from the wood-burning oven—try the version topped with caramelized onions, thyme, and Gorgonzola. Desserts might include hazelnut crème brûlée with chocolate cookies, Italian-style ice creams, and sorbets. The wine list features an all-star selection of Italian and California wines with a number of smaller producers among them, plus great grappas and dessert wines. ◆ Italian ◆ Daily, lunch and dinner. Reservations recommended. 1050 Charter Oak Ave (just east of Main St). 963.4444; fax 963.1233

Within Tra Vigne's courtyard:

CANTINETTA TRA VIGNE

★★★$ Have a glass of wine or an ice-cold draft beer and shop for hard-to-find Italian groceries at this upscale wine bar and shop. The wood-paneled bar on one side has a wonderful selection of wines by the glass and bottle from little-known wineries. They offer 110 wines by the glass in 2-ounce to 5-ounce tastings. They even pour hard-to-find "cult" wines from Bryant Family, Harlan Estate, and Shafer Hillside Select. The Wine Bar usually offers complimentary tastings with the owner or winemaker on hand on Sunday from 6PM to 8PM. Call ahead to confirm. The perfect wine-country gift? **Tra Vigne**'s own dried tomato conserves, or one of the flavored olive oils or wine vinegars. There is also a good selection of top California and Italian wines, plus books on wines and cooking. ◆ Wine bar ◆ Daily, lunch. 963.8888

32 TAYLOR'S REFRESHER

$ Since 1949 this roadside stand with a picnic area has been dishing out hamburgers (and now veggie burgers), hot dogs, corn dogs, fries, and homemade burritos and tacos. You can get shakes, malts, and floats here too. ◆ Fast food ◆ Daily, breakfast, lunch, and dinner. 933 Main St (between Charter Oak Ave and Mitchell Dr). 963.3486

33 NAPA VALLEY FARMERS' MARKET

Shop for exotic leaf lettuce, vine-ripened tomatoes, and handmade cheeses and breads at this Friday-morning certified farmers' market in the parking lot behind the high school. (*Certified* means that all goods must be grown or made by the farmer selling them.) This is a chance for a firsthand look at some of the top-notch ingredients that go into wine-country cooking. It's also fun to rub elbows with innkeepers, chefs, vintners, and other locals who make a point of shopping here. ◆ F, 7:30AM-11:30AM, May-Nov. Main St and Grayson Ave (park and follow the crowds). 963.7343

34 NEWTON VINEYARDS

Set on a knoll overlooking the valley, this winery was designed by owners Su Hua Newton and Peter Newton, founders of **Sterling Vineyards**, and features a spectacular formal roof garden of old roses and boxwood. The winery uses grapes from the steeply terraced vineyards on Spring Mountain to produce consistently good Chardonnay, Cabernet, and Merlot. The cellar is laid out along classic French lines, with the oak barrels all housed underground. ◆ Tours, F at 11AM by appointment only. 2555 Madrona Ave (south of Fir Hill Dr). 963.9000; fax 963.5408

35 EL BONITA MOTEL

$$ Built in the 1930s and remodeled in 1994, this 41-unit motel retains its original Art Deco feel on the outside, whereas inside, the rooms are more contemporary, decorated in pastels, with such modern conveniences as private baths, cable TV, microwaves, and refrigerators, plus whirlpools in some rooms. The units with kitchens are the best deal in the valley for families. The gardens surrounding the motel are always in bloom; there's also a kidney-shaped pool. ◆ 195 Main St (at El Bonita Ave). 963.3216, 800/541.3284

36 HARVEST INN

$$$ If the Catalán modernist architect Antoni Gaudí worked in brick, he might have created something like this fantasy hotel just off Route 29. The bricks came from turn-of-the-century San Francisco houses, old cobblestones were used to build the fireplaces, and more than $1 million was spent on antiques. Alas, the effect is just a bit ho-hum. Fifty-four rooms, with names such as **Romeo and Juliet**, the **King of Hearts**, and the **Count of Fantasy**, are scattered in several buildings on the spacious grounds and feature private baths, ornate fireplaces, hardwood floors, and decks or patios. West-facing rooms have hillside views. Leather sofas are pulled up around a baronial fireplace in the main hall, which sports a wine bar with a dozen wines by the glass. The inn has two swimming pools with Jacuzzis, plus private Jacuzzis in some of the deluxe rooms. ◆ 1 Main St (at Sulphur Springs Ave). 963.9463, 800/950.8466. www.harvestinn.com

37 WHITE SULPHUR SPRINGS RESORT

$$ The oldest hot-springs resort in California, established in 1852, is 3 miles west of Main Street on a 330-acre estate in a quiet valley. This family-owned resort offers rustic lodging in the nine-room inn (shared kitchen and shower, private toilets and sinks), a carriage house that sleeps 30 (shared bath and kitchen), or eight cabins (private baths; most have kitchens). The resort really feels like the country, and for the times when racing around the valley is too taxing, settle in for a soak in the outdoor mineral-spring pool or 15-person Jacuzzi, picnic in the secluded redwood grove, take on your fellow guests in a friendly game of basketball or horseshoes, or indulge in a massage or mud, herbal, or seaweed wraps and facials at the health spa (spa reservations, 963.4361). This is a great spot

More than 200 years ago Franciscan missionaries planted not only the first grape vines in California but also the first olive trees. Today, with olive oil enjoying lofty status as a heart-healthy food, the industry is experiencing a surge in sales. Boutique olive oil producers—a number of them operate in wine country—make oils from manzanillo, sevillano, mission, picholine, and frantonio olives grown throughout the state.

for bicycling too. No smoking is allowed. ◆ 3100 White Sulphur Springs Rd (west of Spring St). 963.8588. www.whitesulphursprings.com

sive herb garden. The visitors' center is a big operation: T-shirts, jackets, specialty foods, umbrellas—they've got it all. ◆ Tasting and sales daily. 277 St. Helena Hwy (at Lewelling Ave). 963.3104

Villa St. Helena

1995

38 Villa St. Helena

$$$ You might feel like Jane Eyre approaching Gateshead mansion as you enter this expansive Tuscan-style villa high in the hills of the Mayacamas Mountains above St. Helena. Internationally known architect **Robert M. Carrere** was commissioned in 1941 to create this fantastic villa—his last major work—on a 20-acre site. In the 1940s and 1950s, Hollywood celebrities and the political elite favored it as their country hideaway. Now three of the rooms are a bed-and-breakfast for those who want to experience true peace and solitude while enjoying panoramic views of Napa Valley. The unusual but beautiful architecture of this grand house is its strong point; the ambiance, however, is rather cold and eerie. As you stroll through the wide hallways and peer into the many rooms, you can't help but imagine what the likes of Gloria Swanson or Rita Hayworth and their entourages would have brought to this great villa. It's an intriguing place but definitely not for everyone; you may want to inquire about a quick tour before planning a long retreat here. A continental breakfast is served, and hiking trails and tennis courts are nearby. ◆ 2727 Sulphur Springs Ave (between St. Helena Hwy and White Sulphur Springs Rd). 963.2514

39 Sutter Home Winery/ Trinchero

Established in 1874 by Swiss-German immigrant John Thomann and purchased by the Sutter family in 1906, this winery, housed in a complex of gussied-up Victorian buildings, has been under the sole ownership of the Trinchero family since 1947. It is best known for Zinfandels, with its Amador County Zinfandel and White Zinfandel, a wine created specifically for wide consumption, being the most popular. Chardonnay, Cabernet, and a flock of other wines are also produced here. Visitors are welcome to take a self-guided tour of the **White Zinfandel Garden**, with more than 800 varieties of flora, including roses, day lilies, azaleas, columbines, and an exten-

40 Louis M. Martini Winery

This is one of the oldest wineries in Napa Valley, founded in 1922 by Louis M. Martini and still run by the Martini family. (It was sold to Ernest and Julio Gallo in 2002.) The founder's granddaughter, Carolyn, is now president; his grandson, Michael, is the winemaker. Its Los Niños, a Cabernet Sauvignon made from the oldest vines on **Monte Rosso** vineyard high in the Mayacamas Mountains, is meant to age until *los niños*—children born the year of the vintage—are at least 21 years old. It is Martini's benchmark wine; the regular bottling is called North Coast Cabernet. ◆ Tasting, sales, and tours daily. 254 St. Helena Hwy (at Chaix La). 963.2736; fax 963.8750

41 Heitz Wine Cellars

Established in 1961 by Joe and Alice Heitz, this winery is known for its big, full-bodied Cabernets, especially those made from three specially selected Cabernet Sauvignon vineyards—**Bella Oaks**, **Trailside Vineyard**, and **Martha's Vineyard**; the last is noted for its unique bouquet of eucalyptus and mint. ◆ Tasting and sales daily; tours M-F, 2PM, by appointment only. 436 St. Helena Hwy (between White and Chaix Las). 963.3542. www.heitzcellar.com

42 Dean & DeLuca

It's telling that America's foremost purveyor of fine food, wine, and kitchenware has an outpost in Napa Valley, one of only five stores nationwide. Joel Dean and Giorgio DeLuca in 1977 opened their first food emporium in lower Manhattan and introduced the public to balsamic vinegar, sun-dried tomatoes, and extra-virgin olive oil. If you share the owners' passion for quality and taste, anticipate a culinary adventure. The store stocks the latest cook's tools plus a vast array of caviar, foie gras, chocolates, herbs, spices, teas, and vinegars. Or you can shop local for Napa Valley nuts, honey, cheese, bread, and seasonal produce for your pantry or picnic basket. There are 600 cheeses, and 13,000 labels of California wine. The staff prepares box lunches with pasta salads and gourmet sandwiches. Among the most popular: roasted turkey breast with applewood-smoked bacon on a Dutch crunch roll; and pear and brie with watercress on sliced walnut bread. ◆ Daily. The store is on Hwy 29 north of Inglewood St and a mile south of St. Helena. 607 S St. Helena Hwy (Hwy 29). 967.9980. www.deandeluca.com

Cabernet Sauvignon, and dry Chenin Blanc. (Girard is one of the last to produce this wine.) ◆ Tasting and sales daily. 677 St. Helena Hwy (between Inglewood and Lewelling Aves). 967.8032

SHADY OAKS COUNTRY INN

43 V. Sattui Winery

The fourth generation of the Sattui family offers 10 of its wines to taste at this 1885 winery with yard-thick stone walls, hand-hewn timbers, and four underground cellars. It's also a popular stop for people who want great picnic fare: The large, well-organized cheese shop and deli offers more than 200 imported and domestic cheeses, cold cuts, straightforward salads, and desserts such as truffles and oversize cookies. Enjoy your booty at the winery's shady picnic area alongside the highway. Wine- and cheese-related gifts are available too. ◆ Tasting daily. 1111 White La (at St. Helena Hwy). 963.7774; fax 963.4324

44 St. Helena Wine Merchant

A wide range of California and imported wines are sold at good prices in this large shop specializing in vintages from small-production wineries—often hard to find outside of California. You can choose from 400 to 500 estates (more than 300 Cabernets alone). You'll also find the latest releases from up-and-coming wineries. The knowledgeable staff members are ready to advise and will ship your purchase home. ◆ Daily. 699 St. Helena Hwy (at Inglewood Ave). 963.7888; fax 963.7839

44 Flora Springs Wine Co.

Founded in the 1880s by the Rennie brothers of Scotland, the old stone winery now houses a state-of-the-art cellar. The present winery, owned and run by three generations of the Komes and Garvey families, produces top-rated Chardonnays in a French Burgundy style and an exceptional Sauvignon Blanc. Winemaker Ken Deis's blend of Cabernet Sauvignon, Merlot, and Cabernet Franc is called Meritage Red Napa Valley Trilogy. You can taste these at the **Flora Springs/Girard** tasting room on St. Helena Highway. Here you may also taste Girard's Chardonnay,

45 Shady Oaks Country Inn

$$ This inn features two guest rooms in a 1920s house and two more in an 1800s stone winery building, all with private baths and furnished with antiques; three have fireplaces. A champagne breakfast, including eggs Benedict and Belgian waffles, is served in the parlor or on the patio overlooking the gardens and vineyards, which is shaded with wisteria. ◆ 399 Zinfandel La (between Silverado Tr and St. Helena Hwy). 963.1190

46 Arger-Martucci Vineyards

Viognier (a white Rhône Valley varietal), Cabernet Sauvignon, and Dulcinea (a late-harvest dessert wine with a blend of Sémillon and Sauvignon Blanc) are the specialties of this small producer. ◆ Tasting and sales daily in the summer. 1455 Inglewood Ave (west of St. Helena Hwy). 963.4334; fax 963.4748

47 Milat Vineyards

Chardonnay, Chenin Blanc, Zinfandel, Zivio (a blush Zinfandel), and Cabernet are produced by this small winery. ◆ Fee. Tasting and sales daily. 1091 St. Helena Hwy (between W Zinfandel La and Inglewood Ave). 963.0758, 800/54.MILAT; fax 963.0168

48 Zinfandel Inn

$$$ Don't let the fancy stonework and formal entrance fool you: Inside lies not a stuffy castlelike interior but a quaint, quiet, three-room bed-and-breakfast inn. The property is well tended by proprietors Jerry and Diane Payton. Two of the rooms feature fireplaces; all have private baths, and the **Zinfandel Suite** also has a large indoor whirlpool tub and a private balcony. A swimming pool provides welcome relief on hot summer days, and there's an outdoor Jacuzzi. A full breakfast is served in the formal dining room. ◆ 800 Zinfandel La (at Victoria La). 963.3512; fax 963.5310

Restaurants/Clubs: Red | **Hotels: Purple** | **Shops: Orange** | **Outdoors/Parks: Green** | **Sights/Culture: Blue**

49 RAYMOND VINEYARD AND CELLAR

Full-bodied Chardonnay and Cabernet, plus Sauvignon Blanc, Merlot, and Pinot Noir, are made here by one of the oldest wine-making families in the valley. Fourth-generation vintners Roy Raymond Jr. and Walter Raymond, along with Kenn Vigoda, oversee all aspects of the vineyard and winery operation. Their top wines are the Raymond Generations and Napa Valley Private Reserves; older vintages of their notable Cabernet Sauvignon Private Reserve are sometimes available here. ♦ Tasting and sales daily; tours by appointment only. 849 Zinfandel La (between Silverado Tr and St. Helena Hwy). 963.3141; fax 963.8498; 800/525.2659

50 THE INK HOUSE

$$$ Wealthy local landowner Theron H. Ink built this Italianate Victorian bed-and-breakfast in 1884. The inn boasts understated period décor and antique furnishings. The seven guest rooms have private baths and brass-and-iron beds. The observatory on the third floor is a perfect place to watch hot-air balloons floating over the valley. A full breakfast is served, as are wine and appetizers in the afternoon. ♦ 1575 St. Helena Hwy (between Whitehall and W Zinfandel Las). 963.3890. www.inkhouse.com

50 WHITEHALL LANE WINERY

Winemaker Arthur Finkelstein founded this small winery on the northern edge of the Rutherford Bench district in 1979. The Leonardini family now owns the place. Dean Sylvester is the winemaker. The winery produces a good Cabernet and Merlot, as well as Chardonnay and Sauvignon Blanc. ♦ Tasting and sales daily; tours daily, 1PM and 4PM. 1563 St. Helena Hwy (between Whitehall and W Zinfandel Las). 963.9454; fax 963.7035

51 BURGESS CELLARS

In a two-story wood-and-stone winery building on the site of a vineyard planted around 1880, former IBM corporate jet pilot Tom Burgess and winemaker Bill Sorenson produce big, bold wines from Burgess's Chardonnay, Cabernet, and Zinfandel vineyards. The Cabernet Sauvignon Napa Valley Vintage Selection and the barrel-fermented Chardonnay from **Triere Vineyard** both age well. ♦ Tasting and tours daily by appointment only. 1108 Deer Park Rd (between Silverado Tr and Howell Mountain Rd). 963.4766; fax 963.8774

52 DEER PARK WINERY

This small, state-of-the-art winery is housed in a venerable two-story stone building erected in 1891. The winery, owned by the Robert Knapp and David Clark families, produces Sauvignon Blanc and Zinfandel from a rocky hillside vineyard. It also produces Chardonnay and a small amount of Petite Sirah and Cabernet. ♦ Tasting and sales by appointment only, F-Su. 1000 Deer Park Rd (between Silverado Tr and Howell Mountain Rd). 963.5411

53 LAKE BERRYESSA

Creek Canyon was dammed at one end to create this 26-mile-long artificial lake, the largest in Northern California. **Oak Shores Park** and resorts around the lake offer an array of recreational opportunities. Anglers will find plenty of trout, bass, catfish, and salmon. The lake's marinas have docks, berths, and boat launches. Most marinas rent fishing or ski boats, Jet Skis, and sailboards, and one leases houseboats. Tent and RV camping, picnic areas, and barbecue facilities are available at the lake's resorts. ♦ Berryessa Knoxville Rd (between Sage Canyon and Pope Canyon Rds). For information, call the Lake Berryessa Chamber of Commerce at 800/726.1256

54 BOTHE–NAPA VALLEY STATE PARK

This 1,800-acre park has more than 100 picnic sites, all with tables and barbecues, situated under huge maple and Douglas fir trees. After lunch, swim in the park's pool or work off your picnic by taking a hike. The 1.2-mile **History Trail**, rated as moderately strenuous, leads past a pioneer cemetery and the site of Napa County's first church, built in 1853, to the **Bale Grist Mill State Historic Park** (see page 75). Originally a country retreat built in the 1870s by Dr. Charles Hitchcock and his wife, the estate was bought by Reinhold Bothe after Hitchcock's daughter Lillie Coit died in 1929. Bothe deeded it to the state in 1960, and today the park is a haven for wine-country vacationers, offering the ultimate bargain in Napa Valley budget accommodations. There are 50 family campsites, including 10 remote, walk-in sites suitable for tent camping. The remaining 40 sites can accommodate tents or RVs. Campsites have flush toilets, hot showers, laundry sinks, picnic tables, barbecues, and use of the swimming pool. Evening campfire programs

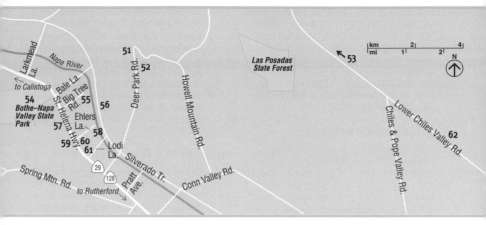

and talks about the stars and planets are held on Wednesday and Saturday. Reservations for campsites are accepted 8 weeks in advance. ◆ Fee. Park: daily. Pool: daily mid-June through Labor Day. 3801 St. Helena Hwy (between Birdhill and Tucker Rds). 942.4575, 800/444.PARK (for reservations)

55 TUDAL WINERY

This winery consistently produces well-made Cabernet from a small property where two generations of the Tudal family work side by side. ◆ Tasting and tours daily, by appointment only. 1015 Big Tree Rd (east of St. Helena Hwy). 963.3947; fax 963.9288

56 ROMBAUER VINEYARDS

Founded in 1982 by Koerner Rombauer, the great-nephew of Irma Rombauer, author of *Joy of Cooking*, and his wife, Joan, this well-equipped winery custom-crushes wines for a number of aspiring winemakers and also produces a smooth, rich Chardonnay, Cabernet Sauvignon, and proprietary red wine of Cabernet blended with Cabernet Franc and Merlot under the name Le Meilleur du Chai ("the best of the cellar"). There's also a crisp Merlot and zesty Zinfandel. ◆ Tasting daily; tours by appointment only. 3522 Silverado Tr (between Lodi and Bale Las). 963.5170; fax 963.5752

57 STONY HILL VINEYARD

Founded in 1951, this small vineyard on the rocky hillside of the western ridge of Napa Valley has a cult following for its voluptuous Chardonnay. Despite the wine's high quality and the difficulty in finding this wine, sold only to a mailing list of faithful customers, the prices remain moderate. White Riesling and Gewürz-

traminer are also produced. The winery is hard to find; ask for directions when you call to make your appointment. ◆ Sales by mail only; tours by appointment only. 3331 St. Helena Hwy (north of Birdhill Rd). Mailing address: Box 308, St. Helena, CA 94574. 963.2636

57 BALE GRIST MILL STATE HISTORIC PARK

Napa Valley's economy was once based on wheat, not grapes. This historic flour mill was designed and built in 1846 by British surgeon Edward Turner Bale, who served under General Mariano Guadalupe Vallejo, married Vallejo's niece, and settled in Napa Valley. The mill has been restored to working condition, complete with a 36-foot wooden waterwheel and millstones. On weekends at 11:30AM, 1, 2:30, and 3:30PM the immense wheel turns, and you can watch the ranger-miller grind grain with the French buhr (quartz); at times you may linger in the granary to watch baking demonstrations. It's an invigorating walk to the mill from **Bothe–Napa Valley State Park** (see page 74) along the well-marked, 1.2-mile **History Trail**, which passes through a pioneer cemetery and the site of the first church in Napa County, built in 1853. This site may look familiar—it was used by Walt Disney in the 1960 film *Pollyanna*. ◆ Admission; children younger than 6 admitted free. 3369 St. Helena Hwy (north of Birdhill Rd). 963.2236

57 BALE MILL CLASSIC COUNTRY FURNITURE

Owner Tom Scheibal designs about 80% of the handsome country pine furniture, stylish iron

Restaurants/Clubs: Red | **Hotels: Purple** | **Shops: Orange** | **Outdoors/Parks: Green** | **Sights/Culture: Blue**

75

garden chairs, beds, and chaise longues for sale here. More portable are willow and wire baskets. He also has lovely lamps and weathered iron signs. Also in St. Helena, Scheibal's second shop, called **Tivoli** (1432 Main St, between Adams and Pine Sts; 967.9399), has a garden focus. ♦ Daily; closed Tu in winter. 3431 St. Helena Hwy (north of Birdhill Rd). 963.4595; fax 963.4128

58 DUCKHORN VINEYARDS

Margaret and Daniel Duckhorn founded this winery with 10 other families in 1976; their first wines from the 1978 vintage, a Cabernet and a Merlot, were immediately acclaimed. **Duckhorn** remains a headquarters for these rich reds. Wine connoisseurs say the vineyard's Cabernet Sauvignon Napa Valley now even outshines its renowned Merlot—although its Napa Valley Merlot is considered one of California's best crafted and ages well up to 10 years. The winery's Cabernet Blend Howell Mountain is an earthy Bordeaux-style wine; the Sauvignon Blanc is the only white produced here. ♦ Sales, M-F; tours and tastings by appointment. 1000 Lodi La (at Silverado Tr). 963.7108; fax 963.7595

59 NAPA PREMIUM OUTLETS

Within a pleasant tree-lined shopping complex, you'll find clothing and shoes discounted by 25% to 55% at these factory outlets that include, among others, **Donna Karan**, **Brooks Brothers**, **London Fog**, **Joan & David**, **Coach**, and **Movado**. There are rest rooms, a pay phone, and a food cart on weekends. You can bring lunch to enjoy on the patio in front, or in the picnic area in back. ♦ Daily (shop hours may vary). 3111 St. Helena Hwy (between Rockland and Birdhill Rds). 963.7282

60 FREEMARK ABBEY

This small complex features two restaurants, a winery, a shop, and offices. ♦ 3010–3022 St. Helena Hwy (between Lodi and Ehlers Las)

Within Freemark Abbey:

FREEMARK ABBEY WINERY

In 1886, Josephine Tychson established a winery at this historic site. She was the first woman to build a winery in California, and her successor, Antonio Forni, built the present stone structure around 1900. It changed hands several times until the present owners bought it in 1967. Now under the management of partner and winemaker Ted Edwards, the winery is best known for its Cabernet Sauvignon from **Bosché Vineyard** near Rutherford, considered one of the finest vineyards in California. It also produces

Chardonnay, Merlot, and Johannisberg Riesling, which in certain years develops into Edelwein, a rich and extravagantly perfumed late-harvest dessert wine. A lovely room with a wood-beam ceiling and sofas in front of a fieldstone fireplace welcomes you to the tasting area, where you can sample not only new releases but also an occasional older vintage. ♦ Fee. Tasting and sales daily; tours daily at 2PM. 963.9694; 800/963.9698; fax 963.0554

60 FOLIE À DEUX WINERY

The name of this winery comes from a French term used by psychiatrists in the US to describe a fantasy or delusion shared by two people—the duo in this case was Larry and Evie Dizmang (a psychiatrist and psychiatric social worker, respectively). Everyone told them they were crazy to start a winery. In 1981, the winery started producing wine from a 12-acre estate vineyard, and the fruits of the Dizmangs' "folie" was soon winning praise. The winery was sold in 1995 to a group of wine enthusiasts, including the well-known winemaker Dr. Richard Peterson, who is now chairman. Scott Harvey, considered to be one of America's best winemakers, came aboard too; Harvey produces some serious wines, drawing praise and prizes for his Merlot and both Cabernet Sauvignon and Cabernet Sauvignon Reserve, as well as Chardonnay. The roster also includes Sangiovese and Syrah. Two Zinfandels were released in 1998, one partially blended from the oldest Zinfandel vines in California, from the 129-year-old **Grandpère Vineyard** in Amador County. The tasting room is in the original turn-of-the-century farmhouse. Oak-shaded picnic grounds are available here. ♦ Tasting and sales daily. 3070 St. Helena Hwy (between Lodi and Ehlers Las). 963.1160, 800/473.4454; fax 963.9223

60 EHLERS GROVE WINERY

Formerly known as **Stratford Winery**, this winery continues to produce a nice, reasonably priced Chardonnay and also makes Pinot Noir, Merlot, Cabernet Sauvignon, and Sauvignon Blanc. ♦ Tasting and sales daily. 3222 Ehlers La (east of St. Helena Hwy). 963.3200

61 WINE COUNTRY INN

$$ Located off the highway in a quiet meadow, this small hotel was designed in the tradition of the inns of New England. All 24 rooms have private baths and views of the countryside; most have private patios or balconies and/or fireplaces. Country furniture is complemented with fall or spring colors. A full breakfast with fruit, homemade bread and granola, plus quiche or omelettes is served. ♦

1152 Lodi La (just east of St. Helena Hwy). 963.7077; fax 963.9018

62 RustRidge Ranch, Winery, and Bed & Breakfast Inn

$$ Seemingly lost in the hills above the Silverado Trail, this 442-acre vineyard, winery, and thoroughbred-horse breeding facility now operates as a five-room bed-and-breakfast as well, with guests bunking down in the 1940s ranch house. Innkeepers Jim Fresquez and Susan Meyer Fresquez have a collection of arrowheads, leather-grinding bowls, and pestles they've found on the property (which once belonged to the Wappo Indians). The entire ranch house can also be rented to families and groups. Three of the guest rooms are in the left wing of the house; the largest is the sunny **RustRidge Room**, which has its own fireplace, large private bathroom, and floor-to-ceiling windows offering views of the pastures and vineyards. **The Oaks** and **The Vine** each have private baths (although they are off the hall outside the rooms) and direct access to the back deck. In the right wing of the house are the **Chiles Valley** and **Poolside** rooms, both with private baths; the only rooms in this wing, they are near the inn's sauna and spa. The entire inn is decorated in Santa Fe style. The innkeepers offer guests the unusual option of using the professionally equipped kitchen to make a salad or cook dinner for themselves. The ranch also has a tennis court and a swimming pool. The horses on the ranch are not available for riding, but guests may bring their own mounts and stable them here. There are miles of trails for riding or hiking. ♦ There is a two-night minimum stay. 2910 Lower Chiles Valley Rd (between Sage Canyon and Chiles & Pope Valley Rds). 965.9353; fax 965.9263. www.rustridge.com

CALISTOGA

As its legacy of geysers, hot springs, and lava deposits attests, the Calistoga area began life with a bang—a volcanic bang, that is. Some of the eruptions formed the gray stone used in local landmarks such as the **Culinary Institute of America at Greystone** and various bridges. Local Native American tribes healed their sick in steam baths they constructed around the hot springs at the northern end of **Napa Valley**. And when Sam Brannan, California's first millionaire, visited the area in the mid-19th century, he immediately envisioned a first-class spa and set to work designing a lavish hotel to attract wealthy San Franciscans to the site of what is now **Indian Springs** spa and resort. Brannan also brought the first railroad to the valley and dubbed the town "Calistoga," a hybrid of the words *California* and *Saratoga* (the famous New York resort).

Set in the midst of rolling vineyards, with extinct volcano **Mount St. Helena** standing guard in the distance, this small country town is shedding its Old West image in favor of one as a spa resort town. The mineral water and mud baths of Calistoga are a splendid side attraction of a wine-country trip.

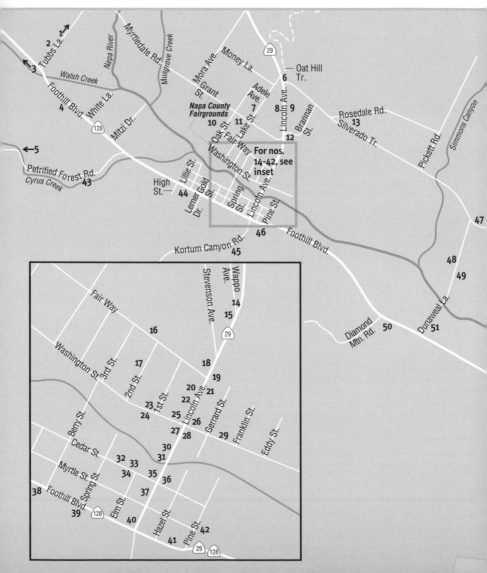

1 OLD FAITHFUL GEYSER

Just 2 miles north of Calistoga, you'll find one of the town's prime attractions, one of three faithful geysers (so called because of their regular eruptions) in the world. Every 40 minutes, thar she blows—a column of 350-degree water and vapor goes roaring more than 60 feet into the air. The geyser became a paying attraction at the turn of the century, when people would arrive in their Model T's, spread lavish picnics on the ground, and settle in for the show. On request, visitors may see a video explaining how geysers are formed. You will also find a wishing well and a picnic area nearby. ◆ Admission. Daily. 1299 Tubbs La (between Rte 128 and Bennett La). 942.6463

1 CHÂTEAU MONTELENA WINERY

Don't miss this historic winery at the foot of Mount St. Helena. It was built of local and imported stone in a grandiose French-château style in 1882 by Alfred L. Tubbs, one of California's first state senators. A Chinese engineer bought the property in the 1950s and added the 5-acre lake with three islands. In 1972 the Barrett family and partners replanted the vineyards, restored the cellars, and hired Mike Grgich (now at his own winery, **Grgich Hills**) as winemaker. His second vintage, the 1973 Chardonnay, brought the establishment fame and fortune in the famous 1976 Paris competition, when expert French tasters rated it first over several world-famous French White Burgundies in a blind tasting. The winery, with Bo Barrett as winemaker, continues to produce classic Napa Valley Chardonnay and Cabernet Sauvignon with plenty of aging potential, plus Riesling. Don't rule out this lovely spot on a rainy or misty day, when the Chinese pavilion in Jade Lake looks especially ethereal. ◆ Fee. Tasting and sales daily; tours daily, 11AM and 2PM, by appointment only. 1429 Tubbs La (between Bennett La and Rte 29). 942.5105; fax 942.4221

1 ROBERT LOUIS STEVENSON STATE PARK

This largely undeveloped area at the northern end of the valley contains an abandoned silver mine where Stevenson and his wife, Fanny, spent their honeymoon in 1880, staying in a bunkhouse. He later wrote about his experiences and the area's beauty in *The Silverado Squatters*. He also modeled Spyglass Hill in *Treasure Island* after Mount St. Helena, which, at 4,343 feet, is the highest of the Bay Area's peaks. A rigorous 5-mile trail to the top offers unsurpassed views of the wine country below—on a *very* clear day, you can see all the way to Mount Shasta and the Sierra Nevada. Plan your hike for the cool morning hours and bring plenty of drinking water. The park has no developed facilities, and the entrance is marked by a small sign and a gravel parking lot, which is easy to miss. On your way here, don't miss the spectacular lookout over Calistoga on the right side of the road about 1 mile after the

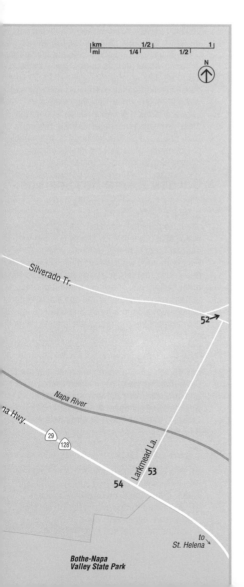

Silverado Tr.

52

Napa River

na Hwy.

29
128

Larkmead La.

53

54

to
St. Helena

Bothe-Napa
Valley State Park

highway veers to the right and heads uphill. Best visited in spring and fall. ◆ 3801 Hwy 29 (north of Tubbs La). 942.4575

2 SUMMERS WINERY

Take a moment for this tiny family winery where you can taste and talk Italian-style wines with the owners, Jim and Beth Summers. Their first crush was 1997. The hospitable Summerses produce small lots of Merlot and Chardonnay under their own label. **Villa Andriana**'s estate-bottled wines are Charbono and Zinfandel. ◆ Tasting and sales daily, summer; winter, by appointment only. 1171 Tubbs La (between Rte 128 and Bennett La). 942.5508. www.summerswinery.com

3 STORYBOOK MOUNTAIN VINEYARDS

This small winery is entirely devoted to producing Zinfandel—and owner Bernard Seps does a knockout job, consistently making one of the top California Zinfandels in both a regular bottling and a reserve bottling that improves with age. ◆ Tasting, sales, and tours, M-Sa, by appointment only. 3835 Hwy 128 (west of Petrified Forest Rd). 942.5310

4 FOOTHILL HOUSE

$$ Nestled in the foothills of Calistoga, this small turn-of-the-century farmhouse is a romantic, comfortable, and tastefully decorated hideaway. Each of the three large guest suites, featuring a private entrance and bath, takes its color scheme from the quilt on the antique bed. Each room has a radio, CD player, and TV, a refrigerator, a wood-burning fireplace or stove, and soundproof walls. The **Evergreen Suite** features a Jacuzzi and a private sundeck. The owner's cottage is even more private and boasts a fireplace and a kitchenette so you can settle in for a longer stay. Innkeepers Doris and Gus Beckert deliver a great gourmet breakfast to your room. ◆ 3037 Foothill Blvd (north of Petrified Forest Rd). 942.6933, 800/942.6933; fax 942.5692

5 PETRIFIED FOREST

Six miles from Calistoga are gigantic redwoods that turned to stone more than three million years ago when Mount St. Helena erupted and molten lava coursed through the valley that is now known as the **Petrified Forest**. Silicates in the ash that blanketed the area seeped into the tree fibers, replacing wood cells with crystallized silica. Highlights along the well-marked trail include "The Giant," a tree that's 60 feet long and 6 feet in diameter and was 2,000 years old when it was petrified three million years ago; the 105-foot-long Monarch tunnel tree,

also 6 feet in diameter; a wishing well; a museum; and a nature store. A bronze plaque marks where Charles Evans discovered the first stump of petrified wood in 1870; his meeting in 1880 with Robert Louis Stevenson is immortalized in Stevenson's book *The Silverado Squatters*. There is wheelchair access to part of the trail. Smoking is not allowed on the trail. ◆ Admission; children younger than 10 are admitted free. Daily. Group tours are offered and picnic tables are available on a first-come, first-served basis. 4100 Petrified Forest Rd (southwest of Mountain Home Ranch Rd). 942.6667

6 OAT HILL TRAIL

Oat Hill Road was once the service road for 60 mines that lay between Calistoga and Pope Valley. Many residents do not know that $15 million of cinnabar, the ore from which mercury/quicksilver is processed, traveled this road. It is now properly known as Oat Hill Trail because vehicle traffic is banned, as the sign warns on the metal gate. Follow the trail up under black oak and scrub oak and marvel at the open vistas and old mines. The 10-mile round trip has an elevation gain of 1,900 feet, making it moderately strenuous. The trailhead is a half mile north of Calistoga's main business district. ◆ Park on Lake St near the three-way-stop junction of Hwy 29, Silverado Trail, and Lake St. The trailhead is at the back of Trailhead Café's parking lot. No official agency can be called for information.

7 GOLDEN HAVEN HOT SPRINGS

$ It's not Southern California's sybaritic Golden Door Spa, but it does have the requisite mud bath that you may take with your mate. Also offered are a deeply relaxing hot mineral Jacuzzi, herbal mineral baths, European body wraps, massages, acupressure treatments, herbal facials, and a whole lot of other treatments. The warm mineral pool is topped with a sun deck. The spa's accommodations are akin to a motel and hardly glamorous. The 26 rooms have private baths and sliding-glass doors opening onto a minuscule patio overlooking a parking lot; some rooms have kitchenettes and/or a private Jacuzzi and sauna. Guests have use of the swimming pool, hot mineral-water pools, and sundeck. No children are allowed on weekends or holidays. ◆ Spa: daily. 1713 Lake St (between Grant St and Adele Ave). 942.6793

8 COMFORT INN

$$ This comfortable motel has a hot mineral-water swimming pool and spa, a sauna, and steam room. The 54 rooms have modern décor, private baths, and cable TV; upstairs rooms have decks with views of the hills. A continental breakfast is provided. ◆

1865 Lincoln Ave (between Wappo Ave and Lake St). 942.9400; fax 942.5262

9 CALISTOGA VILLAGE INN & SPA

$$ Another full spa-inn combo, this one offers mud baths, mineral baths, steam and blanket wraps, body massages, natural facials, and salt scrubs. The comfortable accommodations include use of the mineral-water swimming pool, spa, sauna, and steam rooms. All 41 rooms and suites have cable TV and private baths, and some of the suites have whirlpools. Spa-and-lodging deals are available. ♦ Spa: daily. Reservations recommended. 1880 Lincoln Ave (between Brannan St and Silverado Tr). 942.0991; fax 942.5306

10 NAPA COUNTY FAIRGROUNDS

Each Fourth of July weekend the Napa County Fair kicks off for 5 fun-packed days. Choose between live music and entertainment or auto racing at night; leave the day for touring exhibits on domestic arts and watching the homemade wine competition. ♦ Call for information on other events during the year. 1435 Oak St (between Washington and Grant Sts). 942.5111; fax 942.5125.

11 CARLIN COUNTRY COTTAGES

$$ These 15 cozy cottages on a quiet side street are the Carlin family's pride and joy. Innkeeper Gina Carlin's dad acted as general contractor and all the other Carlins got into the act, working on the carpentry, bathroom tiling, and garden design. With the help of her mother, Gina decorated the pin-neat rooms with Shaker-style furniture and Irish country motifs, with handsome quilts whose colors dictate each room's color scheme. Similar quilts are on sale in the lobby and are made by yet another member of the Carlin clan. Guests can choose from studios, one-bedroom, or large one- and two-bedroom suites with kitchens. The kitchen cottages are ideal for families. In seven cottages, Jacuzzis fed by the Calistoga mineral springs refresh the weary traveler. There's a heated mineral-spring water swimming pool and outdoor mineral-spring-fed Jacuzzi. ♦ 1623 Lake St (at Grant St). 942.9102. www.carlincottages.com

12 INDIAN SPRINGS SPA

$$ Founded in 1860 by millionaire Sam Brannan, this spa and resort is named for the Wappo Indians, who built sweat lodges around the springs long ago. To the left of the spa building you can see one of the three active geysers that provide the spa with a constant supply of 212-degree mineral water, which is cooled for use in the spa and pool. Treatments include mud baths, massages, facials, and mineral-water baths in a thoroughly professional setting. This is also the home of California's oldest operating swimming pool—a huge, beautiful, hot-spring pool that was built in 1913. The pool is kept at 102 degrees in the winter and 90 degrees in the summer. Its use is complimentary for spa guests. Owner Erin Donnelly has decorated the 17 cottages in country style, and hammocks hang about the grounds. The cottages are studios and one-bedrooms, most with gas fireplaces; there also is a three-bedroom house. Other amenities include a clay tennis court, a playground with slides, shuffleboard, croquet, Surrey bikes, and barbecues. ♦ Spa and pool: daily. Reservations recommended for spa. 1712 Lincoln Ave (just south of Brannan St). 942.4913

13 SILVER ROSE INN SPA & WINERY

$$$ Two separate inns offer guests a choice of 20 spacious rooms. The **Inn on the Knoll** was the original inn and spa facility; the **Inn on the Vineyard** adjoins a well-equipped conference center. Each inn has its own dignified "gathering" rooms, dining areas, fireplaces, and cozy corners. All rooms have private baths; five have fireplaces, seven feature both fireplaces and Jacuzzis, and most have balconies. Sally and J-Paul Dumont have had fun decorating the rooms and suites—each has a different theme, such as teddy bears, dolls, safaris, carousel, Mardi Gras, Oriental furnishings, and a tribute to Greta Garbo. The original swimming pool with a Jacuzzi was carved out of the natural rock in the shade of a 300-year-old oak tree. The other pool is in the shape of a wine bottle and also has a Jacuzzi. Mineral water from the inn's own hot springs is available for drinking and bathing. A new spa decorated in earth tones offers a full range of services. Some spa services also are offered in the guest rooms. At breakfast time, the Dumonts offer fresh fruit and homemade bread, and during their evening wine-and-cheese hour, they serve Silver Rose Cellars Napa Valley wine. No smoking is allowed. ♦ 351 Rosedale Rd (between Pickett Rd and

---

Restaurants/Clubs: Red | Hotels: Purple | Shops: Orange | Outdoors/Parks: Green | Sights/Culture: Blue

Silverado Tr). 942.9581, 800/995.9381; fax 942.0841

14 COTTAGE GROVE INN

$$$ You would swear these 16 Craftsman-style cottages have been sheltered by these old elms for centuries. In fact, they are the recent designs of architect **Tom Simpert**, who fashioned them to fit into the grove's natural landscape. The cottages in this bed-and-breakfast have wood-burning fireplaces, comfy reading chairs, vaulted ceilings with skylights, overhead fans (plus air conditioning), and gleaming hardwood floors. They're also well soundproofed against traffic noise. The spacious bathrooms include two-person Jacuzzis under skylights, double vanities and well-lighted mirrors, and tub ledges that hold sea salts, candles, and a white orchid plant, and thick terry robes provide cocoons of comfort. Cable TV with VCR, a stereo with CD player, a wet bar, a refrigerator, and a coffeemaker and freshly ground coffee are all at hand. What impresses most is the way in which interior designer Monica Bootcheck has lent each cottage a distinctive theme: Golden yellow and blue, the charming **Audubon Cottage** has an iron head-board with sculpted birds, handcrafted lamps, and an antique birdhouse. Audubon prints, books on birds, and copies of *Audubon* magazine complete the theme. The **Botanical Cottage** features 18th-century florilegia artwork, floral furnishings, and trellis bedside lamps. Accenting the **Music Cottage** are an old violin and antique drum cocktail table. A replica of the scale model of a yacht is on the mantel in the **Nautical Cottage**, which also has yachting fabrics. The other cottages are equally enchanting. Each porch cottage has two wicker rocking chairs, a basket with a tarp for a car (a parking space is provided), and firewood. You can meet guests over a continental breakfast or afternoon wine and cheese and preserve your privacy in cottages made for romance. This is a nonsmoking inn. ♦ 1711 Lincoln Ave (north of Stevenson Ave). 942.8400, 800/799.2284; fax 942.2653

14 CALISTOGA ROASTERY

★$ Clive Richardson runs this friendly spot where you can get a cappuccino with a

Wine country is best maneuvered by car, but there are streets just meant for walking: Main Street, St. Helena (shops, cafés, restaurants); Lincoln Avenue, Calistoga (spas, saunas, shops, restaurants); Main Street, Mendocino (galleries, cafés, and historic sites); Historic District, Petaluma (historic and architectural treasures); Sonoma Plaza (historic), and Santa Rosa's Historic Railroad Square.

wicked pastry, or a sandwich or other snack. Take it to the deck and watch the gliders overhead. ♦ Coffeehouse ♦ Daily. 1721 Lincoln Ave (at Wappo Ave). 942.5757

15 BRANNAN COTTAGE INN

$$ When Sam Brannan opened his **Calistoga Hot Springs Resort** in 1860, he built 14 cottages. Of the three cottages remaining today, only the one housing this charming inn remains on its original site. Listed on the National Register of Historic Places, this bed-and-breakfast was originally owned by the Winn sisters, Brannan's cousins. Its restoration was a labor of love for former innkeepers Jay and Dottie Richolson (they sold the inn, and the current owner is Dieter Back). The Richolsons had help from local residents, who donated matching porch lights and provided early photos that were enlarged to make templates for the gingerbread gable. Each of the six rooms is stenciled with a different wild-flower border and decorated with antiques and wicker furnishings. Clock radios and air conditioners add modern comforts to this yesteryear world. All rooms have their own entrances, private baths, and queen-size beds with down comforters. On sunny mornings, a full breakfast is served in the courtyard under the trees; in inclement weather guests dine indoors. No smoking is allowed. ♦ 109 Wappo Ave (at Lincoln Ave). 942.4200

16 HIDEAWAY COTTAGES

$$ On a quiet residential street off Lincoln Avenue, this place offers overnight lodging, mostly for clients of **Dr. Wilkinson's Hot Springs** spa (see page 83) around the corner. The 15 cottages have private baths and picnic tables and barbecues outside; some also have kitchenettes. The bonus here is the outdoor mineral-water Jacuzzi and a mineral-water swimming pool (heated in winter) with chaise longues, tables, and umbrellas in a lawn and garden area. Recent renovations have brightened some rooms; work is continuing on others. No children are allowed. ♦1412 Fair Way (between Lincoln Ave and Park St). 942.4108

17 SCOTT COURTYARD

$$ A great wine-country find, this classy bed-and-breakfast will please even those folks who don't much care for the typical bed-and-breakfast experience. You'll get plenty of privacy and space here—and you won't feel as if you have to tiptoe around for fear of

disturbing other guests. The five spacious suites are comfortable and attractive; each one has a sitting room, queen-size bed, private bath, and its own entrance. The Werretts show off their love of cooking with large breakfasts, which may include lemon poppy-seed French toast and maple syrup, eggs, ham, fresh fruit, freshly squeezed orange juice, coffee and tea, bread pudding, and even some Mexican specialties. There's also late-afternoon wine, cheese, and hors d'oeuvres. Best of all, it's located in a quiet neighborhood, and it's an easy walk to Calistoga's shops, spas, and cafés. Another plus: The Werretts can provide information on the wine country and what's happening around town. ♦ 1443 Second St (between Washington St and Fair Way). 942.0948, 800/942.1515; fax 942.5102

18 Dr. Wilkinson's Hot Springs

$ "Doc" Wilkinson was a young chiropractor when he came to Calistoga and established this spa in 1946. His spa-resort features a variety of treatments, including facials, acupressure face-lifts, back and shoulder cleansing, mud baths, aromatic mineral whirlpool baths, a steam room, blanket wraps, massage, and special spa packages. There are 42 modern, motel-like units, five Victorian-style rooms, and four bungalows, all with private baths, mini-refrigerators, coffeemakers, and color TVs; several rooms also have kitchens. There are an additional 17 rooms in the **Hideaway Cottages** (see page 82). Spa guests may use the three mineral-water pools (indoor whirlpool, outdoor soaking pool, and outdoor cool swimming pool). The patio area is furnished with chaise longues and tables. ♦ Spa: daily. 1507 Lincoln Ave (between Fair Way and Stevenson Ave). 942.4108

19 Palisades Market

This ranch market has good-looking produce, a small wine section, and imported chocolate, gourmet groceries, and boxed lunches. ♦ Daily. 1506 Lincoln Ave (between Washington and Brannan Sts). 942.9549; fax 942.6476

20 Mount View Hotel

$$ Built in 1917, this hotel, which is on the National Register of Historic Places, has been restored in the Art Deco style of the 1920s and 1930s. There are eight fantasy suites, which are furnished with handsome period pieces, and three private cottages, each featuring a patio and hot tub as well as a wet bar. The 22 standard doubles, all with private baths, are less glamorous—Deco on a budget. But everybody gets to enjoy the pool and

Jacuzzi, and there's a full-service spa that's open to the public. ♦ 1457 Lincoln Ave (between Washington St and Fair Way). 942.6877; fax 942.6904

Within the Mount View Hotel:

Mount View Spa

Time for some R&R? Treat yourself to one of this spa's many services—a Swedish massage, a customized whirlpool bath, a Dead Sea mud wrap, or a deep pore-cleansing facial. Or you can go whole hog and sign up for one of the spa's Silverado Indulgences, which combines all of these services. Relaxation is guaranteed. ♦ Daily. Reservations recommended. 942.5789; fax 942.9165

21 Calistoga Depot Railroad Station

Established in 1868 and restored a century later, this historic landmark is believed to be the oldest railroad depot in California. The clapboard building is now a mini shopping gallery that's home to the **Chamber of Commerce** (see below), a restaurant, and several shops. Six restored Pullmans are parked alongside the station and house some of the stores. ♦ Daily (some store hours vary). 1458 Lincoln Ave (between Washington and Brannan Sts)

Within the Calistoga Depot Railroad Station:

Calistoga Tasting Room

Housed in railroad car 12, the tasting room for the hand-crafted Pope Valley wines is outfitted with antiques and original art. The $5 tasting fee is refunded with a purchase. Daily. 942.6999. www.popevalleywinery.com

Calistoga Wine Stop

Parked in the middle of the depot, this bright yellow train car trimmed in green makes an ingenious space for a serious, small wine store with more than a thousand Napa and Sonoma wines. Some rare and older bottles are available, and the store ships. ♦ Daily. 942.5556

Chamber of Commerce

You can get all kinds of information here on Calistoga and Napa Valley. ♦ Daily. 942.6333. www.calistogafun.com

Treasures of Tibet

You may never meet the Dalai Lama in Calistoga, but you can feel his aura in this shop filled with Tibetan treasures—beautiful tankas (scrolls); jewelry; rugs; clothing in lustrous

---

Restaurants/Clubs: Red | Hotels: Purple | Shops: Orange | Outdoors/Parks: Green | Sights/Culture: Blue

silk, cotton, and hemp; books; rice paper; and more. A portion of the profit from each sale goes to help the Tibetan people. ♦ Daily. 942.8287

EVANS DESIGNS / CALIFORNIA

22 EVANS DESIGNS GALLERY

Exotic handmade pottery, many pieces over-sized or one of a kind, are all discounted by 40% to 90% at this outlet. Note their New Age twist on raku ware. The shop also has hand-blown glass pieces. ♦ Daily. 1421 Lincoln Ave (between Washington St and Fair Way). 942.0453

23 ROMAN SPA

$ You'll find motel-like accommodations at this no-frills establishment. A lounge and chairs are set out on AstroTurf around a mineral pool. Yes, it's as ugly as it sounds, but people come here for the facilities at the adjacent **Oasis Spa** (see below), which is one of the best in town, and the staff is friendly. There's also a sauna and Jacuzzi. ♦ 1300 Washington St (at First St). 942.4441

At Roman Spa:

OASIS SPA

This spa offers mud baths for singles and couples, Jacuzzi mineral tubs with a choice of five herbal oils, Swedish and Esalen massages, foot reflexology and acupressure treatments, herbal facials, and herbal blankets—all in an unassuming bungalow directly behind the **Roman Spa** hotel. You'll find some of the most reasonable spa rates in the city here. ♦ Daily. 942.6122

24 SHARPSTEEN MUSEUM AND BRANNAN COTTAGE

After 30 years at Walt Disney Studios as an animator (*Pinocchio*, *Fantasia*) and Oscar-winning producer, Ben Sharpsteen retired to Calistoga and created this museum. With the help of friends from his Disney days, he designed and constructed elaborate dioramas re-creating the arrival of the railroad, Calistoga's former Chinatown, and more. The largest depicts Calistoga as it looked when millionaire Sam Brannan opened the town's first spa in 1860. Hailed by Brannan as the "Saratoga of the Pacific," his Calistoga included a hotel, dining hall, stables, and racetrack, plus an indoor pool, a pavilion for dancing and roller skating, a distillery, a winery, and a cooper's workshop. One of the

14 original cottages is part of the museum, furnished as it would have been in the 1860s. Books on the history of Napa Valley are for sale too. ♦ Free. Daily. 1311 Washington St (between Lincoln Ave and Berry St). 942.5911

25 WAPPO BAR BISTRO

★★$$ You won't find a full bar at this popular neighborhood restaurant, but you will discover Wappo's delicious *chiles rellenos* (*poblano* chilies stuffed with cheese with walnut-pomegranate sauce), *éscliva* (Spanish-style roasted vegetables), seared Chilean sea bass with garam masala, and other interesting dishes. When the weather is mild, dine on the pretty brick patio shaded by a grapevine-laced trellis. ♦ Continental ♦ M, Th-Su, lunch and dinner; W, lunch. 1226-B Washington St (between Lincoln Ave and First St). 942.4712

25 HYDRO BAR AND GRILL

★★$ Those who prefer a light meal to a heavy repast would do well to sample the cleverly named "nibbles, appetizers, bites, and bigger bites menu" served here. This special menu, served between 3PM and 5PM daily and after dinner, is the answer to those small cravings—burgers and thin-crust pizza, as well as vegetables with a hummus dip, inventive salads, chili, and soup. Attractive, with a beamed ceiling and brick walls, the restaurant also serves breakfast, lunch, and dinner, with menus ranging from American standards to international specialties. Owners Gayle and Alex Dierkhising (who also own the **All Seasons Café**—see page 85) offer a good selection of high-quality wines and draft beers, and there are 25 single-malt Scotches and 15 tequilas. ♦ Continental ♦ M-W, F-Su, breakfast, lunch, and dinner; Th, dinner. Light bites, 3PM-5PM and after dinner. 1403 Lincoln Ave (at Washington St). 942.9777

café SARAFORNIA

25 SARAFORNIA

★$ What's in a name? Millionaire Sam Brannan's tipsy tongue twisted when he declared the area the Calistoga of Sarafornia (trying for *Saratoga of California*), but there's nothing confusing about this modern-day, friendly family restaurant. Appropriately, the décor boasts an early Calistoga street scene along one wall. Breakfast packs 'em in here. Omelettes are served about 20 different ways, and the waffles, granola, and oatmeal are first-rate, as is the French toast in orange-brandy batter. A lunch favorite is five-alarm chili; there also are great salads—Thai vegetable or Bombay chicken among them—and pastas. Kids love having their own menu. ◆ California ◆ Daily, breakfast and lunch (until 3PM weekdays, 4PM weekends). 1413 Lincoln Ave (between Washington St and Fair Way). 942.0555

26 ALL SEASONS CAFÉ

★★$$ This café is a favorite not only because of its innovative menu but also for its great wine list and enlightened wine pricing policy. Instead of doubling or tripling the price (what most restaurants do), owner Alex Dierkhising adds a $10 corkage fee to each bottle and sells it at the retail price. Needless to say, they sell a lot of wine from a list of top-notch Burgundy, Bordeaux, and Napa Valley producers. And choices abound: The wine list changes many times during the year. Executive chef John Cobb—expert at selecting dishes that complement different styles of wines—varies his menu with the seasons. Early fall dinner entrées might include duck breast, flavored with huckleberries and served with roasted garlic gnocchi and autumn vegetables; or lamb shank with pomegranate and red wine on a bed of beans, root vegetables, and leeks. More straightforward dishes include steak with Cabernet glaze and a salad of organic greens. For dessert, he uses a different fruit daily in deep dish pie (topped with ice cream, of course), and the sorbet flavors also vary. Good dessert wines top off the meal. This is a great spot for lunch, offering pasta, pizza, and excellent sandwiches. ◆ California ◆ M-Tu, Th-Su, lunch and dinner; W, dinner. Reservations recommended for dinner. 1400 Lincoln Ave (at Washington St). 942.9111; fax 942.9420

Within the All Seasons Café:

ALL SEASONS WINE SHOP

Go to the back of the café and turn left for this shop, which manager Dan Dawson stocks with an inspired array of Burgundies, Rhônes, and Loire Valley wines and top California wines from small producers. He loves to talk

wine and will put together a mixed case of hard-to-find wines at very good prices and ship them home for you. He also produces an informative newsletter. For picnics, he has some chilled white wines. ◆ M, Tu, Th Su. 942.6828

26 FLATIRON GRILL

★★$$ Polished wood, deep banquettes, an open kitchen, and whimsical artwork set the stage for a memorable steak. Classic flatiron steak with red wine jus and beef brisket with red potatoes and button mushrooms calls for a glass of Napa Valley Cabernet. Among the red wines on the menu is a $150 bottle of Opus One Meritage. The casual ambiance of this steak house appeals to diners with sophisticated palates but who wish to forgo formal attire. The all-American desserts include triple chocolate pie, apple crisp, and peanut-caramel sundaes. ◆ American ◆ Sa, Su, lunch; daily, dinner. 1440 Lincoln Ave (at Washington St). 942.1220

26 CHECKERS

★$ This trendy, informal spot has a polished wood floor, black-and-white tile details, and fanciful wood sculptures, and offers 10 or more thin-crust pizzas. Choices include a pizza topped with sun-dried tomatoes, artichokes, thyme, and pine nuts, and a Thai pizza with chicken, cilantro, and peanuts. The calzone are large enough for two. At night, pasta and chicken dishes, as well as specials, are offered. For dessert, try the chocolate brownie sundae with vanilla gelato or the fruit crisp. This is a very kid-friendly place. Espresso drinks and a short wine list are offered too. Takeout is available. ◆ Italian ◆ Daily, lunch and dinner. 1414 Lincoln Ave (just north of Washington St). 942.9300

27 THE CANDY CELLAR

To please your inner child or a real child, Michael and Donna Clark have assembled an enchanting world of "penny" candy, past and present. The array of tempting sweets overflows barrels and fills display cases. ◆ Daily. 1367 Lincoln Ave (between Cedar and Washington Sts). 942.6990; fax 546.3459

Restaurants/Clubs: Red | Hotels: Purple | Shops: Orange | Outdoors/Parks: Green | Sights/Culture: Blue

27 CALISTOGA MASSAGE CENTER

You can probably find relief for your aching back or whatever ails you at this immaculate shop, where massage therapy ranges from 30 minutes for back, neck, shoulders, and feet to 1.5 hours for the full-body treatment. Check out the center's aromatherapy shop next door for mineral bath salts, aromatherapy essences, and tension-reducing herbs to take home. ♦ Daily. 1219A Washington St (between Lincoln Ave and Berry St). 942.6193

28 BOSKO'S RISTORANTE

★$ This casual dining spot with oilcloth-covered tables and sawdust on the floor offers a dozen fresh pasta dishes—everything from spaghetti and meatballs to fettuccine with shrimp. You may have your pasta cooked to order. (Speak up if you prefer it al dente.) The best deal at lunch is a half order of pasta with a salad. Other dishes include a variety of pizzas and generous-size sandwiches. Espresso drinks are available too. There's also a pleasant counter, or you can order food to go. ♦ Italian ♦ Daily, lunch and dinner. 1364 Lincoln Ave (between Cedar and Washington Sts). 942.9088

28 BRANNAN'S

★★$$ Mark Young and Ron Goldin have named their restaurant after Sam Brannan, Calistoga's founding father. A charming blend of old and new, the restaurant's hand-forged suspended ceiling and 19th-century bar seem right at home with furnishings made by local artisans—wood furniture, mica lampshades, and a stone fireplace. Sculptor Jack Chandler fashioned the handles for the front doors from hydraulic airplane cables, and Calistoga muralist Carlo Marchiori created the trompe l'oeil mural in the dining room. Executive chef Rob Lam offers diners an interesting mélange of ethnic flavors. Starters include skillet clams and mussels with lemongrass curry sauce, seared Sonoma foie gras with melon and huckleberries, and ahi tempura roll with caviar. We loved the caramelized onion soup and seafood mine-strone. A sophisticated dish is a crispy whole fish with white corn and potato risotto. And Lam serves meat and fish dishes cooked on a wood-burning grill; also try the asparagus with Dungeness crab in citrus vinaigrette. And if you have room for dessert, indulge in lemon pudding with blueberry sauce or a slice of pie. The six-page wine list features selections from Napa and Sonoma, empha-sizing wineries in and about Calistoga. There's a short list of microbrews. ♦ American ♦ Daily, lunch and dinner. 1374 Lincoln Ave (at Washington St). 942.2233. www.brannansgrill.com

29 CALISTOGA SPA HOT SPRINGS

$ This is the people's spa—relaxed, fun, unpretentious, and a great base for exploring. It has the amenities of a resort at budget prices, including kitchenettes and cable TV. The best rooms have king-size beds, high ceilings, and larger kitchens. All open onto the pool area, which has four mineral pools: a giant 80-degree pool for lap swimming, a 100-degree soaking pool, a 105-degree pool with Jacuzzi jets, and a 90-degree wading pool with a fountain. There are barbecues near the pool area, but no restaurant. Make an appointment in advance for a volcanic-ash mud bath, mineral bath, steam bath, blanket wrap, or massage. Exercise equipment and aerobics classes are also available. Families are welcome. If you plan to stay elsewhere and still want to enjoy the pools, the resort has day passes; stop by early in the day to buy one, as they go fast. ♦ Spa and pools: daily. 1006 Washington St (between Franklin and Gerrard Sts). 942.6269

30 MAIN ELEMENT

This inspiring gallery features crafts by top West Coast artists, including handblown glass, ceramics, jewelry, wooden objects, and textiles such as painted silk scarves and handwoven shawls. The prices match the quality. ♦ Daily. 1333-A Lincoln Ave (between Cedar and Washington Sts). 942.4743

The first Napa Valley vineyards were planted in 1838.

Pinot Noir is one of the oldest grape varieties known, dating back some 2,000 years. The grape came to California in 1885 but didn't catch on for quite some time, as it is one of the most difficult varieties in the world to grow and make into wine. California vintners now produce distinctive Pinot Noirs, similar to those from Bordeaux, France.

When is a goblet a gobelet? When it is a technique of training vines: a single trunk terminates in several arms rising in the shape of a goblet.

Good Reads on Wine, Wine-Making, and California Wine Country

American Wine: A Comprehensive Guide, by Anthony Dias Blue (Harper & Row, 1988): Here is an exhaustive reference volume devoted to wines, their characteristics, and the top American vintners.

Backroad Wineries of Northern California: A Scenic Tour of California's Country Wineries, by Bill Gleeson (Chronicle Books, 1994): This volume lists 60 lesser-known wineries throughout northern California wine country. Areas covered include **Napa**, **Mendocino**, **Sonoma**, and **Lake Counties**.

California's Great Cabernets: The Wine Spectator's Ultimate Guide for Consumers, Collectors, and Investors, by James Laube (M. Shanken Comm., 1989): Cabernet Sauvignon made in California is the focus of this well-written guide. Laube, a leading wine authority, comments on how to judge this type of wine, offers a history of California Cabernets, and rates more than 1,200 vintages.

The Jimtown Store Cookbook: Recipes from Sonoma County's Favorite Country Market, by Carrie Brown (Harper-Collins Publishers, 2002): Lore and recipes from this Alexander Valley landmark.

Making Sense of California Wine, by Matt Kramer (Morrow, 1992): Kramer, who also wrote *Making Sense of Wine* (see below), here describes the innovative wine-making techniques of California vintners, lists the best grapes and winemakers in each region of the state, and notes the specific varieties that can be found.

Making Sense of Wine, by Matt Kramer (Morrow, 1992): A general guide to wine and wine tasting, this book discusses the process of wine-making, the standards for choosing and judging the quality of a vintage, and the proper way to serve wine.

Napa, by James Conaway (Houghton Mifflin, 1990): Written in a lively, interesting style, this is a history of the people who settled in the Napa Valley and began producing wine.

The New Frank Schoonmaker Encyclopedia of Wine, by Alexis Bespaloff (Morrow, 1988): Here is an encyclopedic listing of wine terms, including explanations of the different varieties and the history of wine-making in general. There's also a handy chapter about how wine drinking can complement meals.

Parker's Wine Buyer's Guide, by Robert Parker Jr. (Fireside, 1999): This detailed manual is an up-to-date, worldwide guide to wines produced in a given year. Organized by region, each chapter describes and rates the current vintages being made, lists the area's best producers and growers, and gives retail prices.

Vintage: The Story of Wine, by Hugh Johnson (Simon & Schuster, 1992): Everything you might want to know about wine or wine history can be found in this fascinating book. Topics include technological breakthroughs such as the evolution of the wine bottle, the development of the different varietals, and biographical information about such figures as Dom Pérignon and Baron Rothschild.

The Wine Atlas of California and the Pacific Northwest: A Traveler's Guide to the Vineyards, by Bob Thompson (Simon & Schuster, 1993): Thompson, a renowned wine expert, provides a comprehensive guide to the wine districts of California, Oregon, and Washington, including history, climatic information, and the leading vintners in each area.

The Wine Spectator's California Wine, by James Laube (Wine Spectator Press, 1996): A comprehensive guide to the wineries, wines, vintages, and vineyards of America's premier wine-growing state. This book is a winner of the James Beard Award.

30 Lincoln Avenue Spa

Relax at this spa offering herbal-mud treatments with 34 herbs imported from India, herbal blanket wraps, facials, Swedish/Esalen massages, acupressure face-lifts, and foot reflexology treatments. A variety of spa packages is also available. ♦ Daily. Reservations recommended. 1339 Lincoln Ave (between Cedar and Washington Sts). 942.5296

30 Calistoga Bookstore

Here's a comfortable place to browse through books on wine and California travel and history, with a good section of paperback mysteries, children's books, Celtic books, and art supplies. The inviting sofa in the back of the store is sometimes adorned with a sleeping cat named Sara. ♦ Daily. 1343 Lincoln Ave (between Cedar and Washington Sts). 942.4123

Restaurants/Clubs: Red | Hotels: Purple | Shops: Orange | Outdoors/Parks: Green | Sights/Culture: Blue

THE BEST

Jan J. Shrem
Proprietor, Clos Pegase Winery

Driving from **Yountville** to **Calistoga** on the **Silverado Trail** and watching the valley carpeted in vines wall to wall and the mountains closing in and meeting just north of **Calistoga**.

And 1 mile past **Calistoga**, taking the **Old Toll Road** up the mountain for the most romantic drive in wine country. Lilly Langtry used it to visit her estate in Lake County.

Taking a hike to the top of the **Palisades** from the end of **Calistoga**'s main street.

Visiting **Napa Valley** in February and March and seeing the valley carpeted in mustard yellow flowers.

Taking a mud bath and massage at **Indian Springs** in **Calistoga**.

Walking or bicycling to **St. Helena** from **Calistoga** via **Bothe–Napa Valley State Park** and the old mill.

Shopping at the **Farmers' Market** in **St. Helena**.

Visiting wineries of spectacular contemporary architecture: **Codornìu Napa**, **Dominus Estate**, **Clos Pegase**.

Visiting wineries of striking classical architecture: **Robert Mondavi**, **Beringer**, **Sterling**.

Visiting the caves of **Schramsberg** and **Clos Pegase**, the latter with an art-laden cave theater.

Admiring world-class modern sculptures and paintings at **Hess Collection** and **Clos Pegase**.

Dining at the **French Laundry** and **Domaine Chandon**.

Beautiful-people watching—cosmopolitan and creative—at **Tra Vigne** restaurant.

Dining on the **Napa Valley Wine Train**.

Shopping at factory outlets in **St. Helena** and **Napa**.

30 WEXFORD & WOODS

Handsome antique pine furniture imported from Ireland provides an elegant setting for the quality skin-care products featured in this attractive, sweet-smelling shop. ♦ Daily. 1347 Lincoln Ave (between Cedar and Washington Sts). 942.9729, 800/919.9729; fax 942.0536

31 THE BIRD'S EYE

Kelly Larson's shop is replete with women's apparel—some items are made with natural fibers; others boast beading. More exotic offerings include Japanese kimonos. The range of sizes and prices is equally varied. ♦ Daily. 1307 Lincoln Ave (between Cedar and Washington Sts). 942.6191

32 PIONEER PARK

Tired from touring the town? This small, quaint park offers a peaceful place to rest your dogs. It sports a white Victorian gazebo, several benches, and a well-equipped and fenced-in playground. ♦ Cedar St (between Lincoln Ave and Spring St)

33 THE ELMS

$$ Built in 1871 by Judge A.C. Palmer, this truly elegant three-story French Victorian house with a formal parlor and tall windows has been furnished with grace and style by innkeepers Stephen and Carla Wyle. The Wyles owned and operated a hotel in Germany before moving to the Napa Valley in 1994, and both know how to make guests feel welcome. Beautiful European-style furnishings and Oriental rugs fill each room. Though some bed-and-breakfasts have just one exceptional guest room, here all seven have something special—for example, one room has a canopy bed, another has a view of the mountains. The cottage in back is ideal for honeymooners. Each morning, a two-course gourmet breakfast is prepared by Carla Wyle. The inn is located in a peaceful neighborhood very close to Calistoga's main street. ♦ 1300 Cedar St (between Lincoln Ave and Spring St). 942.9476, 800/235.4316

La chaumière
a country inn

34 LA CHAUMIÈRE

$$$ This turn-of-the-century house remodeled in the 1930s in the style of a Cotswold

During the Renaissance, both kings and monks were brewers.

To store unfinished wine, recork it and put it in the refrigerator; the cold will stop the chemical reactions that lead to deterioration. But don't keep it too long (no more than a day or two), and be sure to bring it to the proper temperature before drinking it.

Getting Down and Dirty in Calistoga: A Guide to the Famous Mud Baths

Say "mud bath," and some people will fall into a fit of giggles at the idea of lying in a tub, covered in warm, gooey mud. Well, keep in mind that this is not just any mud—this is Calistoga's famous volcanic-ash mud mixed with mineral water and, in some cases, imported peat. The mud is first heated to sterilize it and then cooled to just over 100 degrees. The mud bath, taken in individual tubs, lasts only 10 to 12 minutes. It's usually followed by a warm mineral-water shower and a whirlpool bath, then a steam bath. At that point, relaxation sets in as attendants swathe you in warm blankets, leaving you to rest and slowly cool down.

If soaking in a mud bath is just not your idea of a good time, the spas also offer other treatments, starting with massages. You can get a full-body massage or a neck-and-shoulder massage, which can be combined with seaweed or herbal body wraps. Or perhaps you'd prefer to indulge in a facial, be scrubbed with a loofah, or soak in an herbal bath. Every spa has its specialties, and staff members will explain them in detail. Don't plan on doing anything too rigorous immediately afterward—you'll probably be too relaxed to move.

Calistoga Spa Hot Springs ♦ 1006 Washington St (between Franklin and Gerrard Sts). 942.6269

Calistoga Village Inn & Spa ♦ 1880 Lincoln Ave (between Brannan St and Silverado Tr). 942.0991

Dr. Wilkinson's Hot Springs ♦ 1507 Lincoln Ave (between Fair Way and Stevenson Ave). 942.4102

Eurospa ♦ Eurospa and Inn, 1202 Pine St (north of Foothill Blvd). 942.6829

Golden Haven Hot Springs ♦ 1713 Lake St (between Grant St and Adele Ave). 942.6793

Indian Springs ♦ 1712 Lincoln Ave (just south of Brannan St). 942.4913

Lavender Hill Spa ♦ 1015 Foothill Blvd (east of Kortum Canyon Rd). 942.4495

Lincoln Avenue Spa ♦ 1339 Lincoln Ave (between Cedar and Washington Sts). 942.5296

Mount View Spa ♦ Mount View Hotel, 1457 Lincoln Ave (between Washington St and Fair Way). 942.5789

Oasis Spa ♦ 1300 Washington St (at First St). 942.2122, 800/404.4772

cottage is located on a quiet residential street near the heart of town. It features two guest rooms, each with a queen-size bed and private bath. The upstairs suite has its own sitting room; the downstairs room has French doors leading to a private deck. The honeymoon cottage has a king-size bed, bath, and kitchen. A large redwood shades a hot tub surrounded by decks. Innkeeper Gary Venturi serves a fabulous breakfast. Open on weekends only. ♦ 1301 Cedar St (at Elm St). 942.5139, 800/474.6800; fax 942.5199

35 Ca'toga Galleria D'Arte

Enter Carlo Marchiori's world and lift your eyes to his amazing ceiling mural of whirling constellations with associated myths. Lower your eyes to the terrazzo floor: a pre-Copernicus chart of the sun, moon, stars, and comets. The planet earth is marked *In Hic Es*: "You are here." Shelves overflow with paintings, bowls, tiles, sculptures, and furniture, all created by Marchiori, Maestro d'Arte. You can also tour the artist's Palladian villa in the Calistoga foothills for a glimpse of Marchiori's trompe l'oeil frescoes. Tours Saturday at 11AM from May to Oct. Sign up at the desk or call. ♦ Daily. 1206 Cedar St (at Lincoln Ave). 942.3900. www.catoga.com

36 Calistoga Inn

$ For travelers on a budget, this turn-of-the-century building located on Calistoga's main street offers 18 clean, basic rooms with double beds and two bathrooms down the hall. The rooms, which can be noisy until the bar below settles down at night, include electric fans in the summer and small heaters in the winter. A continental breakfast (juice, coffee, and fresh pastries) is included in the price. ♦ 1250 Lincoln Ave (at Cedar St). 942.4101; fax 942.4914

Within the Calistoga Inn:

Calistoga Inn Restaurant

★$$ When the sun is out and it's not too hot, the garden patio here is one of the most pleasant spots in town to kick back and sip a

---

beer made at the inn's brewery. If you're hungry, stick to the simple stuff—salads, sandwiches, and items from the grill. ◆ American ◆ M-Sa, lunch and dinner; Su, brunch and dinner. 942.4101

NAPA VALLEY BREWING COMPANY

Founded in 1987, this was the valley's first brewery since Prohibition. It's housed in an old water tower in the back of the garden, and the shady patio in front offers a great place to sit and sample the suds. Brewmaster Randy Gremp creates a good Calistoga Golden Lager, a Calistoga Red Ale, and a Calistoga Wheat Ale that won a gold medal at the prestigious 1994 Great American Beer Festival in Denver. The beer is served with the **Calistoga Inn Restaurant**'s lunch and dinner menus and is also available in bottles to go. ◆ Tours by appointment only. 946.4101

37 PACIFICO

★$ Terra-cotta floors and potted palms set the tone for this Mexican restaurant serving traditional cuisine. The menu includes tacos, tamales, fajitas, enchiladas, and burritos; fish with salsa on grilled corn with rice and tortillas; and sirloin with corn, beans, and tortillas. A fiesta hour is held Monday through Friday between 4:30PM and 6PM. Brunch is served on weekends, and the long bar is pleasant. ◆ Mexican ◆ M-F, lunch and dinner; Sa, Su, brunch and dinner. 1237 Lincoln Ave (between Myrtle and Cedar Sts). 942.4400

37 HURD BEESWAX CANDLES

Candlemakers roll, dip, and cut pure beeswax into fanciful shapes and decorate classic candles with leaves and flowers. Peek through the window at the bees swarming around a hive. From slender tapers, to votives, to pillar candles, the selection mesmerizes every candlephile. ◆ Daily. 1255 Lincoln Ave (at Cedar St). 963.7211, 800/977.7211

38 CALISTOGA WAYSIDE INN

$$ Set on a wooded hillside, this Spanish-style 1920s house has three guest rooms, all with private baths and featuring down comforters and feather pillows. There's also a small library of reading material. Owner Robert Lewin serves a full breakfast in the dining room, as well as wine, cheese, and hors d'oeuvres in the evening and sherry and sweets at bedtime. ◆ 1523 Foothill Blvd (between Berry and Silver Sts). 942.0645. www.calistogawaysideinn.com

Calistoga Wayside Inn

The Pink Mansion

39 PINK MANSION

$$ Built in 1875 by the pioneer William F. Fisher, who founded Calistoga's first stagecoach line, this extravagant pink house is now a six-room inn run by Leslie and Toppa Epps. Each room has its own bath and views of the valley or forest behind; three have fireplaces. The **Rose Room** has a sunken sitting room and a private redwood deck; the **Angel Room** holds a sampling of previous owner Alma Semic's collection of decorative angels. There's also a heated indoor pool and a Jacuzzi, and a substantial breakfast is served. ♦ 1415 Foothill Blvd (between Kortum Canyon Rd and Lerner Dr). 942.0558, 800/238.7465; fax 942.0558. www.pinkmansion.com

40 GETAWAY ADVENTURES

This tour company offers visitors views of California wine country on 1- to 6-day bike tours that include visits to wineries, overnight stays in bed-and-breakfasts, dining at fine restaurants, and gourmet picnic lunches. Some tours include canoeing or kayaking, biking, and wine tasting. Getaway also rents bikes and mountain bikes on an hourly and daily basis and tailors tours for hikers, canoers, and kayakers. ♦ Daily. 1117 Lincoln Ave (between Foothill Blvd and Myrtle St). 942.0332, 800/499.2453; fax 763.3040. www.getawayadventures.com

41 CHRISTOPHER'S INN

$$$ Laura Ashley interiors and antiques dress up the 22 rooms in this bed-and-breakfast. Rooms are in the main building and annexes on the grounds. Each room has a private bath (some with Jacuzzis), and some have fireplaces and small patios. Although the inn is on the side of Route 29, the rooms are in the back, and Calistoga's main shopping street is around the corner. A hearty breakfast featuring such homemade treats as fruit cobbler, soufflé, croissants, juice, tea, and freshly ground coffee is delivered to your room. After a hot summer's day of touring the valley, you'll find the swimming pool refreshing. ♦ 1010 Foothill Blvd (between Pine and Hazel Sts). 942.5755

42 EUROSPA AND INN

$ On a quiet Calistoga side street, this 12-room inn and spa consists of several stucco bungalows with flower boxes and parking in front. Though the spa package—the *only* option on Friday, Saturday, and holidays—looks pricey, when you consider it includes an overnight stay, spa treatments of your choice, plus continental breakfast, the rates are actually quite reasonable. Guests who visit Sunday through Thursday can arrange for

---

Restaurants/Clubs: Red | Hotels: Purple | Shops: Orange | Outdoors/Parks: Green | Sights/Culture: Blue

lower-priced spa–hotel packages or opt for room-only reservations. Some bedrooms at the inn are small but ample; most have pine armoires and are attractively decorated in pastels; some have kitchenettes. New owner Paul Schreiner has renovation plans that include making rooms "evergreen," by adding filtered water and air ionizers. With abundant plants, he has turned the patio into a tropical garden café where guests enjoy breakfast (cereal, eggs, pastries, juices, coffee, tea). There's a heated outdoor pool surrounded by a small, grassy, shaded area. ♦ 1202 Pine St (north of Foothill Blvd). 942.6829

At Eurospa and Inn:

EUROSPA

This spa specializes in a very different sort of treatment called the European fango mud bath. A private tub is filled with a dehydrated compound that is mixed with water; it has a looser consistency than a regular mud bath and is taken in a double Jacuzzi so you also get the benefits of hydrotherapy. (The tub is drained and cleaned between each treatment.) Herbal oils and extracts can be added to the mud, and the spa offers other special baths, seaweed wraps, herbal body wraps, and Dead Sea mud wraps. Massage options include either a 55-minute full-body massage or a 25-minute massage that concentrates on the back, neck, and shoulders, and 25 minutes of reflexology. The spa also offers 25-minute mini-facials and 55-minute aromatherapy facials. ♦ Daily. 942.6829

43 MEADOWLARK

$$ This 1886 farmhouse has been remodeled into a bed-and-breakfast set on a wooded, 20-acre estate with a swimming pool and sundeck. Innkeeper Kurt Stevens raises horses too (though not for guests' use). The four guest rooms have queen-size beds and private baths; furniture throughout the inn is an eclectic mix of contemporary and antique. *Comfort* is the key word here. Guests share the downstairs area, which includes a large living room, refrigerator, and a shady veranda overlooking an English garden. The sign near the swimming pool says "Clothing Optional"—and many guests take advantage of the option. The full breakfast includes orange juice, fruit, muffins, and scones, plus a main dish such as quiche. No smoking is allowed. Dogs are welcome (with prior approval). ♦ 601 Petrified Forest Rd (west of Foothill Blvd). 942.5651; fax 942.5023

44 CULVER'S COUNTRY INN

$$ Major John Oscar Culver, a Milwaukee newspaperman, built this beautifully restored Victorian house in the early 1870s. The period décor is refreshingly understated in the six guest rooms, all with private baths and comfortable custom-made mattresses. A medium-size swimming pool is open in season. British-born innkeepers Meg and Tony Wheatley prepare a three-course country breakfast and serve sherry and hors d'oeuvres in the evening. ♦ 1805 Foothill Blvd (between Lerner Dr and High St). 942.4535

45 FALCONS NEST

$$ It's only a quarter of a mile up steep Kortum Canyon Road from Calistoga, but you feel like you're a world away at this bed-and-breakfast. There's a panoramic view from the three guest rooms (all with spare, modern décor, private baths, and sliding glass doors), located on the lower floor of a contemporary home. The outdoor Jacuzzi has the same view. A full breakfast is served. ♦ 471 Kortum Canyon Rd (south of Foothill Blvd). 942.0578; fax 942.1188

46 CALISTOGA POTTERY

You'll find traditional, functional stoneware here. Jeff Manfredi and his wife, Sally, specialize in ovenproof dinnerware decorated with lead-free glaze. They take custom orders too. ♦ W-Su or by appointment. 1001 Foothill Blvd (east of Kortum Canyon Rd). 942.0216

46 LAVENDER HILL SPA

This *très élégant* establishment is *the* couples spa, where everything is designed with partners in mind, except for the massages, which are given in privacy. The specialties here include therapeutic massage treatments that combine Chinese foot reflexology with Swedish and acupressure massages. This is one of the only spas in town featuring a one-time-use mud bath (the mud is not reused by other patrons) combining volcanic ash, white sea kelp, salts, and essential oils. Also offered here are seaweed baths using seaweed imported from France, herbal bath wraps, oil massages, and aromatherapy treatments and facials. Don't miss the terraced backyard that's laced with lavender and features a picnic area—the final touch that makes this spa setting second to none in Calistoga. ♦ Daily. Reservations required. 1015 Foothill Blvd (east of Kortum Canyon Rd). 942.4495; 800/528.4772

46 WINE WAY INN

$$ From the moment you enter this cozy bed-and-breakfast, you'll feel like the special guests of innkeepers Cecile and Moye Stephens. Their Craftsman-style abode was built in 1915 and has been a bed-and-breakfast since 1979. The Stephenses set up shop in mid-1990 and have been upgrading this homey place ever since. The five small rooms upstairs come complete with quilts, antique decorations, and creaky floorboards—enough to make you feel you're in Grandma's guest room. And for those seeking ultraprivacy, there's a cottage in back. Each room has its own bath and shower. A multilevel wood deck juts into the backyard, and a gazebo nestled on the hillside is an ideal spot for tasting wines. You can don one of the bathrobes provided and stroll through the backyard gate into **Lavender Hill Spa** next door (see page 92). You can hear traffic from Route 29, but night brings relative peace. The advantage of this location is that Calistoga is accessible by foot. There's a tasty full breakfast, plus late-afternoon hors d'oeuvres and wine. ♦ 1019 Foothill Blvd (east of Kortum Canyon Rd). 942.0680, 800/572.0679

47 CUVAISON WINERY

Founded in 1969, this Spanish Colonial–style winery is Swiss-owned and specializes in Chardonnay, although winemaker John Thacher's Cabernet, Merlot, and Pinot Noir are first-rate too. The tasting room offers an inspired collection of wine books for sale, plus insulated wine bags and picnic carriers, corkscrews, and local jams and condiments. Visitors may use the picnic tables set out under moss-covered oaks. ♦ Fee. Tasting and sales daily; tours by appointment only. 4550 Silverado Tr (between Lommel and Pickett Rds). 942.6266; fax 942.5732

CLOS PEGASE

48 CLOS PEGASE

Michael Graves designed and built the winery and house here in 1986. The commission resulted from a major architectural design competition sponsored by the owner, international businessman Jan Shrem, and the San Francisco Museum of Modern Art. It was won by the architect–artist team of Graves and Edward Schmidt. Widely recognized for his postmodernist architecture as well as for designs of household objects, Graves built Shrem's house on a secluded knoll overlooking the winery east of Calistoga. The design of the stunning winery buildings, done in tones of earth and russet, is rooted in ancient Mediterranean architecture, with rows of columns (treated to look ages old) arranged around a courtyard. Sculptures are incorporated into the landscape; the most remarkable is an oversize bronze thumb that appears to be planted in the vineyard. The highlight of a tour of the winery building is the cylindrical room that Schmidt covered with frescoes depicting allegorical scenes of wine-making. Visitors may also watch a slide show called "A Bacchanalian History of Wine Seen through 4,000 Years in Art," which covers images of wine-making in art ranging from Egyptian reliefs and medieval illuminated manuscripts to Cubist works. The winery produces straightforward Chardonnay, Cabernet Sauvignon, Merlot, and Hommage, a Meritage-style red wine. The best vineyard lots of all Bordeaux varieties (Cabernet Sauvignon, Merlot, Cabernet Franc, Petit Verdot, and Malbec) go into the Hommage blend. Pegase Circle Reserve wines are available only at the winery. ♦ Fee. Tasting, sales, and outdoor self-guided tours daily; guided tours daily 11AM and 2PM. Slide presentation, third Saturday of the month (except December and January) 11AM, free; with lunch, $25. 1060 Dunaweal La (between St. Helena Hwy and Silverado Tr). 942.4982; lunch reservations 942.4981; fax 942.4993. www.clospegase.com

---

Restaurants/Clubs: Red | **Hotels: Purple** | Shops: Orange | **Outdoors/Parks: Green** | Sights/Culture: Blue

STERLING
VINEYARDS

49 STERLING VINEYARDS

An aerial tramway zips up a 300-foot knoll valley to the flagship winery of the Seagram Corporation. This dazzling white, Mykonos-inspired building was built in 1969. At the end of the ride, follow the self-guided tour of the winery and then take a seat in the tasting room to sample the top-flight wines: Chardonnay, Merlot, and especially the Cabernet Reserve and Diamond Mountain Cabernet. In addition, winemaker Rob Hunter makes limited bottlings of Chardonnay from the **Diamond Mountain** vineyard, Pinot Noir from the legendary **Winery Lake** vineyard in the Carneros District, and a blend of Cabernet Sauvignon, Cabernet Franc, and Merlot. ♦ Fee for the tramway. Tasting, sales, and self-guided tours daily. 1111 Dunaweal La (between St. Helena Hwy and Silverado Tr). 942.3344; fax 942.3467. www.sterlingvineyards.com

Within Sterling Vineyards:

STERLING VINEYARDS SCHOOL OF SERVICE AND HOSPITALITY

This professional school for training restaurant employees in the expert service of food and wine is directed by Evan Goldstein—who in 1987, at the age of 26, was the youngest person ever to pass the prestigious Master Sommelier exam, making him one of only 31 master sommeliers in the world at the time. The school offers a variety of seminars for professionals only. ♦ The Sterling Vineyards School of Service and Hospitality, Box 365, Calistoga, CA 94515. 800/955.5003

50 QUAIL MOUNTAIN

$$ Nestled high above Napa Valley on a forested mountain range, this comfortable, contemporary three-room bed-and-breakfast offers king-size beds, private baths and decks, a small lap pool next to a rose garden, and an inviting hot tub. Proprietors Don and Alma Swiers prepare a full breakfast and, aside from other guests, your only companions will be deer, raccoons, squirrels, hummingbirds, and quail. No smoking is allowed. Call far in advance for reservations. ♦ 4455 St. Helena Hwy (between W Dunaweal La and Diamond Mountain Rd). 942.0316

51 TWOMEY CELLARS

Founded in 1973 by Jim and Barbara Spaulding to produce wine from hillside vineyards near Diamond Mountain, this establishment makes consistently good Cabernet and Merlot, especially from the **Spaulding** vineyard. Winemaker David Spaulding also crafts both a regular and a late-harvest Sauvignon Blanc, plus a Chardonnay, Cabernet Franc, and Meritage. ♦ Fee. M-Sa. Tasting and sales daily. 1183 Dunaweal La (just north of St. Helena Hwy). 942.2489. www.twomeycellars.com

52 CALISTOGA RANCH

$$$$ The long-awaited Calistoga Ranch, set in a secluded canyon in Upper Napa Valley, began welcoming guests and part-time vacationers in August 2003. In the transition from campground to luxury lodging club, construction barely disturbed this serene canyon. At campsites scattered throughout the 157-acre canyon around Lake Lommel, owners Claude Rouas and Robert Harmon of Auberge du Soleil installed prefabricated guest lodges. To maintain the rustic ambiance, each lodge encloses an outdoor living room that guests walk through from the bedroom to the kitchen. Aside from the 47 guest lodges, 35 owner lodges priced at $650,000 for a 20 percent share also debuted in August. Since the campground was not zoned for residential use, no one can live here year-round. Guests and owners dine at the private Lakehouse restaurant, and enjoy a dip at the Bathhouse Spa, fed by the ranch's geothermal springs. ♦ 580 Lommel Rd (off Silverado Tr, past Zinfandel La). 942.8108. www.calistogaranch.com

53 LARKMEAD COUNTRY INN

$$ This delightful country inn is tucked into vineyards 3 miles south of Calistoga. The Palladian-style Victorian with an octagonal loggia is built on two levels, with the main part of the house upstairs, the better to catch the afternoon breezes. The three guest rooms, all with private baths and vineyard views, are in one wing of the house. The **Beaujolais Room** has a queen-size bed, cushioned wicker-and-cane chairs, and a private veranda; the **Chenin Blanc Room** features a queen-size bed and a chaise longue; and the **Chablis Room** has its own solarium. Innkeeper Tim Garbarino serves an excellent continental breakfast on china and sterling. ♦ 1103 Larkmead La (between St. Helena Hwy and Silverado Tr). 942.5360

53 FRANK FAMILY VINEYARDS

Specializing in sparkling wines made by the traditional French *méthode champenoise*, this cellar was founded in 1958 by German immigrant Hanns Kornell; Rich Frank, former head of Disney Studios, now owns it. An instructive guided tour of the two-story stone winery takes you through every aspect of sparkling-wine production and is followed by a tasting of a broad range of vintages. ♦ No fee. Tasting, sales, and tours daily. 1091 Larkmead La (between St. Helena Hwy and Silverado Tr). 942.0859, 800/574.9463. www.frankfamilyvineyards.com

Schramsberg FOUNDED 1862 ®

54 SCHRAMSBERG VINEYARDS

Follow in the footsteps of Robert Louis Stevenson, who paid a visit in the late 1880s to this winery founded by itinerant barber Jacob Schram in 1862. The place was in ruins by 1965, when Jack and Jamie Davies fell in love with it and restored it as a producer of sparkling wines. The original winery building stands next to the old Schram home; the tunneled-out hillside is now a modern wine-production cellar. In 1972 Schramsberg sparkling wine was chosen for the banquet President Richard Nixon gave for Premier Zhou En-lai in Beijing. The winery makes half a dozen sparkling wines, including Blanc de Blancs, Blanc de Noirs, and a rosé called Cuvée de Pinot. The tour here thoroughly covers the art of making sparkling wine. ♦ Fee. Tasting and tours daily by appointment only. 1400 Schramsberg Rd (south of St. Helena Hwy). 942.4558 www.schramsbergvineyards.com

SONOMA COUNTY

The crescent-shaped Sonoma Valley—a swath of vineyard-friendly territory 7 miles wide and 22 miles long within the much larger Sonoma County and the birthplace of the California wine industry—extends from **San Pablo Bay** through a small cluster of old hot-springs towns, past tiny, bucolic **Glen Ellen** and **Kenwood**, and stops just short of **Santa Rosa**. Bounded to the east by the **Mayacamas Mountains** and to the west by the **Sonoma Mountains**, Sonoma County is slightly larger than the state of Rhode Island. Currently, the federal government recognizes 10 viticultural areas: Alexander Valley, Carneros/Sonoma, Chalk Hill, Dry Creek, Green Valley, Knights Valley, Russian River Valley, Sonoma Coast, Sonoma Mountain, and Sonoma Valley. Sonoma is an easy hour's drive from San Francisco—close enough for a one-day jaunt through the wine country. It is also ideal for a long weekend of winery visits paired with a stroll through the town of **Sonoma** and a drive through the pastoral **Valley of the Moon**.

The earliest vineyards on the North Coast were planted in 1824 by the Franciscan fathers at the **Mission San Francisco Solano de Sonoma**, which had been founded the previous year. The fathers planted the Mission grape, which they used to produce sacramental wines. When Mexican *comandante* General Mariano Guadalupe Vallejo closed the mission in 1834 under orders from the Mexican government, he took over the existing vineyards, planted more vines behind the presidio barracks, and in 1841

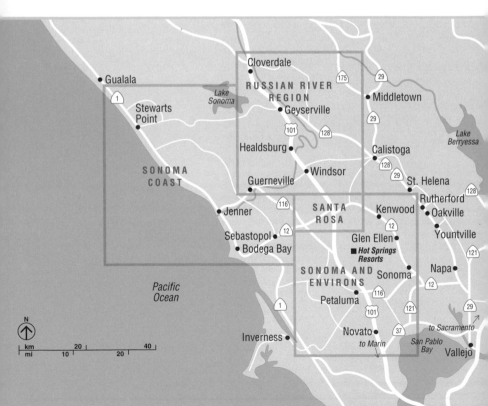

became Sonoma's first commercial vintner. His cellar, wine presses, and sales outlet were housed in the barracks, and he bottled his wines under the **Lachryma Montis** label (the name means "tears of the mountain"). More than a decade later, when the flamboyant Hungarian political exile Agoston Haraszthy arrived in Sonoma, he quickly realized the possibilities this fertile valley held for wine-making, having already tried and failed to grow grapes in Wisconsin, San Diego, and San Francisco. In 1857 he planted the first major vineyard of European grape varietals in California at his **Buena Vista** estate on the eastern outskirts of Sonoma. Today Haraszthy, who cultivated 300 varieties of grapes, is widely viewed as the father of California wine. Other wine-savvy immigrants soon followed, including Jacob Gundlach of **Gundlach-Bundschu Winery**. By 1870 Sonoma was already considered the center of California's burgeoning wine industry. Among the world's wine-growing regions, Sonoma County has the most diverse appellations. The county also touts America's newest viticulture area: the Rockpile, an odd but appropriate name for the rugged, northwest mountains planted with vineyards of Cabernet, Petite Sirah, and Zinfandel. Here elevation, terrain, climate, and soil conspire to make distinctive red varietals.

Reminiscent of southern France, the Sonoma Valley has attracted famed writers and celebrities since the legendary Jack London named one of his books after Sonoma's Indian-given name, Valley of the Moon. Today Sonoma Valley is home to more than 150 grape growers and 35 wineries, including some of the most familiar names in California wine-making: **Buena Vista, Sebastiani**, and **Benziger**. Like many wineries, Benziger is converting to fully organic farming methods to protect the county's environmental resources. Several of the smaller estates are also noteworthy, such as **Ravenswood**, which just happens to make one of the best Zinfandels in California. Together they produce about 25 types of wines, ranging from crisp Sauvignon Blancs and buttery Chardonnays to robust Cabernets and spicy Zinfandels. Some vintners are experimenting with Sangiovese from Tuscany, Italy, and with Syrah and Viognier from the Rhône Valley in southern France. This region also produces premium sparkling wines and luscious late-harvest dessert wines made from Johannesburg Riesling. And you might sip them from the Sonoma Valley appellation's blue-stemmed wineglass created especially for them. Both large and small wineries here tend to be much more casual than those in Napa Valley about drop-in visits. Most may be visited without calling ahead; those who ask for an appointment do so only to make sure someone will be around when visitors arrive.

As in Napa Valley, Sonoma producers have taken special pains to provide visitors with lovely picnic spots. Many wineries have picnic supplies on hand too; most notably, Sam and Vicki Sebastiani go all out with an upscale Italian marketplace and deli at **Viansa**, their hillside property at the gateway to Sonoma Valley. With its red-tile roof and grove of olive trees, Viansa seems like a slice of Italy transplanted to Sonoma—and indeed, the countryside here is reminiscent of Tuscany. Much of the valley's food, too, is Italian-influenced, a legacy from the Italian stonecutters who originally emigrated to the valley in the 19th century to quarry stone and later turned to the career of wine-making. You may choose from restaurants serving hearty, old-fashioned Italian-American fare and from a newer generation of restaurants concentrating on regional Italian cuisine and California wine-country cooking.

Sonoma County also has a number of state parks and nature reserves, including these in Sonoma Valley: **Jack London State Historic Park** in Glen Ellen, **Sugarloaf Ridge**

PEACEFUL PETALUMA: THE PERFECT EXCURSION

A visit to California wine country without a stop in Petaluma is a bit like going to New York City and skipping SoHo or Greenwich Village. Perched beside the **Petaluma River** off **Highway 101**, mere miles from **Sonoma**'s wineries, charming Petaluma is the quintessential American town.

For a century, Petaluma was a vital shipping port between San Francisco to the south and Sonoma County to the north. Today poultry and dairy are the main industries here. The river is still used to ship cargo, however, and pleasure craft often dally here; if you enter the town via D Street you may see a drawbridge open to allow a boat to pass through.

Petaluma's history is written in its bite-size **Victorian Historic Downtown**, perfect for strolling. The 1906 earthquake that devasted many Northern California cities left the town unscathed, so this area offers an amazingly well-preserved collection of graceful old buildings, some with iron fronts. Movie buffs may feel a familiar twinge here: This part of Petaluma appears frequently in movies as a stand-in for "Smalltown USA." Guided walking tours of Petaluma's Historic Downtown take place most Saturdays, and the first and third Sunday of the month, at 10:30AM from May through October. Costumed docents tell of Petaluma's past as they lead visitors past 1880s iron-front buildings. Numerous antiques stores beckon, as do wonderful boutiques. Petaluma Boulevard North has become a mecca for shoppers in pursuit of style, quality, and sophistication in home design. **Chelsea Antiques** (148 Petaluma Blvd N, 763.7686) and **Sienna** (119 Petaluma Blvd N, 763.6088), both owned by Patrick Easley, carry rustic American and European furniture, carpets, and a variety of decorative items.

The town also is a trove of residential architectural treasures. Every style of house built in the US during the Victorian era can be found along the tree-lined streets. These old homes all stand in well-manicured gardens, many with beautiful and rare trees; a pamphlet, available from the **Petaluma Visitor Center** (see below), describes a walking tour of the town's arboreal treasures. For lodging within walking distance of downtown, book a room at **Metro Hotel** (508 Petaluma Blvd S, 773.4900; www.metrolodging.com), a renovated 1870 mansion with 15 rooms furnished in eclectic French antiques.

Petaluma has a number of delightful restaurants along the river, but the must-stop is **Dempsey's** (★★★$$; Golden Eagle Center, 50 E Washington St, between Weller St and Petaluma Blvd N, 765.9694), where umbrella-shaded tables are set on a patio facing the water. This is a brew pub, but the food is a far cry from pub grub. Chef-owner Bernadette Burrell serves innovative California fare made from the freshest ingredients; menu offerings range from country-style pork chops to Thai noodles. Also recommended is **Della Fattoria Downtown Café** (141 Petaluma Blvd N, 763.0161; www.dellafattoria.com), in a quaint storefront open throughout the day from morning *caffè latte* to the evening wine hour. Here the Weber family sells the wine country's most highly acclaimed artisan bread, which they bake on their 14-acre Petaluma ranch.

At night, downtown bustles with bars and clubs. Or you might choose an evening of innovative opera, dance, or music at the **Cinnabar Performing Arts Center** (3333 Petaluma Blvd N, at Skillman La, 763.8920), housed in a converted Mission-style schoolhouse just outside of town.

As a finale to your visit, amble down to the **River Walk** in the center of town. It includes a pedestrian bridge connecting the east and west sides of the river and a boardwalk by old commercial buildings now filled with trendy shops.

Other area attractions include **Garden Valley Ranch** (498 Pepper Rd, between Stony Point and Jewett Rds, 795.0919), a Victorian ranch surrounded by 8,000 rosebushes; **Adobe State Historic Park** (3325 Adobe Rd, at Manor La, 762.4871), General Mariano Vallejo's estate, restored to its 1840s glory; and **Petaluma Village Premium Outlets** (2200 Petaluma Blvd N, between Cinnabar Ave and Corona Rd, 778.9300), a shopping center featuring designer clothing at discount prices.

Keller Estate Winery, a 600-acre ranch in Petaluma's eastern hills above the Petaluma River, spans open range, olive orchards, and vineyards with views extending to San Francisco and east to Mount Diablo. Keller Estate, Sonoma County's southernmost winery, produces a rich oaky Chardonnay that won 89 points from *Wine Spectator*. New vineyards allow them to add Syrah and Pinot Noir to their winery collection. Winemaker Ted Lemon is often on hand to talk about Petaluma Valley's long, cool growing season. Tastings, cave tours, and vineyard walks are available by appointment, M-F, 9AM-4PM. 707.765.2117. www.KellerEstate.com

For more information, contact the **Petaluma Visitor Center** (800 Baywood Dr, suite A, 94954; 769.0429, 877/273.8258; www.visitpetaluma.com). For a tour schedule, call the events hotline at 762.4247.

THE BEST
Bob Beck

Real Estate Broker, Beck & Taylor Realty, and Owner, Cottage Grove Inn

Hiking up the **Oat Hill Mine Trail** near **Calistoga**.

Visiting hand-dug caves at **Schramsberg Vineyards**.

Mountain-biking down **Mount St. Helena** with Getaway Bike Tours.

Taking a cooking class at the **Culinary Institute of America** in the historic **Greystone Building**.

Soaking in the hot mineral water pools at **Calistoga Hot Springs**.

A day trip to **Healdsburg** through the pristine **Knights Valley**.

Sunset cocktails on the deck at **Auberge du Soleil**.

Rating the morning buns at **Model Bakery** (St. Helena), **Downtown Bakery** (**Healdsburg**), and **ABC Bakery** (**Napa**).

Seeing a scale model of **Calistoga** as a late-1800s spa resort at the **Sharpsteen Museum**.

State Park in Kenwood, and **Annadel State Park** just outside of Santa Rosa. If you like, you can take a break from wine tasting and wander through fields of wildflowers and groves of redwoods, spend the afternoon basking in the sun, or go for a hike or a horseback ride. The valley is compact enough to make bicycling a great way to explore the wine country.

The riches of Sonoma County—which nudges Napa to the east and Lake and Mendocino Counties to the north—include more than abundant vineyards and wineries. What sets Sonoma County apart from neighboring Napa is its diverse pleasures. Drive along its rugged, 76-mile coastline to experience some of America's most memorable scenery, where sea lions and heart-stopping views abound. There also are a hundred working farms that welcome visitors, and numerous historic sites. There's no better place to begin than the valley. The Sonoma County Tourism Program provides complimentary visitors' guides (800/380.5392, or online at www.sonomacounty.com). The web site offers the largest database of visitor attractions because it is a nonmembership marketing organization.

Restaurants/Clubs: Red | Hotels: Purple | Shops: Orange | Outdoors/Parks: Green | Sights/Culture: Blue

SONOMA AND ENVIRONS

The wine-country town of Sonoma, whose name is said to come from a Suisun Indian word meaning "valley of many moons," began as Mission San Francisco Solano de Sonoma, founded by Franciscan Padre José Altimira in 1823. In 1834 the Mexican government sent the young General Mariano Guadalupe Vallejo to oversee the secularization of the mission and to establish a Mexican pueblo and presidio. It was Vallejo who laid out Sonoma's lovely Spanish-style plaza and the clus-

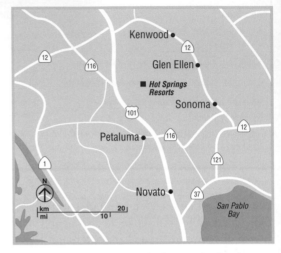

ter of rustic adobe buildings that grew up around it. By 1845 the little town had 45 houses and a population of more than 300. Sonoma was incorporated as a city in 1850.

This was also the site of the short-lived Bear Flag Revolt, in which disgruntled American settlers, who had been lured to the area by rumors of free land, rebelled against the Mexican government when they discovered noncitizens were prohibited from owning property. For 25 days in 1846, a ragtag band of immigrants who called themselves the Bear Flag Party seized control of Sonoma, jailed Vallejo, and raised their flag (the grizzly bear–emblazoned banner later adopted by the state of California) over the plaza, declaring the independent Republic of California. The revolt ended less than a month later when the American government stepped in and took over.

Today this city at the very end of **El Camino Real** (the royal Spanish road that connected the missions of California) offers visitors a glimpse into California's past, as well as a chance to visit several interesting vineyards; browse through antiques shops, galleries, and country stores; and dine at some of the best restaurants in **Sonoma Valley**.

Also near the city are parklands and wineries enough to satisfy oenophiles and outdoors-lovers' appetites. Just a sampler: Bird watchers can delight in the more than 200 species that call the **San Pablo Bay National Wildlife Refuge** home, whereas grape aficionados may taste the wines at the **Viansa, Gundlach-Bundschu,** and **Roche** wineries.

There's plenty to see beyond Sonoma too. The stretch of the **Sonoma Highway (Route 12)** that heads north toward **Santa Rosa** is a state-designated scenic route, marked with signs depicting an orange poppy (California's state flower) on a blue background. The half-hour drive runs along an old stagecoach and railroad route, past rolling hills, neatly manicured vines, and old barns and farmsteads. Along the way are several noteworthy places, including the hot-springs resorts of **Fetters Hot Springs, Boyes Hot Springs, El Verano,** and **Agua Caliente,** as well as **Glen Ellen,** writer Jack London's old stomping grounds, and the bucolic little town of **Kenwood.** The natural springs no longer exist, but Sonoma Mission Inn spa in Boyes Hot Springs still pumps up the mineral water.

SONOMA

The center of this small, quiet town (population 8,900) is its 8-acre, parklike plaza surrounded by historic adobe buildings that house boutiques, antiques stores, restaurants, food shops, and several renovated Gold Rush–era hotels. The **Sonoma State Historic Park** comprises a half-dozen sites in and around the plaza, including the old mission; the Indian and Mexican army barracks; the **Toscano Hotel**, a restored mining hotel; and General Vallejo's Gothic Victorian–Revival home at his estate, **Lachryma Montis**. There's plenty for wine lovers to see here too—such as **Sebastiani Vineyards**, perhaps Sonoma's best-known winery and where the practice of aging wines in French oak barrels began in California. And after a long day of sightseeing, nothing tops a great dinner at **Della Santina's**, or **The Girl & the Fig**.

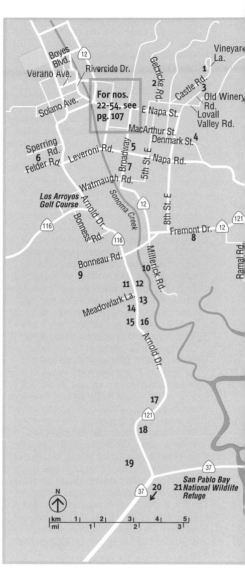

1 BARTHOLOMEW PARK WINERY

Buena Vista Winery's founder, Agoston Haraszthy, really knew how to pick a site. The first building at the end of the grand drive is not the winery but a reconstruction of the Pompeian-style villa Haraszthy built here in 1857. A plaque commemorates a masked ball held on this site at the original building (which was presumably destroyed by fire) on 23 October 1864, the first formal vintage celebration in California history—General and Señora Vallejo were guests of honor. Farther along is the winery, a Spanish colonial building built in 1921 as a hospital for indigent and "fallen" women (later a community hospital). The building was the home of **Hacienda Wine Cellars** (founded in 1973 by Frank Bartholomew) until 1994, when the label was sold to a large Central Valley wine company. The interior of the building has been extensively renovated; an airy, light-filled tasting room, a museum filled with wine memorabilia from the days of Haraszthy in the 1850s to the present, and a photo gallery of grape growers have been added. Under winemaker Antoine Favero (formerly of **Gundlach-Bundschu**), the winery completed its first crush in 1994. Visitors can sample 1994 and 1995 vintages of Chardonnay, Zinfandel, Merlot, Cabernet Sauvignon, and Pinot Noir in the tasting room or in the picnic area outside. ♦ Tasting, sales, and self-guided tours daily. 1000 Vineyard La (north of Castle Rd). 935.9511. www.bartholomewparkwinery.com

2 RAVENSWOOD

A rustic stone building with a sod roof is the headquarters of this winery specializing in Zinfandel. Visitors can enjoy a spacious tasting room or picnicking outdoors. Winemaker Joel Peterson and W. Reed Foster, president of the San Francisco Vintners Club, started the winery in 1976. Its name came from two ravens who scolded Peterson during his first day of harvesting—and from the opera *Lucia di Lammermoor*. The winery has established a reputation as one of California's leading Zinfandel producers. Grapes come from several very old, dry-farmed vineyards, yielding rich, concentrated wines. The winery also produces Cabernet Sauvignon, Merlot, and a small amount of Chardonnay, Gewürztraminer, and Claret. The distinctive label (shown opposite) was designed by the renowned Bay

---

Restaurants/Clubs: Red | Hotels: Purple | Shops: Orange | Outdoors/Parks: Green | Sights/Culture: Blue

Area poster artist David Lance Goines. ♦ Tasting and sales daily; tours by appointment only. Weekend barbecues, May–Sept. 18701 Gehricke Rd (north of Brazil St). 938.1960. www.ravenswood-wine.com

3 BUENA VISTA WINERY

Founded by flamboyant Hungarian émigré Colonel Agoston Haraszthy, California's oldest premium winery shouldn't be missed. Widely acknowledged as the father of California wine, Haraszthy imported thousands of cuttings of European grape varietals and turned this site into a showcase wine estate. The winery's current owner is the Moller-Racke family of Germany. Anne Moller-Racke, director of vineyard operations, has been instrumental in developing Buena Vista as the largest estate vineyard in Carneros. The vineyards supply 90% of the winery's grapes. From the parking lot, follow the tree-covered pathway to the winery grounds. Picnic tables are set up in front of the cellars and in the shady grove just beside them. The original press house now serves as the tasting room, where visitors can sample most of the winery's current releases, including a good Chardonnay and a graceful Sauvignon Blanc produced by winemaker Judy Matulich-Weitz. The new releases of Grand Reserve and Estate Cabernets and Pinot Noirs are consistently top-notch. For a small fee, visitors can taste older vintages of the Private Reserves along with Bricout Champagne from the owner's French wineries. The winery also stocks picnic supplies: Sonoma jack and cheddar, local goat cheese, salami, pâtés, and even Muscovy duck breast. The wine is not processed here, but you can take a self-guided or guided historical tour of the stone winery. ♦ Fee for older vintages. Tasting, sales, and self-guided tours daily. Guided tours daily at 2PM. 18000 Old Winery Rd (north of Lovall Valley Rd). 938.1266, 800/926.1266. www.buenavistawinery.com

Within the Buena Vista Winery:

PRESSHOUSE GALLERY

Visit this gallery upstairs in the tasting room and see painters at work Monday through Friday as part of the artists-in-residence program sponsored here. Monthly shows display their works. ♦ Daily

4 GUNDLACH-BUNDSCHU WINERY

California's second-oldest bonded (state-licensed) winery was founded in 1858 by Bavarian-born Jacob Gundlach, who planted 400 acres of vineyards and introduced the German varietal Johannisberg Riesling to California at his **Rhinefarm** vineyards. Soon he and son-in-law Charles Bundschu had created a worldwide market for their wines,

sold under the Bacchus label. The family had to shut down its operations after the 1906 earthquake destroyed the winery and Prohibition effectively ended their business, but in 1967 Jacob's great-great-grandson, Jim Bundschu, reopened the historic winery, rebuilding the original cellar and restoring the Rhinefarm vineyards. Jim's sons, Jeff and Robbie, have entered the family business as the sixth generation to carry on their family's proprietorship. The specialty is Kleinberger, a little-known white German varietal, but Bundschu also makes Chardonnay and a fairly dry, distinctively flavored Gewürztraminer. The Cabernet from Rhinefarm and the Rhinefarm Estate Merlot, Pinot Noir, Cabernet Franc, and Zinfandel are excellent. After your visit, hike up a short trail to the landmark **Towles' Eucalyptus**, a tree on a hill with a panoramic view of the valley. The tree was planted by 10-year-old Towels Bundschu, a fourth-generation Californian Bundschu, in 1890. Picnic tables are set out on a grassy knoll. ♦ Tasting and sales daily. 2000 Denmark St (between Napa Rd and Eighth St E). 938.5277. www.gunbun.com

5 TRAINTOWN RAILROAD

Kids—and train buffs of all ages—will love this meticulously crafted railroad system. Every 20 minutes a scaled-down reproduction of an 1890s steam (or diesel) train leaves the depot, carrying passengers through 10 acres landscaped with miniature forests, tunnels, bridges, and lakes. At the halfway point, the little steam engine stops to take on water in **Lakeville**, a small replica of an old mining town, where passengers may disembark and hand-feed a menagerie of farm animals. ♦ Admission. Daily in the summer; F–Su in the winter. 20264 Broadway (at Napa Rd). 938.3912; fax 996.2559

6 HAPPY HAVEN RANCH

Locals, savvy mail-order shoppers, and tourists in the know make it a point to seek out this source for delicious jams. ♦ Daily, by appointment only. 1480 Sperring Rd (west of Arnold Dr). 996.4260

7 LOS ARROYOS GOLF COURSE

This nine-hole, par-29 course is open to the public on a first-come, first-served basis. ♦ Daily. 5000 Stage Gulch Rd (just west of Arnold Dr). 938.8835

8 CHERRY TREE COUNTRY STORE

Every other car heading down Route 12 seems to pull in at this larger and fancier version of the original **Cherry Tree Country Store** (see page 105). This one features a deli and picnic area. Skip the sandwiches, but buy as much of the delicious, unsweetened cherry juice as you

A WACKY WINE AUCTION

Bored by the same old Labor Day barbecue? Yearn for something outrageous and fun? Come to the Sonoma Valley Harvest Wine Auction.

The wackily wicked auction, held at the **Fairmont Sonoma Mission Inn & Spa** in **Boyes Hot Springs**, is the highlight of a weekend of Labor Day events including wine tastings, picnics, dinners, and dancing—all charity fund-raisers sponsored by the Sonoma Valley Vintners & Growers Alliance.

The headliner wine auction presents 80 or so unique lots, including precious releases signed by winemakers. Also auctioned off are dinners at local wineries and restaurants, and culinary and wine-themed vacation trips. In attendance are several hundred wine fans who have deep pockets for local charities.

Auction organizers pride themselves on the outrageousness of it all and every year try to outdo the previous auction's antics. Inevitably there will be a sexy model or two, and wine lots to be auctioned off often have sugges-tive, double-entendre titles. Perhaps a vintner will do a strip-tease, auctioning off his clothes down to his skivvies, or a group called the Raging Hormones on Horseback may perform a raunchy line dance. The auction might also include spoofs on popular game shows like *Let's Make a Deal*. The always-enthusiastic participants—many wearing costumes—raise a sea of paddles in boisterous bidding. It's an innocent kind of auction too, where the auctioneer may stop to remind an overeager participant not to bid against himself.

Such shenanigans result in hefty dollars for several Sonoma charities. (The 1997 auction rang up nearly $400,000.) Generous bids abound: $10,000 might buy "A Year of Moderate Consumption" from Sebastiani; $7,500 might get a custom-labeled Barbera from Cale or rare bottlings of Syrah from Arrowood; and $7,000, a collection of wines from various Sonoma wineries. Lower bids do good too. For instance, 105 individual pledges of $100 each combined buy a new van for a needy group.

For information about attending the next Sonoma Valley Harvest Wine Auction, contact the **Sonoma Valley Vintners & Growers Alliance** (9 E Napa St, Sonoma, CA 95476, 935.0803; fax 935.1947).

---

can carry. ♦ Daily. 1901 Fremont Dr (between Burndale and Millerick Rds). 938.3480. Also at Arnold Dr, Hwy 121 (between Sears Point Rd and Meadowlark La). 938.3480

9 SCHUG CARNEROS ESTATE WINERY

Originally located in Napa, Walter Schug's winery has been reestablished in Sonoma, just north of **Gloria Ferrer Champagne Caves**. The half-timbered building, which pays tribute to Schug's German heritage, includes an underground cellar dug into the hillside for aging the casks of wine. The winery concen-trates on Carneros District Chardonnay and Pinot Noir. There are picnic facilities on a sometimes windy site. ♦ Tasting and sales daily; tours upon request. 602 Bonneau Rd (west of Arnold Dr). 939.9363, 800/966.9365; fax 939.9364

10 LARSON FAMILY WINERY

This family-owned Carneros District winery with vineyards first established in the late 19th century specializes in barrel-fermented, estate-bottled Chardonnay. The owner-winemaker is Tom Larson, but the business is definitely a family affair: His father and brother have vine-yards supplying the winery, and two sisters

also help around the winery. ♦ Daily, tasting and sales. 23355 Millerick Rd (south of Fremont Dr). 938.3031.
www.larsonfamilywinery.com

11 GLORIA FERRER CHAMPAGNE CAVES

By the time America declared its independence in 1776, the family of José Ferrer (the vintner, not the actor) had already accumulated 15 generations of wine-making experience in Catalonia. Because *cava* (sparkling wine) from the family's well-known Spanish producing house, Freixenet, had become such a runaway success in this country, the firm decided to start its own California facility in 1986. Named for Ferrer's wife, this Carneros District winery boasts extensive subterranean aging cellars. In the **Sala de Catadores** (tasting room), enjoy the sparklers. In the winter, settle in at the green marble bistro tables in front of the massive fireplace; in warmer weather, sit on the terrace

---

overlooking the vineyard. The winery's popular cellar tour gives visitors an overview of the art of making sparkling wine. Catalán oil and vinegar, olives, anchovies, and other Spanish delicacies are sold in the winery's store. Spanish cooking classes are occasionally offered, and every July the winery hosts a Catalán Festival. ◆ Fee. Tasting, sales, and tours daily. 23555 Arnold Dr, Hwy 121 (between Meadowlark La and Bonneau Rd). 996.7256

12 ANGELO'S WINE COUNTRY MEAT & DELI

Pull up to this deli for sandwiches made with Angelo Ibleto's own roasted and smoked meats, plus 15 varieties of homemade sausages. Hikers and campers swear by Angelo's flavored beef jerkies; he makes a half-dozen now, including a dynamite Cajun style. (Ask for a taste before you buy.) For picnics, consider the small boneless ham or the smoked Cornish game hen. ◆ Daily. 23400 Arnold Dr, Hwy 121 (between Sears Point Rd and Fremont Dr). 938.3688

12 FESTIVAL OF GARDENS

If you want to take the artistic approach to taming an ugly-duckling backyard, visit this 9-acre gallery of gardens. Ever-changing exhibits are installed by recognized talents in the world of landscape design. Andy Cao and Xavier Perrot, Tom Leader, and Martha Schwartz are a few of the landscape artists who have been showcased here. Founder Chris Hougie has created an important resource for people interested in gardens, garden design, and art. Surprises greet you at every turn on a leisurely walk among the traditional gardens and modern, abstract installations. Also stop by the market café and a nursery that sells unique plants, tools, pots, outdoor furniture, books, and gifts. You can't miss the turn at the bright turquoise tree. ◆ Fee. Daily. 23570 Arnold Dr (near Hwy 12/121 junction). 933.3010. www.cornerstonegardens.com

13 VINTAGE AIRCRAFT CO.

Take an exhilarating 15- to 20-minute ride over Sonoma in a 1940 Stearman biplane once used to train World War II combat pilots. Unlike balloons, which depend on wind currents, these  little planes can take off anytime. Based at **Schellville Airport**, this company offers all sorts of rides (most for just one or two people), ranging from leisurely flights over Sonoma Valley or an extended scenic ride over both Napa and Sonoma Valleys to an aerobatic ride with loops, rolls, and assorted dizzying maneuvers. Or you can stay safely on the ground and hire one of the pilots to skywrite a message to your honey. ◆ Daily. 23982 Arnold Dr, Hwy 121 (between Hwy 37 and Fremont Dr). 938.2444. www.vintageaircraft.com

14 FRUIT BASKET

Bins overflow with Sonoma's fresh bounty at this produce stand. Stop here for farm-fresh eggs, milk from Clover-Stornetta Farms, artichokes, asparagus, luscious strawberries, dried fruit and nuts, and other staples. There is also a selection of Sonoma Valley wines, some of them chilled. ◆ Daily. 24101 Arnold Dr (between Sears Point Rd and Meadowlark La). 938.4332

14 SONOMA COUNTRY ANTIQUES

Country kitchen pine tables and armoires (either English antiques or modern reproductions) are sold in this gracious shop, along with antique kitchen utensils, teapots, vases, and country-style dinnerware. The wooden plate racks are handy additions for any kitchen. ◆ Daily. 23999 Arnold Dr, Hwy 121 (between Sears Point Rd and Meadowlark La). 938.8315; fax 938.0134

15 CLINE CELLARS

California Rhône-style wines are the specialty here. Winemaker Matt Cline, a University of California Davis graduate, makes three blends of Zinfandel with Carignane or Mourvèdre (both varietals from France's Rhône Valley), along with terrific unblended Zinfandels, a barrel-fermented Sémillon, and a lush dessert wine made from Muscat of Alexandria. Certain special varietals and reserves are only available at the tasting room. The surrounding vineyards are planted with Syrah and the rare white Rhône varietals Viognier and Marsanne. You can also sample wines from the unique Contra Costa County appellation. Cline Cellars owns and manages acres of 100-year-old vines of Zinfandel, Petite Sirah, and Carignane planted by Italian and Portuguese immigrants, who recognized the region's potential. The property was a Miwok summer camp 5,000 years ago. The picnic area has views of Sonoma Valley. ◆ Tasting and sales daily; tours by appointment only. 24737 Arnold Dr, Hwy 121 (near Meadowlark La). 935.4310; fax 935.4319. www.clinecellars.com

16 VIANSA WINERY AND ITALIAN MARKETPLACE

Sam Sebastiani, a third-generation vintner from one of Sonoma's oldest wine families, and his wife, Vicki, have created a

THE BEST

Ray Lewand

Innkeeper/Owner, Camellia Inn

In Healdsburg:

Morning coffee or lunch at **Costeaux French Bakery**. Take home a loaf of the best sourdough bread anywhere.

Spend a summer Sunday afternoon at the concert on the plaza.

Shop the many antiques stores.

Tour the museum exhibits in the historic **Healdsburg Carnegie Library** building.

Have an early dinner at the **Restaurant Charcuterie** or **Ravenous Café**, then attend a first-run movie at the **Raven Theater** complex.

On the plaza, sample tastings of wine at **Belvedere, Kendall Jackson, Trentadue**, and **Windsor** tasting rooms.

Do a walking tour of historic homes.

Recreation:

Bicycle the **Dry Creek** and **Alexander Valleys**.

Hike or horseback-ride the **Armstrong Redwoods State Reserve** trails.

Canoe the **Russian River**.

Golf at **Tayman Park Municipal Golf Course**.

---

fantasy Tuscan village on the top of a Carneros District hill. The russet-colored winery with terra-cotta roof tiles and green shutters is surrounded by a grove of olive trees, and inside the Italian theme continues with evocative frescoes of vineyard scenes by San Francisco artists Charlie Evans and Charley Brown. Sam and Vicki's son, Michael, is the winemaker and continues to experiment with the Italian grapes grown on the estate. Varietals produced here include Chardonnay, Arneis, Freisa, Nebbiolo, and Merlot. Vicki, an accomplished cook and gardener, offers elegant Italian picnic fare—sandwiches, country pâtés, pasta salads, imported Italian cheeses, and cold cuts—in the marketplace. Enjoy the informal picnic fare at a bistro table inside, or dine alfresco in the olive grove with its sweeping view of the valley. The marketplace also features local food products—jam, mustard, olive oil, and vinegar. ♦ Tasting, sales, and guided tours daily. 25200 Arnold Dr, Hwy 121 (between Sears Point Rd and Fremont Dr). 935.4700, 800/995.4740. www.viansa.com

At the Viansa Winery and Italian Marketplace:

SONOMA VALLEY VISITORS' BUREAU

This is *the* stop in Sonoma for information on wineries, lodging, restaurants, shops—you name it, they've got it. For a free copy of the *Sonoma Valley Visitors' Guide*, send a request to Sonoma Valley Visitors' Bureau, 453 First St E, Sonoma, CA 95476. Stop by the welcome center in the old **Carnegie Library** on Sonoma Plaza. ♦ Daily. 996.1090

17 CHERRY TREE COUNTRY STORE

The pure, unsweetened black bing cherry juice sold here is a Sonoma tradition. In fact, the juice is so addictive that you may want to pick up a case on your way out of Sonoma. The recipe is said to mix cherry juice with apple cider. Olives, wines, jellies, and country gifts are also featured here. ♦ Daily. Arnold Dr, Hwy 121 (between Sears Point Rd and Meadowlark La). 938.3480. Also at 1901 Fremont Dr (between Burndale and Millerick Rds). 938.3480

18 ROCHE WINERY

Established in 1988, this winery is surrounded by 25 acres of Chardonnay and Pinot Noir vines. Owners Joseph and Genevieve Roche believe in producing estate wines at reasonable prices; their winemaker, Steve MacCrostie, also makes wines under his own label. Picnic facilities are available. ♦ Fee for tasting special or older wines. Tasting and sales daily; tours by appointment only. 28700 Arnold Dr, Hwy 121 (between Sears Point Rd and Fremont Dr). 935.7115; fax 935.7846

19 INFINEON RACEWAY

This is one of the most demanding courses in the country, offering automobile, bicycle, and motorcycle racing at its best. Pros such as Mario Andretti and Al Unser have raced frequently on the 12-turn 2.5-mile course, along with celebrities such as Tom Cruise, Paul Newman, Clint Eastwood, and Candice Bergen. Most events are held from March

---

Restaurants/Clubs: Red | Hotels: Purple | Shops: Orange | Outdoors/Parks: Green | Sights/Culture: Blue

through October; call for schedules and more information. ◆ Arnold Dr (Hwy 121) and Hwy 37. 938.8448, 800/870.RACE. www.infineonraceway.com

At Infineon Raceway:

RUSSELL RACING SCHOOL

This school specializes in go-carts. Call for more information. ◆ 939.8000

20 PORT SONOMA-MARIN

This diverse port offers a combination of open bay, tidal salt marsh, and freshwater wetlands. It is mainly a boat marina, and there also is a picnic area. ◆ Daily. 270 Sears Point Rd (just northeast of Petaluma River), Petaluma. 778.8055

21 SAN PABLO BAY NATIONAL WILDLIFE REFUGE

Bird watchers and wildlife photographers frequent Tubbs Island, a largely undeveloped 332-acre marsh on San Pablo Bay that is part of the refuge. Park your car in the parking lot on the south side of Route 37, approximately half a mile east of the Route 121 turnoff, and then hike in 2.75 miles to the bird sanctuary on Tubbs Island; from there, more trails lead to the bay and the salt marshes (where shorebirds and water-fowl live). Bring your binoculars and a good field guide to identify canvasback ducks, the endangered California clapper rail, and the more than 280 species of other resident and migrating birds that call this preserve home. It's a good idea to bring drinking water, because there is none here. If you plan to linger awhile, tuck some sandwiches in your knapsack. The best times to visit are in the fall, winter, and spring when the weather is cool and the birds are plentiful. Waterfowl and pheasant hunting is permitted in speci-fied areas during the legal hunting season (months vary; call for regulations). No rest rooms. ◆ Daily, during daylight. Sears Point Rd (east of Arnold Dr). 562.3000

22 HANZELL VINEYARDS

James D. Zellerbach established this boutique winery in the late 1950s and set out to emulate the wines he had admired in Burgundy. The tradition continues today under the ownership of Great Britain's de Brye family

with winemaker and manager Bob Sessions, who makes one of California's most renowned Chardonnays, as well as an acclaimed Pinot Noir. Convinced that California could produce wines that would rival those in France, Zeller-bach planted 14 acres of Chardonnay and Pinot Noir vines on the winery's south-sloping hillsides in 1953 and 1957 and ordered a shipment of French oak barrels in which to age the Chardonnay. Zellerbach is often credited with changing the course of modern wine-making—he designed the first stainless steel fermentation tanks to be used in conjunction with French oak barrels. Today the winery's 32 acres produce 3,000 cases of handcrafted wines. ◆ Tasting, sales, and tours by appointment only. 18596 Lomita Ave (north of Donald St). 996.3860. www.hanzell.com

23 SONOMA OVERLOOK TRAIL

The hillside oak woodlands a few blocks from the plaza were, in turn, a Muchi Indian hunting ground, a community cemetery, a basalt quarry, and a city dump. Sonoma resi-dents successfully fought off developers in the 1990s and undertook the cleanup and trail construction. Throughout the year, the Sonoma Ecology Center holds docent-led hikes from the cemetery parking lot on First Street West. The gently graded trail is just under three miles. Once atop the hill, follow the loop trail and scan the view. When the morning haze lifts, you can often see the San Francisco skyline in the distance. Wildflowers blanket the meadow in spring. Park at the cemetery, a few minutes' drive north of the plaza, and you'll see the trailhead. ◆ First St W. 996.9744

24 LACHRYMA MONTIS

A visit to General Vallejo's Victorian home and gardens is well worth the price of the museum ticket. Set in the shelter of a hillside, the steep-gabled, yellow-and-white wood house designed in Gothic Revival style is twined with rambling roses. One yellow variety has climbed a 30-foot tree and is considered the oldest rosebush in Sonoma. The illusion inside is that the family is only out for the afternoon. The table is set and a bottle of the general's wine is decanted; his wife seems to have laid out her shawl on one of the beds upstairs. The former wine-and-olive storehouse has been turned into a little museum, with the general's silver epaulets, books, and photos on display, along with examples of his wine label, also called Lachryma Montis. It means "tears of the mountain"—a reference to a mineral spring on the property. You may picnic at shaded tables on the terraced hillside and spend the after-noon at the 20-acre estate, which has been incorporated into the **Sonoma State Historic**

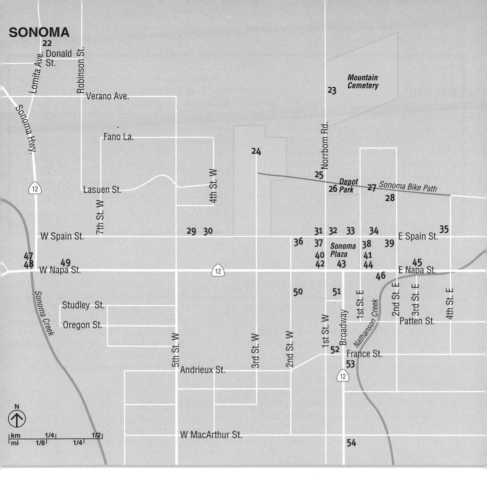

SONOMA

22 Donald St.

Lomita Ave.

Robinson St.

Verano Ave.

Sonoma Hwy

12

Fano La.

24

23 Mountain Cemetery

Norrbom Rd.

25

26 Depot Park 27 Sonoma Bike Path

28

Lasuen St.

7th St. W

4th St. W

29 30

W Spain St.

31 32 33 34 E Spain St. 35
36
37 Sonoma 38 39
40 Plaza 41
42 43 44
45

47
48

49

W Napa St.

12

E Napa St.

46

50 51

Studley St.

Oregon St.

Sonoma Creek

5th St. W

3rd St. W

2nd St. W

1st St. W

Broadway

1st St. E

Nathanson Creek

2nd St. E

3rd St. E

Patten St.

4th St. E

52 France St.
53

Andrieux St.

12

N

km 1/4 1/2
mi 1/8 1/4

W MacArthur St.

54

Park. ♦ One ticket valid for same-day admission to this site as well as to the Mission San Francisco Solano de Sonoma, Toscano Hotel, Sonoma Barracks, and Casa Grande Indian Servants' Quarters. Daily. W Spain St and Third St W. 938.1519

25 DEPOT HOTEL AND CUCINA RUSTICA

★★$$ Built in 1870 with stone from nearby quarries, this restaurant was originally a three-bedroom home with a saloon operating out of the living room. Once a station was built across the street, the railroad purchased the house and saloon to accommodate travelers. Now it's been transformed into a spacious, casual Northern Italian dining spot. The severe stone façade gives no hint of the surprises inside. The dining room is dressed in blue and white; outside, a glassed-in garden room and terrace overlook a pool and formal garden. There's alfresco dining in warm weather on the decks or around the pool. The most popular lunch dishes are salads and pastas. Dinner specialties include *ravioli al bosco* (filled with

shiitake mushrooms, herbs, and spices in a white-wine sauce), grilled New York cut sirloin, roasted chicken with fresh mushrooms, or one of the fresh seafood specials. For dessert, try the tiramisù or housemade gelati or sherbets. Symbols on the menu highlight heart-healthy and oil- and fat-free dishes. Wine is also served in the fireside parlor. ♦ Italian ♦ W-F, lunch and dinner; Sa, Su, dinner. 241 First St W (at Sonoma Bike Path). 938.2980. www.depothotel.com

26 DEPOT PARK

A few old train cars are pulled up alongside the replica of an old train station, which is now a museum (see below). The park includes a playground area, gazebo, picnic tables, and barbecue pits. ♦ Sonoma Bike Path (between First St E and First St W)

Within Depot Park:

SONOMA DEPOT MUSEUM

A replica of the old **Northwestern Pacific Railroad** station now houses Sonoma's impromptu historical museum. The volunteer

---

Restaurants/Clubs: Red | Hotels: Purple | Shops: Orange | Outdoors/Parks: Green | Sights/Culture: Blue

THE BEST

Rick Theis

Executive Director, Sonoma County Grape Growers Association

When I want some hard-to-find or "what's new" Sonoma County wines, I go to **Traverso's Gourmet Foods & Wine** (Third and B in Santa Rosa) and have Bill Traverso or Les Ferguson pick out a case for me.

The **Sonoma County Harvest Fair** on the first weekend of October is an annual celebration I won't miss. It is always fun, especially the wine pavilion. The best time to taste wine is Friday afternoon when the fair arranges the gold medal- and silver medal-winning wines by variety. The wine pavilion is usually more crowded on Saturday and Sunday, when the wines are arranged by winery.

I love watching the expression on people's faces when I tell them that wines made from **Sonoma County** grapes win more medals than **Napa** in major US wine competitions year after year—nearly two to one in 1997.

---

docents are eager to show off the restored stationmaster's office, where the big clock still ticks away. Show an interest and they'll conduct you around the museum, pointing out a map and memorabilia tracing the railroads in this part of the West. A re-creation of the kitchen and other rooms in a typical Victorian household and photos of local historical figures (including members of the infamous Bear Flag Party) complete the display. The museum has a good selection of historical books and monographs on Sonoma, plus California history coloring books for kids. ♦ Free. W-Su. 270 First St W (north of Sonoma Bike Path). 938.1762

SONOMA FARMERS MARKET

There's no better place to shop for a picnic than this lively outdoor market, held once a week throughout the year. A vibrant evening market is held spring through early fall; pick up something tasty for a snack or the next day's outing. ♦ F, 9AM-noon, Arnold Field parking lot, year round; Tu, 5:30-dusk in front of city hall on Sonoma Plaza, Apr-Sept. 538.7023

27 SONOMA BIKE PATH

No cars are allowed on this path, making it ideal for bicyclists and pedestrians. The bicycle trail takes you past the **Vella Cheese Company**, the **Sonoma Depot Museum** and **Depot Park**, and General Vallejo's home, **Lachryma Montis**. ♦ Between Fourth St E and Maxwell Farms Park, El Verano

28 VELLA CHEESE COMPANY

When Tom Vella arrived in California from his native Sicily in 1922, he sold butter, eggs, and cheese in San Francisco until he saved enough to open his own cheese-making business in Sonoma in 1931. His Monterey jack cheese and the Bear Flag dry Monterey jack have long been wine-country favorites. Under the direction of Tom's son Ig, the company now makes at least a half-dozen cheddars, an Oregon blue, and several flavored jacks (as well as sweet butter) at its headquarters in an old stone building. Call ahead to arrange to watch the entire artisanal cheese-making process; Ig often conducts the tours himself. A mail-order catalog is available. ♦ M-Sa. 315 Second St E (between E Spain St and Sonoma Bike Path). 938.3232, 800/848.0505. www.vellacheese.com

29 RAMEKINS

At Sonoma Valley Culinary School, home chefs learn wine-country cuisine from the chefs at Ramekins. You can sign up for individual classes or the Culinary Weekend. The complete schedule of cooking classes is listed online. There is also a bed-and-breakfast. The kitchen store carries the latest gadgets and cookbooks and is an easy 4-block walk west of the plaza. ♦ 450 W Spain St (between Fourth and Fifth Sts W). 933.0450, ext. 10. www.ramekins.com

30 THE GENERAL'S DAUGHTER

★★★$$$ Built in 1852 as a home for General Vallejo's third daughter and restored to its former glory, this dining spot garners high praise for its food and ambiance. Gardens, including a century-old rose arbor, and patio surround the building. The light and airy interior has a stately, yet unstuffy, feel— French provincial paintings adorn the walls. The seasonally themed "Wine Country" menu offers such starters as crisp buttermilk-and-cornmeal onion rings with lemon pepper aioli, and seared rare ahi tostadas with lime cream vinegar. The restaurant's homemade infused vodka is just the right thing to sip with these dishes. The dinner menu features several delicious meat dishes cooked in a variety of ways, and the grilled brochette of fall vegetables with wild mushroom risotto and thyme vinaigrette is a true delight. The California wine list is varied and reasonably priced. Pastry chef Lisa Lytle prepares flaky pastries, luscious puddings, and her outrageously rich

"One Heckuva Hot Fudge Sundae" with ice cream, hot fudge topping, whipped cream, and hazelnuts. ♦ American ♦ M-Sa, lunch and dinner; Su, brunch and dinner. Reservations recommended. 400 W Spain St (at Fourth St W). 938.4004

31 SONOMA HOTEL

$$ Completed in 1880, this corner structure has had a checkered past. As in many buildings of the era, the downstairs was used for shops and saloons. Upstairs, it featured a hall and a stage for social occasions. When Samuele Sebastiani bought it in the 1920s, he added a third floor and a balcony encircling the second floor and made himself a hotel, which he dubbed the **Plaza**. There are now 16 rooms, and the upstairs rooms, with shared baths in the European tradition, are wine-country bargains. Maya Angelou wrote *Gather Together in My Name* in **No. 21**, a small, cozy room with a pitched ceiling. Rooms with private baths on the second floor have deep claw-foot tubs. The grandest is the **Bear Flag Room**, which is furnished with a bedroom suite of carved mahogany from the Bear Flag era. The plus here is Veronica Enders, the helpful, knowledgeable manager. Continental breakfast is included. ♦ 110 W Spain St (at First St W). 996.2996, 800/468.6016; fax 996.7014. www.sonomahotel.com

Within the Sonoma Hotel:

THE GIRL & THE FIG

★★★$$ Chef Sondra Bernstein has won a local following for her grilled fig salad with goat cheese and crudité salad topped with cold poached salmon. She has a gift for whipping up healthy, imaginative salads and brasserie fare. Two inspired dishes are the steak frites—grilled ribeye with tarragon butter, matchstick frites—and mussels steamed with Pernod. Lively artwork of voluptuous women and ripe fruit adorn the dining room's pale-yellow wall. Try a wine flight with dinner. The restaurant promotes Rhône-style wines such as Roussanne, Marsanne, Cinsault, and Carignane, which also pair well with the cheese platter. Don't pass up the opportunity to taste fig and port ice cream, another local favorite. You may want to take home a bottle of fig and balsamic vinegar, and fig and port vinaigrette so you can make their famous grilled fig salad at home. ♦ California/French ♦ Daily, lunch and dinner. Late-night brasserie menu until 11PM. 110 W Spain St (at First St), 938.3634. www.thegirlandthefig.com

32 SONOMA CHEESE FACTORY

The plate-glass windows at the back of this crowded shop offer a good view of workers in white hard hats and yellow aprons making cheese. Famous for its Sonoma jack, the factory has developed a growing line of cheeses, including jack spiked with pepper, garlic, or caraway seeds; a mild cheddar; and a tender cheese called teleme. Many of them are cut up for free tasting. The store is filled with all sorts of picnic fare, not only cheeses (already wrapped) but also cold cuts sliced to order; the prepared salads are less tempting. You can have the staff make you a sandwich and then retire to the shady patio or the plaza out front for lunch. Crackers, local mustards, jams, and Sonoma wines are also offered, some arranged in gift baskets. ♦ Daily. 2 W Spain St (between First St E and First St W). 996.1931. www.sonomajack.com

32 BAKSHEESH

Look here for an interesting array of handicrafts from the world over—bags, boxes, decorative stone and wood carvings, chess sets, jewelry, toys, games, and more. The store is committed to trading fairly (eliminating as many of the middlepersons as possible) with artisans in more than 30 developing countries who supply these creations. ♦ Daily. 14 W Spain St (between First St E and First St W). 939.2847. www.vom.com/baksheesh

32 SWISS HOTEL

$$ Small and full of authentic charm, this property has five antiques-filled guest rooms with views of the plaza or garden patio and access to the balcony. The building, now a California Historical Landmark, was built in 1850 for General Vallejo and has been an inn since 1909. Rates include continental breakfast. ♦ 18 W Spain St (between First St E and First St W). 938.2884. www.swisshotelsonoma.com

Within the Swiss Hotel:

SWISS HOTEL RESTAURANT

★★$$ Don't be fooled by the name—this restaurant turns out very good Northern Italian dishes. At lunchtime, try the spinach salad or a stick-to-your-ribs sandwich—roasted eggplant Parmesan and Italian sausage with provolone are two examples. Dinner highlights include grilled lamb and roasted rosemary chicken. Pizza and pasta dishes are featured on both lunch and dinner menus. The patio is a perfect summer lunch or dinner place. Most of the wines served are from Sonoma. ♦ Northern Italian ♦ Daily, lunch and dinner. 938.2884

33 SONOMA BARRACKS

Between 1836 and 1840, Native American laborers built this two-story Monterey-Colonial

FLIGHTS OF FANCY: SONOMA COUNTY FROM THE AIR

Whether by balloon or small plane, flightseeing tours are a memorable way to explore the Sonoma Valley. Most trips that depart from Sonoma County travel over the **Russian River Valley**, and the farther north you go, the more stunning the views become. Here are some companies that offer scenic aerial excursions:

Hot-Air Balloons

One-hour tours in Sonoma County cost about $140 per person.

AIR FLAMBUOYANT   Hot-air balloon flights over the **Sonoma** wine country are followed by a champagne brunch. ♦ Daily by reservation. 250 Pleasant Ave, Santa Rosa, CA 95403. 838.8500, 800/456.4711

ADVENTURES AEROSTAT   Hot-air balloon rides above the **Healdsburg** area include a continental breakfast before and a champagne brunch after the flight.♦ Daily by reservation. ♦ 2414 Erickson Ct, Santa Rosa, CA 95401. 579.0183, 800/579.0183

ABOVE THE WINE COUNTRY BALLOONING   Flights are followed by a champagne celebration.♦ Daily by reservation. 829.9850, 800/759.5638

Small Planes

For one to two people, 30- to 60-minute flights cost $80 to $120.

VINTAGE AIRCRAFT CO.   Passengers ride in a Stearman plane once used to train World War II combat pilots.♦ Daily, by reservation. Schellville Airport, 23982 Arnold Dr, Sonoma, CA 95476. 938.2444

PETALUMA AEROVENTURE   Offers scenic flights aboard one- or three-passenger planes. ♦ Daily, by reservation. 561 Sky Ranch Dr, Petaluma, CA 94954. 778.6767

adobe to serve as General Vallejo's Mexican troop headquarters. Seized by the Bear Flag Party when they set up a short-lived independent republic in 1846, it was a US military post until the 1850s. A century later, the state bought and restored it as part of the **Sonoma State Historic Park**. ♦ One ticket valid for same-day admission to this site as well as to the Mission San Francisco Solano de Sonoma, Toscano Hotel, Lachryma Montis, and Casa Grande Indian Servants' Quarters. Daily. First St E and E Spain St. 938.1519

33 TOSCANO HOTEL

Originally built as a general store and lending library in the 1850s, this early California wood-frame building became a hotel in 1886, its name a tribute to the proprietors' Tuscan heritage. In 1957 a descendant of the hotel's original owners sold it to the state, and now it's part of the **Sonoma State Historic Park**. The Sonoma League for Historic Preservation stepped in to help restore the old mining hotel, endowing it with a certain raffish charm. Whiskey glasses and hands of cards sit on the tables, as if the players had just slipped out for a minute or two, and ragtime music plays in the background. Upstairs, the six bedrooms are furnished with period antiques and authentic touches. The turn-of-the-century kitchen in back displays a quirky collection of cookware and gadgets. ♦ One ticket valid for same-day admission to this site as well as to the Mission San Francisco Solano de

Sonoma, Sonoma Barracks, Lachryma Montis, and Casa Grande Indian Servants' Quarters. Daily. Tours: M, Sa, Su, 1PM-4PM. 20 E Spain St (between First St E and First St W). 938.9560

33 CASA GRANDE INDIAN SERVANTS' QUARTERS

Part of the **Sonoma State Historic Park**, this two-story Monterey-Colonial structure, once used as servants' quarters, is all that's left of General Vallejo's early Sonoma home. The imposing **Casa Grande**, built circa 1835, featured a three-story tower from which the general could survey the surrounding countryside. In 1867 a fire destroyed Casa Grande's main buildings, leaving only these servants' quarters, where a small Native American exhibit is now housed. ♦ One ticket valid for same-day admission to this site as well as to the Mission San Francisco Solano de Sonoma, Toscano Hotel, Lachryma Montis, and Sonoma Barracks. Daily. 20 E Spain St (between First St E and First St W). 938.1519

34 MISSION SAN FRANCISCO DE SOLANO

One of the five sites that comprise the **Sonoma State Historic Park**, this is the northernmost and the last of the 21 Franciscan missions built along the length of California. Named after a Peruvian saint, it was constructed on a site chosen by Padre José

Altimira in 1823, when California was under Mexican rule. Construction of the original church began in 1823, but all that survives from that time is the adobe building that served as the padre's quarters. (The present church was built under the direction of General Vallejo in 1840.) You can walk through the mission fathers' former rooms and tour black-smith, weaving, and bread-baking workshops to get a sense of what life was like in this mission outpost. ♦ One ticket valid for same-day admission to this site, as well as to the Sonoma Barracks, Toscano Hotel, Lachryma Montis, and Casa Grande Indian Servants' Quarters. Daily. 114 E Spain St (between Second St E and First St E). 938.1519

35 SEBASTIANI VINEYARDS

When Samuele Sebastiani arrived in the area from his native Tuscany in 1895, he worked at a number of odd jobs—from quarrying stone in the Sonoma hills to laying the San Francisco cable car tracks— before turning to wine-making.  Within a few years he had produced his debut wine, a Zinfandel, and sold it around town by the jug from his horse-drawn wagon. The third generation of the family runs the winery, and the antique crusher, basket press, and 500-gallon redwood tank that was used to make that first batch are prominently on display. Sam Sebastiani opened his own winery, **Viansa**, in the Carneros District several years ago, leaving his brother Don in charge here. The guided tour lasts about 20 minutes and takes visitors through the fermentation room and aging cellar, with its extensive collection of ornate carved cask heads, all crafted by local artist Earle Brown. The tour also includes a view of the crushing pad and interesting commentary about the valley and the Sebastiani family. The winery is the largest premium-varietal in Sonoma. After a multimillion-dollar renovation, the winery now includes a spacious hospitality center. Aside from tasting and retail sales of current releases, reserve and library wines, you can spend an afternoon here in the art gallery or historic museum, on the winery and vineyard tours, or in the wine education programs. The tasting room offers samples of the producer's full line of wines, from Cabernet to Merlot and more. There are several picnic areas on the property. Take the Sebastiani cable car from Sonoma Plaza to the winery. ♦ Tasting, sales, and tours daily. 389 Fourth St E (between E Spain and Brazil Sts). 938.5532, 800/888.5532. www.sebastiani.com

36 THISTLE DEW INN

$$ This 1910 California Arts and Crafts house offers six guest rooms (two in the main house, four in the back house), each with a private bath. The four rooms in the back house have private entrances; three have gas fireplaces, three have two-person whirlpool tubs, and two have both. The **Rose Garden** is furnished with antique oak furniture and a fan-patterned Amish-style quilt; the smaller **Cornflower** is, of course, blue with a matching Star of Texas quilt. **Wisteria**, a two-room suite overlooking the subtropical fern garden, has a private entrance, gas fireplace, falling-leaves quilt, and two-person whirlpool tub. Most of the original Arts and Crafts furniture is by Gustav Stickley or Charles Limbert; lamps, textiles, and rugs were made during the same period. Guests may use the cozy parlor, complete with a wood-burning stove, or relax in the hot tub in the plant-filled garden. Innkeepers Bethany and Greg Johns cook a full breakfast. Bicycles, picnic baskets, and passes to a local health club are available to guests. No smoking is allowed. ♦ 171 W Spain St (between First St W and Second St W). 938.2909, 800/382.7895; fax 996.8413. www.thistledewinn.com

37 EL DORADO HOTEL

$$ A great location and a heated outdoor lap pool in the courtyard are two pluses at this hotel on the plaza that dates from the days of the Gold Rush. The 26 rooms, each with a private bath, are fairly small and, wisely, uncluttered; each has terra-cotta tile floors and simple furniture. French doors lead to balconies overlooking the plaza or the court-yard in back. Be forewarned: Rooms above the restaurant may get cooking odors. A continental breakfast (coffee, fruit, breads, and pastries) is served buffet-style in the lobby; in nice weather enjoy your morning meal in the courtyard. ♦ 405 First St W. 996.3030, 800/289.3031; fax 996.3148. www.hoteldorado.com

WINE COUNTRY GIFTS

Stop here for gifts with a grape motif: California and Italian pottery, wine bags, picture frames, cards, and jewelry. ♦ Daily. 996.3453

COFFEE GARDEN CAFÉ & GIFT SHOP

★$ This is a pleasant place on the plaza to pick up inexpensive sandwiches, soups, salads, pastries, and, of course, an assort-

---

Restaurants/Clubs: Red | **Hotels: Purple** | **Shops: Orange** | **Outdoors/Parks: Green** | **Sights/Culture: Blue**

ment of well-brewed java. Hidden behind the deli is a pretty vine-laced patio where you can settle in with your fare when the weather is fair. ◆ Café ◆ Daily, continental breakfast, lunch, and dinner. 415 First St W. 996.6645

38 PLAZA BISTRO

★$$ The tried-and-true Italian-American fare here keeps the regulars coming back. The menu features fresh pasta dishes, chicken Parmesan, turkey scaloppine, and osso buco, among other items. The wine list is perfunctory. ◆ Italian ◆ Daily, lunch and dinner. 420 First St E (between E Napa and E Spain Sts). 996.4466

38 EL PASEO

Pass under an archway of plum stone from local quarries to this series of small shops off a charming courtyard. ◆ 414 First St E (between E Napa and E Spain Sts)

Within El Paseo:

VASQUEZ HOUSE

Built in 1855 by the Civil War hero "Fighting" Joe Hooker, who later sold it to early settlers Catherine and Pedro Vasquez, this small steep-gabled house is now the headquarters of the Sonoma League for Historic Preservation. It contains a library that is devoted to the town's history and a changing exhibit of historical photos gleaned from the town archives. Homemade desserts and tea are served in the tea room or at umbrella-shaded tables outdoors. You can also pick up books on Sonoma's history and copies of the indispensable guide Sonoma Walking Tour. ◆ W-Su, 1PM-5PM. 938.0510

38 SONOMA WINE SHOP

Come here for one-stop shopping for wine-related paraphernalia from many of the valley's wineries, plus corkscrews, wine carriers, picnic baskets outfitted with wineglasses, and a selection of wine. You can taste several different vintages by the glass in the tasting room. Shipping is available. ◆ Daily. 412 First St E (between E Napa and E Spain Sts). 996.1230; fax 944.2710

38 CUCCINA VIANSA

★★$ At this sleek café, deli, and wine bar run by **Viansa** winery, panini are made on herbed focaccia or sourdough bread and stuffed with a variety of fresh ingredients in delicious combinations. To complete your treat, buy a glass of Arneis, a crisp Italian

The beer can was introduced in 1935. This is the least desirable way to treat or drink a great beer—it is best enjoyed from a bottle or microbrewery tap.

white, rarely found in California, or Freisa, a light Italian red, and settle in at the counter along the windows and enjoy eating with a Mission view. In fair weather, dine outdoors. Salads and pastas are arrayed in delicious abundance, and rotisserie items are done to perfection. For those desiring lighter fare, have a breakfast pastry and cappuccino, or a gelato. ◆ Italian ◆ Daily, breakfast and lunch. 400 First St E (at E Spain St). 935.5656

39 LA CASA

★★$$ Chef José "Pepe" Loza makes delicious traditional and nouvelle Mexican fare in this family-owned restaurant across from the **Mission San Francisco de Solano**. Entrées include enchiladas, tamales, fajitas, and other classic Mexican dishes, but the grilled salmon served over Spanish rice is also a good bet. End the meal with a simple flan. The lovely back patio in the **El Paseo** courtyard is a treat in warm weather, especially on weekends when strolling Latin musicians serenade diners. ◆ Mexican ◆ Daily, lunch and dinner. 121 E Spain St (between Second St E and First St E). 996.3406

39 BLUE WING INN

This two-story Monterey-Colonial adobe was built by General Vallejo to lodge troops and travelers. During the Gold Rush, the inn became an infamous saloon where Ulysses S. Grant, Kit Carson, and bandit Joaquin Murrietta stopped to hoist a few. In the spring, cascades of wisteria blossoms hang from the hand-hewn balconies. ◆ 125-139 E Spain St (between Second St E and First St E)

40 SIGN OF THE BEAR

This friendly, unpretentious store is filled with all kinds of kitchen equipment—pot and wine racks, gadgets of all kinds, and cook- and bakeware are just some of the items sold. Check out the cookbooks and opera CDs too. ◆ Daily. 435 First St W (between W Napa and W Spain Sts). 996.3722; fax 966.2046

40 BATTO BUILDING

This three-section, glazed-brick building designed in the Classic Revival style dates from about 1912. ◆ 453-461 First St W (between W Napa and W Spain Sts)

Within the Batto Building:

KABOODLE

Designer-owner Beth Labelle has stuffed her charming shop to the rafters with gift items, including her exquisite dried-flower wreaths and romantic straw hats decorated with silk ribbon from France. Her choice selection of children's books and one-of-a-kind handmade toys will tempt the child in anyone. Also irresistible are the old-fashioned topiaries and locally made birdhouses, some large enough for 16 families. ♦ Daily. 453 First St W. 996.9500

SONOMA SPA ON THE PLAZA

The owners of two Calistoga spas have set up shop on Sonoma's plaza, allowing you to pamper your body with a wide range of treatments—from full-body massages and foot reflexology treatments to facials and mud baths. ♦ Daily. Reservations recommended. 457 First St W. 939.8770

41 SPIRITS IN STONE GALLERY

You'll find one-of-a-kind treasures among the basketry, African stone sculpture, paintings, and jewelry. Mata Ra'a, a descendant of Tahitian royalty who most recently worked at Place Vendôme in Paris, is the resident gemologist. ♦ Daily. 452 First St E (between E Napa and E Spain Sts). 800/474.6624. wwwspiritsinstone.com

42 HOMEGROWN BAKING

★$ Order a bagel with a schmear or a made-to-order sandwich to eat at the counter or at any of the half-dozen tables squeezed into this small shop. Takeout is available too. ♦ Deli ♦ Daily, breakfast and lunch. 122 W Napa St (between First St W and Second St W). 996.0166. Also at Maxwell Village, 19161 Sonoma Hwy (between W Napa St and Verano Ave). 996.0177

43 SONOMA PLAZA

ⓟ The real heart of Old Sonoma is this 8-acre Spanish-style plaza, a state and national landmark. General Mariano Vallejo, the Mexican *comandante*, laid it out with a pocket compass in 1835 as the nucleus of a square-mile town. At first it was a bare, dusty place where Vallejo drilled his troops. Later it was used to graze livestock and provide soil to make adobe bricks. Then at the turn of the 19th century the Ladies' Improvement Club took it over and turned it into the verdant park it is today, with more than 200 trees and an intriguing mix of native and exotic plants, including a salmon-colored rose that became known as the Sonoma rose. With its shady areas, playground, duck pond, and wooden tables and benches, the plaza is an appealing spot for a picnic. The **Sonoma Valley Visitors Bureau** is located in the **Carnegie Library**. Parking spots on the sides of the plaza have a 2-hour limit; a lot behind the Sonoma barracks building permits longer stays. ♦ Bounded by First St E and First St W and by Napa and Spain Sts

In Sonoma Plaza:

SONOMA CITY HALL

To avoid slighting any of the merchants on the plaza, when San Francisco architect **A.C. Lutgens** drew the plans for Sonoma's new city hall in 1906, he designed the square Mission-Revival building to be identical on all four sides. Built of locally quarried basalt, the eccentric golden-stone building is the subject of Sonoma schoolchildren's drawings at the annual art show. If the building looks familiar, it might be because you saw it as the Tuscany County Courthouse on TV's long-running wine-country soap opera, *Falcon Crest*. ♦ Napa St (between First St E and First St W)

BEAR FLAG MONUMENT

This bronze statue of a figure raising the Bear Flag commemorates 14 June 1846, when a band of American immigrants rode into Sonoma, imprisoned General Mariano Vallejo, and proclaimed California an independent republic. Bear Flagger John Sears contributed the white cloth for the banner's background; the flag's red stripe came from a petticoat; and Abraham Lincoln's nephew, William Todd, painted a large bear, a single star, and the name "California Republic" on the flag. The audacious band's new republic lasted just 25 days, when the US government stepped in to halt the rebellion. In 1911 the California state legislature voted to adopt the design as the official state flag. ♦ E Spain St and First St E

44 ROBIN'S NEST

A paradise for serious cooks, this shop features an ever-changing array of cookware at discount prices. Sort through a wide array of wooden utensils, baking pans, and gadgets galore. Also stop here for wine paraphernalia—including handsome blue-stemmed Sonoma Valley stemware and acrylic glasses (perfect for picnics). ♦ Daily. 116 E Napa St (between Second St E and First St E). 996.4169

44 LEDSON HOTEL

$$$$ On the historic plaza next to the ornate Sebastiani Theatre stands the Ledson Hotel, Ledson Winery's latest venture. Despite its modern construction, this small six-suite hotel evokes the golden era of hostelry with an ornate stone façade. Each suite is uniquely decorated in the style and grandeur offered resort-goers a century ago. Not only richly appointed with antiques and balcony views, the suites also have modern amenities such as gas fireplaces

---

Restaurants/Clubs: Red | Hotels: Purple | Shops: Orange | Outdoors/Parks: Green | Sights/Culture: Blue

and whirlpool tubs. Harmony Club on the lobby level provides evening entertainment. Wine tasting throughout the day and a deluxe continental breakfast are included in room rates. ♦ 480 First St E. 344.1318. www.ledson.com

44 THE CORNER STORE

The former home of **Pinelli's Hardware Store** houses a tasting room featuring wines of the **Mayo Family Winery**. The attractive room is in a historic 1861 building. There are also interesting gift items on sale, including table linens, dishes, clocks, and candles. ♦ Daily. 498 First St E (at E Napa St). 996.2211

44 PLACE DES PYRENEES

Inside this peaceful courtyard are several shops, an Irish pub, and a coffee roaster. ♦ 464 First St E (between E Napa and E Spain Sts)

Within Place des Pyrenees:

JEANINE'S COFFEE & TEA COMPANY

Enjoy a cappuccino or espresso at tables outside in the cobblestone courtyard. Proprietors Jeanine and Bruce Masonek buy the beans and roast their own coffees in an old-fashioned drum roaster to get the slow-roasted flavor they prefer. To compensate for flavor lost in the decaffeination process, they roast their decaf coffees a bit darker. ♦ Daily. 996.7573

BRIAR PATCH TOBACCONIST

The other half of **Jeanine's Coffee & Tea Company** is devoted to hand-crafted cigars and custom-blended tobaccos. ♦ Daily. 996.7573

44 BASQUE BOULANGERIE CAFÉ

★$ Fresh-baked breads and pastries fill the shelves of this bustling bakery and café that has a few tables and a marble bar. Locals gather for coffee and sourdough Basque bread, sticky buns, a bowl of oatmeal, or granola in the morning and for homemade soups, salads, sandwiches, or tasty potato omelettes at lunch. A rack behind the bar holds a large selection of Sonoma County wines, available by the glass. ♦ Café ♦ Daily, breakfast, lunch, and early dinner. 460 First St E (between E Napa and E Spain Sts). 935.7687

44 THE MERCATO

Mercato is Italian for "market," and this post-modernist building bathed in stylish pastels contains a number of interesting shops. Note the 16-by-13-foot mural on the side of the building depicting a bird's-eye view of Sonoma Valley; it was painted by local artist Claudia Wagar. ♦ 450-452 First St E (between E Napa and E Spain Sts)

Within The Mercato:

ARTIFAX

Proprietors Candace Tisch and Tom Rubel travel all over the world buying crafts for this elegant gallery with a special emphasis on offerings from Asia and Africa. Japanese flower-arranging tools, African musical instruments, woven platters from the Philippines, tribal dolls from Kenya, Tibetan singing bell bowls, and bamboo trays from Japan all make special gifts. ♦ Daily. 996.9464

PAPYRUS

This stationery store has a collection of appealing cards, writing materials, and ornate wrapping papers, many from museums around the world. ♦ Daily. 935.6707

WINE EXCHANGE OF SONOMA

Spacious and well organized, this shop offers a dynamite array of more than 500 California wines selected by the knowledgeable staff. This is the place to go for some serious wine talk—or beer talk, for that matter, as the shop also features a superb collection of more than 250 brews from around the world. (It also stocks about 50 different kinds of cigars.) There is a comfortable, informal wine bar at the back. The store gives case discounts and will ship orders. ◆ Daily. 938.1794, 800/938.1794

45 VICTORIAN GARDEN INN

$$ The white picket fence and posies in front of the inn only hint at Donna Lewis's carefully tended Victorian-style garden beyond. The inn has four guest rooms, one in the main house and the rest in a 19th-century water tower. Lewis has left the architecture as it was, adding only private baths and decorating the rooms in period décor (guests in the main house may occasionally have to share the bathroom with the owner's personal visitors). The **Garden Room**, decorated in Laura Ashley rose-colored prints, has white wicker furniture and a claw-foot tub. The most requested accommodation is the **Woodcutter's Cottage**, which has a sofa and armchairs set in front of the fireplace, and a private entrance. Breakfast features juice, eggs, granola or muffins, and fresh fruit from the garden. ◆ 316 E Napa St (between Fourth St E and Second St E). 996.5339, 800/543.5339; fax 996.1689. www.victoriangardeninn.com

46 DELLA SANTINA'S

★★★$$ It's a trattoria, grill, and pastry shop all in one, run by cousins of the same family that operates the Joe's restaurant dynasty of San Francisco's North Beach. The kitchen prepares a good minestrone, Caesar salad, and handmade pastas. But the real stars here are the grilled meats—chicken, Sonoma rabbit, pork loin, duck, veal, and turkey breast. The plate of mixed roasted meats will go with just about any wine. At lunch try that savory meat tucked into a roll brushed with olive oil and fresh herbs. Dessert offerings include a wonderful tiramisù and tarts made with fresh fruit. There is a list of Italian and Sonoma wines. Takeout is available. ◆ Italian ◆ Daily, lunch and dinner. 133 E Napa St (between Second St E and First St E). 935.0576

47 RANCH HOUSE

★★$$ A real find, this restaurant serves flavorful Yucatecan cuisine in a relaxed, informal setting. Aficionados line up for the succulent *came adobada* (beef braised with onions and a mix of Yucatecan spices) or the *pollo mole* (chicken in a sharp chocolate-chili sauce). Burritos get an interesting twist with a filling of spicy prawns spiked with bay leaves and orange extract, yet you can still find such familiar well-prepared standards as enchiladas, tostadas, and crisp, not soft, tortillas. ◆ Mexican ◆ W-M, lunch and dinner. 875 West Napa St (note: West Napa St is also Hwy 12). 996.8756

48 TROJAN HORSE INN

$$ Innkeepers Joe and Sandy Miccio take great pride in their historic blue wood-frame bed-and-breakfast, which was built in 1880 as the home of a Sonoma pioneer family. Though replete with antique furnishings, the six light and airy rooms all have such modern-day conveniences as private baths. Each room is individually decorated: The spacious first-floor room has a wood-burning stove and a canopy bed; on the second story, one room features red mahogany, an antique armoire, and a queen-size brass bed. The other, in shades of silver, lavender, and silver rose, has a border of stenciled grapes, a fireplace, a queen-size high oak bed, and its own Jacuzzi. The inn has bicycles for guests' use, an outdoor Jacuzzi, and a large garden. There's also a full breakfast, and complimentary wine and hors d'oeuvres in the evening. ◆ 19455 Sonoma Hwy (just north of W Napa St). 996.2430, 800/899.1925. www.trojanhorseinn.com

49 ARTISAN BAKERS

Tear into a crusty loaf of dry jack and garlic sourdough or one of the other award-winning loaves of bread at this bakery. The Ponsford and Jones families bake more than a dozen types of fresh bread daily, including potato rosemary, multigrain, and pugliese, all of which have won gold medals at the Sonoma County Fair. Pastries, pizza by the slice, and cold drinks are also sold. ◆ Daily. 750 W Napa St (between

---

Restaurants/Clubs: Red | Hotels: Purple | Shops: Orange | Outdoors/Parks: Green | Sights/Culture: Blue

Seventh St W and Sonoma Hwy). 939.1765. www.artisanbakers.com

50 SONOMA VALLEY INN

$$ On a busy street one block from Sonoma Plaza, this Best Western property has 75 comfortable rooms and suites, all with private baths and no-nonsense modern décor; some have wood-burning fireplaces, Jacuzzis, or kitchenettes. There's a pool and spa, and a continental breakfast is provided.♦ 550 Second St W (between Andrieux and W Napa Sts). 938.9200, 800/334.KRUG in CA; 800/528.1234 elsewhere in the US; fax 938.0935. www.sonomavalleyinn.com

51 BEAR MOON TRADING COMPANY

In an 1880s building with an Italianate false front, this women's apparel shop carries a good selection of natural-fiber sweaters, socks, and lightweight, hot-weather clothing. Consider one of the handsome Panama hats to ward off the summer sun. ♦ Daily. 523 Broadway (between McDonell and W Napa Sts). 935.3392

52 MAGLIULO'S ROSE GARDEN INN

$$ The Magliulo family turned this cornflower-blue Victorian into a charming bed-and-breakfast, decorating the four guest rooms with brass beds, armoires, and ceiling fans, and antique quilts hung on the walls. Rooms have either private or shared baths. The parlor features a fireplace framed in copper with cozy chairs pulled up in front. A continental breakfast is served in the inn's dining room. No smoking or pets are allowed. ♦ 681 Broadway at Andrieux St. 332.1031

53 INN AT SONOMA

$$ One of a dozen Four Sister inns that span the state from Dana Point to the wine country, this new property is a hop, skip, and a jump from the historic town square ringed with nationally acclaimed restaurants and tantalizing shops. The inn's 19 rooms cosset guests in stylish comfort with fireplaces, queen-size beds, and wine-country oil paintings by Impressionist artist Wendy Johnson. All but a few rooms have furnished private patios. If you like to share experiences, you'll run into other guests soaking in the rooftop Jacuzzi. In the spacious dining room, you can help yourself to a three-course gourmet breakfast, tea-time cookies, and evening wine and hors d'oeuvres. Four Sisters' hospitality also extends to complimentary bicycles. The Inn offers discount rates weekdays and during winter. ♦ 630 Broadway (at Perkins), two blocks south of the town square.

939.1340 or 888/568.9818. www.foursisters.com

54 MACARTHUR PLACE

$$$$ What was once a 300-acre vineyard and working ranch is now the quintessential wine-country inn. Located on a 7-acre estate, MacArthur Place offers first-class service, plush bedding, and original artwork. Restored Victorian buildings with covered porches and new cottages house 64 rooms, 10 of which are in the original 1850s residence. Formal gardens surround the pool and spa. Rates include breakfast, which is served in **Saddles** restaurant, a 100-year-old converted barn. The choices are muffins, cereal, mandarin oranges, cottage cheese, scones, yogurt, bagels and cream cheese, coffee, and juice. ♦ 29 East MacArthur St (at Broadway, Hwy 12). 938.2929, 800/722.1866; fax 933.9833. www.macarthurplace.com

HOT SPRINGS RESORTS

At the northwest end of Sonoma are the old resort towns of **Boyes Hot Springs**, **Fetters Hot Springs**, **Agua Caliente** (Spanish for "hot water"), and **El Verano** (see the map below). Local Indians discovered the hot springs and brought their sick to bathe in the healing waters, but it was the young British naval officer Captain Henry Boyes, urged on by General Mariano Vallejo, who developed the sites as resort areas. By the turn of the century, San Franciscans were taking their families north by train—and later in their private cars—to spend summers at the popular resorts. These vacation destinations became less family-oriented during Prohibition; speakeasies served bootleg liquor, the atmosphere was rowdy, and madams such as Spaniard Kitty Lombardi set the tone. Today only a few vestiges of the hot springs' heyday remain, notably the **Fairmont Sonoma Mission Inn & Spa** in Boyes Hot Springs.

HOT SPRINGS RESORTS

55 MOON MOUNTAIN VINEYARD

This estate's steep, terraced vineyards near the crown of the Mayacamas Mountains date from the 19th century. They were reworked in 1981 when Chalone, a small premium-wine company that also owns top-rated Chalone Vineyard, Edna Valley Vineyard, and Acacia, bought the property. Chalone replanted the vineyard with Bordeaux varietals and began making the kind of blends the Bordelaise refer to as *carmenet*, hence the name. Cool, underground aging cellars hold French oak barrels of Carmenet estate red, a Bordeaux-style wine made from a blend of Cabernet Sauvignon, Merlot, and Cabernet Franc that consistently earns high marks. Winemaker Jeffrey Baker's white reserve is mostly Sauvignon Blanc blended with a small amount of Sémillon; the inexpensive, well-made Colombard comes from old vines just off the Silverado Trail in Napa Valley. ♦ Tours by appointment only. 1700 Moon Mountain Dr (east of Sonoma Hwy), Sonoma. 996.5870. www.moonmountainvineyard.com

THE BEST

Healdsburg Chamber of Commerce & Visitors' Bureau

Pick and choose to visit 60-plus wineries.

Canoe trips down the **Russian River—W.C. "Bob" Trowbridge Canoe Trips**.

Fishing in **Lake Sonoma** and the **Russian River**.

Hiking at Lake Sonoma and **Armstrong Redwoods State Reserve** in **Guerneville**.

Boating at Lake Sonoma.

Hot-air ballooning.

Local farmers' market.

Plenty of antiques shops.

Many fine art galleries.

Historic **Healdsburg** homes walking tours.

56 FAIRMONT SONOMA MISSION INN & SPA GOLF CLUB

Originally designed in 1926 by Sam Whiting and Willie Watson (who also designed the Lakeside Course at San Francisco's Olympic Club), this 18-hole championship course has been completely restored by the renowned golf-course architect Robert Muir Graves. Now part of Sonoma Mission Inn, the course has a spectacular setting: more than 177 acres and three lakes bordered with centuries-old oak and redwood trees with the majestic Mayacamas Mountains in the background. The clubhouse restaurant offers a regional California cuisine with a few Japanese dishes. ♦ Daily. 17700 Arnold Dr (north of Boyes Blvd), Sonoma. 996.0300 (tee times)

57 FAIRMONT SONOMA MISSION INN & SPA

$$$$ Native Americans were the first to appreciate this Boyes Hot Springs site, using the area as a sacred healing ground for many years. Then in the mid-1800s, an eccentric San Francisco physician, Dr. T.M. Leavenworth, built a water-storage tank and a small bathhouse here, creating a small spa of sorts. It's rumored that right after the doc built his little spa, he promptly burned it down, because of a tiff with his wife. It wasn't until 1883 that English adventurer Captain Henry Boyes constructed a posh hot-water spa at this site, which became a fashionable summer retreat for San

Francisco's wealthy Nob Hill set. About 40 years later, the spa was hit by another devastating fire, and the present California Mission–style inn wasn't built until 1927. It was completely renovated in the 1980s, and more rooms were added in 1986. Today it's Sonoma's premier luxury retreat, drawing such stars as Barbra Streisand, Harrison Ford, Oprah Winfrey, Tom Cruise, Jerry Seinfeld, Roseanne, Helena Bonham-Carter, Sarah Ferguson, and Billy Crystal, to name a few. The décor of the 200 guest rooms and suites blends country elegance with luxurious appointments—plantation shutters, down comforters, and TVs. The newer rooms have grand, granite bathrooms; some boast fireplaces and terraces, and most overlook the eucalyptus-shaded grounds. The new suites have rose and avocado color schemes carried out in quilted bedspreads, slipper chairs, wood-burning fireplaces, wet bars, whirlpool baths, and balconies or terraces. The primary draw here, however, is the state-of-the-art European-style spa (see page 118). The 10-acre site also includes a spring-fed stream (the source of the inn's privately bottled water); two pools (the pool by the spa is heated to a toasty 92 degrees year-round); two lighted, championship tennis courts; a fully equipped fitness room; and two restaurants. The resort pipes naturally hot artesian mineral water from 1,100 feet underground into its pools and whirlpools. The water was discovered after a 2-year search for a source of hot, mineral-rich water on the property. (The springs used by local Native Americans and subsequent residents became dormant in the early 1960s.) The establishment is a member of the prestigious Preferred Hotels & Resorts Worldwide organization. ◆ 18140 Sonoma Hwy (at Boyes Blvd), Boyes Hot Springs. 938.9000, 800/862.4945. www.fairmont.com/sonoma

Within the Fairmont Sonoma Mission Inn & Spa:

THE SPA

Expanded in 1999, the spa is now better equipped to serve its many patrons. Reserve well ahead, especially on weekends, for a wide range of spa treatments in a glamorous, pristine coed setting complete with soft lights and soothing music. The possibilities here range from individual body treatments and aerobic and yoga classes to custom-designed 1- to 5-day packages of diet and exercise programs. There's a wide choice of full-body, aromatherapy massages; reflexology, citrus body scrubs, herbal body wraps, various facials, or a go-for-broke, all-in-one treatment are available as well. Other amenities include full beauty salon services, fitness and nutrition evaluations, and a weight room with exercise machines. The exercise regimen includes morning and afternoon hikes and bicycle rides to scenic locations in Sonoma Valley. Mind–body treatments include guided meditation and tarot card readings, stress management, and energy balancing. One favorite therapy is a body massage topped off with a purifying wrap of steaming Irish linens infused with fragrant herbs. Afterward, become even more relaxed (if that's possible) in the bathhouse sauna, steam room, whirlpool bath, or outdoor swimming pool. The pool and both the indoor whirlpools are filled with hot artesian mineral water. The large roster of famous and not-so-famous guests swear by the spa's restorative powers. ◆ Day guests pay a $45 facility fee in addition to their treatment. Must be 18 years old to use the spa facilities. Reservations required for body treatments. 938.9000, 800/862.4945

SANTÉ

★★★$$$$ Chef Bruno Tison's expertly produced California cuisine is paired with wines from the inn's 7,500-bottle wine cellar. He keeps an eye on what's fresh at Sonoma County's gardens and farms for his seasonal and spa menu. He fills the beef pot-au-feu with market-fresh vegetables and beef tenderloin, and serves it in truffle broth. Two other winning entrées are Petaluma chicken paillard with roasted potatoes and olive-and-pistachio tapenade, and bluenose bass wrapped in eggplant served with squash ragout. For starters, the farmers' market salad is tossed

with preserved lemon oil and clabbered cottage cheese from the Strauss Family dairy. The wheat berry salad is a healthy mélange of vine-ripened tomatoes, brocconcini, olives, and basil. Desserts are inventive. The Gloria Ferrer rouge champagne gelée is a light but sensuous choice. Or try the raspberry clafouti with lavender-infused cream and red raspberry compote. The warm dining room, with a high-beam ceiling and abundance of light through tall pocket doors that open to the terrace, is the perfect place to enjoy the bounty of Sonoma County. ◆ Wine-country cuisine. ◆ M-F, dinner; Sa, lunch and dinner; Su, brunch and dinner. Reservations recommended. 938.9000, 800/862.4945

THE BIG3

★★$$ Famous for its generous breakfasts and varied lunch fare, this handsome café on the inn's grounds includes a wine bar and adjacent market. In summer, it's a refreshing spot for lunch, with its open kitchen, green-and-white décor, and old-fashioned ceiling fans. Chef Philip Breitweiser offers a nice selection of salads, burgers, sandwiches, and California pizzas. Smoothies and shakes are served too, and the wine bar features about 25 Sonoma wines by the glass. A "spa" menu is available as well. Take home an inn sweatshirt from the marketplace, along with books and all the appurtenances of country life in the Californian style. ◆ American ◆ Restaurant: M-F, breakfast, lunch, and dinner; Sa, Su, brunch and dinner. Wine bar: daily, 11:30AM-9:30PM. Reservations recommended. 938.9000, 800/862.4945

58 FRUIT BASKET

Stop here for a veritable cornucopia representing the best of Sonoma County produce at good prices, plus dried fruits and nuts, bulk foods, farm-fresh eggs, cherry juice from the **Cherry Tree**, and an array of Sonoma wines. ◆ Daily. 18474 Sonoma Hwy (between Verano Ave and Boyes Blvd), Boyes Hot Springs. 996.7433; also at 24101 Arnold Dr. 938.4332

59 GOOD TIME BICYCLE COMPANY

Owner Doug McKesson will deliver his well-maintained rental bikes to your hotel or bed-and-breakfast by prior arrangement. Back at the shop, he rents and sells bicycles, racing gear, accessories, and books on local biking routes. Stop in or pedal this way for updated route advice and information on guided tours. ◆ Daily. 18503 Sonoma Hwy (between Siesta Way and E Thomson Ave), Boyes Hot Springs. 938.0453. www.goodtimetouring.com

60 MAXWELL FARMS PARK

Picnic spots, hiking trails, and a playground for kids are just minutes from downtown Sonoma in this regional park with about 85 acres of woods and meadows along Sonoma Creek. The farm once belonged to turn-of-the-century conservationist George Maxwell, an advocate for small farmers. A footpath runs along the creek; the **Sonoma Bike Path**, which runs from **Sebastiani Vineyards** past **Depot Park** and Lachryma Montis, is a scenic route into the park for bikers and pedestrians. Shady picnic facilities are available. ♦ Parking fee. Verano Ave and Riverside Dr, El Verano. 938.2794

61 ROB'S RIB SHACK

★$ This casual dinerlike place serves generous portions of hardwood-smoked ribs, chicken, and sausages. Baked macaroni and cheese, as well as shakes, root beer floats, cherry cider, and beer and wine, are offered too. ♦ Barbecue ♦ Daily, lunch and dinner. 18709 Arnold Dr (between Verano and Craig Aves), El Verano. 938.8520

62 LITTLE SWITZERLAND

Kick up your heels to the live polka, tango, and waltz music at this popular weekend dance hall. All the fun people are here—they'll even tell you so on the phone. The menu's continental selections please popular tastes. ♦ Cover. Sa, Su. Reservations recommended. Grove St and Riverside Dr, El Verano. 938.9990. www.lilswiss.com

GLEN ELLEN

The nucleus of early Glen Ellen was the sawmill General Vallejo built on **Sonoma Creek** in the mid-19th century. Before long, winemakers from all over Europe had followed pioneering vintner Joshua Chauvet to the area, planting vineyards and establishing landmark wineries in the heart of the **Valley of the Moon**. When the narrow-gauge railroad tracks reached the town of Glen Ellen in 1879, the rural community was invaded by scores of San Franciscans, and the saloons, dance halls, and brothels that opened to serve the city slickers turned Glen Ellen into a country cousin of the Barbary Coast. Author Jack London came to have a look and stayed to write at the place he dubbed **Beauty Ranch** (now known as **Jack London State Historic Park**). The diminutive town, which for many years was home to the late food writer and novelist M.F.K. Fisher, is a quiet backwater now, its bawdy days left far behind.

63 BELTANE RANCH BED & BREAKFAST

$$ This restored 1892 bunkhouse painted buttercup-yellow and white once belonged to

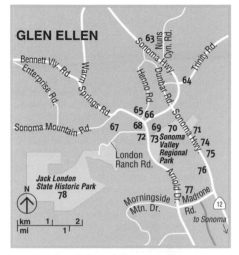

the former slave and abolitionist Mary Ellen Pleasant—who, at one time or another, was also a madam, a cook, and the mistress of British millionaire Thomas Bell. Innkeeper Rosemary Wood reopened the house as a bed-and-breakfast inn in 1981. Daughter Alexa Wood now manages the property, which has five guest rooms: two simply decorated suites, another guest room upstairs, and two bedrooms downstairs. (Try to get the suite with a king-size bed and wood-burning stove.) All have private baths, queen-size beds, and doors opening onto the porch. Wood keeps a library of books on local history, fauna, and flora and sets up chairs in the shade of a venerable old oak. There are tennis and volleyball courts and a hammock perfect for snoozing. Guests have the run of the 1,600-acre estate, which extends to the Napa County line and includes 8 miles of hiking trails. There's also a full country breakfast. ♦ 11775 Sonoma Hwy (north of Nuns Canyon Rd). 996.6501. www.beltaneranch.com

64 TRINITY ROAD— OAKVILLE GRADE

Buckle up for this 12-mile scenic drive from the Sonoma Highway near Glen Ellen over the Mayacamas Mountains to St. Helena Highway in Napa Valley at Oakville. The twists and turns, along with the panoramic views of the valley and mountains, make for an exciting ride. Be sure your brakes—and stomach—are up to the task before you set off. ♦ Between St. Helena Hwy, Oakville, and Sonoma Hwy

65 GLENELLY INN & COTTAGES

$$ Originally built as an inn for train travelers in 1916, this charming place on a rural road retains the ambiance of another era with its

---

Restaurants/Clubs: Red | Hotels: Purple | Shops: Orange | Outdoors/Parks: Green | Sights/Culture: Blue

long verandas furnished with wooden chairs. The inn consists of two peach-and-cream buildings set on a hillside, with a terrace garden shaded by old oaks in back. A hot tub is sheltered by an arbor twined with grapevines and old roses. All eight rooms have private baths and entrances. Pine armoires, ceiling fans, and claw-foot tubs add to the country feel; some rooms also have wood-burning stoves. Innkeeper Kristi Hallamore's breakfast includes freshly squeezed juice, a hot dish, fruit, and fresh-baked muffins. ◆ 5131 Warm Springs Rd (west of Arnold Dr). 996.6720. www.glenelly.com

GAIGE HOUSE INN

66 GAIGE HOUSE

$$$ Built in 1890 for the town butcher, A.E. Gaige, this brown-and-beige Italianate Queen Anne Victorian home is now a glamorous bed-and-breakfast inn in the heart of old Glen Ellen. New owners Ken Burnet and Greg Nemrow describe the place's evolving décor as "Indonesian plantation." An attractive mix of antiques, period reproductions, and hand-carved teak makes a welcome change from the abundance of Victoriana in these parts. Each of the 15 rooms and suites has a private bathroom with separate showers; some also feature Jacuzzis, others deep claw-foot tubs. The beautiful **Gaige Suite** on the second floor has a canopied bed, whirlpool, and balcony. Room 10 has a bathroom with a double Jacuzzi and a two-headed shower. A gourmet chef prepares country breakfasts that rate raves. The inn grows its own herbs in a large garden. ◆ 13540 Arnold Dr (just east of Warm Springs Rd past Glen Ellen). 935.0237, 800/935.0237. www.gaige.com

67 BENZIGER FAMILY WINERY

Young winemaker Mike Benziger was scouting vineyard properties in Sonoma Valley when he came across this historic estate, established

When Jack London bought his Beauty Ranch in Glen Ellen, improvements to the property and agricultural experiments became a passion. In the early 1900s, he devoted 2 hours a day to writing and 10 hours to farming.

by the carpenter Julius Wegener, who received the land as payment from General Vallejo for constructing his Sonoma home. Benziger was so taken with the steep, terraced vineyard site that he convinced his father, Bruno Benziger, to buy it. The straightforward wines, especially the ready-to-drink, modestly priced Proprietor's Reserve Chardonnay and Cabernet Sauvignon, have won an unassailable place on the market; the best wines are those made from grapes grown on the steep, terraced **Home Ranch Vineyard**. Sauvignon Blanc, Merlot, and Zinfandel are also produced here. The property includes a folksy tasting room, a classic California-barn winery building, and a picnic grove. Tram tours give visitors a ringside view of the vineyard's insectary and recycling ponds, two important elements of biodynamic farming. An art gallery displays original works, many of which served as the inspiration for wine labels. ◆ Tasting, sales, and tours daily. 1883 London Ranch Rd (west of Arnold Dr). 935.3000. www.benziger.com

68 GLEN ELLEN INN RESTAURANT AND COTTAGES

★★★$$ Christian and Karen Bertrand prepare a variety of cuisines in their cozy restaurant, using the freshest local produce and ingredients available to make some original dishes. Entrées might include California jambalaya—a saucy potpourri of prawns, chicken, sausage, honey-smoked ham, and vegetables simmered in cayenne and served on a bed of basmati rice. More conservative diners might choose a grilled New York steak with roasted garlic and shallots and a Zinfandel beurre rouge sauce. Among the desserts might be a warm French bread pudding, studded with pecans and served with a brandy-caramel sauce. The dessert sampler for two is always a fitting finale. Sip dessert wine with whatever you order. Dine outside in the garden with a lovely waterfall in pleasant weather. Sonoma wines are featured. ◆ International ◆ Daily, dinner. Reservations required. 13670 Arnold Dr (between Warm Springs and London Ranch Rds). 996.6409; for Cottage reservations, 996.1174. www.glenelleninn.com

68 JACK LONDON LODGE

$ Set beside a creek and the entrance to **Jack London State Historic Park**, this two-story motel has 22 fairly large guest rooms, all with private baths and functional country antique décor brightened with country prints; ask for one of the upstairs rooms. It's hardly luxury, but it's just fine for the budget traveler, and it even has a creekside swimming pool and the Wolf House café (996.4401). ◆ 13740 Arnold Dr (at London Ranch Rd). 938.8510. www.jacklondonlodge.com

Adjacent to the Jack London Lodge:

JACK LONDON SALOON

Plaid shirts, hiking boots, and the lumberjack look are de rigueur at this historic saloon. The bar has been pouring drinks for locals and city slickers alike since Jack London's days, and the saloon seems to have saved every bit of memorabilia from those rowdy years. On warm summer evenings, it's fun to linger over drinks outside on the patio beside the creek. ◆ Daily. 996.3100

69 VILLAGE MERCANTILE

An ever-changing selection of teapots and cups, plus other items collected by owner Raegene Africa, can be found in this shop. Some are choice pieces from the 1930s and 1940s; others are reproductions of antique pieces. Specialty teas are available too. ◆ Tu-Sa. 13647 Arnold Dr (at Carquinez Ave). 938.1330

69 GLEN ELLEN VILLAGE MARKET

Now an all-purpose grocery market, this store dates back to Glen Ellen's pioneer days. The basics are all here, plus a bakery, wine section, meat department, and catering services. ◆ Daily. 13751 Arnold Dr (west of Carmel Ave). 996.6728

70 SONOMA VALLEY REGIONAL PARK

In the springtime, the wildflower preserve in this park 6 miles north of Sonoma is a carpet of California poppies, lupines, wild irises, and other native flowers. There's a picnic area and hiking and bike paths. ◆ Sonoma Hwy (between Madrone Rd and Arnold Dr)

71 GARDEN COURT CAFÉ

★★$ Breakfast for lunch or vice versa? Both are served throughout the day at this simple, cheerful roadside café. New owners Rich and Stacy Treglia have introduced five different eggs Benedict (try Pacific Coast smoked salmon) to the menu. Other breakfast options include omelettes, scrambles, pancakes, waffles, French toast, cereals, and bagels. Or try one of Rich's sticky buns with a cup of French roast coffee. Lunch fare features such standards as soup, burgers (beef, turkey, and veggie), and a variety of sandwiches. Salads are served with freshly baked bread and homemade dressings. The Treglias also pack picnics. ◆ American ◆ Daily, breakfast and lunch. 13875 Sonoma Hwy (between Cavedale and Trinity Rds). 935.1565. www.gardencourtcafe.com

72 JACK LONDON BOOKSTORE

Established by Winifred Kingman and her late husband, Russ, this bookstore is filled with works by and about Glen Ellen's famous writer. Russ Kingman was one of the country's leading experts on Jack London, and some of his large collection of memorabilia about the writer is displayed in the store. Here you can find first editions by London, rare and out-of-print works, and other books not relating to London. It's a cozy, unintimidating place to spend an afternoon and is one of an endangered species: a serious small bookstore. ◆ M, W-Su. 14300 Arnold Dr (south of London Ranch Rd). 996.2888

73 JACK LONDON VILLAGE

Almost hidden in the hoary oaks along Sonoma Creek, this complex of ramshackle redwood buildings is home to a series of small shops and artisans' workshops. ◆ 14301 Arnold Dr (south of London Ranch Rd). 888/996.5582

Within Jack London Village:

THE OLIVE PRESS

Experience the ancient ritual pressing of olive oil on the state-of-the art equipment featured here. Following the pattern of the cooperatives in southern France and northern Italy, dozens of local olive growers bring their crops here to have them made into extra-virgin olive oil. Visitors may sample and buy premium oils, as well as cured olives, tapenades, and other delicacies. Olive-themed gifts, some specially commissioned from around the world, fill the gift shop. In the spring, young olive trees and cuttings are available for planting. ◆ Shop: Daily. Pressing: Daily, Oct-Mar. 939.8900. www.theolivepress.com

ART FOR LIVING

The handsome gallery of well-known interior designer Julie Atwood, located in the old **Chavenet Mill Building**, showcases American crafts, fine art, home furnishings, and accessories. The shop is filled with objects made from several different media—pottery, wood, glass, and stone—as well as fine art and interesting furniture, including pieces produced from the lumber of torn-down buildings. ◆ Daily. 935.2311

Restaurants/Clubs: Red | Hotels: Purple | Shops: Orange | Outdoors/Parks: Green | Sights/Culture: Blue

74 ARROWOOD VINEYARDS AND WINERY

When **Chateau St. Jean**'s longtime winemaker Richard Arrowood first founded his own small winery in 1987 with his wife and partner, Alis Demis Arrowood, he decided to make just one Chardonnay and one Cabernet Sauvignon, using a blend of grapes from several Sonoma County regions. But his passion for producing wine led him to expand and include Merlot, Viognier, Malbec, late-harvest Riesling, Pinot Blanc, and Syrah—all are consistently excellent. Opened in 1998, the **Hospitality House** maintains the winery's New England farmhouse theme, with a wraparound veranda, wood plank floors, a two-story limestone fireplace, and a large marble tasting bar. The maple-leaf flag flies out front right next to the US flag because Alis, who devotes her time to sales and marketing, was born in Canada. The Arrowoods' daughter, Kerry, has become involved in all aspects of the business. ♦ Tasting and sales daily; tours by appointment only. 14347 Sonoma Hwy (between Cavedale and Trinity Rds). 938.5170. www.arrowoodvineyards.com

74 IMAGERY ESTATE WINERY

The Benziger family has launched a new winery with a unique walking tour of Sonoma County's diverse viticultural regions called the Appellation Trail. Check out the art gallery that houses the original art commissioned for the famous Imagery Artist Collection. The Imagery Vineyard Collection features single-vineyard wines. Releases for 2001 include Cabernets from Ash Creek and Sunny Slope vineyards. ♦ Fee. Tasting, sales, and tours daily. Seasonal hours in effect in winter. 14335 Sonoma Hwy

Two of the most popular books on Sonoma are cookbooks. Both of them feature fresh food that you can easily prepare in your own kitchen. *The New Cook's Tour of Sonoma*, by Michele Anna Jordan, showcases Sonoma's bounty in 200 recipes. Jordan's notes and observations have won her a loyal following. *From the Earth to the Table: John Ash's Wine Country Cuisine*, by John Ash and contributor Sid Goldstein, encourages home cooks to prepare beautiful seasonal dishes.

(between Cavedale and Trinity Rds). 935.4500. www.imagerywinery.com

75 OAK HILL FARM

Stop here for organic summer fruits and vegetables, including vine-ripened tomatoes and fresh garlic, plus bouquets of flowers and dried wreaths. ♦ Th-Sa, mid-June through Dec. 15101 Sonoma Hwy (between Cavedale and Trinity Rds). 996.6643

76 B.R. COHN WINERY

As manager of the rock 'n' roll band the Doobie Brothers, Bruce R. Cohn guided the group to fame and fortune. He used his share of the fortune to buy this beautiful property, then known as **Olive Hill Vineyards**, in 1974. In 1984 he released his first wines. Winemaker Merry Edwards heads a team that turns out highly rated Cabernet with grapes from Olive Hill Vineyards. Cohn also produces two Chardonnays, plus Merlot and Pinot Noir, and continues to manage both his music enterprises and the winery from an office in Sonoma. Cohn recently started producing elegantly bottled and distinctively labeled high-quality olive oils—"Sonoma Estate" from the 120-year-old French Picholine trees surrounding the winery, and "California Extra Virgin," a blend of Picholine with California Mission olive oils. Exceptional champagne, red wine, and white wine vinegars are also made and packaged here. ♦ Tasting and sales daily; tours by appointment only. 15140 Sonoma Hwy (between Madrone Rd and Arnold Dr). 938.4064. www.brcohn.com

77 VALLEY OF THE MOON WINERY

Long a landmark with its enormous gnarled (over 400 years old) California bay laurel tree out front, **Kenwood Vineyards** took over this well-established winery in 1997. Renovations were made to incorporate state-of-the-art technology, but the original structure, a low-slung stone building with a galvanized tin roof, was retained. Pat Henderson, a former assistant winemaker at Kenwood, heads up the wine-making operations. The newly reborn winery had its first releases in March 1998—Zinfandel and smaller lots of Syrah, Sangiovese, Pinot Blanc, Chardonnay, and Merlot. The current manager is Harry Parducci, a grandson of Enrico Parducci, the winery's founder. The elder Parducci bought a defunct property in 1941 with 500 acres of vineyards laid out in 1851 by Civil War hero "Fighting"

Joe Hooker. The Parducci family began making affordable estate-bottled premium wines here in the early 1980s. The property was owned at one time by newspaper tycoon William Randolph Hearst's father, Senator George Hearst, who introduced varietals from France and enjoyed pouring his own wines at his home in the nation's capital.♦ Tasting and sales daily. 777 Madrone Rd (between Sonoma Hwy and Arnold Dr). 996.6941; fax 996.5809. www.valleyofthemoonwinery.com

78 Jack London State Historic Park

Just as Robert Louis Stevenson is associated with Napa Valley, Sonoma Valley is Jack London territory. It was London who, in his 1913 novel *The Valley of the Moon*, recounted an Indian legend that says Sonoma means "valley of many moons." This 800-acre park, a memorial to the adventurer and writer, is located on what was once London's beloved **Beauty Ranch**. The highest-paid author of his time, with *Call of the Wild* (1903) and *The Sea Wolf* (1904) under his belt by the age of 28, London settled permanently on his Glen Ellen ranch in 1909. Here visitors can experience the unspoiled landscape much as it was during London's time. Just off Sonoma Highway on the west side of the valley, the well-maintained park is a paradise for hikers and horseback riders, with 9 miles of trails. You can visit the restored white-frame cottage where London and his wife, Charmian, lived and where he wrote many of his books, as well as the log cabin and artificial lake he constructed in tribute to his Klondike days. And don't forget to visit the remarkable **Pig Palace** with its two nearby 40-foot-high silos. You'll also see the eerie remains of **Wolf House**, the dream home built by London and his wife, which mysteriously burned down days before they were to move in. Charmian later built a scaled-down version of Wolf House, which she dubbed the **House of Happy Walls**. Now a touching museum of London memorabilia, it is filled with the furniture, art, and personal photographs the Londons had planned to keep in Wolf House—it even includes a collection of the successful author's rejection slips. Nearby is the tranquil grove of oaks where London is buried. In the 40 years of his life, London managed to write 51 books and 193 short stories (and somehow he also fit in two lifetimes of travel and adventure in exotic locales). Bring a picnic, because you'll want to linger in this magnificent park. A rigorous 3-mile trail leads to the summit of

Sonoma Mountain and a breathtaking view of the Valley of the Moon. ♦ Admission fee per car. 2400 London Ranch Rd (west of Arnold Dr). 938.5216

Within the Jack London State Historic Park:

TRIPLE CREEK HORSE OUTFIT

One of the best ways to see the park is on horseback, riding down trails Jack London once used to survey his Valley of the Moon domain, past lush meadows, redwood groves, and vineyards now owned by London's descendants. The company provides horses for riders of all levels and takes them out in groups of two to 20. You may sign on for a 2-hour horseback ride followed by a personal tour and a picnic at **Benziger Family Winery**. Tourgoers can then proceed in their cars for a beer tasting at **Sonoma Mountain Brewery** and wine at **Kunde Estate Winery**. Children must be at least 8 years old; no previous riding experience is required. This outfit also offers rides in nearby **Sugarloaf Ridge State Park** (see page 124), **Bothe–Napa Valley State Park** in Calistoga (see page 74), and **Annadel State Park** (see page 126). ♦ Jack London State Historic Park rides: Apr-Oct, weather and trails permitting. Sugarloaf Ridge State Park rides: year-round. Reservations required. 933.1600.
www.triplecreekhorseoutfit.com

KENWOOD

The town of Kenwood, the surrounding valley, and what is now **Annadel State Park** were once part of the vast **Rancho Los Guilicos**. The name was a Spanish corruption of Wilikos, the name the Wappo Indians had given their village. In 1834, just after General Vallejo established the Sonoma presidio, smallpox and cholera epidemics reduced the local Native American population by thousands. Those who survived were later driven away or relocated to the Mendocino reservation. Juan Alvarado, the Mexican governor of California, ceded the 18,883-acre ranch to Captain John Wilson, a Scottish sea captain who had married General Vallejo's sister-in-law, Romona Carrillo. Wilson sold the vast holding shortly after the 1846 Bear Flag uprising in Sonoma; the buyer was William Hood, another Scotsman, who had fallen in love with the valley as a young man. Hood was a shipwright, carpenter, and cabinetmaker who made his fortune in real estate in Australia, South America, Canada, and California. The old Indian settlement was soon renamed Kenwood. Laid out in the 1880s, Kenwood was built around a small central plaza where the Gothic **Kenwood Community Church** still stands. On Warm Springs Road is the valley's only stone railroad depot, built in 1887 of basalt quarried in the surrounding hills.

Restaurants/Clubs: Red | **Hotels: Purple** | **Shops: Orange** | **Outdoors/Parks: Green** | **Sights/Culture: Blue**

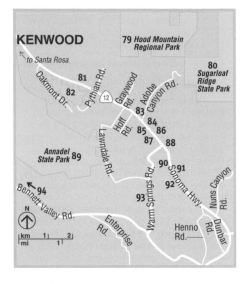

KENWOOD

79 *Hood Mountain Regional Park*

to Santa Rosa

80 *Sugarloaf Ridge State Park*

81

82

Oakmont Dr.

Pythian Rd.

12

Graywood Rd.

Adobe Canyon Rd.

83

84

Hoff Rd.

85 86

87 88

Lawndale Rd.

Annadel State Park 89

90 91

92

93

Warm Springs Rd.

Sonoma Hwy.

Nuns Canyon Rd.

94

Bennett Valley Rd.

N

Enterprise Rd.

Henno Rd.

Dunbar Rd.

km 1 2
mi 1

areas that Congressman John King Luttrell used for the production of charcoal in the late 1890s. The park includes 50 family campsites, each with a tent space, barbecue, and picnic table. There are corrals for horses too. A rigorous foot trail (**Goodspeed Trail**) leads to the adjacent **Hood Mountain Regional Park** (see opposite), but "good speed" here means several hours of hiking. ♦ Admission. 2605 Adobe Canyon Rd (northeast of Sonoma Hwy). Camping reservations: 800/444.7275

Within Sugarloaf Ridge State Park:

81 LEDSON

Kenwood's castle beyond the estate vineyards houses a beautiful tasting room, gourmet market, and gift center. Originally built as a residence, Steve Ledson decided his dream home should become a winery. The Ledsons emigrated from England and have been farming the area and growing grapes since 1862. The tasting menu features Michele's Cuvée, Chardonnay, and Merlot, which is the signature wine from the vineyard on the property. Dark purple in color, with rich chocolate-cherry aromas, this Merlot usually wins the annual Tasters Guild gold medal. Walk in the rose garden or enjoy your wine and food selections in an oak-sheltered picnic area. Special events, which are posted on the web site, include weekend barbecues with live entertainment and invitations to the Reserve tasting room. ♦ Fee. Daily. 7335 Sonoma Hwy (near Pythian Rd). 537.3810. www.ledson.com

79 HOOD MOUNTAIN REGIONAL PARK

🄿 This 1,300-acre park in the Mayacamas Mountains offers hiking and riding trails, campgrounds, and picnic sites. Clamber up Gunsight Rock Lookout for heart-stopping views of Sonoma Valley all the way to San Francisco Bay and, on occasion, the Sierra Nevada. To get to the park, follow Los Alamos Road about 5 miles up to the steep ridge that marks the park boundaries. ♦ Day-use fee. Sa, Su, holidays, Oct-May. 3000 Los Alamos Rd (northeast of Sonoma Hwy). 527.2041

THE
OAKMONT
GOLF CLUB

82 OAKMONT GOLF CLUB

🄿 This semiprivate club offers two 18-hole courses, both designed by Ted Robinson. The 72-par, 6,000-yard **West Course** is championship quality, and the par-63, 4,300-yard **East Course** is the finest executive-style (shorter, faster than a traditional green) course in Northern California.♦ Daily. Oakmont Retirement Community, 7025 Oakmont Dr (off Pythian Rd). West, 539.0415; East, 538.2454

80 SUGARLOAF RIDGE STATE PARK

🄿 The conical ridge that rises behind **Chateau St. Jean** in the heart of the Mayacamas mountain range is known as Sugarloaf Ridge. Follow Adobe Canyon Road as it winds into the hills to the entrance of this spectacular state park. Archeologists believe Sugarloaf Ridge was first inhabited 7,000 years ago. The steep hills of the 2,700-acre park, covered in redwood, fir, oak, and chaparral, offer more than 25 miles of hiking and riding trails. From the park's highest elevations, views extend to Sonoma and Napa Valley— you can even spot San Francisco Bay and the Sierra Nevada. Near the entrance to the park, look for the remains of old charcoal-burning

83 LANDMARK VINEYARDS

The whitewashed California Mission–style complex houses one of the first wineries in the state that concentrated primarily on Chardonnay. The current owners are Damaris Deere Ethridge, the great-granddaughter of John Deere (famous for his tractor company), and her son Michael Colhoun. There's a picnic

Sonoma County boasts 15 golf courses, all within driving distance of Santa Rosa. Ten are 18-holers; the other five are 9-hole courses.

area and a boccie court near the winery's pond. Ask about the hayrides with tastings. For those wishing to spend the night, the winery offers two kinds of accommodations: a comfortable one-bedroom guest cottage, with kitchen, bath, and sitting room overlooking the vineyard; and an elegantly decorated guest suite in its own little cottage-style building with a private patio, cozy fireplace, and eye-popping views of Sugarloaf Ridge and Hood Mountain. ♦ Tasting and sales daily; tours by appointment only. 101 Adobe Canyon Rd (at Sonoma Hwy). 833.0053. www.landmarkwine.com

84 CHATEAU ST. JEAN

One of the best-known boutique wineries of the late 1970s, this establishment now produces well over 235,000 cases per year. The winemaker since 1997 is Steve Reeder, previously wine master at **Kendall-Jackson**, where he played a key role in the development of vineyard-designated wines. Here he also concentrates on single-vineyard wines, notably those from designated wineries: Chardonnay from the acclaimed **Robert Young** and **Belle Terre Vineyards** and a Fumé Blanc from **La Petite Etoile**. The winery also produces Cinq Cépages, a Bordeaux-style blend of "Five Varieties," labeled Cabernet Sauvignon. The Sonoma County line consists of varietal wines blended from various vineyard sources, and small amounts of reserve wines are also produced from each vintage. The winery is renowned for its late-harvest Johannisberg Riesling as well. The 250-acre estate in the shelter of Sugar-loaf Ridge was once the preserve of a wealthy businessman; his former living room is used as the tasting room, and visitors may picnic on the lawn in front of the country mansion. The view of Sonoma Valley from the mock medieval tower is one of the highlights of a visit here. In 1996, the winery was acquired by Beringer Wine Estates, joining **Beringer Vineyards**, **Chateau Souverain**, Meridian Vineyards, Napa Ridge, and Wine World Imports in an impressive portfolio of premium wines. ♦ Tasting, sales daily; tours by appointment only. 8555 Sonoma Hwy (between Warm Springs and Adobe Canyon Rds). 833.4134, 800/543.7572. www.chateaustjean.com

85 ST. FRANCIS WINERY AND VISITORS' CENTER

The original vineyard, planted in 1910, was part of a wedding gift to Alice Kunde (of the prominent grape-growing family) and her husband, Will Behler. The hundred-acre estate is now owned by Lloyd Canton and former

San Francisco furniture dealer Joe Martin and his wife, Emma. Top wines include a fine Merlot (regular and reserve), a Barrel Select Reserve Chardonnay, and a Sonoma Mountain Cabernet. The winery also makes Gewürztraminer. In summer the patio area beckons with picnic tables and views of the surrounding vineyards. ♦ Fee for reserve wines. Tasting and sales daily. 100 Pythian Rd (at Hwy 12). 833.4666; fax 833.6534; 800/543.7713. www.stfranciswine.com

86 SL CELLARS

An eye-catching 1890 blue schoolhouse set behind a rose-bordered picket fence is home to this winery's tasting room. The interiors, though modernized, are hung with historic photos of the school in its heyday and of Kenwood's yesteryear. Tasting lessons are given at the sleek bar. The winery has an award-winning winemaker, Rebecca Martinson, and a national reputation for value. Best known for its Merlot (California and French), it also offers a highly respected Cabernet Sauvignon. The roster includes a Zinfandel, White Zinfandel, and Chardonnay as well. There are many gift items on sale here and a pleasant picnic grove, garden, and resident cat. ♦ Tastings and sales daily. 9380 Sonoma Hwy (between Warm Springs and Adobe Canyon Rds). 833.5070. www.slcellars.com

87 CAFE CITTI

★★$$ Luca and Linda Citti cook their hearts out at this small, casual Italian takeout and trattoria. Lunch features sandwiches on homemade focaccia and pasta dishes with a choice of sauces. For picnics, try one of the spit-roasted chickens. Table service may be slow when it's busy, but the food tastes authentically Italian. Italian groceries are available too, and the espresso is good and strong. There's a lovely garden and outdoor seating. ♦ Italian ♦ Daily, lunch and dinner. 9049 Sonoma Hwy (between Warm Springs and Hoff Rds). 833.2690

KENWOOD

88 KENWOOD VINEYARDS

Originally built in 1906 by the Pagani brothers from Italy who peddled their jug wines door to door, the property's name changed from **Pagani** to **Kenwood** in 1970 when newcomers to the business John Sheela and Mike Lee bought it. They restored and modernized the wood barns that still serve as the cellars and started producing a series of

---

Restaurants/Clubs: Red | Hotels: Purple | Shops: Orange | Outdoors/Parks: Green | Sights/Culture: Blue

excellent wines with Lee as winemaker. In partnership with fourth-generation vintner Gary Heck, Sheela and Lee currently produce 275,000 cases annually. Some of their award-winning wines include Cabernet, Zinfandel, Merlot, Pinot Noir, Sauvignon Blanc, and Chardonnay. The vineyard's most acclaimed wines are the artist Series Cabernet Sauvignon, a collector's item since its first vintage in 1975. Its labels feature work by a renowned artist every year. Artists have included Sam Francis, Miró, Alexander Calder, Joseph Neary, and James Harrill. ♦ Tasting and sales daily; tours by appointment only. 9592 Sonoma Hwy (at Warm Springs Rd). 833.5891. www.kenwoodvineyards.com

89 ANNADEL STATE PARK

The Pomo and Wappo Indian tribes gathered food and obsidian in the wilderness here 3,000 years before Europeans arrived in the area. In 1837 Scottish sea captain John Wilson (who was also General Vallejo's brother-in-law) received a land grant of 18,883 acres from the Mexican government; that parcel included what is now this state park. Between the 1870s and the 1920s Italian stoneworkers cut paving stones from the basalt rock quarried here; production stepped up dramatically just after the 1906 earthquake, when the rebuilding of San Francisco was under way. Today this 5,000-acre park bordering the city of Santa Rosa offers nearly 40 miles of trails for hikers, horseback riders, and mountain bikers. **Getaway Adventures** provides guided mountain biking (568.3040,800/499.2453; www.getawayadventures.com) on single-track and fire trails through meadows, oak, and Douglas fir forests. On hot days they set up lunch by the lake, where you can enjoy a swim. Most trails interconnect and include a wide range of terrain and landscape, from rigorous mountain hiking to leisurely walks through meadows of wildflowers. Head to Lake Ilsanjo for fishing or go bird watching in Ledson Marsh. Camping is available in nearby **Sugarloaf Ridge State Park** (see page 124). ♦ Day-use fee. Entrances at Lawndale Rd (between Keiser Rd and Sonoma Hwy), Kenwood, and Channel Dr (south of Montgomery Dr), Santa Rosa. 539.3911

90 KENWOOD RESTAURANT AND BAR

★★$$ The view is all vineyards from the outdoor terrace here, where you can eat in the shade of large canvas umbrellas. Inside, this California roadhouse with polished wood floors and a natural pine ceiling is simply furnished with white linens and bamboo chairs. Chef Max Schacher features the same appealing California wine-country menu at both lunch and dinner. There's also a large,

reasonably priced wine list to choose from. For white wines, Schacher might offer oysters on the half shell; crab cakes with cress and herb mayonnaise; poached salmon in a creamy caper sauce; or rabbit braised in white wine. The Caesar salad is also excellent. Red-wine aficionados can select from lamb, New York steak with shallot–herb butter, a burger with thick-cut fries, and roasted duck in cherry sauce.♦ California ♦ Tu-Su, lunch and dinner. 9900 Sonoma Hwy (between Dunbar and Warm Springs Rds). 833.6326; fax 833.2238

91 KUNDE ESTATE WINERY

The 2,000 acres of rolling hills at this over-a-century-old winery are covered with grapevines, oak trees, and grazing pastures. Another attraction is the romantic stone ruin of a winery that was built here in 1882. The Kunde family is one of the largest grape growers in Sonoma County, supplying the fruit to several other wineries. In 1990 the vineyard made its first Chardonnay, Sauvignon Blanc, Cabernet Sauvignon, and Zinfandel, and today winemaker David Noyes produces a range of distinctive wines, all aged in Kunde caves. They include Chardonnay, Sauvignon Blanc, Cabernet Sauvignon, Merlot, Viognier, Syrah, and Zinfandel. All the winery's vintages can be sampled in its tasting room. There are picnic facilities on the grounds. ♦ Tasting and sales daily; F-Su, guided cave tours. 10155 Sonoma Hwy (between Nuns Canyon and Warm Springs Rds). 833.5501; fax 833.2204

92 KENWOOD INN & SPA

$$$$ Former San Francisco contractor Terry Grimm and his wife, Roseann, a restaurateur who owns the Anchor Oyster Bar in San Francisco, transformed an old antiques store into this posh *pensione* with 12 rooms and suites. The living room and kitchen area are defined with Italianate colors—rusts and ambers—and the full breakfast continues the Italian theme, with Mediterranean egg dishes, polenta, and freshly baked fruit tarts and pastries. Each of the suites is very different in size, décor, and feeling, though all have fireplaces and private baths. Sensualists will appreciate the down comforters and Egyptian cotton sheets. The **Tuscany Suite** upstairs is the most private, featuring a small stone balcony overlooking the swimming pool, a separate living room deco-

rated in honey-colored hues, and a view of the **Kunde Estate Winery**. A potpourri of spa treatments is another attraction, including a range of massage techniques, mud and enzyme wraps, sea salt scrubs, facials, and ancient ayurvedic body ritual purification. There's also a Jacuzzi and steam room. The spa is also open to nonguests (with reservations). ♦ 10400 Sonoma Hwy (between Dunbar and Warm Springs Rds). 833.1293. www.kenwoodinn.com

93 MORTON'S WARM SPRINGS

This spot provides the setting for a local family tradition in Kenwood for summer swimming and picnics. It has been open since 1887, and was recently remodeled. The three swimming pools are heated by the naturally warm springs. Indians used to bring their sick to bathe in its waters, and early pioneers created an impromptu bathhouse by putting up a burlap sack around a wooden tub. At the turn of the century, the springs were a popular resort. The water still bubbles out of the ground at 87 degrees (too cool to be classified as a hot spring), and is cooled a bit for use in the swimming pool. Plan on spending the day here; there are 25 or so barbecues and picnic tables, plus a baseball diamond, volleyball and basketball courts, and a snack bar. ♦ Fee. Sa, Su, May-Sept. 1651 Warm Springs Rd (between Bennett Valley and Lawndale Rds). 833.5511

94 MATANZAS CREEK WINERY

For a scenic drive, take Warm Springs Road to Bennett Valley Road to get to this showcase winery overlooking the Sonoma Mountains. Owned by Bill and Sandra MacIver, it is an inviting place, with a loggia leading up to the tasting room and tables on a deck sheltered by a centuries-old oak. The winery's Chardonnays have always appeared on the most discerning wine lists in the country; and current winemakers Bill Parker and Susan Reed continue this tradition. The Chardonnays remain among the best in California, and the Sauvignon Blanc is also top grade. The Merlot is very much in demand. You'll also find the Matanzas Creek poster by painter Mary Silverwood on sale here. But this winery is more than a destination for wine connoisseurs. Visitors come for the gardens: a 2-acre terraced lavender garden with 4,500 plants is just part of this, one of Sonoma's most memorable landscapes. Also here are rare perennials and massive displays of foliage, all seemingly part of their natural surroundings. The two million stems of lavender harvested annually produce a wide range of estate-grown products, from sachets and potpourri to silk wands. A self-guided tour covers the garden highlights and includes tips for home gardeners.♦ Tasting, sales, and guided tours daily. 6097 Bennett Valley Rd (west of Sonoma Mountain Rd), Santa Rosa. 528.6464. www.matanzascreek.com

---

Restaurants/Clubs: Red | Hotels: Purple | Shops: Orange | Outdoors/Parks: Green | Sights/Culture: Blue

SANTA ROSA

In 1875 Luther Burbank took his older brother's enthusiastic advice to leave the East Coast and move to Santa Rosa. Burbank immediately liked the place. "I firmly believe, from what I have seen, that this is the chosen spot of all this earth as far as nature is concerned," he wrote. For more than 50 years the world-renowned horticulturist labored here in his greenhouse and gardens, producing more than 800 new varieties of fruits, vegetables, and other plants.

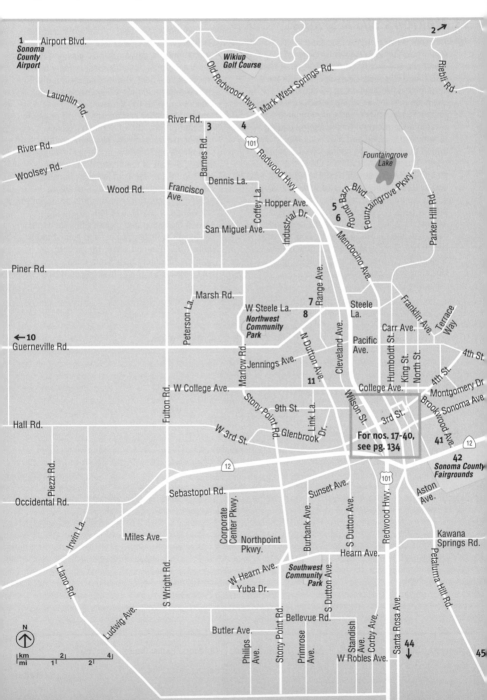

For nos. 17–40, see pg. 134

Santa Rosa was once part of an immense Spanish land grant held by Doña Maria Ignacia Lopez Carrillo, the mother-in-law of General Mariano Guadalupe Vallejo. Americans first came to Santa Rosa to establish a trading post in 1846, and it was incorporated as a town 8 years later.

Santa Rosa, which is Sonoma's county seat, is home to more than 155,000 people and is just minutes from the **Valley of the Moon** and about a half hour from the town of **Healdsburg**, in the heart of the **Russian River Valley**. The city is considered the hub of **Sonoma County** because most of the main roads cross here.

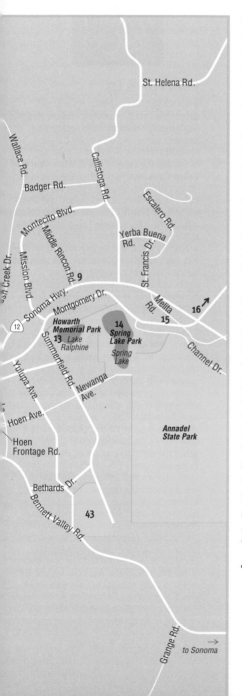

A quiet town that recalls another era, Santa Rosa offers a respite for those who find the country a little too quiet but don't want San Francisco–style nightlife. **Historic Railroad Square**, just west of the freeway in downtown Santa Rosa, is a six-square-block area of restored turn-of-the-19th-century buildings filled with antiques shops, stores, and restaurants. And **Fourth Street**, the main artery of Santa Rosa's restored downtown area, comes alive every Wednesday night from May to September with an exuberant farmers' market featuring music, street food, arts and crafts, and entertainment that attracts 4,000 to 6,000 people per week from near and far. Its tenth anniversary was 1998.

History buffs will want to visit the **Sonoma County Museum** and the **Luther Burbank Home and Gardens**. Across the street from Burbank's home is the **Church Built of One Tree** in **Juilliard Park**, which was entirely constructed from the lumber provided by one enormous redwood. Santa Rosa is surrounded by 5,000 acres of city, county, and state parks offering everything from walking, hiking, and horseback-riding trails to campgrounds and lakes for fishing, swimming, and boating. One of Sonoma County's top restaurants, **John Ash & Co.**, is in Santa Rosa, and bed-and-breakfasts and several comfortable inns lie on the northern outskirts of town, including the deluxe **Vintners Inn**.

1 CHARLES M. SCHULZ SONOMA COUNTY AIRPORT

Only private planes and charter planes fly to this county airport. Rental cars are available from **Avis** and **Hertz.** ♦ 2200 Airport Blvd (just west of Laughlin Rd). 524.7240

2 SAFARI WEST

🐘 Visitors' first impression is one of entering the African savanna. Antelope, zebras, Watusi cattle, giraffes—more than 350 animals—roam the 400-acre preserve. A naturalist drives through the preserve in a safari vehicle, stopping to acquaint visitors with the exotic and extinct-in-the-wild African animals and birds. You'll meet auodads, Thomson's gazelles, and Indian hornbills; you'll learn how to feed a giraffe and how to detect emotion in a zebra's ears. In the early 1990s Peter and Nancy Lang opened their preserve to tours. ♦ 3115 Porter Creek Rd (at Franz Valley Rd, 6.7 mi from Hwy 101). 579.2551, 800/616.2695. www.safariwest.com

Within Safari West wildlife preserve:

SAFARI WEST

$$$ Overnight guests often awake in the morning to the sight of zebras galloping across the hillside. Bedding down in these authentic safari tents from South Africa is quite comfortable. The bedframe, bedside table, clothing rack, and desk are handcrafted from recycled timber at the preserve. The shower is also a canvas enclosure but completely private. Drought-resistant plantings surround the 30 cabins, sited for optimal animal viewing. Complimentary breakfast is served in the **Savannah Café**, which is also open for lunch and buffet-style dinners.

3 VINTNERS INN

$$ Set amid vineyards, this 44-room luxury inn was acquired by Don and Rhonda Carano. The inn blends European style with the ambiance of California wine country. Rooms are furnished with pine antiques and quilts; amenities also include first-class room service, a concierge, TVs, and in-room phones. The four Spanish-style, two-story buildings with red-tile roofs face an inner courtyard with a fountain. All of the rooms are spacious, but those on the upper floor get a great view as well. Suites boast a fireplace and a wet bar, plus a refrigerator for chilling wine. The inn also features a sundeck and an outdoor whirlpool and serves a good-size

A typical oak aging barrel holds enough wine for about 25 cases. Barrels can be used more than once.

breakfast that includes fresh fruit and homemade waffles and muffins. This is a nonsmoking hotel. ♦ 4350 Barnes Rd (just south of River Rd). 575.7350; fax 575.1426. www.vintnersinn.com

Within Vintners Inn:

JOHN ASH & CO.

★★★★$$$$ Save up for a meal at this casual-yet-chic wine-country enclave that has Southwestern-inspired décor, entrancing vineyard views, and an exciting menu. Founder John Ash (who is also culinary director of the **Fetzer Food & Wine Center** at **Valley Oaks** near Hopland) pioneered wine-country cooking, bringing a diversity of influences—French, Italian, Asian, and South-western—to bear on Sonoma's bounty of local ingredients. With executive chef Jeff Madura at the helm, the restaurant carries on Ash's artistically inspired cuisine, turning out dishes with both imagination and flair. The selections on the frequently changing menu are enhanced by fresh herbs and vegetables from the restaurant's vineyard garden. On a chilly night you might start with onion soup with house-made croutons and topped with Gruyère cheese or mixed Sonoma greens topped with candied walnuts and a choice of dressings. Main courses range from a first-class butternut squash risotto with spot prawns, wild mushrooms, and Sonoma jack cheese to grilled fillet of beef with artichoke pesto served with roasted pepper chutney and basil Béarnaise. Seasonal game such as venison is prepared with a black-eyed pea pilaf to be enjoyed with a dried fig and port sauce. Desserts by pastry chef Patricia Di Falco command as much attention as the main courses; highlights might include chocolate raspberry cheesecake in a phyllo nest with raspberry sauce, angel-food cake with lemon curd and strawberries, fresh crisp of the day with vanilla ice cream, vanilla crème brûlée, and a seasonal sorbet. The wine list offers a broad range of Sonoma County vintages, as well as a select few from the rest of Northern California. A special reserve list includes older vintages of California wines, plus Bordeaux and Burgundies. A fine feature is wines by the glass offered in half-glass servings for those who want to pair wines with each of their food courses but do not wish to buy several bottles. ♦ California ♦ Tu-Sa, lunch and dinner; Su, dinner. Reservations recommended. 527.7687

4 LUTHER BURBANK CENTER FOR THE ARTS

The three theaters here are used for guest lectures, concerts, and performances by big-name artists such as the late Ray Charles, Johnny Mathis, Barbara Mandrell, and the late Victor Borge. Call for a schedule of events. ♦ Mark West Springs Rd (between Old Redwood and Redwood Hwys). 546.3600

Sonoma County Hilton

5 SONOMA COUNTY HILTON

$$ The Hilton hotel chain took over this attractive chalet-style property in 1998 and thoroughly renovated it. The 250 spacious guest rooms and suites are pleasantly decorated with a wine-country feel—grapes and winey color schemes—and have a host of in-room amenities, plus a well-equipped business center. A big attraction here is the **Nectar** restaurant, open for breakfast, lunch, and dinner, with an adjoining outdoor bar and smashing view of the Santa Rosa Valley. There's a junior Olympic-size pool, hot tub, and on-site gym and vollyeball courts. ♦ 3555 Round Barn Blvd (north of Fountaingrove Pkwy). 523.7555, 800/445.8667; fax 559.5550

6 FOUNTAINGROVE INN

$$ Understated luxury is the theme at this contemporary inn on the old **Fountaingrove Ranch**. All of the 126 rooms and suites in the original building and similarly styled new wing are decorated with simplicity and taste, featuring custom-designed furniture and attention to details, such as soundproofing, separate dressing alcoves, double closets, and work spaces with modem jacks. Some suites feature a Jacuzzi and a dining area. There is also a beautifully landscaped pool with a waterfall and an outdoor Jacuzzi. A sumptuous California continental buffet breakfast is included, as is afternoon tea and cookies. Special wine-tasting packages bring a double room here into the price range of most of the area's bed-and-breakfasts. ♦ 101 Fountaingrove Pkwy (at Mendocino Ave). 578.6101

Within the Fountaingrove Inn:

EQUUS

★★★$$$$ The hotel's restaurant offers an exceptional seasonal menu. The large room, made to seem more intimate with wooden dividers, has an air of understated elegance. Tables are well spaced for conversation, which makes it a magnet for businesspeople. One of the attractions here is a wine list of nearly 300 selections, including what the management believes to be the most extensive selection of Sonoma wines in the world. Though the menu is seasonal and changes frequently, among the first-rate appetizers might be blackened ahi tuna, perfectly complemented with a salad of green papaya and other vegetables in a soy-ginger-sesame dressing, or rock shrimp cakes with a spicy chipotle sauce. For a main course, try pan-seared Petaluma duck served with braised fennel, spinach, diced tomatoes, and roasted polenta, or grilled swordfish with a pesto-and-olive tapenade. Loretta Patzwald makes incredible desserts—our favorite is the Valrhona triple chocolate torte, a melt-in-the-mouth soufflé confection layered with truffle filling and bittersweet chocolate ganache. Lunch features pizzas, sandwiches—including a first-rate burger—pastas, a selection of appetizers, salads, and a few warm main courses. ♦ California ♦ M-Sa, lunch and dinner; Su, brunch and dinner. Reservations recommended. 578.0149

7 REDWOOD EMPIRE ICE ARENA

Peanuts cartoonist Charles Schulz, one of Santa Rosa's most eminent citizens, came up with the idea for this Olympic-size ice-skating rink, which opened in 1969. You can rent skates here or bring your own. Fans of Schulz's long-running comic strip will want to visit the gallery next door (see below). ♦ Daily. 1667 W Steele La (between Range Ave and Coffey La). 546.7147

7 SNOOPY'S GALLERY & GIFT SHOP

The world's largest collection of Snoopy memorabilia and merchandise is housed here—and Schulz generously permitted Charlie Brown, Lucy, Linus, and the rest of the *Peanuts* gang to hawk their likenesses here too. Don't miss the collection of Schulz's original drawings and personal photos. ♦ Daily. 1665 W Steele La (between Range Ave and Coffey La). 546.3385; fax 546.3764

Restaurants/Clubs: Red | **Hotels: Purple** | Shops: Orange | **Outdoors/Parks: Green** | Sights/Culture: Blue

WINE-TASTING TIPS

- White wine should be served chilled but not icy. If it's too cold, the flavors and aromas will be suppressed. Conversely, a red wine should not be too warm. Reds should be served at room temperature, but not if the room in question is hot (80 degrees Fahrenheit or higher). When red wine is too warm, the alcohol is accentuated and the wine tastes coarser and harsher than it should.

- Before pouring a bottle of wine, sniff the wineglass to make sure it hasn't picked up any odors of wood from the cupboard and that there's no soap residue, which will affect the wine's taste.

- Fill a wineglass only one-quarter to one-third full. If the glass is too full, the wine cannot *aerate* (mix with air) properly, and it will be difficult to swirl the wine and experience its aroma.

- Hold the glass by the base or stem up to the light, and look at the *clarity* of the wine. It should be anywhere from clear to brilliant. Then note its *color*. Whites range from pale yellow to golden, rosés from pink to orange-pink, and reds from light purple to deep ruby.

- Swirl the wine around in the glass. This aerates it, which releases the *aroma*. Hold the glass under your nose and breathe deeply. The aroma should be reminiscent of the grape from which the wine was made. Then note the *bouquet*, which results from the aging process and is stronger in older red wines and dessert wines.

- Take a sip and swirl it around in your mouth. Keeping a sense of the wine's aroma and bouquet in mind, try to determine its *texture* and *balance*. Is it dry or sweet? Soft or tart? Full-bodied?

8 CHARLES M. SCHULZ MUSEUM AND RESEARCH CENTER

Welcome to the *Peanuts* universe, where you can relive the triumphs and trials of a boy, his impish dog, and their oddball neighborhood pals. Atop his dog house Snoopy played out his alter-egos: WWI flying ace, world-famous writer, world-famous attorney, Easter beagle, and Joe Cool. Cartoonist Charles Schulz modeled Snoopy on his boyhood pet: a black-and-white dog named Spike. Across the south wall of the museum's Great Hall spans a tile mural of Charlie Brown and Lucy, while a massive three-dimensional wood sculpture, "Morphing Snoopy," hangs on the east wall. The complex includes the Snoopy Gift Shop and Gallery, outdoor gardens with a labyrinth in the shape of Snoopy's head, and art installations. Nearby is Schulz's studio, where he produced 52 years of comic strips. At Railroad Square, from where the museum offers a free shuttle service, visit Stan Pawlowski's bronze sculpture of Charlie Brown and Snoopy. ◆ W-M. Admission. 2301 Hardies La (exit Steele La from Hwy 101 and follow signs). 579.4452. www.schulzmuseum.org

9 RINCON CYCLERY

You can rent bikes by the hour, by the day, or by the week here. Take one of the 24-speed mountain bikes up to a trail in nearby **Annadel, Sugarloaf Ridge**, or **Jack London State Parks**. Helmets and bike racks are also available. ◆ Daily. 4927-H Sonoma Hwy (between Jack London Dr and Middle Rincon Rd). 538.0868, 800/965.BIKE; fax 538.0879

10 DE LOACH VINEYARDS

Noted for their Russian River Chardonnay, Cecil and Christine De Loach make wines in an easy, accessible style. Their top-of-the-line O.F.S. ("our finest selection") is a rich, barrel-fermented Chardonnay. They also make Sauvignon Blanc, Fumé Blanc, Gewürztraminer, and White Zinfandel, along with the original Zinfandel, red, and Pinot Noir. A few picnic tables are set out with views of the vineyard. ◆ Tasting and sales daily; tours by appointment only. 1791 Olivet Rd (between Guerneville and Piner Rds). 526.9111. www.deloachvineyards.com

10 MARTINI & PRATI

In the Martini family since 1902, this is one of California's oldest wineries in continuous operation. The rambling old ranch-style establishment, situated on 8 acres, produces California-style Italian wines under two labels: Martini & Prati and Fountain Grove. But the history of wine—even more than the wine itself—is the main reason to visit here; in fact, the winery has been mentioned in *The Wine Spectator* as one of California's top 10 historic wineries. Some of the immense redwood tanks here are 100 years old. As did his turn-of-the-19th-century predecessors, vintner Bob Goyette still invites visitors to purchase a jug of their rich red blend of Zinfandel and Carignane and fill it directly from the tank, unrefined and unfiltered, just like in the old days. Though true wine connoisseurs and critics frown at these antics, come with an open mind and you'll enjoy yourself, the wine, and history too. The walls of Elmo's Groceria, which is also the tasting room and shop, are hung with historic family pictures and mementos; the shelves are stocked with picnic victuals. Visitors can sip and /or feast at tables under the old shade trees. The winery is a convenient stop en route to the Russian River Valley. ♦ Tasting and sales daily; tours 11AM or by appointment. 2191 Laguna Rd (between Guerneville and Vine Hill Rds). 823.2404

10 ZAZU

★★★$$$ This roadhouse restaurant, with copper-top tables and large windows overlooking vineyards, has its roots in the kitchens of wine-growing families. Wife-and-husband team Duskie Estes and John Stewart, both accomplished chefs, base their menu on American and Northern Italian cuisine. The menu changes nightly but features authentic, rustic Tuscan dishes like vin santo–braised rabbit with chestnut pappardelle and seared Sonoma duck with goat cheese gnocchi. American classics—updated with local meat, cheese, and seasonal produce—also shine. Try the wild salmon with corn griddle cakes or the side orders of buttermilk mashed potatoes and fried green tomatoes with Tabasco aioli. The chefs also ply their desserts with Sonoma County ingredients. Try the nectarine and blueberry crisp or Scharffen Berger chocolate bourbon cake. ♦ W-Su, dinner; Su, brunch. 3535 Guerneville Rd (at Willowside). 523.4814

11 SASSAFRAS

★★★$$$ A bright newcomer to Santa Rosa's burgeoning restaurant scene, this restaurant and wine bar infuses its menus with Sonoma County products, giving new sparkle to old favorites. The Caesar salad is topped with tapenade and the house salad with Blue Lake green beans. Award-winning Redwood Hill crottin goat cheese in pastry tops lemon-herb green sauce, tomatoes, and baby spinach. You can also order entrées in "starter" portions, a welcome option for gourmands. You don't have to choose between the braised leg of Muscovy

duck with dried figs, olives, and Pinot Noir and the rare yellowfin tuna wrapped in smoked ham. Chef Scott Snyder and manager Michael Hirschberg teamed up to open Sassafras in the Santa Rosa Business Park. Whether you're in for a snack at the wine bar or a five-course dinner complete with specially paired wines, Sassafras fills the bill. ♦ American. ♦ M-F, lunch; daily, dinner and wine bar. 1229 North Dutton Ave (between W College and Jennings Aves). 578.7600. www.sassafrasrestaurant.com

12 FLAMINGO RESORT HOTEL CONFERENCE CENTER

$ Here's a pleasant boon for the budget: 170 spacious, comfortable, attractive rooms and suites at moderate rates divided among the landmark 1957 property and the new convention annex. Additional pluses are a 25-meter heated pool, separate outdoor spa for up to 10 people, five tennis courts, table tennis, and shuffleboard. The **Terrace Grill** overlooks a garden, and the **Cabaret** lounge features live entertainment and dancing on weekends. Guests also have access to the well-equipped **Montecito Heights Health and Racquet Club** (see below) for a modest fee. ♦ 2777 Fourth St (at Long Dr). 545.8530, 800/848.8300; fax 528.1404

At the Flamingo Resort Hotel Conference Center:

MONTECITO HEIGHTS HEALTH AND RACQUET CLUB

This state-of-the-art fitness center offers a cardiovascular room, weight room, aerobics studio, all manner of fitness machines—NordicTrack, Gravitron, treadmills—plus sauna, steam room, and whirlpool facilities. The club also has outdoor full-court basketball, a regulation volleyball court, and a lighted jogging path. Massages are also available. For hotel guests only; not open to the public. ♦ Daily. 526.0529; fax 528.1404

13 HOWARTH MEMORIAL PARK

Pack that fishing pole and cooking gear and head for Lake Ralphine to catch some lunch—catfish, black bass, trout, and bluegill—in this park owned and operated by the city. The park has picnic and barbecue facilities so you can cook your catch right here. After-lunch activities include a hiking trail and, for the kids, a playground, a merry-go-round, pony rides, a miniature train ride, and an animal farm. Canoes, paddleboats, rowboats, and sailboats are available to rent too. ♦ Fee for each ride. Summerfield Rd (between Medica Rd and Montgomery Dr). 524.5115

Restaurants/Clubs: Red | Hotels: Purple | Shops: Orange | Outdoors/Parks: Green | Sights/Culture: Blue

14 SPRING LAKE PARK

This state park is on the east side of Santa Rosa, between Howarth Memorial Park and Annadel State Park; it has campsites, rest rooms, shower facilities, hiking and equestrian trails, and a 72-acre lake. It is open for swimming and boating during the summer and stocked with catfish, black bass, trout, and bluegill for year-round fishing. Launch your own boat or rent a sailboat, canoe, or rowboat for a modest hourly charge; the lake is a popular spot for windsurfing too. Access to the camping area is available via Newanga Avenue; the campsites are available on a first-come, first-served basis. ◆ Park: daily. Campsites: daily between Memorial Day and Labor Day; F-Su and holidays, the rest of the year. 5390 Montgomery Dr (between Channel and Jackson Drs). 539.8092 (general park information), 539.8082 (campground information)

15 MELITA STATION INN

$$ Near **Annadel State Park** on the winding country road that served as the old Sonoma Highway is a six-room bed-and-breakfast in a restored turn-of-the-century train station. This comfortable inn is filled with American folk art and antiques. Five of the six rooms have private baths, and a full country breakfast (juice, fruit, muffins or bread, and an omelette or another main course) is included. The location, at the head of the Valley of the Moon, is ideal for winery touring by bike or car. ◆ 5850 Melita Rd (at Montgomery Dr). 538.7712

16 ADLER FELS WINERY

Founded in 1980 by Dave Coleman and his wife, Ayn Ryan, whose family had a hand in starting **Chateau St. Jean**, this tiny winery sits high atop a 26-foot-wide ridge, very near the outcropping of rock that locals have dubbed Eagle Rock (*adler fels* in German—hence the winery's name). The half-timbered building looks a bit like something from the Rhine or Alsace. White wine is the focus here—Chardonnay, Fumé Blanc, and Gewürztraminer. ◆ Tasting, sales, and tours daily by appointment only, 5325 Corrick La (off Los Alamos Rd), Santa Rosa. 539.3123. Tastings also at The Wine Room, 9575 Sonoma Hwy, Kenwood. 833.6131

17 SONOMA COUNTY MUSEUM

Housed in the old **Post Office and Federal Building** (built in 1909 by James Knox Taylor), the county museum has a permanent collection of 19th-century landscape paintings and a permanent display on the history of Sonoma County. Other exhibits change frequently, but all relate to Sonoma County and the North Bay. On one visit, you may find an exhibit of

Pomo Indian basketry with fine black-and-white photos of the basket-making process, a show of local woodwork, or an exhibit with a Victorian theme. Check the museum gift shop for books on Sonoma history and architecture, work from local craftspeople, and souvenirs of Sonoma County. ◆ Nominal admission. W-Su. 425 Seventh St (between B and A Sts). 579.1500

18 SIZZLING TANDOOR

★★$$ Jessie Singh has filled his menu with specialties from Punjab, the North Indian state from which he hails. Using the eponymous tandoori method—the delicious Punjabi version of barbecue—chicken, meat, or fish is marinated in a blend of yogurt and spices and then cooked in a tandoor (jar-shaped clay oven). Try it with *nan* (the teardrop-shaped tandoori bread). There also are a host of other offerings, including curries, rice pilau (cooked with herbs and spices), a number of delicious vegetarian options, and a daily buffet lunch. ◆ Indian ◆ M-Sa, lunch and dinner; Su, dinner. 409 Mendocino Ave (between Fifth and Ross Sts). 579.5999. Also at 9960 Hwy 1, Jenner. 865.0625

19 CAFE LOLÓ

★★★$$$ Talented chef Michael Quigley and his wife, Lori Darling, work together to make this intimate eatery one of the best in the wine country. The décor is chic and elegant, with crisp white table linen and colorful flowers everywhere. The menu changes according to what fresh ingredients are available each day. The list of appetizers may include salad tossed with balsamic vinaigrette and fresh crab cake topped with remoulade and served with a watercress salad. Entrées might include a sea scallop and potato napoleon with chive butter and roasted beets, oven-roasted chicken breast over caramelized onions and sweet peppers with risotto cakes, and braised beef cheeks with simmered root vegetables. ♦ California ♦ M-F, lunch and dinner; Sa, dinner. 620 Fifth St (between D St and Mendocino Ave). 576.7822

20 LAST RECORD STORE

Rock, blues, reggae, classical, and world music have all found a home in this exceptional store. An amazing assortment of new and used recordings is available, some of them on old-fashioned vinyl. Tapes and CDs also are in stock. ♦ Daily. 739 Fourth St (between E and D Sts). 525.1963

21 TREEHORN BOOKS

This bookstore has a good cookbook section, including the one-volume collection of five books by renowned Glen Ellen food writer M.F.K. Fisher, and books on California wine-country cooking. It also has a wonderful selection of children's books, including old and rare works. ♦ Daily. 625 Fourth St (between D St and Mendocino Ave). 525.1782

22 EPIPHANY MUSICAL INSTRUMENTS

This store sells exotic, little-known African and Asian instruments used by each continent's various cultures. Where else could you purchase a 6-inch thumb piano from Zululand or a 31-inch tong drum mounted on a 4-foot tower from China? A knowledgeable staff of professional musicians and recording artists can answer your questions and offer instruction. ♦ Daily. 640 Fourth St. 543.7008

23 SONOMA COFFEE CO.

The toasty and tantalizing scent of whole-bean coffees pervades this long, narrow shop, where a sandblasted brick wall stands in as an informal photography and print gallery. A collection of thermoses sits atop an old Wedgwood stove for the serve-it-yourself house coffee; they also offer espresso drinks and an array of morning pastries. ♦ Daily. 521 Fourth St (between Mendocino Ave and B St). 573.8022

23 CAFFÈ PORTOFINO RISTORANTE & BAR

★★$$$ The bar at the front of this café is a popular spot for wine tasting. Best bets on the menu are the classic bruschetta (toasted bread rubbed with garlic and olive oil and topped with Parmesan cheese); buffalo-milk mozzarella, garden tomatoes, and basil drizzled with olive oil; and Caesar salad prepared at the table. The linguine with garlic and fresh clams in Chardonnay is decent, and the gnocchi con pesto (potato dumplings with basil pesto and Parmesan) is an authentic Genoese preparation. You can't go wrong with simply prepared grilled items such as fresh salmon or lamb chops served Roman style with a mint sauce. At lunch you might try the special panini (sandwiches), but they're really more American than Italian. In good weather, you can eat either inside or on the sidewalk at umbrella-shaded tables. ♦ Italian ♦ M-Sa, lunch and dinner. 535 Fourth St (between Mendocino Ave and B St). 523.1171; fax 522.8190

24 WEDNESDAY NIGHT FARMERS' MARKET

Between Memorial Day and Labor Day, downtown Santa Rosa's Fourth Street is closed to traffic on Wednesday nights, when it becomes the site of a remarkably successful farmers' market. With live music, jugglers, magicians, and plenty of food, it's a nonstop party that attracts people from miles around. Get down with everything from grilled sausages and beer to fresh pastries and breads. And take home some of the Holy Smokes barbecue sauce and jams from **Kozowski Farms** in Forestville. The farmers set up their stalls along B Street, touting their luscious strawberries, goat cheese, spring onions, Santa Rosa plums, and whatever else the season has to offer. Bring a big shopping bag because it's impossible not to get into the spirit of things. ♦ W, 5:30-7:30PM, 28 May-3 Sept. Fourth and B Sts. 524.2123

25 TRAVERSO'S GOURMET FOODS AND WINE

Since 1929 this Italian deli, opened by Louis and Enrico Traverso, two brothers from Genoa, has been a treasure trove of local and Italian foodstuffs. It has a decent selection of local cheese and cold cuts already sliced for fast service, plus all the standard fixins. To stock the pantry, shop for Californian and Italian olive oils, vinegars, Sonoma County dried tomatoes, and jams. In the well-stocked wine section, vintage photos give a glimpse of Santa Rosa in the 1930s and 1940s. Ask about the used wine-shipment boxes for mailing between two and 12 bottles. ♦ M-Sa. 106 B St (at Third St). 542.2530; fax 542.0736

Restaurants/Clubs: Red | Hotels: Purple | Shops: Orange | Outdoors/Parks: Green | Sights/Culture: Blue

26 A'ROMA ROASTERS & COFFEEHOUSE

This is the best coffeehouse/club in town, with great espresso, cappuccino, *caffè latte*, and house specialties. When it's sweltering outside, come in for a refreshing Italian soda, or iced coffee, or one of the frappés of the day. The bright red French roaster trimmed in brass sits right in the middle of the store, filling the air with the heady scent of fresh-roasted coffee. There are 18 varieties of coffee to choose from; also here to tempt you are organic fruit pies and other scrumptious locally made desserts. Friday and Saturday they feature live music, ranging from flamenco guitar and chamber music to jazz and blues. ◆ Daily. 95 Fifth St (at Wilson St). 576.7765; fax 577.7711

27 HOTEL LA ROSE

$$ Located in a turn-of-the-century stone building in **Historic Railroad Square**, this establishment offers 49 rooms with private baths and simple décor: flowered wallpaper, rose comforters, period reproductions, and TV sets; recently renovated bathrooms, although smallish, boast rich marble walls. The hotel has a sundeck, air conditioning, **Josef's** restaurant (French, 571.8664), a pleasant bar downstairs with a fireplace, and 24-hour room service. Continental breakfast is included. Ask about midweek specials. ◆ 308 Wilson St (between Fourth and Fifth Sts). 579.3200, 800/527.6738. www.hotellarose.com

28 MIXX

★★★$$$ This hot spot features inventive yet homey California-style fare for lunch and dinner with an emphasis on fresh seasonal ingredients and Sonoma delicacies. Chicken potpie; smoked BLT on whole wheat with a choice of salad, fries, rings, or slaw; and a wonderful green chili stew with corn bread might be some of the lunch selections. At dinner, the menu focuses on the freshest of fish and pasta dishes plus some outstanding combinations such as Sonoma rabbit paired with polenta, pancetta (bacon), and wild mushrooms in a Dijon mustard sauce, and chili- and maple-rubbed rack of lamb with wild mushroom tamales in a Zinfandel sauce. Treat your sweet tooth to frozen white chocolate mousse cake on fresh berry coulis or crème brûlée. Some items on the menu are offered as either a "small dish" or "large dish," and heart symbols guide those watching their fat intake. The excellent wine list features vintages that have won gold medals at the Sonoma County Harvest Fair; some of the desserts have gold-medaled there too. Next door at **Mixx Express** (573.5845), you can pick up a scrumptious onion-walnut bread, some of the restaurant's many-splendored desserts, cookies, and morning pastries. ◆ California ◆ M-F, lunch and dinner; Sa, dinner. Mixx Express, M-F, 7AM-3PM; Sa, 8:30AM-3PM. 135 Fourth St (at Davis St). 573.1344

28 OLDE TOWNE JEWELERS

Select a fabulous bauble from this shop's glittering array of antique, estate, and modern jewelry. There's also an extensive collection of antique and vintage pocket and wrist watches. Watch and jewelry repair is also done here. ◆ M-Sa. 125 Fourth St (between Davis and Wilson Sts). 577.8813

29 SYRAH

★★★$$$ The menus at Syrah read like a romance novel. The seared scallops come with truffle carrot broth, the pan-roasted duck breast with andouille sausage and black barley, and the venison with mulled red wine sauce. Chef Josh Silvers creates magic in an unlikely setting: a 1940s Nash Rambler dealership. Save room for the whiskey bread pudding, chocolate orange torte, or ginger spiced cake. Syrah features an exceptional list of late-harvest dessert wines, ports, and ice wine, including the Inniskillin sparkling ice wine from Canada. Desserts are not the only after-dinner indulgence. Sample the chef's personal horde of local and imported cheeses. The St. George from the Matos family's Santa Rosa creamery has a tangy, nutty flavor and a Portuguese-style open texture. ◆ Californian ◆ Tu-Sa, lunch and dinner. 205 Fifth St (at Davis St). 568.4002. www.syrahbistro.com

30 HISTORIC RAILROAD SQUARE

In 1870 the first Santa Rosa–North Pacific train chugged into town, bringing San Franciscans to the countryside. The restored old depot is now home of the **Santa Rosa Convention & Visitors Bureau** and the **California Welcome Center**. Get visitors' information from the well-informed and helpful staff. The surrounding turn-of-the-19th-century stone and brick buildings have been spruced up to house antiques shops, restaurants, and cafés; the depot is listed on the National Register of Historic Places. ◆ Daily; weekends till 3PM. Bounded by Hwy 101 and Santa Rosa Creek, and Third and Sixth Sts. 577.8674

30 CALIFORNIA WELCOME CENTER

The perfect place to plan your journey through the wine country, the center has free visitors' guides, maps, and listings of accommodations. Ask for the calendar of events. The staff also sells same-day, half-price tickets to theater productions. Located off Hwy 101. Take the Downtown/Third Street exit and continue to Fifth Street. Follow the "Traveling Bear" signs west to Historic Railroad Square. ◆ Daily. 9 Fourth St (at the Santa Rosa Convention and Visitors Bureau, at Wilson St), Santa Rosa. 577.8674, 800/404.ROSE. www.visitcwc.com and www.visitsantarosa.com

31 CHEVY'S

★$$ Part of a highly successful chain, this restaurant has an appealing menu of Mexican specialties. If you can handle the summer heat, there's a large deck out back. ◆ Mexican ◆ Daily, lunch and dinner. 24 Fourth St (west of Wilson St). 571.1082

32 OMELETTE EXPRESS

★$ Santa Rosa's casual breakfast spot offers about 50 types of omelettes, from standard combos to vegetarian and seafood, all served with cottage fries. From 11AM on, they serve charbroiled sirloin burgers and classic sandwiches, including roast beef, grilled cheddar cheese, and tuna salad. There's a kids' menu too. ◆ American ◆ Daily, breakfast and lunch. 112 Fourth St (between Davis and Wilson Sts). 525.1690

33 WHISTLESTOP ANTIQUES

Pack rats will have a ball prowling through this two-story 10,000-square-foot antiques collective for old furniture, kitchenware, costume jewelry, and knickknacks. Some stalls specialize in Art Deco plastic jewelry, 1950s cocktail shakers, sleek chrome furniture, and stylish vintage radios. Collectors can also find Russell Wright dinnerware (1939-1959). ◆ Daily. 130 Fourth St (between Davis and Wilson Sts). 542.9474

34 LA GARE

★★$$$ At this family-owned bistro in a charming stone building on **Historic Railroad Square**, you'll find the type of old-style French dishes that have virtually disappeared from trendier menus—standbys such as quiche lorraine, onion soup au gratin, *escalope de veau cordon bleu*, duck à l'orange, and *filet de boeuf Wellington*. Yet the proprietors are savvy enough to include vegetarian and low-

fat, low-sodium specials, and they offer chocolate decadence (that divine combo of dark chocolate and raspberries) alongside that old favorite, cherries jubilee. ◆ French ◆ Tu-Su, dinner. 208 Wilson St (between Third and Fourth Sts). 528.4355; fax 528.2519

35 SONOMA OUTFITTERS

This large store in **Historic Railroad Square** features a friendly, knowledgeable staff and a terrific selection of outdoor gear and apparel, including boots, tents, sleeping bags, and packs. If you're heading for the Russian River, take a look at the bright canoes. Kayaks are also sold here, rental of snowboards is available, and there's also a vertical climbing wall. The staff is well versed in the use of all of the equipment and gear. ◆ Daily. 145 Third St (at Davis St). 528.1920

36 MARIANNE'S ANTIQUES

Handsome tables, sideboards, armoires, and other large pieces of furniture are the specialty at this spacious antiques store. ◆ Th-Tu. 109 Third St (between Davis and Wilson Sts). 528.7293

36 HOT COUTURE

Inveterate vintage clotheshounds are sure to get derailed for an hour or two in this emporium stocked with sequined sweaters, 1940s coats, and glamorous 1950s cocktail dresses. For men, the store offers old-fashioned tuxedo shirts (which look great on women too) and classic jackets and coats à la Bogie. ◆ Daily. 101 Third St (at Wilson St). 528.7247; fax 528.7615

37 COURTYARD BY MARRIOTT

$ Part of the dependable chain, this property has 140 rooms and suites furnished in contemporary style. Guests have use of the pool and outdoor Jacuzzi. The hotel is a block from **Historic Railroad Square** and bordered by the freeway and a residential area. Breakfast is included in the rates. Nonsmoking rooms are available. ◆ 175 Railroad St (at Third St). 573.9000; fax 573.0272

38 LUTHER BURBANK HOME & GARDENS

Visit the home where world-famous horticulturist Luther Burbank worked between 1875 and 1926. The gardens where he conducted his experiments have been completely renovated and feature demonstration garden beds of Burbank's work, extensive labeling of his projects, and a huge pictorial wall constructed with porcelain tiles illustrating the history of

---

Restaurants/Clubs: Red | Hotels: Purple | Shops: Orange | Outdoors/Parks: Green | Sights/Culture: Blue

PREMIER GRAPE VARIETALS OF CALIFORNIA WINE COUNTRY

Cabernet Sauvignon: A transplant from Bordeaux, France, this grape has become California's most famous varietal. It yields medium- to full-bodied red wines that are rich in berry flavor and have a distinct herbaceousness. They may be tannic when young.

Chardonnay: California wine country's most widely planted grape produces medium- to full-bodied dry white wines. Chardonnay ranges in taste from rich to delicate and from fruity to oaky. The grape is also used to make sparkling wines.

Chenin Blanc: This grape creates delicate, light-bodied, and fruity wines. The straw-colored wines vary from dry to semisweet.

Merlot: A relative of Cabernet, although Merlot wines are softer, fruitier, and less tannic. The medium- to full-

bodied wines have a pleasant bouquet reminiscent of cherries.

Pinot Noir: This grape is difficult to grow and convert into wine, but it produces complex, rich red wines with a silky texture. They're fuller and softer than Cabernet and light- to medium-bodied.

Riesling: A popular grape used for fruity white wines that range from dry to sweet and are light- to medium-bodied.

Sauvignon Blanc: The source of crisp white wines that vary in flavor from tart to fruity to slightly grassy. They're light- to medium-bodied.

Zinfandel: Unique to California, this grape produces popular, dark, spicy, and fruity red wines and blush wines that are dry and medium- to full-bodied.

his life and accomplishments. The docent-guided tour that starts on the half hour is an enjoyable ramble through part of the garden, the greenhouse, and the modified Greek Revival house where Burbank's wife, Elizabeth, lived until her death. The carriage house is a mini-museum with photographs of notables who visited Burbank and drawings of his creations, such as the shasta daisy, the russet potato, and the Santa Rosa plum. This brilliant, self-educated man introduced more than 800 new varieties of plants to the world (including over 200 varieties of fruits alone). His objective was to improve the quality of plants and thereby increase the world's food supply. After his death, Congress inducted him into the Hall of Inventors. ♦ Nominal fee for tours. Home: Tu–Su, Apr–Oct; tours every half hour (last tour at 3:30PM). Memorial gardens: Daily. Extensive, guided garden tours available for groups by appointment. Santa Rosa and Sonoma Aves. 524.5445. www.lutherburbank.org

39 JUILLIARD PARK

These 9 acres in the center of the city were once home to wine and fruit broker C.F. Juilliard, a Santa Rosa pioneer. The site is now a park with a self-guided tour of 42 varieties of trees. ♦ Bounded by Santa Rosa Ave and A St and by Juilliard Park Dr and Sonoma Ave

40 PYGMALION HOUSE

$ This restored 2.5-story Queen Anne cottage is tucked away at the end of a quiet residen-

tial street a short walk from **Historic Railroad Square** (see page 136); though it's close to the freeway, it's completely soundproofed. There are six nicely decorated rooms, with private baths featuring showers and old-fashioned claw-foot tubs. A former antiques dealer, owner Caroline Berry has filled her house with antiques from the collections of famous stripper Gypsy Rose Lee and the madam who became Sausalito's mayor, Sally Stanford. ♦ 331 Orange St (south of Laurel St). 526.3407

41 FARMERS' MARKET

The parking lot of the **Veterans Memorial Building** is the site of a lively open-air market. Bring your own shopping bag and stock up on farm-fresh eggs, flowers, produce, and herb and vegetable starts for the garden. ♦ W, Sa, 9AM-noon year-round. Brookwood Ave (just north of Rte 12). 538.7023

42 SONOMA COUNTY FAIRGROUNDS

Summer brings the annual 2-week Sonoma County Fair here, with hundreds of crafts and homemaking exhibits, plants, flowers, livestock, and wool—and blue ribbons galore. It runs from the latter half of July to early August and is a great way to sample Sonoma's bounty. Other events are held here year-round, including horse shows and harvest fairs. ♦ 1350 Bennett Valley Rd (at Brookwood Ave). Events line, 528.3247

At the Sonoma County Fairgrounds:

SONOMA COUNTY FAIRGROUNDS GOLF COURSE

This nine-hole public golf course is a par 29. During the fair, the course is closed. ♦ Daily. 577.0755

43 BENNETT VALLEY GOLF COURSE

This 18-hole municipal golf course (par 72) is shaded by trees and surrounded by mountain views. It's open to the public for individual, club, and tournament play. ♦ Daily. 3330 Yulupa Ave (at Bennett Valley Rd). 528.3673

44 FRIEDMAN BROS.

A Sonoma County fixture, this giant hardware store sells everything from ice chests and portable barbecues to galvanized farm and ranch gates, rural mailboxes, and livestock watering troughs. ♦ Daily. 4055 Santa Rosa Ave (between Mountain View Ave and E Todd Rd). 584.7811, 795.4546

44 ROHNERT PARK

Located just south of Santa Rosa on the 101 Corridor, the town of Rohnert Park is where you go for minor league baseball in summer and concerts by the **Rohnert Park Chamber Orchestra** at the **Spreckels Performing Arts Center**.

In Rohnert Park:

DOUBLETREE HOTEL SONOMA WINE COUNTRY

$$ Updated Mission-style architecture and attractively appointed interiors set the tone here. Near two lush golf courses, the hotel has 245 air-conditioned, well-equipped guest rooms and suites, plus such other amenities as two tennis courts, a pool, a hot tub, and a small workout facility. Also on the premises is **Bacchus Restaurant and Wine Bar**. ♦ 1 Red Lion Dr (at Golf Course Dr). 584.5466, 800.222.TREE; fax 586.4605

45 THE GABLES INN

$$ A historic landmark, this imposing 120-year-old Victorian with 15 (count 'em) gables sits in front of a weathered barn on 3.5 acres. The seven guest rooms, most with a private bath, have Victorian claw-foot tubs and, of course, period décor. The most sought-after accommodation is the two-story cottage in back with a wood-burning stove, a double Jacuzzi, and a kitchenette where you can prepare produce from the local farmers' market. At sunset, guests like to congregate on the deck and take in the view. Innkeepers Michael and Judy Ogne cook a full country breakfast, which may include French toast and fruit compote with coconut cream. ♦ 4257 Petaluma Hill Rd (between Warrington and Kawana Springs Rds). 585.7777, 800/GABLESN

RUSSIAN RIVER REGION

Northwest of **Santa Rosa** is **Sonoma County**'s fastest-growing wine area, the Russian River region, a remarkably diverse landscape of gently rolling hillsides, apple orchards, sandy river beaches, and prime redwood country. Extending from **Cloverdale** in the north to **Sebastopol** in the south, and west to **Guerneville**, this region is so large that it is divided into several subvalleys, each with its own microclimate and appellation, by the **Russian River** and its tributaries.

Explored by the Russians based at **Fort Ross** in the 1840s, the Russian River region— which includes six different appellations—is much broader in both scope and area than either Sonoma or Napa Valley. More than 60 wineries are spread out in many directions, and there is no one wine route to follow.

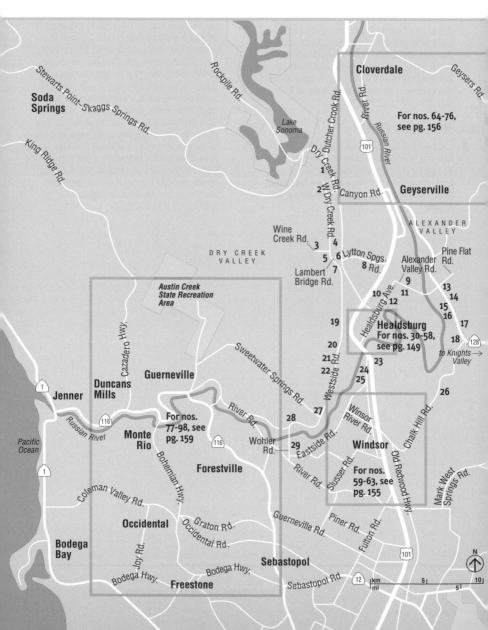

Alexander Valley, more or less parallel with Highway 101 to the west, cradles the Russian River from Cloverdale south to Healdsburg. This stretch of river offers some of the best canoeing in the area, where you can drift past prime vineyards of Chardonnay and Cabernet. The valley is named for Cyrus Alexander, an early settler from Pennsylvania who cultivated grapes and other crops here in the mid-19th century. In the past 3 decades, several top-notch wineries have been built in this scenic wine-growing region.

To the west is Dry Creek Valley, bracketed by serpentine Lake Sonoma to the northwest, the Russian River to the east, and the Russian River growing region to the south. Scattered along the valley are a number of small wine producers. (Many of them require appointments to visit—and it's well worth taking the time to make them.) Dry Creek Valley is primarily Zinfandel country, producing some of California's finest. You'll also encounter excellent Sauvignon Blanc.

Just south of the Dry Creek Valley, the river runs southwest toward the ocean, passing through the Russian River Valley and appellation. With its cooler microclimate, the Russian River appellation is prime territory for Pinot Noir and Chardonnay. It produces the most *méthode champenoise*, or sparkling, wine in the state. This growing region fans out from Santa Rosa in the east, west to Guerneville, and from Healdsburg in the north, toward Sebastopol in the south (wrapping around but not including Green Valley). Westside Road, which more or less parallels the river as it twists south from Healdsburg, then west to join River Road, is an entrancing country drive dotted with small family wineries, old hop-drying kilns, and a few farms where you can buy home-grown fruit, vegetables, and freshly laid eggs. River Road then cuts through the redwoods to Guerneville. Just before arriving at the town, you'll encounter Korbel Champagne Cellars and its heritage rose garden with more than 250 varieties of old-fashioned roses.

The cooler Green Valley (with its corresponding Green Valley appellation wines) provides ideal growing conditions for Pinot Noir and Chardonnay grapes.

There are two other, smaller wine appellations within the greater Russian River area: Chalk Hill, which produces wonderful Chardonnay and Merlot grapes, lies to the east of Healdsburg; and Knights Valley, one of the warmest areas, where excellent Cabernet Sauvignon vineyards and smaller acreages of Sauvignon Blanc grapes flourish, which is situated between the Napa and Alexander Valleys.

The diminutive town of Healdsburg is the hub of the Russian River Valley, with the three major subvalleys fanning out from its boundaries. At its heart is Healdsburg Plaza, a Spanish-style square that resembles Sonoma's famous plaza in miniature. You can swim in the Russian River at Healdsburg Veterans' Memorial Beach, rent a bicycle, or go kayaking on the river. Pack a picnic lunch, because once you're on the wine trail, there are few places to eat, and it can be a long way back into town. Healdsburg offers the most accommodations in the area, but you can also stay in Victorian bed-and-breakfasts in Geyserville and Cloverdale to the north.

You could also make your base the Russian River resort area near Guerneville. It offers family resorts and comfortable bed-and-breakfasts near sunny river beaches and virgin redwood forests. Armstrong Redwoods State Reserve is one of the largest reserves of ancient trees in California, and the rugged Sonoma Coast is just a short drive away, making the Russian River region one of the most dramatic and appealing wine regions in California.

HEALDSBURG

This town lies at the convergence of three famous viticultural regions, the **Alexander**, **Dry Creek**, and **Russian River Valleys**, and there is something here to please every wine-country visitor. Many come for a lazy trek down the Russian River in a canoe rented from **W.C. "Bob" Trowbridge Canoe Trips**. Others prefer to cap off a string of visits to local wineries with dinner at one of the town's good restaurants (such as **Bistro Ralph's** or the **Restaurant at Les Mars**) or a snack at the **Downtown Bakery & Creamery**. And for history buffs, a stop at the restored **Healdsburg Plaza** and the town's museum is a must.

1 FERRARI-CARANO VINEYARDS AND WINERY

Founded in 1981 by Reno attorney and hotelier Don Carano and his wife, Rhonda, this establishment is housed in a state-of-the-art complex at the head of Dry Creek Valley. The 14 winery-owned vineyards are spread over a 50-mile area from the Alexander Valley in northern Sonoma to the Carneros District in Napa Valley. Under winemaker George Bursick, the winery first gained a reputation for its whites, especially the oaky Chardonnay and a well-made Fumé Blanc. The winery then branched out into an array of reds, all widely praised: Cabernet, Merlot, Sonoma County Reserve Red, a rich Meritage, and Siena—an unusual blend of three varietals (Sangiovese, Cabernet Sauvignon, and Merlot). The roster often includes the distinctive Eldorado Gold—a sweet, fruity blend of Sémillion and Sauvignon Blanc. All these and more can be sampled in the handsome Italianate hospitality center with its elegant mahogany and black granite tasting bar, gift shop, and temperature-controlled wine shop. Visitors are invited to walk to the floor below for a view of the barrel aging cellar, which houses 1,500 French oak *barriques* (small wooden barrels). The winery's splendid gardens feature a gazebo, meandering streamlet, plants, and flowers galore. The garden showcases 14,000 tulips in spring. ◆ Fee for tours. Tasting and sales daily; tours by appointment only. 8761 Dry Creek Rd (northwest of Yoakim Bridge Rd). 433.6700; fax 431.1742

2 PRESTON VINEYARDS

Lou Preston first entered the wine scene as a grape grower, and the quality of the grapes coming from his 125-acre Dry Creek Valley estate convinced him to become a winemaker in the late 1970s. The winery focuses on Rhône varietals Viognier and Marsanne, and a red Rhône blend—Faux; and also the Italian Sangiovese and Barbera wines. It makes great Syrah, Zinfandel, and Muscat Canelli (a dessert wine that sells out quickly). Preston also has a wonderful bakery. ◆ Tasting and sales daily; tours by appointment only. 9282 W Dry Creek Rd (northwest of Yoakim Bridge Rd). 433.3372; fax 433.5307

3 MICHEL-SCHLUMBERGER

This Mission-style estate surrounded by a hundred-acre vineyard is owned by Jacques Schlumberger and Jean-Jacques Michel. Schlumberger runs the estate, which produces estate-grown and -bottled Chardonnay, Cabernet Sauvignon, Merlot, and a small amount of Reserve Cabernet Sauvignon under the **Michel-Schlumberger** label, as well as Chardonnay and Cabernet Sauvignon for the **Domaine Michel** label. Winemaker Fred Payne manages the cellar and the estate vineyards. ◆ Tours and tasting daily by appointment only. 4155 Wine Creek Rd (west of W Dry Creek Rd). 433.7427, 800/447.3060; fax 433.0444. www.michelschlumberger.com

4 QUIVIRA WINERY

Owners Henry and Holly Wendt took the name of this stark, modern winery from a legendary wealthy kingdom that early explorers believed was situated somewhere in the Sonoma County area. It is known primarily for its Zinfandel and Sauvignon Blanc. The winemaker is Grady Wann. ◆ Tasting and sales daily; tours by appointment only. 4900 W Dry Creek Rd (between Lambert Bridge and Yoakim Bridge Rds). 431.8333, 800/292.8339 in CA; fax 431.1664

5 A. RAFANELLI

Third-generation vintner Dave Rafanelli still has two of the vineyards his grandfather planted when he first came to this country. The winery is in the redwood barn where Dave Rafanelli's father, Amerigo, made wines with little help from modern-day technology. Today, a fourth generation is involved in the process; Dave and Patty's daughter, Rashell, is assistant winemaker. Dave will take you through the winery, explaining how he makes his beautifully balanced Dry Creek Valley Zinfandels and letting you taste the new vintages from the barrel and from the bottle. The Zinfandels and Cabernets just keep getting better every year. ♦ Tasting and sales daily, Apr-Oct, and by appointment, Nov-Mar; tours by appointment only. 4685 W Dry Creek Rd (just south of Wine Creek Rd). 433.1385

6 DRY CREEK GENERAL STORE & BAR

This old-fashioned general store has a fully stocked deli counter, as well as beer, wine, canned goods, and candy. The store also sells fishing and camping gear, and you can obtain a fishing license here. This classic country bar made the *Men's Journal's* list of 50 top US bars. Cowboy tunes on the juke box, memorabilia hanging from ceiling and walls, and plank wooden floors make this a revered watering hole. Gina Gallo owns the bar and adjoining Dry Creek Store, but assures regulars that this last stronghold of traditional farm culture will be preserved. The bar serves a wide variety of beer and local wines. ♦ Daily. 3495 Dry Creek Rd (northwest of Lytton Springs Rd). 433.4171

6 DRY CREEK VINEYARD

Founded in 1972 by Bostonian David Stare, who studied enology and viticulture at the **University of California, Davis**, this winery is a steady performer producing first-rate Fumé Blanc and Zinfandel. Picnic tables are set out in the midst of an old-fashioned flower garden. ♦ Tasting and sales daily. 3770 Lambert Bridge Rd (between Dry Creek and W Dry Creek Rds). 433.1000; fax 433.5329

6 PASSALACQUA WINERY

This is the tasting room for the Passalacqua family's 133-acre ranch winery and organic vineyards in the sun-drenched, clay-loam hills of Dry Creek Valley—the birthplace of great Zinfandels and Cabernets. Jason and Noelle Passalacqua's winery is a showplace with fountains, pools, waterfalls, and picnic grounds. Their smooth, ripe, and supple Cabernet has received high praise from wine writers and connoisseurs. The Chardonnay

and two Zinfandels from other growers' grapes (Alexander Valley Zinfandel and Dry Creek Valley Zinfandel) also are gaining note. Many top wine-country restaurants offer Passalacqua wines. ♦ Tasting and sales daily. 3805 Lambert Bridge Rd (between Dry Creek and W Dry Creek Rds). 825.5547. www.passalacquawinery.com

7 LAMBERT BRIDGE WINERY

Taking its name from the landmark bridge nearby, this winery's elegant redwood-paneled tasting room has cathedral-high ceilings, glass windows overlooking rows of oak barrels in the aging room, plus a fireplace for chilly days. Under winemaker Julia Iantosca, the winery specializes in Merlot, Chardonnay, Zinfandel, and Sauvignon Blanc. She also produces limited quantities of a proprietary Bordeaux-style blend—Crane Creek Cuvée. Buy a bottle and linger at the handsomely landscaped picnic grounds. ♦ Tasting and sales daily. 4085 W Dry Creek Rd (between Westside and Wine Creek Rds). 431.9600; fax 433.3215

8 RIDGE/LYTTON SPRINGS

This winery has one of the best Zinfandel vineyards in California. Originally planted by Italian immigrants at the turn of the 20th century on a dry-farmed (nonirrigated) hillside, it produces grapes with a rich concentration of fruit and flavor. The sales and tasting rooms are in one corner of the winery. ♦ Tasting and sales daily, F-M. 650 Lytton Springs Rd (between Hwy 101 and Chiquita Rd). 433.7721; fax 433.7751

8 MAZZOCCO VINEYARDS

The first vintage at this family-owned winery was the 1985 Chardonnay. Today Tom Mazzocco and family produce barrel-fermented River Lane Chardonnay, Estate Merlot, a firmly structured Cabernet Sauvignon, and, some years, a Winemaker Select. The winery also produces four Zinfandels—the best known is the Sonoma County Zinfandel, made from grapes from six different vineyards (four in Dry Creek and two in Alexander Valley) and always blended with a small amount of Petite Sirah. Winemaker Phyllis Zouzounis worked at **Dry Creek**

Vineyard up the road (see page 143) before coming here. ♦ Tasting and sales daily. 1400 Lytton Springs Rd (between Chiquita and Dry Creek Rds). 431.8159; fax 431.2369

9 ALEXANDER VALLEY RV PARK AND CAMPGROUND

This family campground by a beautiful stretch of the Russian River features 400 sites that are suitable for either two tents or a trailer (under 30 feet long). There are canoe rentals and acres of sandy swimming beaches. ♦ Fee. Alexander Valley Rd and Russian River. 431.1453

10 SIMI WINERY

Winemaker Nick Goldschmidt produces regular and reserve wines that are well worth seeking out, and you can sample most of them in the tasting room of this winery, across from the **Belle de Jour Inn** (see opposite). Sauvignon Blanc, Chardonnay, Zinfandel, Pinot Noir, Shiraz, Cabernet Sauvignon, Sémillon, and Muscat Canelli (a dessert wine) are for sale here, as are reserve offerings of older vintages of Chardonnay and Cabernet. The tours are well run and informative. Picnic facilities are available too. ♦ Tasting and sales daily; tours daily at 11AM, 1PM, and 3PM. 16275 Healdsburg Ave (at Chiquita Rd). 433.6981; fax 433.6253

11 JORDAN VINEYARD & WINERY

When Denver oilman Tom Jordan opened his winery, everybody hurried to see the grandiose French-style château and to taste the first release, a 1976 Alexander Valley Cabernet, which was full-bodied, lush, and eminently ready to drink—Jordan had the time and capital to age the wine before releasing it. Later wines have kept to the same high standard set by that first release. Jordan also makes fine Chardonnay. ♦ Tastings and tours

---

On a steamy summer's day, there's nothing like a California Wine Country Cooler to lift your spirits.

Combine:

1 quart still or sparkling water
1 cup cucumber, peeled and thinly sliced
½ cup orange or lemon rings with rind, thinly sliced

Cover tightly and refrigerate until chilled and flavors blend (15 minutes). Serve as is or over ice.

"Wine can be considered with good reason as the most helpful and most hygienic of all beverages."

—Louis Pasteur

---

by appointment only. 1474 Alexander Valley Rd (between W Soda Rock La and Lytton Station Rd). 431.5250

12 BELLE DE JOUR INN

$$$ This serene retreat is set on a hill overlooking the Russian River Valley. Innkeepers Tom and Brenda Hearn live in the 1873 Italianate Victorian farmhouse in front. They've turned the caretaker's cottage into a private suite with a king-size bed swathed in lace, a Franklin stove, a whirlpool bath for two, and conveniences such as hair dryers and a refrigerator. Three other cottages are nestled alongside, each with a private entrance and view. The **Terrace Room** offers a king-size bed, a whirlpool tub, and contemporary décor. The snug **Morning Room**, the smallest of the four cottages, has a queen-size bed, paneled walls, shutters opening onto a view, a wood-burning stove, and a shower–steam bath. There is a telephone in each room too. A full breakfast is served in the cheery breakfast room. The fresh, unfussy décor and the privacy make a welcome alternative to Victorian orthodoxy. ♦ 16276 Healdsburg Ave (between Sunnyvale Dr and Alexander Valley Rd). 431.9777; fax 431.7412

Within the Belle de Jour Inn:

BELLE DE JOUR VINTAGE CAR TOURS

Guests can take guided trips in a 1925 Star touring car through the Alexander, Dry Creek, or Russian River Valleys. Itineraries can be custom-tailored to your interests. The chauffeured Star can also be reserved for private trips.

13 JIMTOWN STORE

This place is named for James Patrick, who settled here in the 1860s and ran a country store first at Soda Rock and then here in the Alexander Valley. When John H. Werner and Carrie Brown came across the old country store for sale, they decided to move to the wine country and revive the historic building. First they hired the Berkeley firm **Fernau & Hartman Architects** to restore the lofty space, then painted it an eye-popping yellow and green. Stop in for espresso drinks and coffee cake; on Saturday and Sunday mornings, look for the dried-cherry scones. The deli counter stocks cold cuts and homemade salads. Try the refreshing iced ginseng tea and the old-fashioned chocolate cake. There's a patio eating area in back, where meals are served throughout the summer. Part of the store is stocked with antiques and collectibles, as well as locally made jams, honey, and crafts. Call in advance to order a picnic boxed lunch. ♦ Daily; closed for 2 weeks in January. 6706

Hwy 128 (just southwest of Pine Flat Rd).
433.1212; fax 433.1252

14 SAUSAL WINERY

The Demostene family purchased the 125-acre **Sausal Ranch** in 1956 and began replanting prune and apple orchards with vineyards. In 1973 they turned a building formerly used to dehydrate prunes into a full-fledged winery, which winemaker Dave Demostene initiated with the 1974 vintage, a Zinfandel. Demostene continues to make good Zinfandel, especially an intense, rich private reserve. He also makes a very fine Cabernet, Sangiovese, and Sausal Blanc. Older vintages are for sale too, rereleased for collectors. There's a shady picnic area under the arbor near the tasting room. ♦ Daily. 7370 Hwy 128 (southeast of Pine Flat Rd). 433.2285; fax 433.5136

15 WHITE OAK VINEYARDS & WINERY

Former Alaskan fisherman William Myers pulled up stakes and opened this winery in Healdsburg in 1981. In 1988 the winery was moved to its 30-acre vineyard bordering Sausal Creek, 8 miles east of Healdsburg. Here, winemaker Stephen Ryan produces Chardonnay and Sauvignon Blanc, as well as Cabernet Sauvignon, Cabernet Franc, Merlot, Alexander Valley Zinfandel, and Dry Creek Valley Zinfandel. The tasting room is housed in a Mediterranean-style villa; there are picnic tables just outside and by the creek. ♦ Tasting and sales daily; tours by appointment. 7505 Hwy 128 (southeast of Pine Flat Rd). 433.8429; fax 433.8446

16 JOHNSON'S ALEXANDER VALLEY WINES

The Johnson family purchased this property in 1952 when it was a prune and pear farm. In the late 1960s, they replanted it in grapes, and they began bottling wines in 1974. Their output, which can be purchased only here, now includes Pinot Noir, Cabernet Sauvignon, Zinfandel, White Zinfandel, Chardonnay, and Riesling. Ellen Johnson is winemaker. Note the 1924 theater pipe organ in the tasting room. ♦ Tasting and sales daily. 8333 Hwy 128 (between Chalk Hill and Alexander Valley Rds). 433.2319

17 ALEXANDER VALLEY VINEYARDS

Once owned by Cyrus Alexander, for whom the Alexander Valley is named, this 250-acre ranch and 1841 homestead now belong to the Wetzel family, who produce varietals from grapes grown on their estate. Most of the wines are available only at the tasting room. The age-worthy Cabernet is the one most seen in wineshops. They also make a good Chardonnay and a Merlot, plus small quantities of Pinot Noir, Cabernet Franc, and Chenin Blanc. New wine caves (which can be toured by appointment) have been built for aging and storing the wines. There is a small, shady picnic area beside the parking lot. ♦ Tasting and sales daily; tours by appointment only. 8644 Hwy 128 (northwest of Chalk Hill Rd). 433.7209, 800/888.7209; fax 433.9408

18 FIELD STONE WINERY & VINEYARDS

This family-owned and -operated winery tunneled into the hillside takes its name from the stones used to construct the rustic façade. Known primarily for its Cabernet, Merlot, and Petite Sirah, this high-quality act also produces Sangiovese, Gewürztraminer, Sauvignon Blanc, Viognier, and a barrel-fermented Chardonnay. Picnic grounds are atop the winery on an oak knoll. ♦ Tasting and sales daily; tours by appointment only. 10075 Hwy 128 (at Chalk Hill Rd). 433.7266, 800/54.GRAPE; fax 433.2231

19 EVERETT RIDGE WINERY

Grapes were planted on this Dry Creek Valley estate as early as 1878. The charming old barn, now a tasting room, dates from 1875. New owners Anne and Jack Air have been replanting past-prime vineyards with new vines, and in 1997 they harvested some excellent Russian River and Dry Creek fruit and tucked it away in French and American Oak. The winery produces Old Vine Zinfandel, North Coast Pinot Noir (a Cabernet-based blend), Dry Creek Cabernet Sauvignon, and Russian River Chardonnay. They planned to release a Sonoma Valley Syrah and a Dry Creek Old Vine Zinfandel as we went to press. ♦ Tasting and sales daily; tours by appointment only. 435 W Dry Creek Rd (between Westside and Wine Creek Rds). 433.1637; fax 433.7024

20 MILL CREEK VINEYARDS

This family-owned winery, which overlooks its vineyards in Dry Creek Valley, was founded in 1965. The two-story redwood tasting room

---

Restaurants/Clubs: Red | Hotels: Purple | Shops: Orange | Outdoors/Parks: Green | Sights/Culture: Blue

sits beside the creek, where a wooden mill wheel turns. You can sample the Kreck family's full range of varietal wines: Chardonnay, Sauvignon Blanc, Cabernet Blush, Cabernet, Merlot, and Gewürztraminer. Up a steep path at the back is a large tree-shaded picnic deck with a panoramic view of the valley. ♦ Daily. 1401 Westside Rd (at Mill Creek Rd). 433.5098; fax 431.1714

MADRONA MANOR

20 MADRONA MANOR

$$$ Built in 1881 by John Alexander Paxton, a wealthy entrepreneur and state legislator, this grand, gabled Victorian inn is located on the outskirts of Healdsburg. John and Carol Muir bought the mansion in 1981 and, after a yearlong restoration, opened it as an inn. Bill and Trudi Konrad purchased Madrona Manor in April 1999. They have undertaken further renovations to enhance the elegance of the inn. Their daughter and son-in-law, Maria and Joseph Hadley, are the innkeepers. With the addition of several other buildings, there now are a total of 18 guest rooms, plus three suites—all with baths. The three-story manor contains eight rooms, all with private baths and fireplaces. The elegant rooms on the mansion's second floor are the best— particularly **no. 204**, which has a carved wooden bed, chaise longue, fireplace, claw-foot tub, and French doors opening onto a balcony. Rooms in the carriage house, which dates from 1881, are furnished in a more contemporary style; one of the suites features a king-size bed, a marble-tile bath, and a double Jacuzzi. The most secluded unit is the **Garden Cottage**, furnished in rattan, with a fireplace, a private garden, and a deck area. Guests can relax in the manor's parlor and music rooms, explore the 8-acre gardens, or use the swimming pool. A buffet breakfast is served in the dining room or on the outdoor deck. This inn does allow children in some rooms and in the **Garden Cottage**. ♦ 1001 Westside Rd (at W Dry Creek Rd). 433.4231, 800/258.4003; fax 433.0703. www.madronamanor.com

Within Madrona Manor:

MADRONA MANOR RESTAURANT

★★★$$$$ Executive Chef Jesse Mallgren's wine-country cuisine takes advantage of the greens, vegetables, herbs, and fruit from the garden. House-made breads and pastas, delicious pastries and ice creams, and smoked and cured meats and fish are menu mainstays. The three dining rooms are elegantly decorated with Persian rugs, damask table linens, candles, and flowers. An extensive à la carte menu is now offered in addition to the prix-fixe three-course or the four-course menu. For an additional fee, a selected wine is served with each course. There are seven wines available by the glass, mostly from northern Sonoma County. Appe-tizers might include scallops with artichoke purée and beurre blanc, or a risotto with chard, wild mushrooms, and pumpkin. Entrées range from traditional (beef with garlic mashed potatoes, glazed carrots, and horseradish) to inventive (quail stuffed with spinach, pine nuts, currants, and sun-dried tomatoes)—all superbly prepared. Leave room for the white chocolate mousse cake served with raspberry purée. ♦ California ♦ Daily, dinner

21 MIDDLETON FARM

Nancy and Malcolm Skall sell superb organic fruits and vegetables, many grown from heirloom seeds. Drive past the farmhouse surrounded by flowers and ring the bell in front of the barn for assistance. Also look for Malcolm at the Healdsburg, Santa Rosa, and Sebastopol farmers' markets. ♦ M-Tu, Th-Su, Apr-Nov (call to confirm); call for Dec, Feb, and Mar schedules. 2651 Westside Rd (between Sweetwater Springs and Mill Creek Rds). 433.4755

22 BELVEDERE WINERY

Located in the coastal foothills, this winery's tasting room overlooks the valley and river. The top-of-the-line wines here are Chardonnay, Zinfandel, Merlot, and Cabernet Sauvignon. Guests are welcome to use the picnic tables under the trees and on the deck. ♦ Tasting and sales daily. 4035 Westside Rd (between Sweetwater Springs and Mill Creek Rds). 433.8236. Tasting room also at 250 Center St (between Mill and Matheson Sts). 433.8236

22 RABBIT RIDGE WINERY & VINEYARDS

This winery produces impressively rich wines made from grapes grown on its 45-acre vineyard. Sauvignon Blanc, Zinfandel, Carig-nane, Cabernet Sauvignon, Sangiovese, Barbera, and a port are among the varieties fashioned by owners Erich Russell (Erich is also the winemaker) and Darryl Simmons. They are also opening a winery in Paso Robles. ♦ Tasting and sales daily; tours by appointment only. 3291 Westside Rd (between Sweetwater Springs and Mill Creek Rds). 431.7128

23 CHRISTOPHER CREEK WINERY

Fred and Pam Wasserman are the new owners of this small winery perched on a knoll in the Russian River appellation. Winemaker Sebastien Pochon concentrates primarily on red wines—Petite Sirah and Syrah, made from grapes grown on the 10-acre estate; he also produces small amounts of Chardonnay. ♦ Tasting M, F-Su; tours daily by appointment only. 641 Limerick La (east of Los Amigos Rd). 433.2001; fax 433.9315

24 FOPPIANO VINEYARDS

Founder John Foppiano, an immigrant from Genoa, began making wine from Russian River Valley grapes as early as 1896. Today this remains a family-run winery, with the third and fourth generations in charge. One of California's oldest wineries, the firm began producing varietal wines under its own label in 1970. Primarily known for its Petite Sirah and Sonoma Cabernet, it also produces a Sauvignon Blanc and a Chardonnay. ♦ Tasting and sales daily; tours by appointment only. 12707 Old Redwood Hwy (between Eastside Rd and Hwy 101). 433.7272

25 J WINE COMPANY

The facility here, formerly owned by **Piper Sonoma**, was purchased by **J Wine Company** in 1996. The company farms over 225 acres of vineyards throughout the Russian River Valley, taking advantage of the diversity of soils and microclimates in the region. They focus on the production of Chardonnay and Pinot Noir, along with J Sparkling Wine, which is made in the traditional *méthode champenoise*. Some wines are produced here for Piper Sonoma as well. ♦ At press time, a tasting room, with tasting, tours, and sales, was scheduled to open to the public. 11447 Old Redwood Hwy (just north of Eastside Rd). 431.5400; fax 431.5410

25 RODNEY STRONG VINEYARDS

The vineyards come right up to the base of this monolithic structure built in buff concrete and finished with massive wood beams. The winery, founded by Rodney Strong—who also started **Windsor Vineyards**—is now owned by the **Klein Family Vintners**. Winemaker Rick Sayre produces a wide spectrum of wines: Chardonnay, Sauvignon Blanc, Cabernet Sauvignon, Merlot, Pinot Noir, and Zinfandel—all available for tasting. Summer concerts are held on the picnic lawn in the vineyard. ♦ Tasting and sales daily; tours at 11AM and 3PM. 11455 Old Redwood Hwy (just north of Eastside Rd). 433.6511, 431.1533; fax 433.8635

CHALK HILL
WINERY

26 CHALK HILL WINERY

When Frederick Furth purchased the Donna Maria Ranch in 1980, he replanted the vineyards and constructed a barnlike winery building. Today, winemaker William Knuttel produces Chardonnay, Cabernet Sauvignon, Sauvignon Blanc, and Merlot, plus three estate vineyard selection wines—Chardonnay, Pinot Gris, and Botrytised Sémillon. ♦ Tasting, sales, and tours by appointment only. 10300 Chalk Hill Rd (between Pleasant Ave and Rte 128). 838.4306

27 J. ROCHIOLI VINEYARDS & WINERY

The Rochioli family has been growing premium grapes since the 1930s. They make good Sauvignon Blanc and Pinot Noir as well as Chardonnay and Cabernet Sauvignon. A small gallery offers changing art exhibits. Bring your lunch and picnic at the tables on an outdoor deck. ♦ Tasting and sales daily. 6192 Westside Rd (just north of Sweetwater Springs Rd). 433.2305

27 HOP KILN WINERY

A brass plaque outside this immense building with three towers reads: "This structure served the important hop industry of California's North Coast region, once the major hop-growing area in the West." Built in 1905 by Italian stonemasons, it represents the finest surviving example of its type, consisting of three stone kilns for drying the hops, a wooden cooler, and a two-story press for baling hops. Listed on the National Register of Historic Places, the hop-kiln barn was restored and converted to a winery in 1974 by Dr. Martin Griffin, who is still the owner. The tasting room pours the winery's Chardonnay, Sauvignon Blanc, and A Thousand Flowers (a blended table white), along with its robust reds, among them Primitivo Zinfandel and Marty Griffin's Big Red (made from four unidentified grapes found growing on the property). With its picnic grounds beside a duck pond, this is a popular stop for bicyclists. ◆ Tasting and sales daily. 6050 Westside Rd (between Sweetwater Springs Rd and Foreman La). 433.6491; fax 433.8162 www.hopkilnwinery.com

28 DAVIS BYNUM

Many of the organic wines available for tasting here are sold only at the winery. Chardonnay, Sauvignon Blanc, and Cabernet are good bets. Vintner Gary Farrell also produces other quality wines—Merlot, Pinot Noir, Fumé Blanc, Zinfandel, and Gewürztraminer. Occasionally visitors may be treated to a special "future wines" barrel tasting. There is a shady picnic area with tables at the edge of a ravine. ◆ Daily. 8075 Westside Rd (between Wohler and Sweetwater Springs Rds). 433.5852; fax 433.4309

29 RAFORD HOUSE

$$ Raford W. Peterson built this two-story farmhouse northwest of Santa Rosa in the 1880s. Called the **Wohler Ranch** at the time, the property was surrounded by more than 400 acres of hops, which Peterson processed for beer brewing. In 1981, after a year of restoration, the house, which now sits on a knoll overlooking vineyards and the valley, was converted to a bed-and-breakfast inn. Flanked by palms, this Sonoma County Historical Landmark has seven guest rooms. All are decorated with period décor and have queen-size beds; five rooms have a private bath, and two share a bath. Two of the guest rooms also have fireplaces—the bridal suite is the most private, with its own patio. Innkeepers Carole and Jack Vore provide a full breakfast. Evening wine and hors d'oeuvres are also served. ◆ 10630 Wohler Rd (between

Sonoma County's yield is more varied than that of Napa. Eggs, chicken, cattle, apple orchards, walnuts, peaches, and plums coexist with vineyards.

"I like Champagne because it always tastes as if my foot's asleep."

—Art Buchwald, quoted in *Alexis Lichine's New Encyclopedia of Wines & Spirits* (Alfred A. Knopf, 1967)

The rugged North Coast is renowned for lush forests of redwoods and Douglas fir. The redwoods are among the world's tallest trees, growing as high as 367.8 feet.

Eastside and Westside Rds). 887.9573, 800/887.9503 (US and Canada); fax 887.9597

30 BYRON GIBBS PARK
This 2.5-acre park offers tables for picnicking and a children's playground. ◆ 1520 Prentice Dr (between Sunnyvale and Poppy Hill Drs)

31 BEST WESTERN DRY CREEK INN
$ This vaguely Spanish-style contemporary inn on a busy street not far from the freeway has 102 rooms (choose between a king-size or two queen-size beds). If standard comforts such as in-room coffee, satellite TV, and a heated (mid-April through November) pool are more important than wine country ambiance, this is the place for you. A continental breakfast is included. Ask about AAA or seniors' midweek discounts. ◆ 198 Dry Creek Rd (at Hwy 101). 433.0300, 800/222.KRUG; fax 433.1129

32 TIP TOP LIQUOR WAREHOUSE
There's a great selection of Sonoma County wines here. Shipping is available too. ◆ Daily. 90 Dry Creek Rd (between Healdsburg Ave and Hwy 101). 431.0841

33 HONOR MANSION
$$$ Innkeepers Cathi and Steve Fowler, who purchased Dr. Herbert Honor's 1883 Italianate Victorian, are avid cooks and antiques collectors. Have a peek at the eight rooms to admire the period furniture, European linens, and faux paintings. Four of the rooms are upstairs and one is on the ground floor. Outside, the **Poolside Suite** has a leather-upholstered sleigh bed and a private whirlpool tub. The **Squire's Cottage** has a king-size canopy bed, and the **Garden Suite** has three private outdoor areas; one patio has a garden spa tub. Cathi serves a royal breakfast in the dining room on English china and antique silver. Poached sliced pears drizzled in espresso sauce, cherry-orange scones, caramel-apple French toast, and Mexican egg crepes are some of the elegant fare that she whips up in her professional kitchen. The dining room remains open to guests so they can help themselves to the espresso machine and to the sideboard that Cathi keeps stocked with fruit and snacks. ◆ 14891 Grove St (between Grant St and Dry Creek Rd). 433.4277, 800/554.4667; fax 431.7173. www.honormansion.com

34 TAYMAN PARK MUNICIPAL GOLF COURSE
This nine-hole, par-35 public golf course set on 60 acres overlooks the town. ◆ Daily. 927 S Fitch Mountain Rd (between Hidden Acres Rd and Greens Dr). 433.4275

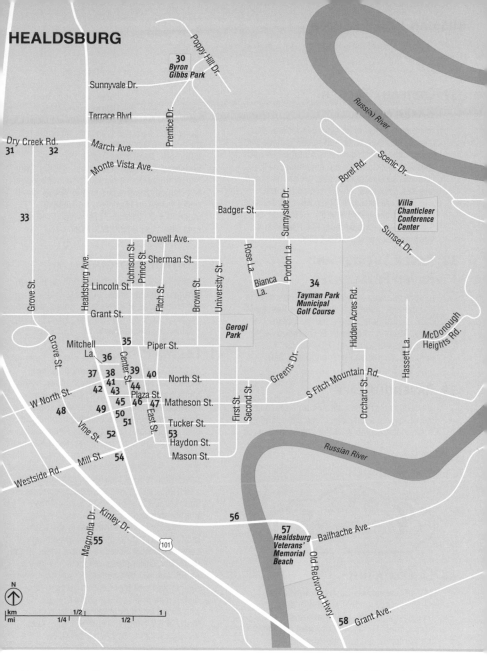

HEALDSBURG

Byron Gibbs Park
30

Poppy Hill Dr.

Sunnyvale Dr.

Terrace Blvd

Prentice Dr.

Russian River

Dry Creek Rd.
31   32

March Ave.

Monte Vista Ave.

Borel Rd.

Scenic Dr.

33

Badger St.

Sunnyside Dr.

Villa Chanticleer Conference Center

Sunset Dr.

Powell Ave.

Rose La.

Pordon La.

34
Tayman Park Municipal Golf Course

Johnson St.
Prince St.
Sherman St.

Healdsburg Ave.

Lincoln St.

Fitch St.

Brown St.

University St.

Bianca La.

Hidden Acres Rd.

Grant St.

Gerogi Park

Hassett La.

McDonough Heights Rd.

Grove St.

Mitchell La.
35
Piper St.

Center St.

Greens Dr.

S Fitch Mountain Rd.

Orchard St.

36

37 38 39 40

North St.

First St.
Second St.

Grove St.

41
42 43 44
45 46 47
49
50
51

Plaza St.

East St.

Matheson St.

W North St.

48

Vine St. 52

Tucker St.

53
Haydon St.

Mill St. 54

Mason St.

Russian River

Westside Rd.

Magnolia Dr.

Kinley Dr.

55

101

56

57
Healdsburg Veterans' Memorial Beach

Bailhache Ave.

Old Redwood Hwy.

N

km   1/2   1
mi   1/4   1/2

58 Grant Ave.

35 SONOMA COUNTY WINE LIBRARY

This special collection at the Healdsburg branch of the **Sonoma County Library** brings together a wide range of materials on wine-related subjects. The library subscribes to more than 80 periodicals, and its collection numbers well over 3,500 books, ranging from technical works on viticulture and enology to books on wine appreciation and cooking. There's a file containing current information on California wineries too. ♦ M–Sa. 139 Piper St (between Johnson and Center Sts). 433.3772; fax 433.7946

36 WESTERN BOOT

★$$ You can order down-home portions of steak, ribs, chicken, and seafood at this family-owned restaurant. ♦ American ♦ M–F, Su, lunch; daily, dinner. 9 Mitchell La (off

---

Restaurants/Clubs: Red | Hotels: Purple | Shops: Orange | Outdoors/Parks: Green | Sights/Culture: Blue

Healdsburg Ave, between North and Piper Sts). 433.6362

37 COSTEAUX FRENCH BAKERY

This bakery displays its signature latticed fruit tarts, lemon curd tarts, and pecan tartlets, but sourdough bread, strawberry-rhubarb pie, and chocolate mocha cake are the stars. You'll also find sandwiches, salads, soups, chili, and cheeses. Espresso, wine, beer, coffee, tea, and soda are available. There are tables inside and out on the patio. ◆ M-Sa, 6AM-6PM; Su, 7AM-4PM. 417 Healdsburg Ave (between W North and Grant Sts). 433.1913

38 RAVEN THEATER AND RAVEN FILM CENTER

Current releases dominate the marquees here. You can eat before the show at the **Ravenous Café** next door to the theater (see below). ◆ Daily. Theater: 115 North St (between Center St and Healdsburg Ave). Film Center: 415 Center St (between North and Piper Sts). 433.5448

39 RAVENOUS CAFÉ

★★$ This great little café has an appealing mix of salads, sandwiches, and light entrées. ◆ American/Italian ◆ W-Su, lunch and dinner. 420 Center St (between North and Piper Sts). 431.1302

40 CAMELLIA INN

$$ Del Lewand, her husband, Ray, and daughter Lucy run this elegant bed-and-breakfast inn in the center of town. Horticulturist Luther Burbank was a friend of the former owner, and the camellias surrounding the house are attributed to him. The Lewands have painted the 1869 Italianate Victorian pale pink, cream, and rose; two pines flank the entryway, and the stone wall in front is bordered with roses. The house features a double parlor with two marble fireplaces and a dining room with a fireplace framed in tiles depicting the seven

---

Native Americans brewed beer from corn sprouts.

"Wine is a food."

—Oliver Wendell Holmes

---

ages of man. All guest rooms have a private bath, and seven of the nine rooms are furnished with antiques and Oriental carpets. The remaining two rooms have their own special charm: The **Tiffany**, papered in silkscreened wallpaper, features a queen-size four-poster bed, gas fireplace, whirlpool tub for two, and a stained-glass window in the bathroom. **Demitasse** features an iron bedstead, antique dresser, and 1920s bath across the hall. Out back, the swimming pool is surrounded with trees and an arbor. A full buffet breakfast is served. No smoking indoors. ◆ 211 North St (between Fitch and East Sts). 433.8182, 800/727.8182; fax 433.8130

41 VINTAGE ANTIQUES

At this antiques cooperative, browse through furniture, vintage linen, prints, and other remembrances of things past. This is a good place to score a fabulous find. ◆ Daily. 328 Healdsburg Ave (at North St). 433.7461

41 LES MARS HOTEL

$$$$ This new 16-room luxury hotel one block from Healdsburg's historic town plaza bears the stately presence of a European château. After many years of travel, owners David and Sarah Mars decided to bring the best of European hospitality to Healdsburg. Their boutique hotel has a mansard slate roof with zinc dormers, wrought-iron window work, and a convincingly aged façade. Antiques and fine reproductions create an authentic 18th- and 19th-century décor for each room. Italian linens drape four-poster beds and Italian marble shines throughout the bathrooms. Amenities include bathrobes, luxury bath products, and state-of-the-art entertainment centers. Sample Sonoma County wines at the lobby bar. Other pleasures include a year-round heated pool, sun deck, spa treatment rooms, and a fitness center. **Cyrus**, a fine-dining restaurant run by chefs Douglas Keane and Nick Peyton, is steps away from the lobby. ◆ 27 North St (at Healdsburg Ave). 707/433.4211, 877/431.1700. ㅎ www.lesmarshotel.com

42 RESTAURANT CHARCUTERIE

★$$ Chef Patrick Martin and his wife, Robin, own this contemporary eatery serving French-Mediterranean fare with a California accent. At lunchtime, sandwiches are a good bet, served with soup or salad, or select a pasta or salad. The dinner menu changes frequently, but, if it is available, try the baked, nut-crusted brie with roasted garlic for an appetizer. Entrées, which are served with your choice of soup or salad, might include a soul-satisfying roasted chicken with mustard-tarragon cream sauce. For those who want a light evening meal, salads are an option too. Check the board for daily specials and wines by the glass. ♦ French-Mediterranean/California ♦ M-Sa, lunch; daily, dinner. Closed Su, Feb-Mar. 335 Healdsburg Ave (between W Matheson and W North Sts). 431.7213

43 KENDALL-JACKSON TASTING ROOM

This is the tasting outpost for Lake County's Kendall-Jackson Winery. The roster of wines includes several barrel-fermented Chardonnays, a Johannesburg Riesling, and an excellent Sauvignon Blanc. Reds run the gamut from Cabernet, Merlot, and Zinfandel (including fine vineyard-designated wines from old mountain vineyards) to a great Syrah. In addition to wine, the store stocks glasses, cookbooks, wine books, and a slew of tempting California gourmet products. The Kendall-Jackson organization also has another tasting facility in Fulton (see below). ♦ Daily. 337 Healdsburg Ave (between W Matheson and W North Sts). 433.7102; fax 433.6215

Between Santa Rosa and Windsor on the west side of Hwy 101:

KENDALL-JACKSON'S CALIFORNIA COAST WINE CENTER

If you're a novice in wine country, start your education by stopping at this unique center. The sensory herbal gardens here will help you to identify flavors and to determine which wines marry well with specific foods and regional cuisines. The gardens (one for red wines, one for whites) contain herbs called descriptives and others called affinities. Descriptives help you to recognize the wine's flavor (some might have a peach, pear, or dill flavor or scent, others a tobacco taste); affinities show which wines go well with regional cuisines or certain types of foods. There also are four regional vegetable gardens, featuring produce used in these areas. Guides explain the complementary relationships between wines and food. There is a tasting room, where the same wines featured at the Healdsburg store may be sampled and purchased. ♦ Tasting and sales daily. Garden tours; self-guided tours daily; guided tours daily, June-Oct. 5007 Fulton Rd (at Hwy 101), Fulton. 525.6222 ext 578; fax 546.9221

43 BISTRO RALPH

★★★$$$ In the short time since its opening, this intimate bistro on the north side of the plaza has become a big hit with locals and visitors. Well-prepared food in a casual setting—exposed brick walls, brass fixtures, and expansive windows—is the draw here. Owner Ralph Tingle wears the chef's hat; seasonal produce and the freshest ingredients are hallmarks of his menus, which please meat-eaters and vegetarians alike. Lunch choices include a four-cheese calzone, a lamb burger, and a fiery Szechuan pepper calamari. Innovative soups such as carrot soup with ginger crème fraiche are served both at lunch and dinner. Top dinner entrées include lamb chops with *flageolets* and braised fennel, and pan-seared duck breast with *cassis* sauce and polenta. Finish with a light crème brûlée or a rich chocolate marquise with hazelnut cream. Please note that the menu changes frequently. ♦ California ♦ M-F, lunch; daily, dinner. 109 Plaza St (between Center St and Healdsburg Ave). 433.1380

43 SEASONS OF THE VINEYARD

This beautifully appointed shop reflects the taste of its owner: Rhonda Carano, co-owner of Ferrari-Carano Vineyards Winery. Browse among a seasonal selection of bed and bath accessories, locally crafted ceramics, and wine country–inspired jewelry. ♦ Daily. 113 Plaza St (between Center St and Healdsburg Ave). 431.2222

44 ZIN RESTAURANT AND WINE BAR

$$★★ Zinfandel lovers have a place to revel in the pleasures of this remarkable wine. Scott Silva, who oversees the wine bar, has an obvious passion for Zinfandel. He pours different flights of Zinfandel each week, and nearly half of the wines on the list are devoted to this lusty full-bodied wine. Not surprising, chef Jeff Mall's seasonal menu pairs well with Zinfandel. Coq au Zin is chicken braised in red wine with bacon, mushrooms, and pearl onions, served over celery-root mashed potatoes. As a farmer's son, Mall grew up eating farm-raised products. He grows herbs, heirloom tomatoes, corn, and peppers in the restaurant garden in Alexander Valley. For starters, try the beer-battered green beans with mango salsa, or the spicy sautéed shrimp with white grits. The buttermilk blue-cheese dressing is delicious over organic greens. The Friday-night blue-plate special—seafood cioppino over soft polenta with fried calamari and rouille—packs the place with locals. Join the fun. ♦ Californian ♦ Daily, lunch and dinner.

Reservations recommended. 344 Center St (at North St). 473.0946. & www.zinrestaurant.com

45 HEALDSBURG PLAZA

Crisscrossed with walkways and shaded by redwood and palm trees, this lovely plaza that was laid out in 1856 features a gazebo at one end and is the focus of special events throughout the year, including summer concerts, September Beer in the Plaza, and an annual Christmas tree–lighting ceremony. Like Sonoma's historic Spanish-style square, the plaza is bordered by shops and restaurants. ♦ Bounded by Center St and Healdsburg Ave and by Matheson and Plaza Sts

46 CENTER STREET CAFÉ & DELI

★$ For a hearty breakfast, order from a menu filled with omelettes, skillet dishes, or something more inventive, like sweet potato pancakes with two eggs any style. At lunchtime, select from sandwiches, soups, salads, juices, and smoothies—to eat in or take out for a picnic. ♦ Deli ♦ Daily, breakfast and lunch. 304 Center St (between Matheson and Plaza Sts). 433.7224

46 LEVIN & COMPANY

Book lovers will want to make time to browse the aisles of this new- and used-book store, which now also carries music CDs and tapes. Classics share shelves with books in many categories, including travel and gardening. History and architecture buffs may want to pick up a copy of Historic Homes of Healdsburg, which provides a self-guided tour of 70 representative houses. ♦ Daily. 306 Center St (between Matheson and Plaza Sts). 433.1118

46 DOWNTOWN BAKERY & CREAMERY

Lindsey Shere, the longtime pastry chef at Berkeley's famous Chez Panisse restaurant and author of Chez Panisse Desserts, and co-owners Therese Shere and Kathleen Stewart, have graced the plaza with this old-fashioned bakery. Everything is top-notch—from the yeasty pecan rolls sticky with caramel to the fruit-drenched sorbets and ice creams. You won't be disappointed by any of their wonderful breads, fragile tarts, irresistible

cookies, and skillfully baked cakes. Don't miss dipping the crunchy biscotti into cappuccino, and nothing beats the old-fashioned milk shakes. There's only a stand-up marble bar and a bench inside and two garden benches out front, but the plaza's inviting lawn and ample park benches are just steps away. ♦ Daily. 308-A Center St (between Matheson and Plaza Sts). 431.2719; fax 431.1579

46 WINDSOR VINEYARDS

A pioneer in the direct marketing of wines, this establishment sells wines only from its tasting room and by mail order. The winery produces a wide range of wines—from Fumé Blanc, several Chardonnays, and sparkling wines to Cabernet, Merlot, Zinfandel, and late-harvest dessert wines. You can also order personalized wine labels (for three or more bottles). ♦ Daily. 308-B Center St (between Matheson and Plaza Sts). 433.2822; fax 433.7302; 800/204.9463. www.windsorvineyards.com

46 EL FAROLITO

★$ The standard Mexican menu offers no surprises, but everything from the tamales and burritos to the vegetarian tacos is well prepared and reasonably priced. And there is a good list of Mexican beers. Takeout is available too. ♦ Mexican ♦ Daily, breakfast, lunch, and dinner. 128 Plaza St (between East and Center Sts). 433.2807

47 HEALDSBURG MUSEUM

Housed in the former 1910 **Healdsburg Carnegie Library** building, the museum displays the town's historical collection, much of it donated by local families. Permanent displays showcase the culture of the area's Pomo Indians, the Mexican land-grant era, the town's founding, and the Westside squatters' wars. Special exhibits highlighting 19th-century tools, costumes, and other treasures change several times a year. At Christmastime, the focus is on the annual antique toy and doll exhibit. Check the museum gift shop for reproductions of old-time toys, replicas of Indian crafts, and books on local history and lore. ♦ Free. Tu-Su. 221 Matheson St (at Fitch St). 431.3325

48 FARMERS' MARKET

You'll find all the makings for a sumptuous picnic here. It's a marvelous, sociable event as well as a vibrant showcase for the country-side's bounty. Special annual festivities (at the Saturday market) include the market's birthday celebration in mid-July, zucchini festival in August, pumpkin festival in late October, and holiday crafts in November. Call for dates. ♦ Tu, 4-6PM, June-Oct; Sa, 9AM-noon, May-Dec. Tu, market on Matheson St;

Sa, market in the city parking lot, W North and Vine Sts. 431.1956

49 Hotel Healdsburg

$$$ No amenity has been overlooked at this four-star hotel, which provides visitors a home in this wine country village. With 70 wineries less than a 10-minute drive from the plaza, visitors keep the hotel hopping. From the outdoor pool, Mediterranean garden and pergolas woven from grape vines, spa, exercise studio, and hearth room, to the modern eye-catching design, this hotel is worth a stay, even for locals. Walk along the corridors on the third floor to appreciate the hotel's ingenious sight lines. A glass-enclosed bridge connects the two buildings, mimicking the letter H of the hotel's insignia. The hotel has a restful spice-island ambiance which carries you down avocado-green hallways, over polished wood floors to rooms furnished with teak desks and rattan chairs. The effect is austere, spare, luxurious. Bathrooms have polished concrete counters and floors, stall showers, and deep soaking tubs. Other luxuries: Frette robes and Pacific Coast featherbeds. Request a room on the third floor overlooking Healdsburg Plaza. When you open the French doors and step onto the balcony, you'll receive a satisfying welcome from the plaza's century-old redwoods, bustling shopping scene, and the distant Mayacamas Mountains. Adjacent to the hotel, the Dry Creek Kitchen touts the cuisine of Charlie Palmer, but enthusiasm for the restaurant has waned since the initial burst of reviews. Lunch provides a good dining experience. ♦ 25 Matheson St (at Healdsburg Ave), 431.2800 or 800/889.7188. www.hotelhealdsburg.com
Within Hotel Healdsburg:

The Spa

Located off a walled garden, the spa offers a full menu of treatments that couples can also enjoy together. The menu draws from the elements of fire, earth, water, and air. The earth-based treatment—the wine-and-honey wrap—uses local products to refine and moisturize the skin, improve circulation, and purify the pores. All the while, you relax in a cocoon of warm blankets as a therapist massages your face, neck, scalp, and feet.

50 Toyon Books

Visit this bookstore for bedside reading and a selection of books on wine and travel with an emphasis on Sonoma County and the North Coast. ♦ M-Sa, 9AM-10PM; Su, 10AM-6PM. 104 Matheson St (between Center St and Healdsburg Ave). 433.9270

50 Robinson & Co.

This well-stocked cookware store offers kitchenware, some great cookbooks, decorative items, and whole-bean coffees. ♦ M-Sa, Su, 11AM-3PM. 108 Matheson St (between Center St and Healdsburg Ave). 433.7116

50 Healdsburg Inn on the Plaza

$$$ This Victorian, built as a Wells Fargo bank at the turn of the 19th century, is now a 10-room bed-and-breakfast inn. Most attractive are the large rooms that have bay windows and overlook the plaza. All guest rooms have private baths, king- or queen-size iron and brass beds, and romantic Victorian décor; nine have fireplaces. A continental breakfast is laid out in the solarium at 7:30 every morning; guests can sit down to a hot breakfast at 9AM. No smoking is allowed. ♦ 110 Matheson St (between Center St and Healdsburg Ave). 433.6991, 800/431.8663. www.healdsburginn.com

Within the Healdsburg Inn on the Plaza:

Innpressions Gallery

Fine arts and crafts by North Coast artists are for sale at this compact gallery, which also carries jewelry and gift items. ♦ Daily. 433.7510

50 Friends in the Country

Jane Oriel's shop is filled with an enchanting collection of dinnerware, linens, cushions and throws, and etchings by local artists. ♦ Daily. 114 Matheson St (between Center St and Healdsburg Ave). 433.1615

50 Fabrications

This small shop is crammed from floor to ceiling with bright fabrics for summer frocks or quilt making. You'll also find supplies for textile arts and Victorian ribbon work. Quilting classes are offered year-round. ♦ M-Sa. 118 Matheson St (between Center St and Healdsburg Ave). 433.6243

51 Spoke Folk Cyclery

Rent 21-speed touring bikes, tandems, and racing bikes, by the hour or day; helmets, packs, locks, and a map are provided at no extra cost. There are no guided tours, but the store will advise on the best route. ♦ M, W-Su. 249 Center St (between Mill and Matheson Sts). 433.7171

Restaurants/Clubs: Red | Hotels: Purple | Shops: Orange | Outdoors/Parks: Green | Sights/Culture: Blue

52 HEALDSBURG CHAMBER OF COMMERCE AND VISITORS BUREAU

The staff here provides information on lodging, restaurants, and events in the Healdsburg area, plus maps (with a wine road map of the three appellations of the Russian River area), Sonoma Farm Trails, and more. ♦ Daily. 217 Healdsburg Ave (between Mill and W Matheson Sts). 433.6935; fax 433.7562, 800/648.9922 (in CA). www.healdsburg.org

53 HAYDON STREET INN

$$ It seems like you go back to another era when you walk up to the white picket fence and find guests chatting on the wraparound veranda of this 1912 Queen Anne Victorian. The eight individually decorated rooms have a tranquil ambiance, with pastel colors, lace curtains, wood floors with handmade rugs, down comforters and matching bed linens, and French and American antiques. Six rooms are in the main house, all with private baths (the **Blue Room**'s large bath is two steps across the hall). The **Turret Suite**, an under-the-eaves charmer, features a claw-foot tub next to the fireplace, a comfortable sitting area, queen-size bed, and bath with shower. The two largest rooms, both in the two-story cottage behind the house, feature vaulted ceilings and private baths with whirlpool tubs: the **Pine Room** has a four-poster bed with a lace canopy and a skylight above the tub in the bathroom, whereas the **Victorian Room** has a queen-size wicker bed, a rocker, antiques, and a double whirlpool tub in the bathroom. The full country breakfast might include fresh fruit, muffins, and strawberry crepes. Refreshments are also served in the parlor every afternoon. ♦ 321 Haydon St (at Fitch St). 433.5228, 800/528.3703; fax 433.6637

54 VINTAGE PLAZA ANTIQUES

This is one of the largest antiques collectives in Sonoma County, with more than 50 dealers showing their wares in Healdsburg's "Big Blue Building." Browsers will find everything from china and quilts to antique tools, rare buttons, and old hats. Two booths carry only 1950s nostalgia items; another specializes in goods with Coca-Cola logos. Furniture restorers, upholsterers, and clock specialists here will fix your own treasures. On one Saturday a month (which varies), from spring through fall, the parking lot is the site of a fair and flea market, open to any dealer. ♦ Mall: daily. Flea market: one Sa a month, 9AM-3PM, Apr-Nov (weather permitting). 44 Mill St (at Healdsburg Ave). 433.8409

55 ALDERBROOK WINERY

Award-winning Pinot Noir, Merlot, Gewürztraminer, Chardonnay, and Sauvignon Blanc are produced at this winery west of Highway 101 and downtown Healdsburg. The 1996 Pinot Noir won a gold medal in the New World International competition in 1998; in 1997, the winery's Kunde Vineyard Merlot 1995 vintage and the 1996 Sara Lee's Vineyard Gewürztraminer won the highest number of medals in their classes. Cabernet Sauvignon, Zinfandel, and Viognier are also produced here. Bring a picnic to enjoy on the veranda. ♦ Tasting and sales daily. 2306 Magnolia Dr (just south of Kinley Dr). 433.9154; fax 800/440.0165

56 W.C. "BOB" TROWBRIDGE CANOE TRIPS

Since the 1960s, this company has been renting canoes along the Russian River. This is said to be the most popular canoeing river in the world—and on summer weekends, it truly appears to be. Sign up for any of five 1-day canoe trips or the 2-day trips with overnight camping. You can drop off your car at your destination point and catch a shuttle to the starting area for a minimal fee. Canoe from Cloverdale to the company's **Alexander Valley Campground** (which is on the river) or to the town of Guerneville, or choose shorter segments in between. One of the most scenic routes starts at the campground and winds back to Healdsburg through the heart of the valley and its vineyards. You don't need to know much about canoeing to set off safely, but bring plenty of sunblock and a hat. Sign up for the inexpensive chicken and steak barbecues held Saturday and Sunday between 4 and 7PM. It's highly recommended that you reserve a campsite and a canoe in advance, especially for weekends. Children must be at least 6 years old and proficient swimmers to go on canoe trips. No dogs are allowed on the campgrounds or in the canoes. For a brochure, write to Trowbridge Canoe Trips, 20 Healdsburg Ave, Healdsburg, CA 95448. ♦ Registration: daily, 8:30-11:30AM, Apr-mid-Oct. 20 Healdsburg Ave (between Old Redwood Hwy and Mill St). 433.7247, 800/640.1386

57 HEALDSBURG VETERANS' MEMORIAL BEACH

At this popular park on the Russian River, a beach and swimming lagoon are created by a dam that is erected around Memorial Day and taken down just after Labor Day. In summer, lifeguards are on duty and a snack stand is open. There are some picnic sites with barbecues above the beach. Fishing is permitted 100 yards from the dam; canoes can be rented at **Trowbridge**'s (see above). ♦ Nominal fee. Daily. 13839 Old Redwood Hwy (between Hwy 101 and Healdsburg Ave). 433.1625

58 GIORGIO'S

★$$ Diners craving an uncomplicated yet satisfying meal will enjoy the hearty dishes served in this cozy 1912 farmhouse restaurant. Decently priced and well prepared, the offerings of chicken cacciatore, spaghetti with meatballs, hand-tossed pizza, and other Italian favorites are a welcome respite from designer variations. Enjoy your meal inside by the fireplace or, weather permitting, on the outdoor patio near ponds and a waterfall. ♦ Italian ♦ M-F, lunch; daily, dinner. 25 Grant Ave (just east of Old Redwood Hwy). 433.1106

WINDSOR

Early settler Hiram Lewis thought the landscape in this area resembled the countryside around Windsor Castle in England, hence the name of this sleepy little township that was established in 1855. For wine-country visitors, Windsor offers a country bed-and-breakfast inn, a water-slide park, golfing, and kayaking.

59 COUNTRY MEADOW INN

$$ Only a few minutes from downtown Healdsburg, this two-story, brown-shingle farmhouse, now a bed-and-breakfast inn, was once part of a farm that stretched to the Russian River. The remaining 6.5-acre estate is surrounded by meadows and rolling hills. The inn has five guest rooms, all with private baths; some have fireplaces and/or whirlpool baths. The pleasant Victorian-era décor

features antique furniture and period fabrics. Most romantic is the garden suite, with a king-size bed, a separate sitting area with a fireplace, sunny atrium, double Jacuzzi, private entrance, and deck. Guests can cool off in the in-ground pool at the edge of a vineyard or play a game of tennis on an asphalt court. A full country breakfast is served by innkeeper Susan Hardesty. No smoking is allowed. ♦ 11360 Old Redwood Hwy (between Windsor River and Eastside Rds). 431.1276. www.countrymeadowinn.com

60 WINDSOR WATERWORKS AND SLIDES

There's no turning back once you've started down the 42-foot drop through tunnels and hairpin curves to the pool at the bottom. That's the thrill of the **Doom Flume** and three other ingenious waterslides. If you'd rather swim, there's a large pool and a children's wading pool, plus horseshoes, Ping-Pong, a games arcade, and a snack bar. ♦ Fee. Daily, mid-June–Labor Day weekend. Sa, Su only, May–mid-June, Sept. 8225 Conde La (between Wilson and Windsor River Rds). 838.7760, 838.7360

61 WINDSOR GOLF CLUB

This 18-hole, par 72 golf course sits on 120 acres in a country setting of gentle hills. ♦ Daily. 6555 Skylane Blvd (just north of Shiloh Rd). 838.PUTT

62 SONOMA-CUTRER

Site of the **World Croquet Championship Tournament** every year, **Sonoma-Cutrer** is just as serious about croquet as it is about wine. The winery's three vineyard-designated Chardonnays created by winemaker Terry Adams are found on the best wine lists worldwide. Les Pierres is its top wine. ♦ Sales M-F; tasting and tours by appointment only. 4401 Slusser Rd (between River and Mark West Station Rds). 528.1181

63 MARTINELLI WINERY

Located on the scenic road to Guerneville and the Russian River, this family-owned winery housed in a rustic hop-drying barn produces Chardonnay, Sauvignon Blanc, Gewürztraminer, Pinot Noir, and more, all of which can be tasted. It also stocks a good selection of local foods and picnic supplies and has a picnic area. ♦ Tasting and sales daily; tours by appointment only. 3360 River Rd (between Woolsey and Olivet Rds). 525.0570; fax 525.WINE

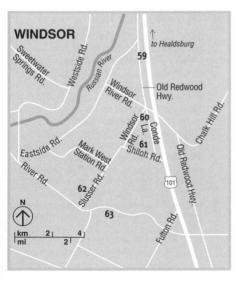

Restaurants/Clubs: Red | Hotels: Purple | Shops: Orange | Outdoors/Parks: Green | Sights/Culture: Blue

CLOVERDALE

An agricultural community just 20 miles north of Healdsburg, Cloverdale was settled in the mid-1800s and is home to one of California's oldest newspapers, *The Cloverdale Reveille*, founded in 1879. From Cloverdale, it is only 1.5 hours to the Mendocino Coast by way of the Anderson Valley.

64 VINTAGE TOWERS BED & BREAKFAST INN

$ This renovated blue-and-white Queen Anne Victorian sits on a quiet residential street in downtown Cloverdale. Listed on the National Register of Historic Places, the house has a side veranda overlooking a rose garden and a lawn where guests play croquet. The inn features a library with chaise longues and a parlor with a TV, stereo, and phone for guests' use. The seven guest rooms and three upstairs tower suites are furnished with antiques and lavish fabrics. Two rooms share a bath; the rest have their own. The largest is the **Vintage Tower** suite, with a sitting room, queen-size bed, claw-foot tub, and Eastlake Victorian furniture. Innkeeper Polly Grant prepares a full breakfast. ◆ 302 N Main St (at E Third St). 894.4535. www.vintagetowers.com

64 RUTH MCGOWAN'S BREWPUB

★$ As expected in such culinary-conscious environs, pub-grub undergoes a transformation. Along with a glass of Ruth's Stout or Cloverdale Pale Ale you can order tapas from Susan Hayward-Keith's creative menu. She makes delicious empanadillas (tiny meat pies) and red potatoes stuffed with smoked turkey salad. The dinner menu offers cioppino,

lamb shank, and smoked pork tenderloin. ◆ Brewpub ◆ W-M, lunch and dinner. 131 E First St (at Main St). 894.9610

65 SHELFORD HOUSE

$ Built in 1885 by Eurasthus M. Shelford on part of a large ranch, this charming Victorian bed-and-breakfast inn is just a short walk from the Russian River. The porch in front looks west across a sea of vines. The inn offers seven guest rooms, three in the main house and four in the carriage house. All have private baths and air-conditioning, some with fireplaces. The rooms are furnished with antiques and handmade quilts, giving the inn a cozy, country feel. Guests can use the gazebo for wine tasting while watching the sunset from the garden, and innkeepers Stan and Anna Smith will make sure your stay is relaxing and memorable. Anna cooks a full breakfast every morning, and wine tours and dinner reservations can be arranged. No smoking is allowed in the inn. ◆ 29955 River Rd (south of Crocker Rd). 894.5956, 800/833.6479. www.shelford.com

66 KOA KAMPGROUND

One hundred and twenty-seven campsites (77 are RV campsites; 50 are tent sites), plus eight cabins, are available here; all sites are equipped with water and electrical hookups. Set on 60 acres, this well-maintained family campground includes a swimming pool, a mini-golf course, a couple of fishing ponds, and a completely stocked store. ◆ Fee. 1166 Asti Ridge Rd. 894.3337, 800/368.4558

66 OLD CROCKER INN

$$ In 1910, Charles Crocker built sleeping quarters and invited his friends from San Francisco for a wilderness weekend of hunting and fishing. In the 1920s the property became a dude ranch. Then Susan and Michel Degive turned this fine old lodge into a getaway for travelers on the wine-country route. From the spacious porch encircling the lodge, you glimpse a peaceful stretch of Russian River and acres of Alexander Valley vineyards. There are five rooms in the lodge and three cottages, each with its own unique furnishings highlighting the inn's history. Other amenities you'll appreciate: a private entrance, deck seating, gas fireplace, modern entertainment center, high-speed Internet, ceiling fan, private bath (some with Jacuzzi tubs, others with antique claw-foot tub), and luxurious robes. All the beds have feather pillows with soft 400-thread-count sheets and a light down comforter. The Degives set out a full complimentary breakfast in a majestic dining room, built in the 1970s. ◆ 11126 Old Crocker Rd (at River Rd). 894.4000, 800/716.2007. ♿ www.oldcrockerinn.com

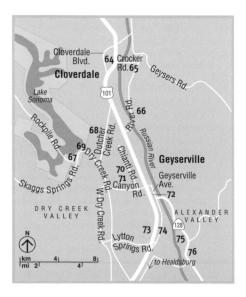

67 LAKE SONOMA AND WARM SPRINGS DAM

This serpentine lake, created by the US Army Corps of Engineers to protect Dry Creek Valley from flooding, was opened in 1985 as a recreational area. The lake and surrounding park total 17,600 acres, with 53 miles of shoreline. Just 10 miles from Healdsburg, the area offers picnic spots, hiking trails, and, in the summer, swimming, camping, and fishing. At the visitors' center you can pick up trail guides and learn about the region's wildlife and the Pomo Indians who settled the area. During the spawning season (generally November through March), salmon return to the adjoining Lake Sonoma fish hatchery to lay eggs; from the second-floor **Interpretive Center**, visitors can watch as eggs are removed from females and incubated. The hatchery's rearing ponds are home to the fish until they are released into Dry Creek. ♦ 3333 Skaggs Springs Rd (west of Dry Creek Rd), Geyserville. 433.9483

On Lake Sonoma:

LAKE SONOMA MARINA

Open to the public, this privately owned marina has boats (including houseboats) and 250 boat slips for rent, a boat launch, a picnic area, and parking. ♦ 433.2200

68 J. FRITZ WINERY

Known for its Chardonnay, this small establishment named for owner Arthur J. Fritz also makes Sauvignon Blanc, Cabernet Sauvignon, Merlot, a late-harvest Zinfandel, and an old-vine Zinfandel; many of the vintages are available only at the winery, which is built partly underground for maximum energy efficiency. Visitors can use the picnic area overlooking the creek. ♦ Tasting and sales daily. 24691 Dutcher Creek Rd (between Dry Creek Rd and Theresa Dr). 894.3389; fax 894.4781

GEYSERVILLE

The little town of Geyserville was founded in 1851 as **Clairville Station**, a stage stop for visitors on their way to see the famous Devil's Canyon geysers on **Geyser Peak**, the world's largest geothermal field, 16 miles to the northeast. Discovered by William B. Elliott in 1846, they are not true geysers but smoking hot springs and hissing steam vents. Between the 1860s and the early 1880s the "geysers" were a prime tourist attraction, and it's remarkable how many people made the difficult journey north to see them—some 3,500 people ventured here in 1875 alone. Ulysses S. Grant, Teddy Roosevelt, and William Jennings Bryan were among the notables who visited. But after 1885, when the more spectacular Yosemite and Yellowstone areas became more accessible, the geysers lost much of their allure. Today PG&E and other companies have plants up there. The geysers are closed to the public, although you can see the steam in the distance.

The town of Geyserville offers two lovely Victorian bed-and-breakfasts, a 60-year-old family-run restaurant, and several wineries, including **Chateau Souverain**. At the **Geyserville Bridge**, you can slip your canoe into the **Russian River** and paddle through the pastoral **Alexander Valley** all the way to Healdsburg.

69 LAKE SONOMA WINERY

Famous champagne maker **Korbel** purchased this winery from the Polson family, who established it in 1977. The tasting room built over the underground cellar is 140 feet above the valley floor and affords a view of Warm Springs Dam and the valley. Sample their range of wines—which includes Chardonnay, Zinfandel, Cinsault, Cabernet, and Zinfandel port—at the bar or on the veranda. ♦ Tasting, sales, and tours daily. 9990 Dry Creek Rd (between Dutcher Creek and Rockpile Rds). 431.1550, 800/750.WINE in CA; fax 431.8356

70 GEYSER PEAK WINERY

You can't miss this ivy-covered stone building with flags flying overhead. The winery is owned by Santa Rosa businessman Henry Trione, and the once-staid wines, particularly the Reserve Cabernet, are getting so good, Geyser Peak received the Golden Winery of the Year award at the California State Fair Wine Competition. Fans of Gewürztraminer made in a softer style should try the winery's version, along with the Riesling, both easy on the wallet. The winery also produces a Sauvignon Blanc, Merlot, Zinfandel, Shiraz, and a Reserve Alexandre (a Red Meritage). Among the cellar selections (featured only at the winery) there is sometimes a late-harvest Riesling. ♦ Tasting and sales daily. 22281 Chianti Rd (northwest of Canyon Rd). 857.9463, 800/255.WINE; fax 857.9402

71 J. PEDRONCELLI WINERY

The original winery and buildings were bought in 1927 by Giovanni Pedroncelli and are still run by his sons John and Jim. The winery produces Dry Creek Valley and Sonoma County varietals; the top seller is the

Zinfandel. Winemaker Gary Martin also makes a Pinot Noir, Merlot, Cabernet, Fumé Blanc, and Chardonnay. After sampling the wines, see the exhibit of local artists' works. ♦ Tasting and sales daily. 1220 Canyon Rd (between Chianti and Dry Creek Rds). 857.3531, 800/836.3894; fax 857.3812

72 SANTI

★★$$ Inside the 1902-vintage brick building is a cheerful room with leaded windows and soft cream walls trimmed in natural wood. Chef-owners Franco Dunn and Thomas Oden have created a European-Italian cuisine that changes seasonally and that complements local wines. For appetizers you may find pickled pink trout, crepes stuffed with mushrooms and chard, and a mini-lasagna with sausage and asparagus. The kitchen is creative with the *contorni*, vegetable side dishes, such as roasted spring onions stuffed with Parmesan cheese and bread crumbs. The menu also features Italian roasts and braised meats, and the restaurant serves a delicious half chicken with sautéed greens, rosemary, and roasted potatoes. For dessert, try the raspberry-muscat trifle. The wine list focuses on local wines, with a half page devoted to Italian wines. ♦ Italian ♦ Daily, dinner. Reservations recommended. 21047 Geyserville Ave (between Hwy 101 and Canyon Rd). 857.1790. www.tavernasanti.com

72 HOPE-BOSWORTH HOUSE AND HOPE-MERRILL HOUSE

$$ In 1997, Ron and Cosette Scheiber purchased these historic houses from Bob and Rosalie Hope. The Hopes had spent more than 4 years restoring the **Hope-Merrill House**, the handsome 1870 Eastlake-style Victorian on Geyserville's main street, doing much of the exterior and all of the interior labor themselves. You can flip through the photo album detailing their work, which was rewarded with a first-place award from the National Trust for Historic Preservation. The stunning hand-silkscreened wallpapers and the carefully chosen antique furnishings make this place very special. Each of the eight guest rooms has a private bath and a different décor. The largest are the **Victorian** and **Briar Rose** rooms upstairs, with antique queen-size beds, bay windows, and chaise longues. Another favorite is the **Bradbury**, with a queen-size bed, a fireplace, a shower for two, and a coffered ceiling papered in an intricate patchwork. The **Hope-Bosworth House** across the street is a 1904 Queen Anne–style Victorian that is furnished less formally; the four guest rooms are smaller and less expensive (all have private baths). Guests at both houses have use of the swimming pool and gardens at the Hope-Merrill House. A hearty breakfast, prepared by Cosette, usually includes fresh fruit, followed by an egg dish and sausages or ham, coffee cake or flaky apple tart, and jams made from fruit trees on the property. With advance notice, she will put together a gourmet picnic lunch. The Scheibers also offer a "Pick and Press" package, including a 2-day stay in the summer while you pick and press grapes, and then a return to the inn in the spring to taste, blend, bottle, cork, and label your own wine. ♦ 21253 and 21238 Geyserville Ave (between Hwy 101 and Canyon Rd). 857.3356, 800/825.4BED; fax 857.HOPE

73 CHATEAU SOUVERAIN

The winery was founded in Napa Valley by Leeland "Lee" Stewart in the old Rossini Winery (now **Burgess Cellars**). In 1970, Pillsbury Corp. acquired Stewart's winery, adding it to other vineyard holdings and then building this chateau. Later, **Wine World Inc.** bought the property, spent millions on new equipment, and planted new vineyards. Designed by **John Marsh Davis**, the architectural complex won an American Institute of Architects design excellence award in 1974 and continues to be admired for its beauty and functionality. The structure boasts a bluish slate roof—an adaptation from the French Chateau style to historic Sonoma hop kilns. Today, winemaker Ed Killian turns out high-quality—and high-priced—wines. Chateau Souverain's whites include Alexander Valley Sauvignon Blanc, Sonoma County Chardonnay, and Winemakers Reserve Chardonnay (the last available primarily at the winery); reds include Dry Creek Valley Zinfandel, Alexander Valley Merlot, Alexander Valley Cabernet Sauvignon, and two reserves—Winemakers Reserve Cabernet and Library Reserve Cabernet (both available only at the winery). There's also a semisweet Zinfandel Blanc, available only here. The winery also has a very good café (see page 159). ♦ Tasting and sales daily. 400 Souverain Rd (west of Hwy 101; take Independence La exit). Tasting room: 857.4245; café: 433.3141 (reservations); fax 433.5174. www.chateausouverain.com

At Chateau Souverain:

CHATEAU SOUVERAIN CAFÉ AT THE WINERY

★★$$ This contemporary café is a great place to eat while on the wine trail. Chef Martin Courtman uses a deft hand preparing dishes that go well with Chateau Souverain wines. His menu changes often, but here's a sampling: For an appetizer, try the Souverain pâté with green peppercorns, or spinach and scallop salad, with almonds, apples, and tarragon. Wines are well paired with entrées, which might include fillet of beef with Gorgonzola potato mousseline (complemented by the 1994 Alexander Valley Cabernet Sauvignon) or eggplant and tomatoes with zucchini noodles and goat cheese fondue (paired with the 1995 Pinot Noir). For dessert, try the chocolate pecan tart. ◆ California ◆ F-Su, lunch and dinner. Reservations recommended. 433.3141

74 TRENTADUE WINERY

Behind the massive red barn doors, the Trentadue family, grape growers in the valley since 1959, produce only estate wines: Petite Sirah, Zinfandel, Cabernet Sauvignon, Old Patch Red (which comes from a patch of century-old vines), Merlot, Sangiovese, Carignane, Merlot Port, and Petite Sirah Port. In the tasting room, pick up picnic supplies, cut-crystal wineglasses, and baskets to tote it all to the picnic area sheltered by a grape arbor. ◆ Tasting and sales daily. 19170 Geyserville Ave (between Lytton Springs Rd and Hwy 101). 433.3104; fax 433.5825. Tasting room also at 320 Center St (at Plaza St), Healdsburg. 433.1082

75 MURPHY-GOODE ESTATE WINERY

Grape growers Tim Murphy and Dale Goode teamed up with wine marketer Dave Ready in 1985 to form a family-owned winery in Alexander Valley. The winery has since earned a reputation for consistently excellent, stylish wines. Christina Benz, the talented winemaker, produces Fumé Blanc, Reserve Fumé, Chardonnay, Reserve Chardonnay, Cabernet Sauvignon, Merlot, and Zinfandel wines. Occasionally there are small lots of "special" reserve wines as well. Tasting-room manager Karen Demostene and the tasting room staff are well informed and will answer questions as they pour wine. ◆ Tasting and sales daily. 4001 Hwy 128 (northwest of Geysers Rd). 431.7644; fax 431.8640

76 STRYKER SONOMA WINERY

This small, family-owned winery has forged a reputation for its estate-grown and -bottled varietals: Chardonnay, Merlot, Cabernet Sauvignon, Zinfandel, and late-harvest Zinfandel. While sampling Stryker's award-winning reds you can view the wine-making process in the next room. There is a bucolic picnic area. One of the staff will take you on a vineyard walk. ◆ Tasting and sales daily; tours by appointment only. 5110 Hwy 128 (between Pine Flat and Geysers Rds). 433.1944, 800/433.1944; fax 433.1948

GUERNEVILLE

This unpretentious little town sits squarely on the site of the logging camp and sawmill George Guerne set up in 1865 to cash in on the redwood logging boom. So many trees were felled that the area around what is now Guerneville was referred to as **Stumptown**; in fact, the center of Guerneville is built on top of the stumps of centuries-old redwoods. Things stepped up when the **San Francisco–North Western Pacific Railroad** chugged into town for the first time in 1877. Soon tremendous trainloads of logs and lumber were heading south, and Guerneville became one of the busiest logging centers in this part of the West. When the area was nearly logged out, entrepreneur A. W. Foster decided to transform the old logging camps into

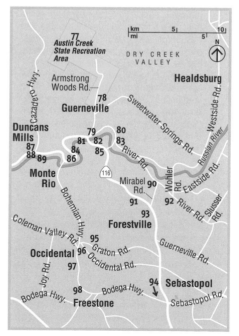

vacation resorts. And so a tradition was born. Guerneville and the **Russian River** remain a popular weekend getaway for San Franciscans bent on fishing, camping, and tramping in the redwoods.

Guerneville offers cafés and restaurants, picnic supplies, canoe and boat rentals, and accommodations ranging from family camping sites to resorts oriented to a gay clientele and Victorian bed-and-breakfasts. Make reservations early, especially between August and October. Annual events include the Russian River Blues Festival in June, the Russian River Jazz Festival in September, and the Russian River Rodeo and Stump-town Days in June.

77 AUSTIN CREEK STATE RECREATION AREA

This 4,200-acre wilderness of oak forests, canyons, and sunny glades surrounds Austin Creek and its tributaries. You can camp at BullFrog Pond (tables, fire rings, flush toilets, and potable water provided, but no washing facilities). For safety reasons, no vehicles over 20 feet in length are allowed. Or hike or ride your horse into one of the four primitive, back-country campsites; preregistration is required. The park sometimes closes in summer because of fire hazards. ♦ Fee. Armstrong Woods Rd (north of Sweetwater Springs Rd). 869.2015, 865.2391

78 ARMSTRONG REDWOODS STATE RESERVE

A county park by 1917, this reserve of stately redwoods along Fife Creek near Guerneville became a state park in the 1930s. The 750-acre property just north of the Russian River offers a number of hikes through the forest. The easiest is the 1.25-mile walk along a marked nature trail, where the highlight is the massive **Colonel Armstrong Tree** (14.5 feet in diameter, 308 feet tall, and estimated to be 1,400 years old). There's also a 1,200-seat amphitheater, shady picnic spots, and barbecue pits. After a morning on the river,

If in your travels through the Russian River Valley you pass through Monte Rio and happen on a 2,700-acre redwood forest, do not think of entering. Owned by the men-only Bohemian Club—an elite group of ex-presidents, cabinet officials, CEOs of major corporations, and a few artists and entertainers—the property affords members a place to escape the workaday world and "camp" in the height of luxury at a 2-week retreat each July. The Bohemian Club counts among its "campers" Henry Kissinger, George H.W. Bush, Walter Cronkite, and William F. Buckley Jr., who come to commune with nature and enjoy the company of other Very Important Persons—with only the trees to whisper their names.

this is a heavenly respite from the heat. ♦ Free parking. Daily, 8AM to 1 hour after sunset. 17000 Armstrong Woods Rd (north of Sweetwater Springs Rd). 869.2015, 865.2391

Within Armstrong Redwoods State Reserve:

ARMSTRONG WOODS PACK STATION

Laura and Jonathan Ayers organize guided horseback rides in the redwood country. Sign up for half-day or full-day rides with a picnic lunch. You can also opt for 2- or 3-day pack trips into the adjoining **Austin Creek State Recreation Area** (see opposite). Brochures are available. ♦ Reservations required. 887.2939

79 KING'S SPORT AND TACKLE SHOP

Serious fishers will enjoy trolling here for gear. Owner Steve Jackson keeps customers informed on river and fishing conditions; he will arrange sportfishing trips with guides. (He is a guide himself.) During the fishing season (around mid-August through February), he opens the shop as early as 5:30 or 6AM. Whether you fish or not, you can find beach gear and attire at this friendly shop. Kayaks are available for rent too. ♦ Daily. 16258 Main St (at Armstrong Woods Rd). 869.2156

79 RUSSIAN RIVER CHAMBER OF COMMERCE AND VISITOR CENTER

Pick up details on Russian River and other Sonoma County restaurants, lodgings, wineries, recreation, and events. ♦ Daily, 16209 First St. 869.9000, 800/253.8800. www.russianriver.com

80 KORBEL CHAMPAGNE CELLARS

Nestled among the redwoods, this gabled brick building covered with ivy overlooks vine-carpeted hills and the Russian River. The winery was built in 1886 by the three Korbel brothers, Czech immigrants who had started out in the logging business along the Russian River felling redwood trees, cutting them into timber and crafting them into cigar boxes. They decided to plant vineyards among the redwood stumps on some of the land they had cleared, first concentrating on still wines and distilling some of them into brandy, and then adding sparkling wines from European grape varietals. The first shipment of their champagne was made in the spring of 1882 and the business remained in the family until 1954, when it was purchased by Adolf Heck, a descendant of a wine-making family from the Alsace area in France. The Heck family has since extended the vineyards and now produces nine vintage and nonvintage sparkling wines, which include a vintage Blanc de Noirs; a Rouge (a medium-dry dark red champagne); a medium-dry Brut; a nonvintage Blanc de Noirs; a Brut Rosé; the original Champagne Sec, first produced in 1882; and the newer Chardonnay Champagne. Korbel Natural has been the sparkling wine poured at the last three presidential inaugurations, and it consistently wins high awards at numerous competitions. More recently, Korbel's new high-priced Vintage Le Premiere was awarded a 91 (on a scale of 1 to 100) by *Wine Spectator* magazine. The Hecks also make the original brandy and some still wines. Fifty-minute tours here guide visitors through the process of making *méthode champenoise* wines from start to finish and end with a tasting of the firm's wines. From May through September, you can also opt for a tour of the hillside rose garden, planted with over 250 varieties of antique roses and a wealth of other flowers and bulbs. ♦ Tasting and sales daily. Tours M-F, every hour on the hour, 10PM-3PM, 3:45PM; Sa, Su, 10AM, 11AM, noon, 12:45, 1:30, 2:15, 3, and 3:45PM, May-Sept; daily, on the hour, 10AM-3PM, Oct-Apr. Tour schedules allow visits to both the champagne cellars and brewery (see below) on the same tour. 13250 River Rd (just north of McPeak Rd). 824.7000; fax 869.2981

At Korbel:

RUSSIAN RIVER BREWING COMPANY

The microbrewery, aglow with copper, is behind the historic brandy tower at **Korbel Champagne Cellars**. Hop growing and micro-brewing were once an important part of Sonoma County's vibrancy. Today brewmaster Randy Meyer and brewer Vinnie Cilurzo reinvent past glories with quality ales to please the most particular palate. The brews are Golden Wheat Ale, Pale Ale, Amber Ale, and Porter, each distinctively flavored and flawlessly brewed. They are available at the **Korbel Delicatessen & Market** (see below) and at restaurants in Northern California. The brewery tours, showing how brews are made, are offered in conjunction with tours of the Champagne cellars. ♦ Daily. 13250 River Rd (just north of McPeak Rd), Guerneville. 824.7000

KORBEL DELICATESSEN & MARKET

★★$$ This restaurant-deli is up-to-the-minute modern with granite tabletops and lots of windows; it also has patio and deck seating. Italian favorites with a California touch predominate: pastas, salads, and specialty entrées like chicken and apple sausage with tomato chutney and polenta.

For quick pick-me-ups there are coffees, espressos, cappuccinos, and snack items. Everything on the menu is available for takeout. Boxed lunches might feature turkey breast with cranberry-horseradish chutney on an herbed sandwich roll, marinated vegetable salad, and fresh fruit and dessert. Don't forget the wine or brew to savor while you admire the view. ♦ Italian/California ♦ Daily. 824.7313

81 JOHNSON'S BEACH

Every summer a temporary dam goes up to create this swimming lagoon along a sandy stretch of beach. It may be foggy and dreary in San Francisco, but it's summer here. When you tire of swimming or sunbathing, you can rent one of the aluminum canoes. This is also the site of the annual Russian River Jazz Festival in September. ♦ First and Church Sts

On Johnson's Beach:

JOHNSON'S BEACH RESORT

$ This family resort sits right on the beach, from which it's only a short walk into town. More than 50 camping spaces are suitable for either tents or RVs; they also have 10 inexpensive, simple rooms with private baths. The campground has hot showers, a laundry, a picnic area, and river access for swimming or fishing. Boats, canoes, and kayaks are also available for rent. Daily and weekly rates. ♦ Daily, mid-May–Sept. 16241 First St. 869.2022

82 APPLEWOOD

$$$ Surrounded by redwood country, this elegant inn offers first-class service in the personal setting of a bed-and-breakfast inn. Owners Jim Caron and A. Darryl Notter have furnished the 10 guest rooms in the Mission Revival–style mansion and six newer rooms in an adjacent building with all the comforts of home. The rooms, traditional yet not fussy, are decorated with antiques, queen-size beds, down comforters, and reading lights. Each room has a private bath, telephone, and cable TV. Most have forest views; several have fireplaces, verandas or balconies, and Jacuzzis. A lavish breakfast is included. The inn has a swimming pool, and the river is only a few minutes away. ♦ 13555 Hwy 116 (between Odd Fellows Park and Drake Rds). 869.9093; fax 869.9170; 800/555.8509. www.applewoodinn.com

Within Applewood:

APPLEWOOD RESTAURANT

★★★$$$ You may choose to dine in the solarium, with forest views, a fireplace, and

Restaurants/Clubs: Red | **Hotels: Purple** | **Shops: Orange** | **Outdoors/Parks: Green** | **Sights/Culture: Blue**

161

marble-topped tables, or in the formal dusky rose dining room at this popular restaurant, touted in *Gourmet* magazine. Dinner is a four-course, fixed-price affair; the menu changes frequently, but chef Brian Gerritsen's dinners always reflect the local bounty and what's ready to be picked in the property's 2-acre organic garden. Appetizers might include butter lettuce and radish salad with avocado dressing, sliced tomatoes with eggplant caviar, and foie gras with grilled brioche and figs. Entrées could be local roast chicken galantine stuffed with bacon, figs, and Bleu d'Auvergen; monkfish braised in lobster–saffron broth; and grilled angus beef rib-eye or pork chop cured in apple cider. The spiced apple fougasse with orange crème fraiche was featured in *Gourmet* and is delicious. You can also end your repast with a cheese course. Guests can bring their own wine ($10 corkage fee) or choose from a list of primarily Sonoma County wines. ◆ California ◆ Daily, dinner. Reservations required.

83 RIDENHOUR RANCH HOUSE INN

$$ Built in 1906 by Louis E. Ridenhour, this turn-of-the-century redwood house was once part of a ranch that extended for 940 acres on both sides of the Russian River. Now an eight-room bed-and-breakfast, it stands on 2.25 forested acres next door to **Korbel Champagne Cellars** (see page 160). Innkeepers Diane Rechberger and her husband, Fritz, had a restaurant in Orange County before moving here, and Fritz, who trained as a chef in Europe, cooks quite a breakfast. Most mornings he bakes at least three pastries and serves them with homemade jam, yogurt, and granola. For the main course, he might prepare an omelette or scrambled eggs with smoked salmon. He leaves cookies out in the afternoon, and guests may arrange for him to cook a five-course dinner. The large living room features a grand piano, a fireplace, and forest views. The most private accommodation is the **Hawthorne Cottage**; it has a queen-size bed, a fireplace, and a window seat. In the main house, the **Spruce Room**, with a queen-size brass bed and antique armoire and dresser, has a forest view. The rooms are more like the guest bedrooms you'd find in a friend's house than the fussy rooms at some bed-and-breakfasts, and all have private baths. There's a hot tub outside. ◆ 12850 River Rd (at McPeak Rd). 887.1033; fax 869.2967

84 FIFE'S GUEST RANCH

$ Nestled among towering redwoods on 15 acres, Fife's is a tranquil, rustic setting with 50 cabins and cottages built in 1905, featuring double-size beds, cotton linens, and simple furnishings. The tent-only campsites along the river are popular with gay and lesbian visitors. **Fife's Road House Restau-** rant and Bar bustles on the weekends. Th-Su, dinner; Sa, Su, breakfast and lunch. ◆ 16467 Hwy 116. 869.0656. & www.fifes.com

85 SANTA NELLA HOUSE

$ Across the river from the **Ridenhour Ranch House Inn** (see opposite), this hotel was formerly the winemaker's residence at the **Santa Nella Winery**. Surrounded by redwoods and only a short walk from the Russian River and **Korbel Champagne Cellars**, the 1870 Victorian features a wraparound veranda where guests can relax. The inn has four guest rooms, all with queen-size beds, private baths, and fireplaces. Innkeepers Kristine and Francis Ranney serve a full breakfast. ◆ 12130 Hwy 116 (at Odd Fellows Park Rd). 869.9488

86 NORTHWOOD GOLF COURSE

Designed by Allistair MacKenzie and Robert Hunter, this regulation nine-hole, 3,000-yard, par-36 course is a golfer's delight, with fairways running through avenues of majestic redwoods. There's a pro shop where you can rent carts and clubs (bring shoes) and a putting green, bar, and restaurant. ◆ Golf: daily, reservations required 2 weeks in advance. Restaurant: daily, lunch and dinner; Sa, Su, brunch. 19400 Hwy 116 (at Redwood Dr). 707/865.1116

86 NORTHWOOD LODGE

$ Next to the golf course, this neat and friendly penny watcher's find has 20 simply furnished rooms grouped around a swimming pool and garden. All rooms have private baths and queen-size or two double beds (one deluxe has a king); some have microwaves and refrigerators. There also are six cabins under towering redwoods, with fireplaces, kitchens, wet bars, dining areas, bunk beds, and decks. ◆ 19455 Hwy 116 (at Redwood Dr). 707/865.1655

87 WINE & CHEESE TASTING OF SONOMA COUNTY

Sonoma County's best wine, cheese, bread, and desserts are arrayed at this quaint 1862 village residence. Wine is available by the taste, glass, or bottle; likewise the cheese is offered by the bite, piece, or pound. People like to take their selection to the parlor in winter, and sit by the fireplace, or in summer onto the porch and garden. ◆ 25179 Hwy 116. 865.0565. www.winetastingsonoma.com

DUNCANS MILLS

As soon as the railroad reached **Guerneville** in 1877, brothers Alexander and Samuel Duncan took apart the sawmill they had been running at the tiny coastal community of Bridgehaven, loaded it on a barge, and headed upriver to meet the railroad at this bucolic spot. Young men looking for logging work followed, and in a short time a flourishing community sprang up around the mill. The 1906 earthquake, which devastated most of the town, was followed several years later by the fire of 1923, in which the mill, Pig Alley (the row of loggers' homes), and, again, most of the town were destroyed. The **Old Railway Station**, the 1971 recipient of the California Historical Society's award for best restoration, is one of the few buildings remaining from the old days. Now it is surrounded by a village reproduced with historical accuracy by the Wallen and Ferreira families. This charming hamlet (just off **Route 116**), with about 20 permanent residents, is filled with art galleries, shops, a quaint inn, the old general store, and more.

87 DUNCANS MILLS GENERAL STORE

This old-time general store dates from the late 19th century. It still offers everything from coffee and pastries to fishing tackle and beef jerky. They also carry newspapers and magazines.♦ Daily. 25200 Hwy 116 (southwest of Cazadero Hwy). 865.1240

87 CHRISTOPHER QUEEN GALLERIES

Showcased here are works of early California artists like the Bohemian Club painters of the 1840s. Their works depict old Duncans Mills, nature, and Sonoma County scenes. You might also find antique prints and nautical scenes. ♦ M, W-Su, also by appointment. John Orrs Garden, Rte 116 (southwest of Cazadero Hwy), no. 4. 865.1318

88 GOLD COAST ESPRESSO BAR

★$ Pull into this pit stop along the road to the coast to find well-made espresso drinks, fresh juices, and pastries. They added a brick oven and the bread is delicious. The place roasts its own whole-bean coffees. On sunny days, take your coffee outside to the garden. ♦ Coffee shop ♦ M-F, 8AM-1PM; Sa, Su, 8AM-5PM. 23515 Steelhead Blvd (off Moscow Rd). 865.1441

88 THE INN AT DUNCANS MILLS

$$ Next to and behind the **Blue Heron**, this delightful inn has four rooms on the second floor, each with its own bath and private entrance, and the **Attic**, with three guest rooms and a shared bath (suitable for friends or relatives). The spacious rooms are decorated with antiques, art, colorful bedspreads, and area rugs; most have queen- or king-size beds (one of the Attic rooms has a double). The **Redwood Room** has two

queen-size beds and a forest view and is accessible for handicapped persons. A hearty breakfast is served in the kitchen; there's an evening social hour in the parlor. Children are permitted only if the entire inn is engaged by one party. No smoking is allowed in the building, nor are pets normally welcomed. ♦ 25233 Steelhead Blvd (off Moscow Rd). 865.1855

88 THE BLUE HERON

★$$ This restaurant and tavern has plenty of old-fashioned charm—a stagecoach stop in former years, it looks like the movie set of an old Western. The menu spans the globe: chowder, steamed mussels Provençale, salmon Catalán, polenta Santa Fe, sushi, and pasta—plus the standard burgers and salads. ♦ American/Continental ♦ Daily, lunch and dinner in summer; Tu-Su, dinner; and Sa, Su, lunch in winter (hours are flexible, so call ahead). 25300 Steelhead Blvd (off Moscow Rd). 865.9135

89 CASINI RANCH FAMILY CAMPGROUND

℗ This huge 125-acre site, surrounded on three sides by the Russian River, offers great family camping. Each of the 225 campsites (suitable for either tents or RVs) has a picnic table and a barbecue pit, and RV hookups include cable TV. George Casini and family have turned the 1862 barn into a recreation hall. There also are showers, a laundry, and store. You can rent a rowboat or canoe; the beach is over a mile long, and there's fishing. Other highlights include volleyball games, and free line dancing and hayrides on Saturday nights between May and September. ♦ Reservations recommended. 22855 Moscow Rd (between Russian River and Russian Ave). 865.2255, 800/451.8400

FORESTVILLE/ SEBASTOPOL

Deep in the heart of redwood country is Forestville, a tiny hamlet that's primarily known for its wines produced in the nearby **Green Valley** appellation, and for its many berry farms. Everybody stops at **Kozlowski Farms** on the way home from the **Russian River** to pick up baskets of raspberries and other homegrown products. Just south of Forestville is Sebastopol, another small town that is known for antique collectives that pop up along Hwy 116 and a bumper crop of apples each year. On the outskirts of town are several wineries, including **Iron Horse Vineyards**.

90 BURKE'S CANOE TRIPS

Canoe down the Russian River for 10 miles through the redwood forests from Forestville to Guerneville. The self-guided trip takes from 3 to 3.5 hours from start to finish, but most people dawdle, turning it into an all-day affair. When you arrive in Guerneville, a shuttle takes you back upriver to your car. There's also a camp-ground in the woods with river views, plus a beach for swimming and a picnic and barbecue area. No dogs allowed. ♦ Daily, May-Sept; Oct, by appointment only. 8600 River Rd (at Mirabel Rd), Forestville. 887.1222

91 HARTFORD FAMILY WINERY

In this château-like winery, you can taste Hartford's hard-to-find wines like the 2000 Sonoma Coast Laura's Chardonnay or the 2000 Arrendell Vineyard Pinot Noir, whose 1994 vintage was served at the White House. This winery specializes in single-vineyard Pinot Noir, Chardonnay, and old-vine Zinfandel. ♦ Tasting daily. Tours by appointment. 8075 Martinelli Rd (between Hwy 116 and River Rd). 887.1756

92 FARMHOUSE INN

$$ This bed-and-breakfast inn lies just off River Road and is nearly hidden in a grove of trees. Designed in the style of English country row cottages, the inn consists of a turn-of-the-20th-century farmhouse and guest cottages built in the 1920s. There are six guest rooms and two suites decorated in restful colors, each with a private entrance, private bath, hot tub, sauna, and fireplace. Rooms here also boast phones, refrigerators, and terry-cloth robes. Spend the day sunbathing around the swimming pool or playing croquet. Innkeeper Rebecca Smith's garden provides ingredients for full country breakfasts; she makes special low-cholesterol or vegetarian dishes on request. She also prepares 2- or 3-day itineraries for guests. ♦ 7871 River Rd (at Wohler Rd), Forestville. 887.3300, 800/464.6642; fax 887.3311

Within the Farmhouse Inn:

FARMHOUSE INN RESTAURANT

★★$$$ Decorated in pinks and greens, this light and airy hotel dining room opens to the public for dinner. The ambiance is informal and rustic without being unsophisticated. Executive chef Jeffrey Young offers an interesting array of appetizers and entrées. Entrées include oven-roasted breast of chicken stuffed with prosciutto, artichoke hearts, and Parmesan cheese, and a roasted vegetable tower of eggplant, mozzarella, and shiitake and Portobello mushrooms with Thai curry sauce. Ask about the evening's dessert selections. ♦ Californian ♦ M, Th-Su, dinner in summer; Th-Su, dinner in winter. Reservations required

93 TOPOLOS AT RUSSIAN RIVER VINEYARD

There's no mistaking this winery, with its eccentric wooden towers. Winemaker Michael Topolos produces Chardonnay, Sauvignon Blanc, Zinfandel, Cabernet Sauvignon, Pinot Noir, and Petite Sirah. Sample them in the tasting room or at the Topolos family restaurant on the property. ♦ Tasting daily; tours by appointment only. 5700 Hwy 116 (between Ross Station and Giovanetti Rds), Forestville. 887.1575; fax 887.1399

Within Topolos at Russian River Vineyard:

TOPOLOS AT RUSSIAN RIVER VINEYARD RESTAURANT

★$$ Though the cuisine here, with flavors of olive oil, garlic, and fresh herbs, is grounded in the Greek heritage of the Topolos family, the menu also reflects a contemporary California touch. Start with the *meze*, a platter of Greek appetizers, or the *saganaki*, imported kasseri cheese flamed at the table, followed by a salad of baby lettuces with blue cheese dressing, or a traditional Greek salad. Main courses range from Petaluma duckling with black currant Madeira wine sauce to *spanakopita* (a spinach and feta cheese phyllo-dough pie). Desserts include a honey-drenched baklava, chocolate mousse, and berry pies. ♦ Greek/Californian ♦ M-Sa, lunch and dinner; Su, brunch and dinner. The restaurant occasionally closes on Monday and/or Tuesday; winter hours vary. 887.1562

93 KOZLOWSKI FARMS

Famous for their wonderful jams, vinegars, and condiments, the Kozlowski family, in business since 1949, runs this shop on the highway between Sebastopol and Guerneville. In season, you can buy organic apples by the barrelful and fabulous berries. They also have homemade berry and apple pies (including their special no-sugar pies), berry tartlets, and cookies. In all, they make 65 food items—every one worth taking home (especially the raspberry fudge sauces). They'll put together a gift basket of Sonoma County products and ship your purchases anywhere in the continental US. A mail-order catalog is available. ♦ Daily. 5566 Hwy 116 (between Ross Station and Giovanetti Rds), Forestville. 887.1587, 800/473.2767; fax 887.9650

93 IRON HORSE VINEYARDS

This winery is responsible for some of California's top sparkling wines, produced exclusively by the *méthode champenoise*. One of the few champagne houses with no French connection, it makes seven cuvées along with Pinot Noir, Cabernet, Fumé Blanc, and Chardonnay. ♦ Sales and tours by appointment only. 9786 Ross Station Rd (west of Rte 116), Sebastopol. 887.1507; fax 887.1337

94 ANTIQUE SOCIETY

You'll find country pricing on the pottery, dolls, quilts, Victoriana, Art Deco, dinnerware, and period furniture at Sonoma County's largest antiques collective. ♦ Daily. 2661 Old Gravenstein Hwy S, Hwy 116 (south of Sebastopol Ave, Hwy 12, between Todd and Bloomfield Rds). 829.1733

94 CALIFORNIA CARNIVORES

This unusual nursery specializes in carnivorous plants from all over the world. You can purchase meat-eating plants such as Venus flytraps, American pitcher plants, cobra plants, sundews, and bladderworts. If you bring your own bugs you can feed the plants. These fascinating botanical oddities fill a spacious new facility. Turn in at the sign for Vintage Gardens. ♦ Th-M, 2833 Old Gravenstein Hwy S, Hwy 116. 824.0433. www.californiacarnivores.com

OCCIDENTAL/FREESTONE

Tucked into the beautiful coastal valley along the **Bohemian Highway** west of **Sebastopol** are the quaint villages of Occidental and Freestone. Both towns were important stops on the **North Pacific Coast Railroad** in the mid-19th century; today, they retain an intimate charm, with historic buildings that house several restaurants, a gift shop, the popular **Osmosis** spa, and the European-style **Inn at Occidental**.

95 MARIMAR TORRES ESTATE WINERY

In a pastoral tableau brimming with natural bounty, a road winds up past the Don Miguel vineyard to Marimar Torres's winery. Torres named the vineyard for her late father, whose family has owned vineyards in Spain since the 17th century. In 1981, investing family money, she proved herself to her skeptical family. Torres bought property in cool Green Valley between mountains and ocean. In the Catalan-style tasting room, you can judge her success as you taste the complex, rich Chardonnay and award-winning Burgundy-style Pinot Noir. And if you love Catalan cuisine, pick up a copy of Marimar's cookbook. Stroll around the vineyards, where

dense clusters hang low to the ground and ripen quickly from the reflected heat. In late afternoon, fog rolls in from the Pacific and cools the vineyards. ♦ M-F, tours and tasting by appointment only; Sa, Su, open to the public for 10AM tour and tastings all day. The winery is 3 miles west of Hwy 116 through the town of Graton. 11400 Graton Rd (between Hwy 116 and Green Hill Rd). 823.4365. & www.marimarestate.com

96 INN AT OCCIDENTAL

$$$ In the 10 years since this lovely place opened its doors, it has established a reputation as one of the best bed-and-breakfasts in the wine country. Gracious innkeeper Jack Bullard has decorated this 1877 Victorian in a delightfully old-fashioned style, with antique furnishings, warm Persian rugs, fireplaces, and fresh flowers. In the mornings, a full breakfast is served in the dining room or on the covered porch; an elegant five-course dinner is offered on Saturday nights to guests only (not included in room rate; reservations required). Many guests combine a stay here with a visit to the **Osmosis** (see below), which is only a few minutes away. ♦ 3657 Church St (at Third St), Occidental. 874.1047, 800/522.6324; fax 874.1079. www.innatoccidental.com

97 NAKED LADY BAKERY & CAFÉ

The bakers keep the brick oven stoked all day, popping out flat bread, pizza, artisan-style hearth bread, and pastries. The café serves delicious focaccia sandwiches. This is a mecca for fresh bread. ♦ Tu-Su. 3782 Bohemian Hwy. 874.2408. www.nakedlady.com

98 OSMOSIS ENZYME BATH AND MASSAGE

The only spa in the country that features enzyme bath treatments, **Osmosis** was voted one of the top 10-day spas in the US by *Travel & Leisure*. You'll love the Japanese ritual. Start by enjoying a cup of herbal tea in the Japanese-style garden; then soak in a hot tub filled with cedar fiber, rice bran, and over 600 plant enzymes. Afterward, you can choose either a warm, relaxing blanket wrap or a 75-minute massage. Communing with nature in the outdoor sanctuary will relax your spirit as well—the entire experience is heavenly. ♦ Daily by appointment. 209 Bohemian Hwy (west of Bodega Hwy), Freestone. 823.8231. www.osmosis.com

Restaurants/Clubs: Red | Hotels: Purple | Shops: Orange | Outdoors/Parks: Green | Sights/Culture: Blue

SONOMA COAST

Just an hour's drive north of San Francisco and a half hour west of Santa Rosa lies **Bodega Bay** and the start of **Sonoma**'s rugged and dramatic coastline— 76 miles of pristine beaches, hidden coves, and grassy headlands covered with wildflowers. Home to the Pomo and Coastal Miwok Indians, this section of the coast was largely ignored by the Spanish for two centuries until Juan Francisco de la Bodega y Cuadro set anchor here on his way to Alaska and "discovered" the bay that bears his name. The Russians actually established the first white settlements on the coast, building outposts at **Fort Ross** and **Salmon Creek Valley** to supply their starving settlers in Alaska with food. But in 1841, after they had killed off the sea otter population and could no longer support their colonies, they pulled up stakes. Today this gorgeous area remains sparsely populated, leaving stretches of uninhabited coastline between small resort towns such as **Jenner** and **Timber Cove**. Most of these hamlets sprang up around lumber mills in the mid-19th century as dog-hole ports, in which lumber was loaded down a chute on the bluffs to ships in the cove below.

More than 5,000 acres and 13 miles of coastline make up the **Sonoma Coast State Beach** system, which encompasses sandy beaches, salt marshes, underwater reserves and parks, and myriad tide pools. There are more than 20 distinct beaches, separated by rocky outcroppings; the most popular include **Doran Beach Regional Park at Bodega Bay**, **Salmon Creek Beach** at the mouth of **Salmon Creek**, **Goat Rock Beach** at the mouth of the **Russian River**, and **Salt Point State Park** just north of **Timber Cove**. You can camp at some of the beaches or find lodging in seaside inns. Wherever you stay, the emphasis is on quiet and relaxation, making the Sonoma Coast an ideal weekend retreat. Bring binoculars for bird watching and spotting wildlife such as harbor seals, California sea lions, and, depending on the season, migrating gray whales. The state park system also includes protected underwater areas for diving. Watch for the brown "Coastal Access" signs with an illustration of bare feet superimposed on a wave to indicate where it's possible to get down to the beach. For more information on this area's parks and campgrounds, call **Sonoma County Regional Parks** at 875.3450. For more extensive information, contact the **California Department of Parks and Recreation**, 1416 Ninth St, room 118, Sacramento, CA 95818, 916/653.6995.

SONOMA COAST

The **Penny Island Bird Sanctuary** is home to ospreys, blue herons, and other shorebirds. Another noteworthy attraction in the area is the **Fort Ross State Historic Park**, centered around the fort that served as the hub of a Russian community in the 19th century. Farther up the coast, a few miles south of **Gualala**, the **Sea Ranch** reserve offers 5,000 acres of wilderness, with walking trails, golf, tennis, swimming, and other recreational activities. The 20-room **Sea Ranch Lodge** is the only hotel in the development, but private vacation homes can be rented through several agencies (see opposite).

1 SEA RANCH GOLF LINKS

Just south of the Gualala River is this privately owned, 18-hole, par-72 championship golf course designed by Robert Muir Graves. It boasts an ocean view from every hole. ◆ Daily. Rte 1 (between Annapolis Rd and Gualala River). 785.2467, 800/SEA.RANCH

2 SEA RANCH LODGE

$$ In 1964 the magnificent 5,000-acre Sea Ranch development was acquired by Hawaii-based Castle & Cook, which did extensive environmental studies before developing the site as a second-home community. The first condominiums were designed by the architectural firm of **MTLW** (**Charles Moore**, **William Turnbull**, **Donylyn Lyndon**, and **Richard Whitaker**), and their simple, elegant designs, with shed roofs and natural-wood interiors, set the tone for much of the other building that followed. Fortunately, the Sea Ranch Lodge, a 20-room inn, was included in the plans so that visitors could also enjoy the serenity and beauty of this unspoiled landscape. All the rooms have private baths; all except one have views of the sea. Most have natural-wood paneling and a rustic, modern décor, with patchwork quilts, bentwood rockers, and window seats. Guests have access to the **Sea Ranch Golf Links** (see above) and to biking and hiking trails. Even if you're not planning to stay here, stop by the bar and sit for a while in front of this unsurpassed view of the headlands and the sea beyond. Within this enormous private reserve are five trails to the beach below, with parking areas west of Route 1. Look for the brown Coastal Access signs to Black Point Beach, Pebble Beach, Stengel Beach, Shell Beach, and Walk-On Beach. In addition, there is a trail into the **Sea Ranch** development from **Gualala Point Regional Park** and another that runs along the bluffs from the same park. ◆ 60 Sea Walk Dr (west of Rte 1, between Stewarts Point–Skaggs Springs and Annapolis Rds). 785.2371, 800/SEA.RANCH

Within the Sea Ranch Lodge:

SEA RANCH LODGE RESTAURANT

★$$ The beautiful dining room, which has views of the bluffs and the sea, is simply and elegantly furnished. There are no surprises on the breakfast menu, and lunch features such standard fare as a chef's salad, seafood pasta, burgers, and several sandwiches. The dinner menu changes seasonally but sticks mainly to the straight and narrow: grilled T-bone steak, pan-seared swordfish, and oven-roasted chicken. ◆ Continental ◆ Daily, breakfast, lunch, and dinner

2 SEA RANCH ESCAPES

This company rents **Sea Ranch** properties for the weekend, week, or month. ◆ 60 Sea Walk Dr (west of Rte 1, between Stewarts Point–Skaggs Springs and Annapolis Rds). 785.2426

2 SEA RANCH VACATION RENTALS

More private homes at **Sea Ranch** can be rented here; write for further information. ◆ Box 88, Sea Ranch, CA 95497. 785.2579

Ever wonder how porter, the toasty blackish beer, got its name? It was originally brewed in London and promoted as a beer for porters and others who toted and hauled and needed a hearty tonic.

Restaurants/Clubs: Red | Hotels: Purple | Shops: Orange | Outdoors/Parks: Green | Sights/Culture: Blue

STARTING YOUR WINE COLLECTION

Inspired by their newfound oenophilic expertise, many visitors to California wine country decide to start wine collections at home. Here are a few guidelines to get you started.

Where to put it?

The words *wine cellar* conjure up a wood-lined subterranean room overseen by a butler in white gloves. But in reality, neither cellar nor servant is needed to establish and maintain a collection of wine. Your "wine cellar" need be nothing more than a simple rack or sturdy box where you can store a few bottles. But even the most modest collection should be stored in a dark, cool place (55 to 65 degrees Fahrenheit). Strong light adversely affects wine, and higher temperatures cause wine to mature too fast. Bottles should lie on their sides (the corks of bottles stored upright dry out too fast and let in air) and in a single layer (moving bottles stacked on top of each other can damage wines). A cool cupboard tucked somewhere quiet is fine, although some collectors opt to build their own wine cellars and others buy one of the ready-made cellars that plug into an electrical outlet. (Check wine magazines for advertisements.)

What goes in it?

One or two bottles of champagne might be in your cache for an unexpected joyous occasion. But sparkling wines don't improve with age (in fact, they get worse), so there's no sense in storing too many bottles. Likewise, there's no need to stock up on distilled spirits—they don't get better in the bottle, so buy them as needed for immediate consumption.

Other than that, the choices are up to your taste, habits, and bank account. If you prefer whites over reds, stock more whites. If you drink your wines young, then buy accordingly. If you're not sure how old you like your wines, buy several bottles of the same wine and allow some to age to see how they mature. Or you might buy a few cases of Chardonnay, Cabernet Sauvignon, Merlot, Pinot Noir, and whatever else strikes your fancy, try a few bottles when you first buy them, and space the others out over several months or years to see how they strike you.

If you can afford it, buy a few high-priced wines and try to blind-taste them along with their less expensive versions. Do this as critics do: Wrap plain opaque paper around the labels and taste the wines with food. You may find that you actually prefer the less expensive wines.

It's both practical and interesting to enter all your purchases in a cellar book, noting the date purchased, wine, merchant, date consumed, and remarks. This will help you define your tastes and prevent you from repeating mistakes. It's a good idea to devote a page to each wine, so you can add notes and comparisons with other wines later.

If you're in doubt about which wines to choose, consult some reviews in the leading wine magazines, take a tasting course, or visit wineries. Eventually you will learn what you like and how much to buy.

A Sample Collection

A well-rounded 36-bottle cellar might include the following:

- 3 bottles of sherry, both dry and medium
- 3 bottles of fortified dessert wine, such as port and Madeira
- 8 red varietals, including Pinot Noir, Cabernet Sauvignon, Merlot, and Zinfandel
- 3 bottles of Italian red wine
- 8 white varietals, including Chardonnay, Sauvignon Blanc, Pinot Blanc, and Fumé Blanc
- 3 bottles of Italian-style white wine
- 3 bottles of late-harvest Sauvignon Blanc, L.H. Riesling, or other sweet white wines
- 2 bottles of champagne or sparkling wine for celebrations
- 3 prized vintages for special occasions

3 STEWARTS POINT

This was an important dog-hole lumber port in the mid-19th century. Cut lumber was sent down a chute here to be loaded onto the ships waiting below. Stewarts Point–Skaggs Springs Road is a scenic but very slow way to get to Dry Creek Valley near Healdsburg and the surrounding wine country. ♦ Rte 1 and Stewarts Point–Skaggs Springs Rd

4 KRUSE RHODODENDRON RESERVE

Spectacular in the spring, this 317-acre reserve shelters a second-growth redwood forest and a large stand of native California rhododendrons. Some of the shrubs are 20 feet high, and when in bloom, mid-April to mid-June, they are quite a sight. There are a few picnic facilities and 5 miles of hiking trails. ♦ Day-use only. Kruse Ranch Rd (between Hauser Bridge Rd and Rte 1). 847.3221, 865.2391

5 SALT POINT STATE PARK

In the past, the Kashaya Pomo and Coast Yuki Indians would take up summer residence here to gather the salt they used to preserve fish—hence the name. The 4,300-acre park offers a wide variety of terrains, from redwood groves and a pygmy forest of stunted cypresses to craggy bluffs and tide pools. The park has trails for hiking and horseback riding too. It is also an underwater reserve, and diving is permitted offshore. Guided whale-watching walks are offered in the winter. ♦ 25050 Hwy 1 (between Timber Cove and Kruse Ranch Rds). 847.3221, 865.2391

Within Salt Point State Park:

GERSTLE COVE CAMPGROUND

This campground has 30 family campsites with picnic tables and fire pits. Gerstle Cove is an underwater reserve; no form of marine life within its boundaries may be removed or disturbed. The rangers are trying to allow the depleted abalone population to recover.

WOODSIDE CAMPGROUND

Also a part of **Salt Point State Park**, this campground has 79 campsites, plus 20 walk-in sites and 10 environmental sites accessible only by hiking. Check in at **Gerstle Cove Campground**.

STUMP BEACH

This is a good spot to observe the breeding of cormorants. No camping is allowed on this beach, but there are picnic facilities with fire pits.

FISK MILL COVE

This beach has picnic facilities with fire pits. There are several trails along the bluffs that lead to the beach below.

6 OCEAN COVE STORE & CAMPGROUND

This campground has 100 sites with hot showers and fire pits; 30 are along the ocean with great views. Hot showers are a fairly recent addition. At the store you can get all the basic groceries, as well as liquor and gas. ♦ Store: daily, Mar-Nov; M, F-Su, Dec-Feb.

23125 Hwy 1 (between Timber Cove and Kruse Ranch Rds). 847.3422

6 SALT POINT LODGE

$ The name sounds fancy, but this is really a 16-room motel with moderately priced accommodations, not easy to find along the Sonoma Coast. Rooms have a standard contemporary décor and distant ocean views; all have private baths and one has a private hot tub; another has a fireplace. There is also an outdoor hot tub and sauna. ♦ 23255 Hwy 1 (between Timber Cove and Kruse Ranch Rds). 847.3234, 800/956.3437; fax 847.3354

Within Salt Point Lodge:

SALT POINT BAR & GRILL

★$$ This family restaurant features a solarium-bar with an ocean view. Breakfast includes omelettes and other egg dishes; at lunch there are burgers, sandwiches, and fish and chips. A bowl of clam chowder and salad is included with such entrées as mesquite-grilled beef, pork ribs, chicken, or a combination of any of the above—all served with the house barbecue sauce. You can also get a steak or a burger, or try the peel-and-eat prawn salad. ♦ American ♦ Daily, breakfast, lunch, and dinner. 847.3238

7 STILLWATER COVE REGIONAL PARK

You'll find a wealth of wildflowers in this park, not to mention ospreys nesting between the cove and Salt Point in the tops of redwood and fir trees. If you take the hiking trail, which runs along Stockhoff Creek, keep an eye out for the Fort Ross schoolhouse, built in Greek Revival style in 1885. There are many good picnic areas, as well as a campground with 23 sites that are available on a first-come, first-served basis. A stairway provides access to the beach. ♦ Fee per vehicle. Rte 1 (between Timber Cove and Kruse Ranch Rds). 847.3245, 524.7175

7 STILLWATER COVE RANCH

$ A former boys' school, this inn offers modestly priced accommodations on a ranch where peacocks, sheep, and deer wander the grounds. One building houses the spacious east and west rooms, both with fireplaces, kitchenettes, private baths, and two double beds. Rustic wooden chairs sit in front of the fireplace, and there's a broad veranda in front. The two white cottages are smaller, but both have private baths, fireplaces, and two double beds. Two other rooms feature king-size beds and private baths; one has a

---

Restaurants/Clubs: Red | Hotels: Purple | Shops: Orange | Outdoors/Parks: Green | Sights/Culture: Blue

fireplace. Groups of fishers or divers often rent the **Dairy Barn**, furnished with eight bunks, a full kitchen, and two showers (bring your own linen for this bargain accommodation). ♦ 22555 Hwy 1 (between Timber Cove and Kruse Ranch Rds). 847.3227

8 TIMBER COVE INN

$$$ Outside the massive timbered lobby, a Japanese pond sets a tone of serenity and contemplation. To complement this peaceful ambience, the rooms originally had no telephones or TV, but they recently have been added in response to guests' requests. Other comments regarding poor maintenance are being addressed as well: In fact, the entire hotel was undergoing renovations—which include new carpeting and a new deck—as we went to press. The property is well designed, from the simplicity of the rooms (though some are rather snug) to the large balconies facing the wild, scenic cove. All 50 rooms have private baths, and a number have built-in hot tubs. Just over half have fireplaces or wood-burning stoves. True romantics will like the large ocean-view units with a hot tub either in the room or on the deck—and a shower with a glass wall facing the ocean. ♦ 21780 Hwy 1 (just northwest of Timber Cove Rd). 847.3231; fax 847.3704

Within the Timber Cove Inn:

TIMBER COVE INN RESTAURANT

★★$$ A few steps down from the bar is the inn's dining room. With its expansive views of the sea, lofty ceiling, and stone walls, it's a dramatic spot for a meal. Eggs, sandwiches, and the like are served for breakfast and lunch, whereas dinner might feature salmon with a mint-basil sauce, filet mignon with Madeira wine-truffle sauce, seafood mixed grill, or steak with a peppercorn sauce. ♦ Californian ♦ Daily, breakfast, lunch, and dinner

9 TIMBER COVE BOAT LANDING

On the weekends, this is one busy place, with divers in wet suits unloading their gear in front and sailors arriving to sling-launch their boats into the cove below. You can obtain a fishing license here, buy bait and tackle, or rent scuba-diving gear or boats. The nominal day-

In Elizabethan England, "the toast" was literally a toasted bread crouton that was dropped into a goblet's dregs to be consumed with the final gulp of wine. Then one day a young man was watching some beautiful maidens bathing and cried out: "I care not for the drink, but I will have the toast," as he dove into the pool with the damsels. Thus, our verbal toasting tradition was born.

use fee includes transportation to and from the cove and use of the hot tub. There's a campground (some sites have hookups), and campers have use of the hot showers, a hot tub, and the laundry facilities. You can also sign up for guided boat tours and fishing or sightseeing trips. ♦ Day-use fee. Daily. 21350 Hwy 1 (at Timber Cove Rd). 847.3278

Within the Timber Cove Boat Landing:

SEA COAST HIDEAWAYS

$$$ The proprietors of the boat landing also rent about 15 private homes in and around Timber Cove, including a rustic redwood cabin overlooking the boat landing with beach access, as well as some much grander places with ocean views. ♦ 847.3278

10 FORT ROSS LODGE

$$ This gray, wood-framed lodge set on a coastal meadow overlooking the ocean has been designed to give most rooms ocean views. Each of the 22 modern units has a color TV and VCR, private patio with a barbecue (the inn provides charcoal), private bath, small refrigerator, microwave, and coffeemaker. Most rooms have a fireplace and some have private hot tubs. Guests have use of a central sauna and hot tub. There's an on-site store with deli items, wine, and beer. The management also rents a two-bedroom ocean-view house. ♦ 20705 Coast Hwy 1 (between Fort Ross and Timber Cove Rds). 847.3333; fax 847.3330

11 FORT ROSS STATE HISTORIC PARK

In 1741, 13 years after he discovered the strait that bears his name, Russian admiral Vitus Bering sailed to the Aleutian Islands and the Alaskan mainland. The Russians were soon exploiting the region for its sea otters. They established outposts on the Aleutian Islands and eventually ventured south along the California coast with the idea of founding a colony to supply the Alaskan settlers with food. In 1812 Ivan Alexandrovich Kuskov, an agent of the Russian-American Fur Company, founded Fort Ross on a high, windswept bluff overlooking the sea. Today the fort (which was abandoned in the mid-19th century) provides a fascinating look at the life and times of the Russian settlers. You should first stop at the **Visitors' Center** for a copy of the walking tour of the fort. Then follow the well-marked path down to the old fort, situated on a dramatic bluff above the sea; little kids will probably be making cannon noises inside the blockhouse as you pass. The small redwood chapel with its cupolas topped with crosses is actually a reconstruction of the original chapel, which was built in 1812 and partially destroyed in the earthquake of 1906. The **Officials'**

Quarters bring the era back to life with Russian furnishings and carpentry and metal workshops. Peek into the kitchen, where the silver samovar for making tea is stored. Guided tours are often available on Saturday and Sunday; call ahead to confirm. **Fort Ross Living History Day**, held annually on the last Saturday in July, re-creates a typical day at the fort in 1836. If you walk out the west gate of the compound and head north along the road, you'll pass the Call ranch house (George W. Call purchased the fort in 1873) and a secluded picnic area in a grove of trees. Adjacent to the park is an offshore underwater park for divers. ♦ Fee per vehicle. 19005 Hwy 1 (at Fort Ross Rd). 847.3286; fax 847.3602

JENNER

The town of Jenner is perched on a high bluff overlooking the spot where the **Russian River** ends its journey to the sea. It was a bustling logging town in the latter half of the 19th century, and it started a new life as a summer resort at the turn of the century. Today Jenner remains a small resort area, popular for its laid-back ambiance and the rugged beauty of the cove, where birds and wildlife abound. Hundreds of harbor seals gather here, and visitors can walk out on the sand spit to watch them loll in the sand and dive through the waves.

12 RIVER'S END

★★$$$ This small, popular restaurant sits atop a cliff where the Russian River empties into the sea, and the many windows afford a terrific view of the scenery. The wood-paneled dining room is decorated with photographs of the Sonoma area, and there's a bar in the solarium. Owner Burt Rangel has attracted a loyal local following for his eclectic cooking, which includes seasonal game such as baby pheasant roasted with juniper berries and filled with fruits and water chestnuts; boneless quail; and venison medallions with the unlikely combination of wild mushrooms and crayfish with a pepper game sauce. The ambiance is fairly informal at lunchtime, but it becomes more elegant in the evening, when the restaurant breaks out linen tablecloths and napkins. The list of local wines is good too. ♦ Continental/Asian ♦ Daily, June-Sept; call for hours the rest of the year. 11051 Hwy 1 (between Rte 116 and Meyers Grade Rd). 865.2484, 869.3252. www.ilovesunsets.com

Within River's End:

RIVER'S END RESORT

$$ There are three rooms underneath the restaurant, four pint-size cabins, and a separate little house that has a full-size kitchen and sleeps up to four people. The

wood-paneled cabins set in a row beside the restaurant are very private and consist of a room with either one or two queen-size beds, a small shower-bath, and a coffeemaker. Sliding glass doors open onto balconies overlooking the river and the ocean beyond. There also are several campsites (no hookups) and a boat-launching facility. Lodging and RV parking throughout the year.

13 GOAT ROCK BEACH

This state beach at the mouth of the Russian River is one of the most popular along the Sonoma Coast. The sand spit that is formed as the river empties into the sea is a haven for seals and is rich in birdlife. In the summer, fish for ocean smelt; in the winter, try the river for trout. Though there is access to the beach on both the river side and the ocean side, swimming is allowed only in the river; sleeper waves, which can surprise the unsuspecting swimmer, make it too dangerous on the ocean side. Picnic areas with fire pits are available. ♦ Day use only. Off Rte 1 (just west of Willow Creek Rd), Bridgehaven. 875.3483

14 SEAGULL GIFTS & DELI

$ Along with espresso drinks, frozen yogurt, and ice cream, this stand-up snack bar dishes out clam chowder, chili, and sandwiches. You can sit at nearby picnic tables and watch the kayakers go by on the river. The gift shop looks touristy but actually carries some good wines. You can also pick up maps and nature books on whales here. ♦ Deli ♦ Daily. 10439 Hwy 1 (between Rte 116 and Meyers Grade Rd). 865.2594

15 JENNER INN & COTTAGES

$$ This comfortable, unpretentious inn invites you to relax on maroon velvet couches in front of a wood-burning stove, with books and games available for whiling away the afternoon. Most of the 16 guest rooms, suites, and cottages are furnished with antiques and quilts and have a warm, lived-in feel. The accommodations range from simple, inexpensive rooms with estuary views to suites with private entrance and deck, a fireplace, and full kitchen. In addition, the inn has a dozen private homes for rent, most with dramatic ocean views and fireplaces. The most romantic are the **Rosewater**, a one-bedroom cottage with a stone fireplace, which is located at the water's edge, and the **Hideaway**, a two-bedroom cottage with a hot tub, at the top of Jenner Canyon. Breakfast—full on the weekends and continental during the week—is included. ♦ 10400 Hwy 1 (between Rte 116 and Meyers Grade Rd). 865.2377, 800/732.2377 (outside CA); fax 865.0829

Restaurants/Clubs: Red | Hotels: Purple | Shops: Orange | Outdoors/Parks: Green | Sights/Culture: Blue

Bodega Bay and Bodega

Bodega Bay (just 68 miles north of San Francisco) is a popular weekend destination for those who enjoy exploring the dunes and beaches, and it has become one of the busiest commercial fishing ports between San Francisco and Eureka. One mile inland is the town of Bodega, a charming haven of Victorian shops and the setting for Alfred Hitchcock's movie classic *The Birds*. The bay was discovered on 3 October 1775 by the Spanish explorer Juan Francisco de la Bodega y Cuadro, for whom it is named. Eighteen years after this discovery, naturalist Archibald Menzies, a member of an expedition led by Captain George Vancouver, disembarked here to collect botanical specimens. The area is still rich in flora and fauna, and during the annual whale migration between November and March, **Bodega Head** draws many visitors to watch the whales as they pass on their way to or from Baja California.

16 Wright's Beach

Thirty campsites with fire pits are available here; sites 0 through 8 are on the beach, and the rest are set back from the ocean. ♦ Fee per vehicle. Rte 1 (between Coleman Valley and Willow Creek Rds). 800/444.PARK (for camping reservations)

16 Shell Beach

This beach is a good spot for observing wildlife. It's directly across from Gull Rock—a nesting area for Brandt's cormorants, Western gulls, and pigeon guillemots—and black-tailed deer, rabbits, and gray foxes can be sighted on the grassy headlands. There's a trail to the beach too. ♦ Day use only. Rte 1 (between Coleman Valley and Willow Creek Rds). 875.3483

17 Duncans Landing

In the mid-19th century, this was where the lumber from Duncans Sawmill in Bridgehaven was loaded onto ships waiting below. (The lumber was transported by carts from the sawmill.) The beach here is accessible via a steep trail. ♦ Rte 1 (between Coleman Valley and Willow Creek Rds)

18 Portuguese Beach

A steep trail leads to this beach. Rest rooms are available. ♦ Day use only. Rte 1 (between Coleman Valley and Willow Creek Rds). 875.3483

19 Sonoma Coast State Beaches/Bodega Dunes State Park Campground

More than 900 acres of gently rolling sand dunes lie covered with soft mounds of dune grasses here. Monarch butterflies winter in the eucalyptus trees, and you can spot alligator lizards, black-tailed deer, jackrabbits, owls, foxes, and badgers throughout the year. Trails include a 5-mile loop for hiking and horseback riding; another trail leads to Bodega Head. The park features picnic areas and a campground with 98 campsites. ♦ Fee per vehicle. Rte 1 (north of East Shore Rd), Bodega Bay. 875.3483, 800/444.PARK (for camping reservations)

19 Salmon Creek Beach

This popular sandy beach at the mouth of Salmon Creek is about 2 miles long and includes a shallow swimming area. The creek is a good spot to fish for steelhead trout, and the saltwater and freshwater marshes are filled with wildlife. A trail leads south to Bodega Head. ♦ Day use only. Rte 1 (north of East Shore Rd), Bodega Bay. 875.3483

19 Children's Bell Tower

One hundred and thirty bells chime from three towers in this moving memorial to a Bodega Bay child who lost his life during a family trip to Italy. Seven-year-old Nicholas Green was traveling through the Italian countryside in 1994 with his parents when he was shot by bandits. His parents donated his organs at the request of the local hospital. The announcement of Bodega Bay's bell project mobilized Americans and Italians to donate bells. You'll see school bells, church bells, ships' bells, mining bells, even cowbells. The Marinelli Foundry, which has been making bells for the Vatican for a thousand years, donated bells inscribed with the names of Nicholas and the seven sick people who received his organs and a new chance to live a full life. ♦ Daily. Coast Hwy 1 (at the entrance to Bodega Dunes State Park), Bodega Bay

20 Chanslor Ranch

$ If you're planning on horseback riding, why not bunk at the bed-and-breakfast on this 700-acre working ranch bordered by Salmon Creek? The suburban ranch-style house has three guest rooms with private baths and color TV sets (two of the bedrooms can be connected to make an impromptu suite) and a two-room loft suite with private balconies and whirlpool bath. A continental breakfast is included. ♦ 2660 N Hwy 1 (between Bay Hill and Coleman Valley Rds), Bodega Bay. 875.2721; fax 857.2785

Within the Chanslor Ranch:

Chanslor Stables

Sign up for guided trail rides through the hills and dunes surrounding Bodega Bay. The hilly 1.5-hour Salmon Creek and Eagle's View Ride affords thrilling Pacific, Bay, and Sonoma views; the Bodega Bay Beach Ride, also 1.5 hours, trails through the dunes on the beach for eye-stopping marina and harbor views.

Beginners are welcome. ♦ Daily. Reservations recommended

CHANSLOR WETLANDS WILDLIFE PROJECT

Within this enormous 700-acre ranch, a 250-acre preserve protects a rare brackish marsh as well as a freshwater marsh, and pools and ponds bordering Salmon Creek. The area has been set aside as a haven for species on endangered or protected, threatened, or special concern lists. These vast wetlands are home to a host of birds, as well as some fish and amphibians and such mammals as river otters and mountain lions. Take a break for a guided tour by foot or horseback here. ♦ Call for reservations. 875.2721

21 SANDPIPER

★★$$$ At this casual café, the service couldn't be friendlier and the bonus is a view of the harbor and bay. For breakfast, try eggs served with home fries or hash browns and link sausage, *huevos rancheros*, or create your own omelette. At lunch try the exceptionally thick clam chowder, a salad, fish and chips, or a burger. The dinner menu includes several more ambitious dishes, such as Mediterranean fish stew in a zesty broth, pasta primavera, and prawns tempura. Desserts change daily. There are children's specials too. ♦ American ♦ Daily, breakfast, lunch, and dinner. 1410 Bay Flat Rd (west of West Shore Rd), Bodega Bay. 875.2278

22 BRANSCOMB GALLERY

This gallery exhibits works by California artists, most notably the wildlife etchings of Mendocino artist James J.D. Mayhew, landscapes by Gerrold Bellaire, and minimalist paintings by Edmund DeChant. ♦ M,Tu, Th-Su. 1588 East Shore Rd (at Rte 1), Bodega Bay. 875.3388.

Within Branscomb Gallery:

BODEGA BAY INN

Original art and comfortable accommodations make a winning combination. Painter and sculptor Ruth Branscomb has created a perfect venue for a weekend getaway. The three rooms have king-size beds, marble-tile bathrooms, TVs, and lovely landscape oil paintings. Ask for a west-facing room with views of Campbell Cove and Bodega Head. Rates include continental breakfast. ♦ 888/875.8733. www.bodegabayinn.com

23 CANDY & KITES

When the wind is good, stop here to pick up dual-control stunt kites, beginners' kites, and colorful dragon kites. A grouping of baskets overflows with saltwater taffy in flavors such as red cinnamon, black licorice, and peanut butter. Believe it or not, the taffy comes in sugar-free versions too. ♦ M, Tu, F-Su. 1415 N Hwy 1 (south of West Shore Rd), Bodega Bay. 875.3777

23 THE BOATHOUSE

$ This seafood snack bar offers fish and chips, clam strips, fried calamari, oysters, prawns, and scallops. Landlubbers can also get burgers and sandwiches. Take your food elsewhere or grab a table on the large deck outside. ♦ Seafood ♦ Daily, lunch and dinner. 1445 N Hwy 1 (south of West Shore Rd), Bodega Bay. 875.3495

At the Boathouse:

NEW SEA ANGLER–JAWS & PREDATOR SPORTFISHING

The Boathouse offers sportfishing trips on the 65-foot *New Sea Angler* or the 55-foot *Jaws*, which carry 49 and 38 passengers, respectively. The larger ship heads out to Cordell Bank, Fanny Shoals, and the Farallon Islands, whereas *Jaws* specializes in light-tackle rock cod trips. Bait and tackle will be provided if desired. Order breakfast and boxed lunches from the restaurant. Whale-watching trips, January–April. ♦ Daily. Reservations required, plus 50% deposit. 875.3344

24 BRISAS DEL MAR

★★$$ Ask locals to recommend a place for lunch or dinner and they will likely say Brisas del Mar. You won't mind the plain-Jane décor when you see the reasonable prices. The exposure to fresh sea air whets the appetite for seafood, and this is the place to assuage it. For lunch, try sandwiches of Dungeness crab cake, grilled snapper, or king salmon. House specialties include *alambres de camarones*, a skewer of jumbo shrimp, bell pepper, onions, mushrooms, and cherry tomatoes. Other seafood delights include crab enchiladas, seviche salad, and taco salad. Order barbecued oysters and imported beer such as Negra Modelo or Tecate, and watch the sun drop into the Pacific. ♦ Mexican/Seafood ♦ Daily, lunch and dinner; also, Sa, Su, breakfast during summer. 2001 Coast Hwy 1 (near Bay Hill Rd), Bodega Bay. 875.9190 ⟁

24 BODEGA HARBOR INN

$ This very basic motel offers 16 rooms and suites in slate-blue bungalows on a hillside overlooking **Porto Bodega Marina**. All have small private baths and cable TV. The inn also rents cottages and houses in the area. ♦ 1345 Bodega Ave (between Windy La and Rte 1), Bodega Bay. 875.3594

24 CRAB POT

Billie and Lynn Douglas have been smoking fish and seafood, providing takeout with flair, at their tiny bright orange shack since 1970. Stop by and most likely you'll find aromatic smoke seeping from the door; they use apple-wood to smoke salmon, tuna, swordfish, sturgeon, and peppered salmon. They'll make shrimp and crab sandwiches, too, and offer a few wines, mostly from Pedroncelli and Geyser Peak. In season, they also have whole cooked Dungeness crabs. ♦ Seafood ♦ Daily, 1750 N Hwy 1 (between Windy La and Bay Hill Rd), Bodega Bay. 875.9970

25 THE INN AT THE TIDES

$$$ Seen from the road, the brown-shingled guest lodges scattered over the hillside to the east of Route 1 look more like condominiums than an inn. There are 86 guest rooms alto-gether, every one with a view of the harbor below. Some have tile fireplaces, and all have small refrigerators, coffeemakers, cable TV, and terry-cloth robes. The décor is somewhat dated, featuring plush carpeting and print comforters. Guests have use of the outdoor lap pool, whirlpool spa, and Finnish sauna. A complimentary continental breakfast is served every morning. ♦ 800 Coast Hwy 1 (between N Harbor Way and Windy La), Bodega Bay. 875.2751, 800/541.7788; fax 875.2669

Within Inn at the Tides:

BAY VIEW RESTAURANT AND LOUNGE

★$$$ This intimate restaurant, serving Cali-fornia fare 5 nights a week, looks out on the bay and a terraced flower garden. The menu, which changes seasonally, might include baked king salmon in a potato crust accented by tomato-dill beurre blanc or pork loin with fresh herbs paired with polenta and wild mushroom sauce. For starters, try the Dungeness crab cakes or Caesar salad for two. And for dessert, sample the flourless chocolate-hazelnut torte. Guests at the inn are served continental breakfast here too. ♦ Cali-fornian ♦ W-Su, dinner. Reservations recommended. 875.2751

26 BODEGA HEAD

The southernmost tip of the peninsula that extends south from Bodega Dunes, this site is characterized by high bluffs and steep, craggy cliffs. Bodega Rock, a half-mile offshore, is a breeding ground for Brandt's cormorants and Western gulls; harbor seals and California sea lions can also be spotted. During the annual whale migrations, this is a prime spot for watching the giant mammals, and talks about the whales are given to the public here on Sundays between mid-December and mid-April. On clear days the rugged area offers fine views of the Marin and Sonoma Coasts. ♦ West Side Rd (west of West Shore Rd), Bodega Bay. 875.3483

27 DORAN BEACH REGIONAL PARK AT BODEGA BAY

Just down the road from the **Bodega Bay Lodge & Spa** (see page 175) is a regional park perched on the narrow, 2-mile-long spit of sand that separates Bodega Harbor from Bodega Bay. Bird watchers haunt the salt marshes and the low sand dunes to gaze at sanderlings, willets, snowy plovers, and other shorebirds. The park has ocean and bay access and is a popular spot for swimming and surfing. It's also a good place for clam digging; razor and horseneck clams are just two of the varieties found here. There's an ocean-fishing pier, a public boat launch, and a fish-cleaning station, along with picnic tables and rest rooms. The park has 134 campsites with space for a car or RV, plus 10 suitable for tents only. ♦ Fee per vehicle. Doran Beach Rd (southwest of Doran Park Rd), Bodega Bay. 875.3540

28 VACATION RENTALS USA

This agency rents approximately 100 private beach houses, ranging from cabins on Salmon Creek to five-bedroom places in a country-club setting. Rentals in the **Bodega Harbour** development include guest privileges at the **Bodega Harbour Country Club**. Rent for 2 or 3 nights or by the week or month. ♦ Daily. 555 Coast Hwy 1 (between Doran Park and West Shore Rds), Bodega Bay. 875.4000, 800/548.7631; fax 875.2204

28 LUCAS WHARF FISH MARKET AND DELICATESSEN

The boats unload their catches right at the wharf, where the fish are cleaned and placed in the market for sale. Picnickers will find smoked salmon, cooked shrimp, pickled herring, and crab meat, along with fresh fish fillets and whole salmon for the grill. You'll also find an array of cold cuts, cheeses, giant pickles, pig's feet, and other fare, and the deli will make up sandwiches to go. ♦ Daily. 595 Coast Hwy 1 (between Doran Park and West Shore Rds), Bodega Bay. 875.3562; fax 875.3032

At Lucas Wharf Fish Market and Delicatessen:

LUCAS WHARF RESTAURANT & BAR

★$$ This is a pleasant spot for a beer or a quick bite. The broad, wooden-plank floorboards and old-fashioned wooden chairs give the restaurant a vaguely nautical theme, but the real décor is just outside the windows: a nonstop view of the busy harbor. A bowl of Boston clam chowder will take the chill off, or try the mussels steamed in white wine, shallots, and garlic, or the standard crab Louis. Entrées might include grilled red snapper fillet with lemon butter, wild king salmon with hollandaise sauce, and a deep-fried seafood mix of calamari, prawns, and oysters. ♦ Seafood ♦ Daily, lunch and dinner. 875.3522

28 TIDES WHARF FRESH FISH MARKET

The same folks who own **The Inn at the Tides** (see page 174) have extensively renovated and improved this property, now the largest fish market in Northern California. In this sleek, clean wharfside setting with a world-class view, you can pick up a cooked whole crab or oysters for a picnic, fresh fish for the grill, packaged cheeses, and chilled Sonoma wines. The fish market also has bait and tackle. ♦ Daily. 835 Coast Hwy 1 (between Doran Park and West Shore Rds), Bodega Bay. 875.3554; fax 875.3285

Within the Tides Wharf Fresh Fish Market:

TIDES WHARF RESTAURANT

★$$ This seafood restaurant's menu runs the gamut from fish and chips and grilled or pan-fried fillets to seafood stew and fresh and deep-fried oysters. At breakfast, you get the usual egg dishes, hotcakes, and side orders. The décor is minimal—modern with brass rails and traditional appointments such as oversize captain's chairs and wooden tables—but the main attraction is the big windows and the view of the bay. Time your visit to see fishing boats unloading their catch. ♦ Seafood ♦ Daily, breakfast, lunch, and dinner. 875.3652

29 BODEGA HARBOUR GOLF LINKS

Robert Trent Jones Jr. designed this privately owned 18-hole, par-70 golf course. Jones laid it out so there would be ocean views from every hole. From the championship tee, the course is 6,265 yards; it is 5,685 yards from the regular tee. ♦ Daily. Reservations taken up to 60 days in advance. 21301 Heron Dr (at S Harbour Way), Bodega Bay. 875.3538; fax 875.9680

29 BODEGA BAY LODGE & SPA

$$$ This lodge adjacent to the golf links consists of a series of two-story, brown-shingled buildings on a secluded, terraced site sheltered by pines and overlooking the salt marshes of Bodega Bay. The showpieces of the main lobby are the massive fieldstone fireplace and two stunning 500-gallon saltwater aquariums filled with tropical fish, starfish, and coral. All 78 of the inn's rooms have patios or balconies, coffeemakers, and cable TV. The décor is clean-cut contemporary, with carpeting, European-style duvet comforters, and tile bathrooms. There's a modest-size swimming pool here and a whirlpool spa that stands in a fieldstone-and-redwood gazebo. Guests also have use of a redwood sauna and a fitness room equipped with Lifecycles and Nautilus equipment. The hotel will make a basket lunch for a day's outing. Complimentary wine is served between 5PM and 6PM. ♦ 103 Coast Hwy 1 (at Doran Park Rd), Bodega Bay. 875.3525, 800.368.2468; fax 875.2428

Within the Bodega Bay Lodge & Spa:

THE DUCK CLUB RESTAURANT

★$$ True to the restaurant's name, duck is the highlight of chef Jeffrey Reilly's menu—our favorite is crisp roasted Liberty duck with Valencia orange sauce. Other culinary highlights include inventive renditions of the Bodega Bay catch of the day, Sonoma Coast lamb, and butternut squash ravioli laced with pine nut–Vermouth cream sauce. For starters try Bodega Bay New England–style clam chowder, seared Sonoma foie gras, or mixed organic greens salad. The crème brûlée and hot fruit crisp with vanilla bean ice cream both make fine finales. ♦ Californian ♦ Daily, breakfast and dinner. Reservations recommended

30 SONOMA COAST VILLA

$$$$ Fashioned of terra-cotta–hued stucco, with a red-tile roof and sweeping veranda, this 60-acre property has the feel and amenities of a luxury Mediterranean villa. Each of the 12 rooms is furnished in a distinctive style with elegant but comfortable furniture, a working fireplace, a queen- or king-size bed, a full bath, and such amenities as TV and VCR, refrigerator stocked with complimentary wine and beer, and coffeemaker. Steps away from the rooms is a landscaped garden with a pool, whirlpool, and the courtyard spa. The full-service menu includes Age-Defying treatment (a foot bath, massage, and facial) and the popular salt scrub. The secluded tower is a fine place to curl up with a book. A full country breakfast is included in the room rate. ♦ 16702 Hwy 1 (between Valley Ford Freestone Rd and Bodega Hwy), Bodega. 876.9818, 888/404.2255; fax 876.9856. www.scvilla.com

---

Restaurants/Clubs: Red | Hotels: Purple | Shops: Orange | Outdoors/Parks: Green | Sights/Culture: Blue

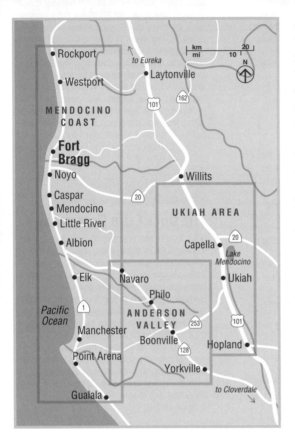

From Cloverdale in the Russian River Valley, it's a short jaunt north on **Highway 101** to the tiny township of **Hopland** and to the dozen or so wineries scattered along the highway close to town and north toward **Ukiah**.

A rural, sparsely populated area, this part of Mendocino County has enjoyed a renaissance of wine-making since the early 1970s. Hopland, the improbable center of it all, was a hop-growing region hit by an economic slump when the sale of hops (the aromatic dried flowers of the hop vine used to make beer) declined in the 1950s. The most visible sign of the current prosperity is the **Fetzer Vineyards**, a remarkable 50-acre complex, with a tasting room, visitors' center, and bed-and-breakfast set in the 5-acre organic **Bonterra Gardens** and vineyard at 13601 East Side Road. Some local wineries also have opened tasting rooms in Hopland. If you have the time, drive the back roads and visit such wineries as **Hidden Cellars, McDowell Valley Vineyards,** or tiny **Whaler Vineyards,** all set in a bucolic, rugged landscape. More wineries are strung along the highway all the way to Ukiah, the county seat. And north of **Lake Mendocino,** a few more remote, small wineries are tucked into the folds of the **Redwood Valley.**

Between visits to favorite wineries, it's easy to fit in some bicycling around the wine country. From Hopland or Ukiah, you can drive over the mountains to **Clearlake,** visiting such wineries as **Steele** in **Kelseyville,** where some wines are made from Mendocino grapes. Depending on which route you take, it's a 30- to 40-minute drive one way. This part of Mendocino is also home to two of the few producers of pot-still brandies (made by the same process used in the Cognac region of France). **Jepson Vineyards** produces brandy and wine, and you may see the copper alambic (or distilling apparatus) when you visit, but, alas, you cannot taste the brandy there. The second producer is **Germain-Robin**; you may purchase Germain-Robin brandy at its sales and tasting rooms in Ukiah.

In Ukiah, the **Grace Hudson Museum and Sun House** is a must-see. As for lodging, try the casually elegant **Bed and Breakfast Inn** at Fetzer, the three-story Victorian **Hopland Inn** in Hopland, or a bed-and-breakfast in Hopland or Ukiah. A less well-known alternative is **Vichy Springs Resort** east of Ukiah, a historic hot-springs inn (which also bottles the naturally effervescent mineral water under the Vichy Springs label).

Good restaurants in the Hopland and Ukiah regions include the **Bluebird Café** for hearty diner fare and the **Mendocino Brewing Company** for casual pub fare and live music on Saturday nights. The wineries in this area are also close enough together for you to spend the morning visiting the tasting rooms in Hopland, plus a few more nearby wineries, and still have time to lunch in **Boonville**. Mendocino County farmers' markets happen May to October in Boonville, Ukiah, Willits, Mendocino, and Fort Bragg. Call Mendocino County Farmers' Market Association for times and locations, 964.6340.

For information on the state parks in Mendocino County, call 937.5804; for camping reservations, call 800/444.7275; and for vacation home rentals, contact **Mendocino Coast Reservations** at Box 1143, Mendocino, CA 95460, or call 937.5033 or 800/262.7801. For information on wineries, call 468.9886, online information at www.gomendo.com. This one-stop web site covers lodging, dining, wineries, attractions, food and wine events, and directions. Order the excellent travel planner.

Ukiah Area

1 Frey Vineyards

Owned by Marguerite Frey and her 12 children, this small winery on a 145-acre ranch was constructed bit by bit with salvaged timber from the old **Garret Winery** in Ukiah. The vineyards are cultivated organically, and winemaker Jonathan Frey makes only small amounts of several different varietals. Gewürztraminer, Chardonnay, Sauvignon Blanc, and a white table wine comprise the whites. Reds include Cabernet, Syrah, Petite Sirah, Zinfandel, and Merlot. This is one of the few wineries in California that doesn't add sulfites. ♦ Tasting and tours by appointment only. 14000 Tomki Rd (between East and Canyon Rds), Redwood Valley. 485.5117, 800/760.3739

2 Gabrielli Winery Vineyards

Winemaker Jefferson Hinchliffe's Nativo Zinfandel was, in February 1997, the first California wine made entirely from native materials—not only pressed from grapes grown in Mendocino but also aged in made-in-Mendocino oak barrels. This small family farm winery turns out only 8,000 cases a year. Praise has often focused on the Sangiovese and Zinfandel Mendocino County Reserve, but the other wines also merit atten-

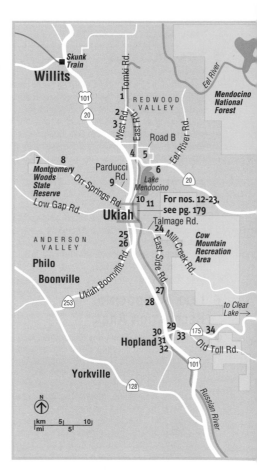

For nos. 12-23, see pg. 179

Restaurants/Clubs: **Red** | Hotels: **Purple** | Shops: **Orange** | Outdoors/Parks: **Green** | Sights/Culture: **Blue**

tion. ◆ Tasting, M-F; weekend tours and tasting by appointment. 10950 West Rd (between East Rd and Hwy 101), Redwood Valley. 485.1221, fax 485.1225

3 QUESERIA MICHOACAN CHEESE COMPANY

Small batches of queso fresco, a firm white cheese, and firm-textured ricotta as well as soft-ripened cheese are sold at this cheese factory. Nicholas Muniz, the cheesemaker, gives tours by appointment. ◆ 9701 West Rd, Redwood Valley. 485.0579

4 REDWOOD VALLEY CELLARS

Locals say the interior resembles an upside-down champagne glass. You decide while treating your palate to various wines of Mendocino all in one tasting room. There is a garden with tables for picnicking, a deli, a shop selling handcrafted gifts, maps, and visitors' information; art exhibits are often held here. ◆ Tasting and sales daily. 7051 N State St (between Rte 20 and Hwy 101), Redwood Valley. 485.0322; fax 485.6784

5 FIFE VINEYARDS

The small rustic winery isn't much to look at, but it offers a hillside terrain of Petite Sirah and Zinfandel vineyards on the Ricetti Bench in the Redwood Valley, known for rich soils and an eye-popping view of Lake Mendocino, plus the unbeatable attraction of John Buechsenstein's well-made wines. Owner Dennis Fife had a long career as a Napa Valley vintner before locating here; his first releases for Fife of Mendocino grapes were in April 1998: a 1996 Redhead Zinfandel and a 1996 Redhead Mendocino Zinfandel. Fife continues to bottle some wines in the Napa Valley. Taste the wines outside at the picnic table and enjoy the views. ◆ Tastings and sales daily; tours by appointment. 3620 Road B (between Rte 20 and East Rd), Redwood Valley. 485.0323. www.fifevineyards.com

6 LAKE MENDOCINO RECREATION AREA

📍 Ten miles north of Ukiah, this recreational lake was created when the Army Corps of Engineers dammed the Russian River at the mouth of the Coyote Valley in 1958. The 1,822-acre lake, bordered by foothills, is a popular destination for boating, waterskiing, windsurfing, and swimming. The lake has two large boat launches and protected beaches for swimming, plus nearly 300 family campsites (available on a first-come, first-served basis), and 100 picnic sites, each with tables and a barbecue pit. In season, there's lots of good fishing for striped bass, large and smallmouth bass, crappie, bluegill, and catfish. Miles of hiking paths wind through the foothills surrounding the lake,

which also includes 689 acres of protected wildlife habitat. ◆ Park entrances: Marina Dr (east of East Side Calpella Rd), Rte 20 and Marina Dr, Lake Mendocino Dr (east of N State St). Recreation area office: 1160 Lake Mendocino Dr (east of N State St). 462.7581

Within the Lake Mendocino Recreation Area:

VISITORS' CENTER

To learn more about Native American traditions and Lake Mendocino, visit this center located in the **Pomo Day-Use Area** at the north end of the lake. It was built by the Army Corps of Engineers in the shape of a ceremonial dance house. The exhibits, films, and programs provide information about local Indian ways. ◆ Free. W-Su, Apr-Sept; Sa, Su, Oct-Mar. Marina Dr (between East Side Calpella Rd and Rte 20). 485.8285

7 MONTGOMERY WOODS STATE RESERVE

📍 There's a self-guided nature trail through groves of redwoods in this 1,142-acre park, as well as several picnic sites with tables. ◆ Day use only. Orr Springs Rd (between Hwy 101 and Low Gap Rd). Call Mendocino State Parks for information at 937.5804

8 ORR HOT SPRINGS

Ukiah's historic hot springs is a wonderful place to take time out from wine tasting. The springs are housed in a restored 1850s building. The water flows from several different springs and is unaltered by chemicals. Bathing suits not required, but bring towels, robes, and slip-on sandals, and your own snacks. This is a bare-bones operation but well worth it. Massage practitioners at Orr offer an eclectic mix of massage styles. ◆ Daily. Reservations required for day use of hot springs and treatments. 13201 Orr Hot Springs Rd (left at N State St, 13.5 miles). 462.6277

9 PARDUCCI WINE CELLARS

After first starting a winery in Cloverdale, Adolph Parducci moved north to Ukiah in 1931 to found this family winery in which four generations of Parduccis have now worked. Rich Parducci, great-grandson of the original owner, is now assistant winemaker. The winemaker is William Henry Hill. The tasting room, a white Spanish-style building, is just north of Ukiah and offers the full gamut of moderately priced wines from this popular producer. The tasting-room complex also houses a small gift shop with wineglasses, decanters, wine buckets, and other related paraphernalia. In back is a picnic area with tables and umbrellas on a sheltered patio. ♦ Tasting, sales, and tours daily. 501 Parducci Rd (west of Hwy 101). 462.3828

10 DUNNEWOOD VINEYARDS & WINERY

Sample winemaker George Phelan's Sauvignon Blanc, Chardonnay, Cabernet Sauvignon, Zinfandel, Merlot, and Pinot Noir at this winery's tasting room in Ukiah. Note their peel-off recipe labels. ♦ Daily. 2399 N State St (between Hwy 101 and Lake Mendo-cino Dr). 462.2987; fax 462.1249

11 VICHY SPRINGS RESORT

$$ Established in 1854 and named after Vichy Springs in France, this 700-acre property, now a California landmark, was well known in the 19th century, attracting the likes of Mark Twain, Robert Louis Stevenson, and Jack London. Current proprietors Gilbert and Marjorie Ashoff recently refurbished the inn and offer their overnight guests recreational activities such as hiking, picnicking, and mountain biking. You may stay in one of the guest rooms in the inn or rent one of the two cottages on the property—which were built in 1854 and are among the oldest existing buildings in Mendocino County. A dozen rooms in the inn are strung along a broad veranda; most have queen-size beds (one has twin beds). Each of these simply decorated rooms has a private bath and shower. The blue cottage has a bedroom with a queen-size bed, a living-room area with a sofa bed and a fireplace, and a full kitchen. The larger white cottage is furnished with a long, overstuffed couch, a wood-burning stove, and a beautiful 1930s-era gas stove. There's a large, shady porch in front and a barbecue. The resort has eight indoor and outdoor bathing tubs, a ther-apeutic massage building, and a refurbished Olympic-size pool (also filled with mineral water). One- or 1.5-hour Swedish massages or foot-reflexology massages are available by appointment only. The Ashoffs also bottle the mineral water under the Vichy Springs label. ♦ 2605 Vichy Springs Rd (east of Redemeyer Rd), Ukiah. 462.9515; fax 462.9516

12 DISCOVERY INN

$ This inexpensive motel provides lodging just 1 mile from downtown Ukiah. The 177 rooms with standard contemporary décor feature queen-size beds, cable TV, a stereo, and direct-dial phones. A heated swimming pool and four whirlpools offer year-round enjoyment; there also are two waterfalls, colorfully illuminated at night. A health club was scheduled for completion as this book went to press. ♦ 1340 N State St (at Empire Dr), Ukiah. 462.8873; fax 462.1249

13 RUEN TONG

★★$ From simple *gai pad-pak* (chicken with fresh vegetables) and the well-known *pad thai* (noodles with prawns, eggs, and bean sprouts) to the more exotic *muk ga praw* (calamari with basil, chili, and crushed garlic), this popular restaurant serves authentically prepared Thai foods in a setting of Thai arti-facts. Even if this is wine country, beers are

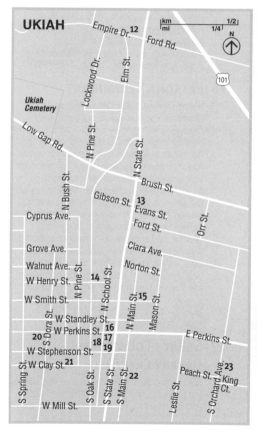

better companions with this spiced food—try the local Red Tail. Fried banana with ice cream is a popular dessert. ♦ Thai ♦ M-Su, lunch and dinner. 801 N State St (at Evans St), Ukiah. 462.0238

14 CHEESECAKE MOMMA

Originally from Philadelphia, Robin Collier, the "Cheesecake Lady," bakes her goods in a large kitchen in Ukiah. Stop by for espresso drinks and her freshly baked croissants, Danish pastries, and bagels. Of her many cheesecakes, the favorite is "the lady's" original version made with a graham-cracker crust and sour-cream topping. Another favorite: the espresso, which has a chocolate cookie crust and sour-cream topping. ♦ Daily. 200 Henry St. 462.2253; e-mail: momma@pacific.net

15 HOYMAN/BROWE STUDIO

In this cheerful shop you can find hard-to-spot seconds of locally made pottery and watch potters working at their craft. Shop here also for handcrafted jewelry by Charlotte Healy (precious metals) and Linda Sandlen (minerals, gems, beads, twigs, and other natural materials). ♦ M-Sa; Su by appointment. 323 N Main St (between E Smith and Norton Sts), Ukiah. 468.8835

16 PATRONA RESTAURANT

★★$$ Owners Bridget Harrington and Craig Strattman pay homage to the earth, their "patron saint," as the ultimate Patrona. Dining here for lunch or dinner is an education on the merits and rewards of sustainable agriculture. You won't find farm-raised fish nor meat pumped with antibiotics but a plethora of fresh, local organic food. The menu varies with the seasons and harvest, with three specials offered daily. Recent dishes on the menu were homemade spinach ravioli with carmody cheese; wild sturgeon with black chanterelles with carrot-and-truffle sauce, and flatbread pizza with Point Reyes blue cheese, pears, and walnuts. For dessert, try the chocolate silk torte. ♦ Californian ♦ Reservations recommended. Th, F, lunch; Tu-Sa, dinner. 130 W Standley St (at School St). 462.9181. Ꮬ www.patronarestaurant.com

17 SCHAT'S COURTHOUSE BAKERY CAFÉ/DELI

★$ Located behind the courthouse, this café is the place to come for overstuffed sandwiches and abundant salads. Standouts include the Melvin Belli sandwich (layers of roast beef, cream cheese, pepperoncini, tomato, and special red sauce on dark rye) and a bountiful cashew chicken salad. ♦ American ♦ M-Sa, lunch. 113 W Perkins St (between S State and S School Sts), Ukiah. 462.1670

17 UKIAH BREWING COMPANY AND RESTAURANT

★$$ Housed in a historic bar in old downtown Ukiah on Courthouse Square, Ukiah Brewing Company is the nation's first certified organic brewery and brewpub and Mendocino County's newest brewery. The brewers are committed to quality organics: meats come from Nieman Ranch and all the food is organic. The menu has 6 to 10 different ales and lagers ranging from pale ale to stout. You can also order tasting portions that pair well with beer. ♦ Daily, lunch and dinner. 102 S State St near Perkins St, across from the courthouse. 468.5898. www.ukiahbrewingco.com

18 CHAMBER OF COMMERCE

You'll get the scoop on restaurants, lodging, wineries, recreation, and other activities in Ukiah Valley here. ♦ M-F. 200 S School St (at W Church St), Ukiah. 462.4705

At the Chamber of Commerce:

MENDOCINO BOUNTY

This specialty café and marketplace carries local foods, Mendocino pottery, and other unusual gift items. ♦ M-Sa. 463.6711

18 DISH

★★$ This countrified storefront café serves gourmet sandwiches at bargain prices. Owner Jane Selover began her culinary career at John Ash & Co. The roasted turkey breast is layered with Vermont white cheddar cheese and roasted red pepper and the salade Niçoise comes with seared tuna, red pepper, green beans, and Niçoise olives. The burritos, made fresh with grilled vegetables or braised pork, are a wholesome meal. ♦ Californian. ♦ M-F, 9AM-5:30PM lunch and take-out dinners.109 S School St (between W Perkins and Church Sts), Ukiah. 462.5700. www.dish-togo.com

19 NEW GARDEN BAKERY

★★$ This tiny, cozy café/bakery with a pint-size garden serves delicious fresh-made vegan soups, luscious chocolate tiens (buns), a range of vegetarian dishes and muffins, cookies, and other treats. ♦ Café ♦ M-F, breakfast and lunch. 210 S State St (between W Stephenson and W Church Sts), Ukiah. 463.0273

20 HELD-POAGE MEMORIAL HOME AND RESEARCH LIBRARY

To get a better sense of Mendocino County history, visit this research library housed in a Queen Anne Victorian, once the home of Mendocino County Superior Court Judge William D. L. Held and Ethel Poage Held.

Dedicated to the collection of archival materials relating to the county's history, the library contains more than 5,000 volumes, with a wonderful collection of historical photographs, plus documents and maps. ♦ Tu, Th, Sa, 1:30-4PM and by appointment. Mendocino County Historical Society, 603 W Perkins St (at S Dora St), Ukiah. 462.6969

21 SANFORD HOUSE BED & BREAKFAST

$ This stately Queen Anne Victorian was built in 1904 as the home of Senator John Bunyon Sanford, a longtime California state legislator. Innkeepers Dorsey and Bob Manogue have five air-conditioned guest rooms, all with private bathrooms and each decorated with antiques and custom fabrics and wallpapers. The Manogues serve a full breakfast of freshly squeezed juice, fruit, homemade muffins and breads, omelettes or French toast, and coffee or tea in the dining room. ♦ 306 S Pine St (at W Stephenson St), Ukiah. 462.1653

22 GRACE HUDSON MUSEUM AND SUN HOUSE

The **Grace Hudson Museum** (1986) and **Sun House** (1911), along with **Hudson-Carpenter Park**, occupy 4.5 landscaped acres in the middle of downtown Ukiah. Bring a picnic lunch and then visit the museum dedicated to artist Grace Hudson (1865-1937) and her husband, anthropologist Dr. John W. Hudson (1857-1936). The museum boasts Hudson's portraits of the local Pomo Indians and a collection of Pomo art and artifacts of anthropological interest; the work of local artists is also displayed here. The Hudsons' house and workshop next door, an Arts and Crafts–style bungalow built by architect-artist **George Wilcox**, may be visited only in the company of a docent, but it's worth taking the 15- to 20-minute tour. Filled with personal touches of the couple, it includes lanterns designed by Grace, a screen with a Mendocino landscape, and Pomo baskets, among other treasures. Tours depart from the museum. ♦ Donation requested. Museum: W-Su (Sun House tours offered hourly between noon and 3PM). 431

S Main St (between E Gobbi and E Clay Sts), Ukiah. 462.3370

23 UKIAH FARMERS' MARKET

Shop for farm-fresh produce at this summer market at **Long's Orchard Plaza**. ♦ Sa, 8:30-noon, May-Oct. S Orchard Ave (between King Ct and E Perkins St), Ukiah. 743.2471

24 CITY OF TEN THOUSAND BUDDHAS

For an enlightening experience, pass through the large pagoda-style gateway to visit this international community of Buddhist monks, nuns, and scholars. First, stop at the reception desk in the administration building for a map of the center and then meander around the grounds. Ten thousand gilded Buddhas can be found standing in niches around the ornate Hall of Ten Thousand Buddhas. The focal point here is the 18-foot-high altar figure of Kuan Yin Bodhisattva, with 1,000 hands and 1,000 eyes, an enlightened being of compassion. Services are open to visitors and present an excellent opportunity to experience the mesmerizing sights and sounds of Buddhist rites. The peaceful grounds house a university, plus secondary and elementary schools. As you wander, you may have unusual company: Occasionally peacocks and pheasants stroll here too. ♦ Daily. Talmage and East Side Rds, Ukiah. 462.0939

Within the City of Ten Thousand Buddhas:

JUN KANG VEGETARIAN RESTAURANT

★$ A serene spot with lovely wall hangings, ideal for reflecting on what you've seen, this place offers delicious vegetarian food from a colorful 20-page menu. ♦ Chinese ♦ M, W-Sa, lunch and early dinner.

25 MOORES' FLOUR MILL & BAKERY

Make a run into Ukiah for bread, flour, and other basics or pick up a deli sandwich made on fresh-baked bread at this unique shop. Through a window in the back, you can see the century-old mill wheel grinding out beautiful whole-grain flour. The store also is a mini-museum of old flour sacks with quaint logos. ♦ M-Sa. 1550 S State St (between Jefferson La and Laws Ave), Ukiah. 462.6550

26 GERMAIN-ROBIN DISTILLERY

As a young man hitchhiking on a backcountry road in Mendocino County, Hubert Germain-Robin got a ride from Ansley Coale. They got to talking and it came out that Hubert's family had been producing cognac since 1782. On Ansley's ranch near Ukiah in 1981 they installed a small antique cognac still to preserve 19th-century distillation methods that have largely disappeared in France. Today, in blind tastings, reviewers rate Germain-Robin brandies as some of the finest spirits ever produced. Anno Domini, chosen as one of "Five Cognacs of the Century" by Richard Carleton Hacker, was blended from barrels set aside for extended aging in 1983 and 1984. ◆ Sales and tasting M-F. Call before coming. 3001 S State St #35. 462.0314. www.germain-robin.com

27 WHALER VINEYARDS

Russ and Annie Nyborg specialize in Zinfandel at their tiny winery on 35 acres near Ukiah. After almost 15 years, they're still fascinated with this intriguing grape, turning out Zinfandels in several different styles. It's fun to visit the weathered redwood barn that houses the winery, and in the small barrel-aging room you might hear how this family came to realize their dream of becoming vintners. The ship on the label is from the Viking Museum in Oslo, Norway. Norwegian-American Russ Nyborg works as a bar pilot, directing large ships into San Francisco's harbor, and his family shares his affinity for the sea. ◆ Tasting, sales, and tours by appointment only. 6200 East Side Rd (between Rte 175 and Ruddick-Cunningham Rd), Ukiah. 462.6355

28 JEPSON VINEYARDS

When Chicago businessman Robert S. Jepson Jr. founded his winery just north of Hopland, he decided early on to specialize in just three products: Chardonnay, sparkling wine, and brandy. The Chardonnay is barrel fermented and aged in small oak barrels; his Mendocino sparkling wine, made entirely with Chardonnay grapes, is produced by the *méthode champenoise*. For his brandies, he distills his spirits from French Colombard, the same grape used in cognac. You may taste everything but the brandy at the fieldstone-and-wood tasting room on the property; when the weather is warm, there are tables outside. ◆ Tasting and sales daily; tours by appointment only. 10400 Hwy 101 (between Hewlitt & Sturtevant and Ukiah

There are many kinds of oak used for barrels and several ways to treat them. Oaks are selected and treated differently depending on the type of wine. For instance, oak for Zinfandel will be treated differently than oak for Cabernet Sauvignon or Pinot Noir. The choice is made based on the desired flavor, the wine style, and the price. (One barrel can cost more than $500!)

Boonville Rds), Ukiah. 468.8936; fax 468.0362

HOPLAND

Just three blocks long, Hopland is billed as the gateway to the Mendocino wine country. It is surrounded by vineyards, with the majority of the valley's wineries strung out along **Highway 101** north of Hopland all the way to **Ukiah** and the **Redwood Valley** beyond. To make their products more easily accessible to visitors, several of the wineries have installed tasting rooms in town. You'll find **Fetzer**, **Zellerbach**, and **Brutacao**, plus a few antiques shops and the restored **Thatcher Inn**.

Before the entire **Sanel Valley** was granted to Fernando Féliz, Indians lived in the area around Hopland. Féliz had come from Pueblo San José south of San Francisco, and the town of Sanel grew up around his home in the valley. The township was established in 1859 and named after an Indian village that once occupied a nearby site on **McDowell Creek**. By the mid-1860s the surrounding area had become the prime producer of hops for the brewing industry, and in 1887 Sanel was renamed Hopland in honor of its best-selling crop.

Despite a setback during Prohibition, farmers continued to grow mainly hops until the 1950s, when the market diminished, and it became more profitable for most of them to replant their fields with pear and prune orchards and grape vineyards. The town was a quiet backwater until **Fetzer Vineyards** opened its original tasting-room complex in 1977, but even today you wouldn't exactly call Hopland a hopping town.

29 HOPLAND INN

$$ This striking, many-gabled property first opened in 1890 as a rest stop for travelers heading by stage or by train from San Francisco to the Oregon border on the old Redwood Highway. Named for its former proprietor, W. W. Thatcher, the restored Victorian hotel offers 21 rooms with private baths, all appointed with original and reproduction antique furniture. The bridal suite features a queen-size bed dressed in pink satin and lace, with a matching armoire, and a large bay window draped in lace curtains; the spacious bathroom has a Victorian claw-foot tub with brass shower fittings. Among our other favorite suites are the **Ornbaum Room** (no. 12), which is located at the back of the hotel and overlooks the patio and pool, and the **Milone Room** (no. 15), which has a brass bed and a claw-foot bathtub tucked in a corner. Downstairs, there's a lovely library room paneled in Philippine mahogany, and the hotel's bar, which scores high when it comes to straight spirits with wonderful collections of single-malt scotches, brandies, cognacs, and tequilas. Be sure to try a taste of **Germain-Robin** or **Jepson**, both locally distilled, fine brandies. All guests are served a complimentary full breakfast in the hotel restaurant. The hotel also has special

weekday escape packages that include accommodations, champagne, fresh fruits, and breakfasts and dinners in the hotel restaurant. ♦ 13401 S Hwy 101 (north of Rte 175). 744.1890; fax 744.1219; 800/266.1891. www.hoplandinn.com

29 MENDOCINO BREWING COMPANY

★$ Installed in the old brick **Hop Vine Saloon Building**, just down the street from the **Hopland Inn**, this brewpub—owned by Michael Laybourn, Norman Franks, John Scahill, and master brewer Don Barkeley—is one of the prime attractions of Hopland. Resembling a rustic English pub, it also has an outdoor beer garden. The partners produce four brews, all made in the traditional manner with 100% malted barley, whole hops, pure yeast culture, and water. Peregrine is the lightest; medium-bodied Blue Heron Pale Ale has a slightly bitter finish; Black Hawk Stout is made from fully roasted black malt; and the most popular brew is the amber, full-bodied Red Tail Ale. Mendocino Brewing is one of the few US breweries asked to participate in the Great British Beer Festival. Appetizers such as buffalo wings and soft pretzels, plus burgers, BLTs, and other sandwiches, are also served here, as are local wines, and the live music on Saturday nights—which runs from blues to country—has become a big drawing card. A shop at the back sells all sorts of beer paraphernalia. ♦ Pub ♦ Daily, lunch and dinner. Tours by appointment only. 13351 S Hwy 101 (north of Rte 175). 744.1361, 744.1015; fax 744.1910

29 McNAB RIDGE

Winemaker John Parducci created a new series of premium wines at the former Zellerbach winery. Parducci named his winery for the pristine McNab Valley 2 miles west of Hwy 101. Chardonnay, Cabernet Sauvignon, and Merlot are produced under the McNab Ridge label and a red Bordeaux varietal under the John A. Parducci Signature Series label. ♦ Tasting room: 13441 S Hwy 101, 2350 McNab Ranch Rd, 462.2423. www.mcnabridge.com

29 PHOENIX BAKERY

Some people drive up from Healdsburg for stuffed fougasse and savory puff pastries filled with everything imaginable from curried shrimp and cracked crab to tri-tip beef, smoked chicken, and smoked salmon mousse. For a treat, try the lobster fougasse. Not all items are available every day, so call ahead. Stone-oven breads are also worth the drive. The black-and-red loaf has roasted red pepper and black pepper. Desserts like apple cake with Calvados and apple tart with caramel are hard to pass up. It's hard to choose among all the treats at Phoenix. ♦ Daily. 13325 S Hwy 101. 744.1944

29 DOMAINE SAINT GREGORY

At this small tasting room, you can sample Pinot Blanc, Pinot Noir, and Pinot Gris, all from grapes grown in Anderson, Redwood, and Potter Valleys. For the red wines, winemaker Greg Graziano bleeds off 10 percent of the juice to intensify color and flavor. Graziano inherited the business from his father and grandfather, who planted vineyards in Mendocino County in 1918. You can also sample Italian varietals produced for the Monte Volpe (fox mountain) and Enotria (land of wine) labels. Enotria wines are crafted in the style of Italy's *Piemonte* region, where Vincenzo grew up. ♦ Daily. 13251 S Hwy 101, Suite 3. 744.VINO. www.domainesaintgregory.com

29 McDOWELL VALLEY VINEYARDS

This small winery owned by the Keehn and Crawford families is a leader in Rhône-style wines. Vintners Richard and Karen Keehn built it in 1979. The Syrah and Grenache grapes grown here are used for many of their wines. Winemakers Bill Crawford and Kerry Damsky make a graceful Grenache Rosé in the style of Provence's Tavel, an intense, concentrated Syrah from vines planted in 1919, a lower-priced Bistro Syrah from a blend of old and new vines, and a rich, perfumed Viognier made from white Rhône varietal grapes. The two generic white and red table wines are ideal for a casual picnic or barbecue. The vineyard's tasting center and sales office is at **Redwood Valley Cellars** (7051 N State St, between Rte 20 and Hwy 101; 485.0322; open daily). ♦ Tours by appointment only. 3811 Hwy 175 (east of Nokomis). 744.1053. The vineyard's tasting room—McDowell Valley Wine & Mercantile—is in downtown Hopland. Daily tasting. 13380 S Hwy 101 (near Hwy 175). 744.8911. www.mcdowellsyrah.com

Restaurants/Clubs: Red | **Hotels: Purple** | **Shops: Orange** | **Outdoors/Parks: Green** | **Sights/Culture: Blue**

183

29 LAWSON'S STATION

$$$ Like the stagecoach inns of early California, Lawson's Station is a happy sight after the long drive up Highway 101. Settling in and getting the kinks out starts the moment you enter your suite. Each of the seven suites has a king-size bed, double-headed shower, private balcony, and spa tub, but all vary in décor and design. Suite 205 has a spacious seating area with a convertible sofa bed, gas fireplace, wet bar, and large-screen Direct TV and DVD. The north-facing balcony overlooks Hopland and the hills beyond. You can order room service from Shotgun restaurant, or dine in the handsome dining room located in the hotel, which offers a seasonal menu for lunch and dinner. ♦ Tu-Sa, lunch and dinner. 13341 S Hwy 101, just north of Hwy 175. 744.1977. 866/744.1977. & www.lawsonsstation.com

30 BRUTOCAO CELLARS HOPLAND TASTING ROOM

Housed in a 1920s former school building, this tasting room has a mural of St. Mark's Plaza in Venice. These grape growers chose the lion from St. Mark's Cathedral as their logo when they established their winery in 1986. Today they farm 187 acres in Mendocino County, with a list that includes Chardonnay, Pinot Noir, Merlot, Cabernet Sauvignon, Sauvignon Blanc, and Zinfandel. Reds are unfiltered and unrefined, and intensely flavorful. The vintners supply primarily to Hopland and Anderson Valley. ♦ Tastings and sales daily. 13500 S Hwy 101 (just north of Mountain House Rd). 744.1664

30 JOHN CARPENTER'S HOPLAND ANTIQUES

Inveterate browsers won't be able to resist poking around the dusty, cluttered rooms of this antiques shop. It has a little bit of everything—and more than a little bit of vintage and estate jewelry; antique fishing lures and reels; fine, old china; and cast-iron doorstops. ♦ Daily. 13456 S Hwy 101 (north of Mountain House Rd). 744.1023

30 BLUEBIRD CAFE

★★$ The menu says "Quality food, big portions, reasonable prices," and this café lives up to that promise. With a 1950s-style décor (Formica tables and vinyl booths and chairs), it serves good, hearty food throughout the day. Breakfast features omelettes, blue-berry blintzes, and whole-wheat pancakes with blackberries. Lunch offerings include salads, burgers, and sandwiches, whereas the dinner menu highlights steak, pizza, pasta, fresh fish, and roast beef with real mashed potatoes and gravy. The café also makes its own fresh juices, plus old-fashioned milk shakes, sundaes, and banana splits. All orders are available for takeout. ♦ American ♦ Daily, breakfast, lunch, and dinner. 13340 S Hwy 101 (north of Mountain House Rd). 744.1633

30 CRUSHED GRAPE

$$ This restaurant is a friendly gathering place for family-style dining. The menu focuses on traditional Italian dishes: lasagna, risotto, osso buco. For an appetizer share a pizza margherita, which comes piping hot and bubbling from the wood-fired oven. ♦ Italian ♦ Tu-Su, dinner. Located in Schoolhouse Plaza, Crushed Grape shares the building with Brutocao Winery. 13500 S Hwy 101 (north of Mountain House Rd). 744.2020

31 MILANO FAMILY WINERY

When winemaker Jim Milone founded this winery in 1977, he incorporated into the winery the old barnlike hop kiln his grandfather and father had built. The winery's name was changed back to the original name of Milano. The new owners are Ted and Deanna Starr. The weathered redwood structure houses the tasting room, where you may sample Chardonnay, Cabernet Sauvignon, and Zinfandel. Also try the special late-harvest dessert wines, if any are left when you visit. Almost all of the winery's vintages are sold here. Also on the property is a self-contained cottage with a small yard, a barbecue, and bicycles. ♦ Tasting daily; tours by appointment only. 14594 S Hwy 101 (south of Mountain House Rd). 744.1396

32 DUNCAN PEAK VINEYARDS

This tiny vineyard makes just one wine: a Cabernet Sauvignon from grapes grown on a few hillside acres on the edge of Sanel Valley near Hopland. Owner Hubert Lenczowski produces only 500 cases of hand-crafted Cabernet each year. ♦ Tasting and tours by appointment only. 14500 Mountain House Rd (between Rte 128 and S Hwy 101). 744.1129

33 FETZER VINEYARDS TASTING ROOM AND VISITORS' CENTER AT VALLEY OAKS RANCH

In this picturesque 50-acre property are a group of old barns, grape vineyards, a gorgeous organic garden, a dining pavilion overlooking Lake Fume, and a modern administration building. When lumber executive Bernard Fetzer bought this vast ranch in 1968, he saw it as a place to raise his family and grow grapes. On

their father's death in 1981, 10 of Fetzer's 11 children took over the winery, which today ranks as one of the most profitable in the US, producing 2.4 million cases annually. In 1992, the Louisville-based Brown Forman purchased the Hopland property. The vineyard produces Sundial Chardonnay, Valley Oaks Cabernet Sauvignon, Eagle Peak Merlot, Echo Ridge Fumé, Home Ranch Zinfandel, and Fetzer Gewürztraminer. Superpremium Reserve wines include Chardonnay, Cabernet Sauvignon, Sauvignon Blanc, Zinfandel, and Pinot Noir. Fetzer also produces a number of critically praised varietals, including Johannesburg Riesling, Gamay Beaujolais, and White Zinfandel. The organically grown brand Bonterra ("good earth") wines are made from 100% certified organically grown Mendocino County grapes. The 5-acre Bonterra gardens also include 1,000 varieties of fruits, vegetables, and ornamental and edible flowers and herbs, all grown without pesticides or synthetic fertilizers. Also within the complex are the **Tasting Room**, a gift shop that offers such items as cookbooks, flavored vinegars, and virgin olive oils, and the **Deli**, a good stop for light breakfast, lunch, or a snack. Overlooking Lake Fume, the **Pavilion** is the site of Fetzer's state-of-the-art demonstration kitchen, which hosts cooking classes conducted by chef-cookbook author John Ash. Special packages, including a picnic lunch and overnight lodging at the **Fetzer Bed & Breakfast** (see opposite), are available. ♦ Tastings, tours, and sales daily; in-depth tours of the property by appointment only. 13601 Eastside Rd and Rte 175. 800/846.8637; fax 744.7488

At Fetzer Vineyards:

FETZER BED & BREAKFAST

$$ The seven rooms in this former carriage house have a pleasant country look—earth tones, comfortable chairs, soft cotton tattersall bedsheets, and thick and thirsty oversized bathsheets. Each room has a private patio or deck and a vineyard view. There's also a swimming pool. A continental breakfast buffet is served in the deli (see opposite). ♦ 744.7418, 800/846.8637; fax 744.7488

33 REAL GOODS SOLAR LIVING CENTER

Ecology is the focus at this 12-acre demonstration center devoted to alternative energy and lifestyles, including exhibits on producing electricity from the sun via solar panels and the resultant recycling of water, and a micro hydrosystem, in which plants from around the world are grown. The 50,000-square-foot solar-powered showroom is itself ecologically correct—made of recycled straw bales and recycled lumber. On sale here are solar panels and wind turbines, plus clothing and accessories—hats, bags, backpacks—made of hemp. Knowledgeable guides show how everything here relates to the environment. Opened in 1996, the site welcomes more than 100,000 visitors annually. They recently opened an alternative fuel station. ♦ Daily. 13371 S Hwy 101 (south of Rte 175). 744.2100

34 SHO-KA-WAH

This Pomo-owned casino has state-of-the-art video machines where visitors can try their hand, albeit electronically, at poker, blackjack, and keno. Lots of smoke. ♦ Daily. 13101 Nokomis (north of Rte 175). 744.1395

MENDOCINO COAST

From the Anderson Valley wine country, it's only a 30- to 40-minute drive—every bit of it scenic—to the coast near **Albion**, where the **Navarro River** opens into the sea. With its ancient redwood forest, steep bluffs, historic towns, and of course, the Pacific Ocean, the Mendocino coast is recognized as one of the nation's most scenic drives.

Head north, and 15 minutes later you'll arrive at the area's prime attraction, the Victorian village of **Mendocino**. All along the **North Coast**, particularly south of Mendocino, are dramatic coves and secret, sheltered beaches inset with tiny seaside villages such as Albion, **Little River**, **Caspar**, and **Westport**. These hamlets were once the centers of the logging industry, which became a booming business after the Gold Rush increased San Francisco's population and created a demand for building materials.

With no superhighway straight to the coast, this area has remained relatively inaccessible; it's a 3.5- to 4-hour drive from San Francisco by way of **Highway 101** and **Route 128** through the Anderson Valley. And the drive from the city up **Route 1** is an even more arduous (though beautiful) trek, taking up to 5 hours on the twisting, narrow road. So when people come to the Mendocino Coast, it's usually for more than a couple of days.

The idea is to find a hideaway near the sea to indulge in relaxed, quiet pleasures—walking in the forests of **Van Damme State Park** or in one of the many coastal parks, or strolling along the headlands watching for seals and, from November through April, migrating whales. There are a few tourist-oriented diversions, such as the **Skunk Train** to **Willits** and some small museums with displays of local history. Many people take advantage of the January crab festival, the march whale festival, springtime garden tours, Gualala art studio open house, the November mushroom fest, and monthlong holiday events, including candlelight inn tours. Contact the Mendocino Coast Chamber of Commerce for information: 961.6300. www.mendocinocoast.com

---

FT. BRAGG

Founded as a military outpost to supervise the Mendocino Indian Reservation, Ft. Bragg, 8 miles north of Mendocino, later became an important logging and fishing town and the largest city along the Mendocino Coast. It's a working-class town and has little of Mendocino's carefully preserved charms, except for the row of restored buildings and historic façades located where **Route 1** turns into **Main Street**. Otherwise you'll just see rows of motels, gas stations, and stores. Ft. Bragg is, however, home of the **Skunk Train**, a narrow-gauge engine that departs from the refurbished **California Western Railroad Station** twice a day for the trip to **Willits**, 40 miles to the east.

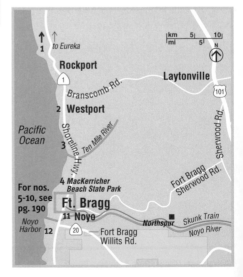

1 SINKYONE WILDERNESS STATE PARK

This 1,576-acre park on the Lost Coast is rugged country, unspoiled and unsettled,

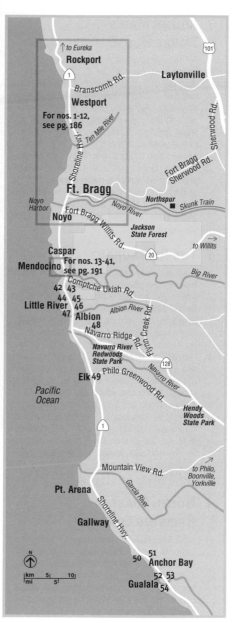

with unforgettable ocean views, secret beaches, and secluded campsites. Inside the park are two dozen backcountry campsites, which can be reached only on foot. Camping in vehicles is permitted only at Usal Beach, at the southern end of the park. The primitive campsites—available on a first-come, first-served basis—all have picnic

tables and barbecue pits. For more details contact the park ranger at the **Visitors' Center** in a turn-of-the-20th-century house at **Needle Rock**. ♦ Usal Rd (northwest of Shoreline Hwy). 986.7711

2 WESTPORT

Fifteen miles north of Ft. Bragg is the coastal town of Westport, with its rich heritage of New England–style architecture left over from the days when this was the largest seaport between San Francisco and Eureka. Once the railroad from Ft. Bragg to Willits was completed in 1911, the seaport lost its importance. Now it's better known as the gateway to Mendocino's Lost Coast, the wild stretch of seashore north of Westport where Route 1 turns inland. The only access to the coast is a dirt road that travels 21 miles into the **Sinkyone Wilderness State Park** (see page 186). ♦ Shoreline Hwy (between Ten Mile River and Branscomb Rd)

2 LOST COAST TRAIL RIDES

Explore spectacular Chadbourne Beach, Bruhel Point Bluff, and coastal redwood forest with local wranglers who know their territory. Novices or expert riders will enjoy this trip because horses are matched to riding levels. Gentle, well-mannered horses ensure a good experience. The cowboys bring horses in trailers and meet you on the coastal bridle path, not back at the ranch, which gives you more time in the saddle. Riders must be at least 10 years old. Call for reservations. ♦ 961.0700. www.lostcoasttrailrides.com

3 PACIFIC STAR

This is a great picnic stop in fine weather. Whales come close to the shore here on their annual migration. Sally Ottoson's winery sits right by the ocean. She says the salty ocean air settles on the barrels, accelerating osmosis and intensifying the flavors. Her wines are dense in flavor and richly concentrated. Appointments aren't necessary, but call ahead. At press time, a tasting room was being built. ♦ Daily. 33000 N Hwy 1, Fort Bragg (12 mi north of Fort Bragg past the Ten Mile River bridge). 964.1155. www.pacificstarwinery

---

Restaurants/Clubs: **Red** | Hotels: **Purple** | Shops: **Orange** | Outdoors/Parks: **Green** | Sights/Culture: **Blue**

4 MacKerricher Beach State Park

Just north of Ft. Bragg lies this state park blessed with one of the longest stretches of sandy beach in California. Picnic among the dunes or explore the miles of trails by foot or bike. Between November and April, follow the wooden boardwalk to the whale-watching platform. Two of the most popular activities here are marveling at the tide pools along the coast and observing the seals from the rocks. The 1,600-acre park includes 153 sites for camping. Laguna Point and Lake Cleone have wooden board-walks accessible to those with disabilities. ♦ Apr–mid-Oct. Shoreline Hwy (between Ft. Bragg and Ten Mile River). 937.5804; 800/444.7275 for reservations

5 The Weller House Inn

$$ Built in 1886, this is the only residence on the Mendocino Coast listed on the National Registry of Historic Places. Luxuries include claw-foot bathtubs, Victorian antiques, English gardens, and breakfast in the former ballroom. Climb up to the restored water tower, the highest point in Fort Bragg. ♦ 524 Stewart St (at Pine St). 964.4415, 877/893.5537. www.wellerhouse.com

6 Skunk Train

Named for the noxious fumes the early gas engines gave off, this narrow-gauge railroad has been making the run from Ft. Bragg to Willits since 1911. Step up to the spiffy restored **California Western Railroad Station** in downtown Ft. Bragg to get tickets for the 6- to 7-hour round-trip ride—through 40 miles of redwood forest and mountain passes, crossing 31 bridges and trestles. For a truly exhilarating experience, you can opt to ride in the cab with the engineer. Less avid rail fans may sign up for a half-day trip, traveling only to Northspur and back, or the summertime Sunset BBQ excursion. Refreshments, such as hot dogs and cold drinks, are available at **Willits Station**, and restaurants are within walking distance. ♦ Day trips are daily except Thanksgiving, Christmas, and New Year's Day. Half-day trips daily, June-Sept, and Sa, Su, Oct-May. Reservations recommended. W Laurel St (west of N Main St). 964.6371, 800/77-SKUNK

7 Round Man's Smoke House

For fans of smoked meats and poultry, it's hog heaven here. At the counter, owners Marilynn Thorpe and Stephen Rasmussen turn out smoked chinook salmon and albacore, plus some terrific peppered salmon jerky. For picnics, consider the small specialty hams, boned and lean, or the smoked chicken breast, both fully cooked and ready to eat. They also have a corned beef brisket. All of their smoked products are vacuum-packed for a shelf life of 6 to 8 weeks. Mail order is also available. ♦ Daily. 412 N Main St (between E Laurel and E Pine Sts). 964.5954, 800/545.2935; fax 964.5438

7 The Restaurant

★$$ Just next door to **Round Man's Smoke House** (see above) is this savvy eatery, where you can get a sandwich made with Round Man's smoked turkey breast, avocado, and fontina cheese, or a burger and salad. Somebody in the kitchen must be Italian, because this place offers a typical Tuscan dessert—a glass of *vin santo* (an amber dessert wine) with biscotti. At dinner, the creative cooks turn out Mediterranean fare along with a few Asian-style dishes. It's a welcome respite from the crowds in Mendocino. Live jazz is featured on Friday and Saturday night. ♦ Continental ♦ M, Tu, Sa, dinner; Th, F, lunch and dinner; Su, brunch and dinner. 418 N Main St (between E Laurel and E Pine Sts). 964.9800

7 North Coast Brewing Company

★$$ A handsome cream-colored building trimmed in green holds this local brew pub. Belly up to the bar for a glass of Scrimshaw, a Pilsner-style beer; Old No. 38, a dry stout; or the firm's best-known brew, Red Seal Ale, a copper-red pale ale. You can eat light or hearty, choosing from a menu of sophisticated pub grub. Try the Route 66 chili (Texas red and New Mexican green combo), the Cajun black beans and dirty rice, or—one of the most unusual dishes on the menu— *cochinita pibil*, Maya roasted pork with chipotle-chili sauce baked in a banana leaf. For plainer fare, there's name-your-cheese burgers served with fries, and char-broiled Noyo snapper with a light lemon-dill sauce. For dessert, try the chocolate mousse cake with raspberry topping if it's on the day's menu; if not, apple crisp, cheesecake, and bread pudding are always satisfying choices. ♦ Pub ♦ Tu-Su, lunch and dinner. 444 N Main St (at E Pine St). 964.BREW

WINE AND SONG: BIRD WATCHING IN WINE COUNTRY

Be sure to take your binoculars and a birding book when packing for a wine-country trip. These hills (and plateaus and shores) are alive with the music of songbirds and the calls of other feathered friends. Here are some good bird-watching locations and checklists to help you keep track of your sightings. For more information on state parks, call 916/653.6995.

Clear Lake State Park (5300 Soda Bay Rd, east of Gaddy La, Kelseyville; 279.4293): With oaks and pines on the high ground and willows and other vegetation along the watercourse, this park is a magnet for up to 150 bird species. In addition to the year-round avian residents, about 500,000 birds spend the winter here. Look for

- Bushtits
- Clark's grebes
- Great horned owls
- Golden eagles
- Herons
- Northern flickers
- Peregrine falcons (winter)
- Western grebes (winter)

Lake Mendocino Recreation Area (entrances at Marina Dr, east of East Side Calpella Rd; Rte 20 and Marina Dr; Lake Mendocino Dr, east of N State St; 462.7581): Rolling hills covered with firs, oaks, conifers, and grasslands surround this lake. Look for

- Acorn woodpeckers (when acorns are present)
- California quail
- Ospreys
- Great blue herons
- Red-tailed hawks
- Waterfowl (in the mornings before boats disperse them)
- Wild turkeys (when acorns are present)

Napa River Ecological Reserve (off Yountville Cross Rd, at the Napa River, Yountville; 944.5500): Huge valley oak and California bays shade the **Napa River** and **Conn Creek**, an old-growth riparian woodland, attractive to more than 200 bird species. Look for

- Anna's hummingbirds
- Acorn woodpeckers
- Downy woodpeckers
- Owls (barn, great horned, and screech)
- Red-breasted sapsuckers
- Tree swallows
- Violet-green swallows
- Yellow-breasted chats

Sonoma Coast State Beach Vista Trail (Rte 1, 4 miles northwest of Jenner; 875.3483): This marine terrace on the edge of the coastal bluffs looms 600 feet above the tide. A mile-long paved hiking loop offers outstanding vistas from **Port Reyes** clear to **Fort Ross**. Look for

- American goldfinches
- Golden eagles
- Hawks (red-tailed, northern harriers)
- Peregrine falcons
- Sparrows (song, savannah, and summer migrants such as barn, tree, and cliff sparrows)
- Turkey vultures
- Western bluebirds

Also consider a visit to the **Viansa Winery** (935.4700), located at the gateway to **Sonoma Valley**. The winery is set on wetlands that are a haven for birds; call for a guided tour (also see page 104). **Chanslor Ranch** (875.2712) on the **Sonoma Coast** offers accommodations in the midst of bird-filled wetlands.

Restaurants/Clubs: Red | Hotels: Purple | Shops: Orange | Outdoors/Parks: Green | Sights/Culture: Blue

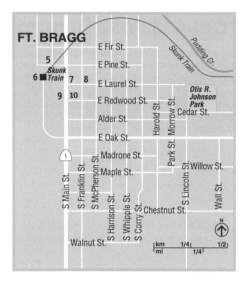

8 Ft. Bragg Farmers' Market

Everyone from backyard growers to high-school agriculture students to farmers sets up shop in front of **City Hall** to hawk fruits, vegetables, and flowers. The produce (almost all organically grown) is sold just hours after being picked. ♦ W, 3:30-6PM, May-Oct. E Laurel and N Franklin Sts. 961.0360

9 Guest House Museum

The home of Charles Russell Johnson, founder of the Union Lumber Company, has been turned into a museum filled with photos, artifacts, and memorabilia from Ft. Bragg's days as a logging and lumber center. ♦ Nominal admission. 10:30AM-2:30PM, Tu-Su, Mar-Nov; and F-Su, Dec-Feb. 343 N Main St (between W Redwood and W Laurel Sts). 961.2840

10 Egghead Restaurant

★$ This tiny storefront café offers over 40 types of crepes or omelettes, in addition to pancakes, eggs Benedict, and other breakfast dishes, along with freshly squeezed juices and espresso drinks. For lunch, there are salads, sandwiches, and half-pound burgers. There's a selection of vegetarian and heart-healthy dishes too. ♦ Café ♦ Daily, breakfast and lunch. 326 N Main St (between E Redwood and E Laurel Sts). 964.5005

10 Carol Hall's Hot Pepper Jelly Company

Try Hall's line of hot pepper jellies, which come in three varieties, along with a half-dozen jams (including the award-winning peach cobbler jam), scrumptious marmalades, two chutneys, two mustards, a garden salsa, herb and fruit vinegars, and all sorts of dressings and condiments, plus top-notch local food products. ♦ Daily. 330 N Main St (between E Redwood and E Laurel Sts). 961.1422. 800/892.4823. www.hotpepperjelly.com

10 Mendocino Coast Chamber of Commerce

The staff members in this storefront office offer good advice on what to see and do along the North Coast. ♦ M-Sa. 332 N Main St (between E Redwood and E Laurel Sts). 961.6300, 800/726.2780 www.mendocinocoast.com

11 Noyo Harbor

Located at the mouth of the Noyo River at the south end of Ft. Bragg, this working fishing village is a good spot to watch boats enter and leave the tiny harbor. A public boat-launching ramp and a sandy beach are beneath the highway. It's fun to go down to look around, maybe stopping for fish and chips or smoked salmon. In January, the crab season is celebrated with crab cruises aboard the Rumblefish (964.3000) or Sea Hawk (964.1881). Every Fourth of July, Noyo Harbor is the site of what's billed as the world's largest salmon barbecue. ♦ N Harbor Dr (east of Hwy 1)

At Noyo Fishing Center:

Nemo's Fish Market

★$ Order fish and chips to enjoy on the outdoor deck with a view of the harbor and the boats. Or buy fresh fish for the barbecue or smoked salmon for a picnic at this fresh seafood market. Takeout is available too. ♦ Seafood ♦ Fish and chips stand: daily, lunch; W-Su, early dinner. Market: daily. 32410 N Harbor Dr. 964.1600

12 Mendocino Coast Botanical Gardens

It took retired nurseryman Ernest Schoefer 16 years to clear the 47 acres he bought on a bluff overlooking the ocean at Ft. Bragg. He purchased the property in the 1960s to create a showcase botanical garden, making the trails and planting rhododendrons and other flowering plants. Spring is the best time to visit, when the rhododendrons and roses are in full bloom. Major plant collections here include heathers, fuchsias, succulents, ivies, and camellias, so there is always something of interest to look at. In all, the garden is home to hundreds of varieties of native and cultivated plants. You can follow a trail into the headlands, where it's possible to see the gray whales on their annual migration. If you want to make an afternoon of it, there is a shady picnic area. The gardens are owned by the nonprofit Mendocino Coast Recreation and Park District and are supported by admission fees, sales of plants, and a volunteer staff. The gift shop sells garden-related items and works by local artists. ♦ Admission. Daily. 18220 N Hwy 1 (south of Old Coast Hwy). 964.4352

AUDUBON AT THE GARDENS

Amateur ornithologists congregate at this friendly store to chat about birds. Shelves are stocked with bird feeders, feed, local wildlife art, and books. The knowledgeable staff will help you pick out the latest birding guides, set you up on a bird-watching tour, or discuss safe havens for birds. ♦ Daily. 962.9413

MENDOCINO

This Victorian village, perched at the very edge of a high bluff overlooking the ocean and flanked on three sides by the wild sea, has captured the imagination of visitors from all over the world. A protected historical area with Cape Cod–style architecture, Mendocino resembles a New England village uprooted and relocated to this Pacific paradise. In the popular television series *Murder, She Wrote*, the fictional town of Cabot Cove, Maine, is actually Mendocino. Many of the town's old homes have been turned into bed-and-breakfasts, restaurants, shops, and galleries. But the headlands, with their marvelous vistas of the sea, have remained unchanged.

Legend has it that *Mendocino* means "path to the sea," but the cape may actually have been named for the Spanish captain who discovered it in the 16th century, or perhaps for his ship. At any rate, the town's history began in 1852, approximately 2 years after German immigrant William Kasten, apparently the sole survivor of a shipwreck off the coast, washed up on a nearby beach. With no rescue in sight, he built himself a cabin on the headlands and lived there for almost 2 years before a ship finally ventured into the bay. The sailors on that vessel noted the vast redwoods surrounding the cape, and Henry Meiggs, a lumberjack then working in Bodega Bay to the south in Sonoma County, organized a party of men to head up the coast to begin logging operations. In 1853, after much difficulty, they constructed a sawmill, and Mendocino (then known as the town of **Big River**) became a logging center.

By 1865 the fledgling metropolis had a population of 700, and a number of hotels and rooming houses had been built for the loggers. Most of the grander homes were built in the 1870s and 1880s for lumber barons and bankers. Mendocino remained a logging town until the 1930s, when the Depression shut down operations. In the 1950s, artists discovered the picturesque little town, and, although it became an artists' community much like Laguna Beach in Southern California and Carmel on the central coast, its population remains at about 1,100.

The Big River Estuary has just become the Big River State Park. When Mendocino Land Trust acquired the property from Hawthorne Timber Co., 50 miles of Big River and its tributaries—plus 100 miles of connected trails—were preserved. The new park includes important wildlife corridors, 1,500 acres of wetlands, and critical habitat for endangered and threatened species. A spectacular inland marsh dubbed the Tuolumne meadows of the north coast (after the famous Yosemite Park meadows) also lies in the new park.

13 CASPAR

Pass through this quiet town, with its white, steepled church and a scattering of old cottages and farmhouses, and it's hard to imagine that this was once the site of one of the busiest lumber mills along the Mendocino Coast. So much lumber was produced here, in fact, that the Caspar Lumber Company, which closed in 1955, ran its own fleet of ships to sail it down to San Francisco. ♦ Point Cabrillo Dr (west of Shoreline Hwy)

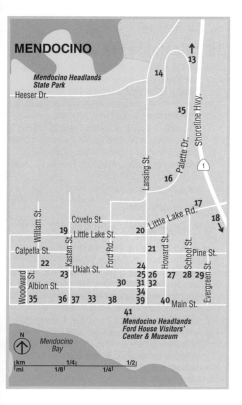

Restaurants/Clubs: Red | **Hotels: Purple** | **Shops: Orange** | **Outdoors/Parks: Green** | **Sights/Culture: Blue**

191

13 JUG HANDLE STATE RESERVE

This park is home to the 5-mile **Ecological Staircase Trail**, a hike through a series of hundred-foot-high terraces that were cut out of the landscape by waves eons ago. Each "step" is 100,000 years older than the next, and at the end of the trail you'll find the **Pygmy Forest**, with dwarfed cypress and pine trees. Pick up a brochure at the rangers' headquarters before setting off to explore. ♦ Shoreline Hwy (north of Fern Creek Rd)

13 RUSSIAN GULCH STATE PARK

This park includes acres of redwood groves, spectacular ocean views, and 12 miles of hiking trails, including a path along the headlands where visitors encounter an ocean blowhole (a hole in the rocks from which water emerges with tremendous force, resembling a whale's spout). There are entrancing views of the village of Mendocino along the path, and some trails head inland to meet the enormous **Jackson State Forest** to the east. The park has specially marked trails for horseback riding and bicycling. There are also 30 campsites, plus a small camp for equestrians. ♦ Fee per vehicle. Apr-Oct. Shoreline Hwy (just north of Woodstock Dr). 937.5804; 800/444.7275 for reservations

14 AGATE COVE INN BED & BREAKFAST

$$ Scott and Betsy Buckwald moved up the coast from Southern California to run this secluded inn overlooking Agate Cove. The hillside property, with an extensive flower garden of old-fashioned varieties, has cottages scattered around the grounds; all but one have fireplaces and private decks where you can settle in to watch the ocean. Most of the 10 rooms have four-poster or canopy beds, an attractive country décor, private baths, and TV sets. There is also a breakfast room at the inn with an old wood-burning stove and a spectacular view of the sea. Breakfast is a cheerful, sociable affair, with hearty offerings such as omelettes, eggs Benedict, or French toast, along with sausages and ham. ♦ 11201 Lansing St (near Palette Dr). 937.0551, 800/527.3111. www.agatecove.com

14 MENDOCINO SPECIALTY VINEYARDS

Three small Mendocino County wineries— Claudia Springs, Eaglepoint Ranch, and Raye's Hill—share this tasting room across from the Boonville Hotel. Eaglepoint Ranch Winery, formerly Lonetree Winery, makes award-winning Syrah, using grapes from John Scharffenberger's Eaglepoint Ranch. The 1,800-foot elevation and shallow moun-taintop soil produces a highly concentrated, lush Rhône-style red. Raye's Hill is known for its Anderson Valley Pinot Noir made from grapes grown 15 miles from the coast. Claudia Springs makes excellent Viognier and Zinfandel. The Boonville General Store (895.9477) is next door in case you want to nibble on some bread and cheese while you are tasting. ♦ Daily. 17810 Farrer La (on Hwy 128). 895.3993

15 MACCALLUM HOUSE SUITES

$$$ If you'd really rather be in a condominium than in rustic Mendocino, this bed-and-breakfast is located on a spectacular piece of real estate overlooking the town, and its guest rooms are furnished with all the conveniences of a big-city hotel—color TV sets (one room even has a second TV in the bathroom for viewing from the tub), VCRs, refrigerators, wet bars, telephones, and answering machines. The five huge rooms and suites boast French-style furniture, cedar-lined closets, and balconies; three have views of the ocean or Mendocino (and telescopes are provided for an even closer look at the scenery). For ultimate privacy, continental breakfast is delivered to each room. ♦ 10691 Palette Dr (east of Lansing St). 937.5446

16 HILL HOUSE INN

$$ The television series *Murder, She Wrote* has made this hilltop hostelry famous by using it as a regular setting. The inn has 44 guest rooms, most furnished with brass beds, reproductions of antiques, and lace curtains— all of which sound innocent enough, but the effect is just a bit dowdy. The views are quite good, though. Continental breakfast is delivered to each room. ♦ 10701 Palette Dr (east of Lansing St). 937.0554 www.hillhouseinn.com

Within Hill House:

SHARON'S BY THE SEA

★$$$ The dining room offers wonderful ocean views, an elegant Victorian atmosphere with antique sideboards, and oil paintings of 19th-century Mendocino. The Italian menu offers such classics as cold and hot antipasti; veal scallopini with mushrooms; prawns *fra diablo*; a mixed grill with steak, Italian sausage, and veal; and a selection of pasta dishes. A more casual menu is available in **Rick's Lounge**: soups, salads, pasta, and sandwiches. ♦ Continental ♦ Daily, lunch and dinner

17 JOSHUA GRINDLE INN

$$ Set on 2 acres overlooking the village, this inn, originally built in 1870 by town banker Joshua Grindle, has a faithful clientele who

come back year after year. The main house has five guest rooms; two more are in a rear cottage; and the water tower out back offers another three rooms. Décor includes Early American and Shaker pieces, antiques, and historical artwork. Soft earth tones predominate, and dried floral wreaths and folk art add attractive touches. All of the rooms have private baths, and some have wood-burning fireplaces. The blue-and-white **Nautical Room** on the second floor, pleasingly furnished with a queen-size bed and captain's table, overlooks the city and a bit of the ocean. The **Library Room** features a four-poster queen-size bed, a fireplace framed in the original tiles, and a floor-to-ceiling bookcase. And the three rooms in the water tower, stacked one on top of the other, are also charmingly decorated. Innkeepers Arlene and Jim Moorehead serve a full breakfast on an 1830s pine harvest table in the kitchen. ♦ 44800 Little Lake Rd (between Shoreline Hwy and Lansing St). 937.4143, 800/GRINDLE. www.joshgrin.com

18 BREWERY GULCH INN

$$$ This redwood-shingle Arts and Crafts lodge sits on a bluff amid pine trees and sight of the sea. Owner Arky Ciancutti, a doctor and lover of redwood forests, built his inn from redwood timbers salvaged from the nearby Big River. The hearth room has a two-story wood-burning fireplace and tall redwood doors swinging out onto a patio above Smuggler's Cove. Guests congregate by the fire for breakfast and wine and hors d'oeuvres when chef Jeffrey Neumeier brings out platters of phyllo empanadas, crab quiche, baked brie, and crusty salt bread. Manager Glenn Lutge pours Mendocino wines every evening at the wine bar and tells intriguing stories about the Mendocino Coast. He discovers guests' interests, then suggests an adventure. He sent one guest on an early-morning bike ride along Big River that was richly rewarding. Of the 10 rooms—furnished with hardwood desks, armoires, queen-size beds, and comfortable brown leather chairs—the ocean-view rooms on the third floor have the most romantic views. Another pleasure: a morning walk through pine trees, redwoods, and rhododendrons along the hillside trail below the inn. Check the web site for packages and seasonal discounts. The inn is one mile south of Mendocino village. Look for the water tower with the inn's name and get ready to turn at the birdhouse mailbox. ♦ 9401 Hwy 1. 937.4752 or 800/578.4454. www.brewerygulchinn.com

---

THE BEST

Paula Gray

Artist

Make your way to Glass Beach just north of **Ft. Bragg**, where an old glass factory dumped its refuse. Spend hours picking through the tiny tumbled smooth treasures.

Take in the annual sheepdog trials at the **Mendocino County Fairgrounds**, then drop in at the **Boonville Hotel Restaurant & Bar** for the best Caesar salad in the West.

Wine tasting at **Navarro Vineyards**. Pick up a bottle of the Chardonnay Verjus to cook with.

Breakfast at the **Bluebird Cafe** in Hopland. Then check out the **Real Goods Solar Living Center** for state-of-the-art alternative energy systems. While in **Hopland**, visit **Fetzer Vineyards'** extensive gardens. Go to **Hendy Woods State Park** off **Highway 128** in **Philo** for old-growth redwoods and make a stop at the **Apple Farm** for organic fruit and ciders.

18 THE STANFORD INN BY THE SEA

$$$ Also known as **Big River Lodge**, this 33-unit inn stands on a meadow leading to a bluff overlooking Big River and the ocean. In addition to great views from all the rooms, the large hillside estate features a greenhouse with an organic garden that provides produce to restaurants, as well as a large pool, a spa, a sauna, and an exercise room. Rooms come with coffeemakers and all sorts of nice touches, including four-poster beds (queen- or king-size), fireplaces, and VCRs (plus a videotape library of classic and current movies). Innkeepers Joan and Jeff Stanford permit guests to bring well-behaved pets—in fact, a few llamas roam the property. Overnight guests may order a hot breakfast entrée or select from the breakfast buffet. Thursday through Sunday, the dining room offers an inventive vegetarian menu at dinner (not included in room rate). ♦ Shoreline Hwy and Comptche Ukiah Rd. 937.5615, 800/331.8884; fax 937.0305

At the Stanford Inn by the Sea:

CATCH A CANOE & BICYCLES TOO!

Both guests and nonguests may rent kayaks or canoes to explore the Big River estuary,

---

Restaurants/Clubs: Red | Hotels: Purple | Shops: Orange | Outdoors/Parks: Green | Sights/Culture: Blue

rated class 1, meaning it's a gentle river suitable for the novice. It's still advisable, however, to get information on tides and river conditions before setting off. The shop also has mountain bikes—free to guests and rented to nonguests—and can suggest various routes. ◆ Daily. 937.0273

19 MENDOCINO ART CENTER

In the 1950s, with its studios, summer study programs, and performing arts, this art center became a hub for artists of many types. Today the educational and recreational programs offered in painting, drawing, ceramics, wood-working, and textiles attract students from around the country. This is also the site of the **Helen Schoeni Theater**, home to the **Mendocino Theater Company**. ◆ Daily. 45200 Little Lake St (at Kasten St). 937.5818

20 NATURAL HERB GARDENS BOUTIQUE

Another of the town's Victorians that house an interesting shop, this boutique carries aromatherapy products, bath and body oils, Ayurvedic remedies, gifts, candles, and soaps. ◆ Daily. 45084 Little Lake St (at Lansing St) 937.4999

21 MENDOSA'S MERCHANDISE & MARKET

This full-service market has plenty of picnic supplies. Choose from cheese, cold cuts, barbecued chicken, and Mendocino County wines, including chilled whites. The hardware division next door stocks fishing equipment, barbecues, picnic baskets, enameled camp cookware, and corkscrews. ◆ Daily. 10501

What's your California wine IQ?

1. Which are the most popular grape varietals in wine country?

2. Which of the above is grown only in the United States?

3. Which is the most widely planted grape species in the state?

4. Which county leads the state in Chardonnay plantings?

5. Which grape is expected to produce one of the best wines in the new millennium?

Answers

1. *Cabernet Sauvignon, Chardonnay, Merlot, Pinot Noir, Sauvignon Blanc, Zinfandel.* 2. *Zinfandel.* 3. *Chardonnay.* 4. *Sonoma, with 11,308 acres.* 5. *Syrah.*

Lansing St (between Ukiah and Little Lake Sts). 937.5879; fax 937.0563

21 MENDOCINO CHOCOLATE COMPANY

Famous for its truffles, which it makes in more than 20 flavors, this homey chocolate company also offers other specialties, including Mendocino toffee (a butter toffee dipped in light chocolate and rolled in toasted almonds) and Mendocino Breakers (chocolate caramels dipped in light chocolate, almonds, and white chocolate). They'll box special assortments and ship them for you from their Ft. Bragg store. ◆ Daily. 10483 Lansing St (between Ukiah and Little Lake Sts). 937.1107; also at 542 N Main St (between E Pine and E Fir Sts), Ft. Bragg. 964.8800

21 MENDOCINO BAKERY & CAFÉ

★$$ Pizza by the slice, garlic and onion bialys, bagels, and an assortment of hefty pastries, muffins, and scones are made in-house at this café. Take your espresso or cappuccino outside on the deck. Early dinner is now served here as well, with entrées ranging from lasagna to glazed chicken with polenta. ◆ Café ◆ Daily, breakfast, lunch, and early dinner. 10483 Lansing St (between Ukiah and Little Lake Sts). 937.0836

21 RAINSONG SHOES

The emphasis here is on comfort and style, with good walking shoes, sneakers, dress shoes, and boots. The Aerosole shoes are good-looking, comfortable, and moderately priced. The slippers shaped like little piggies or schnauzers just might tickle someone's fancy. The same company also has a clothing store just down the street (see page 200). ◆ Daily. 10483 Lansing St (between Ukiah and Little Lake Sts). 937.1710

22 MENDOCINO MARKET

This well-stocked market specializes in gourmet foods to go as well as Sonoma and Mendocino County wines and local microbrews. Stop here for epicurean sandwiches for your picnic hamper. ◆ Daily, Ukiah St at Williams St. 937.3474

23 JOHN DOUGHERTY HOUSE

$$ The severe façade of this hotel, built in 1867, belies its charming interior. There's a small living room with sofas in front of the fire-place and a large veranda with views of the town and the bay, plus ocean views said to be the best in the village. The lovely English garden behind the hotel is planted with old roses, herbs, heirloom plants, and fruit trees.

The **Captain's Room** upstairs has a private balcony with an ocean view, and the sloping ceiling gives it a cozy feel. Like the **First Mate's Room**, it has a private bath and is decorated with pine antiques and hand-stenciled walls and has a village view. Innkeepers Marion and David Wells also offer a two-room suite with a wood-burning stove, a four-poster bed, and a veranda with a view. Another room with a four-poster bed is installed in the water tower; this one has a sitting room and a private bath. They also have two large garden cottages, each with sitting room, private bath, and veranda. A full breakfast is served to guests. ♦ 571 Ukiah St (between Kasten and Woodward Sts). 937.5266

24 MASONIC TEMPLE

Now the **Savings Bank of Mendocino County** (established in 1903), this white wooden building with its single soaring steeple was built as the **Masonic Lodge** in 1866 by **Erik Albertson**, the first Worshipful Master of Mendocino Lodge No. 179. Albertson also sculpted the statue of *Time and the Maiden*, standing atop the steeple, from a single redwood trunk. ♦ Lansing and Ukiah Sts

25 CORNERS OF THE MOUTH

You can't miss the old red **Baptist Church** (constructed in the late 1800s) that houses this natural-foods store. Stop in for organic produce, juices, bottled water, bulk items, or the vitamins you forgot to bring with you. A wood-burning stove keeps the store extra warm. ♦ Daily. 45015 Ukiah St (between Lansing and Kasten Sts). 937.5345; fax 937.2149

25 DÉJÀ VU: THE MENDOCINO HAT CO.

Just what you need to keep your head warm on a foggy day. This shop stocks Stetsons, Akubra felt hats from Australia, rain hats, women's dress hats by Louise Green, and an assortment of boiled wool and crocheted raffia hats by local artisans. ♦ Daily. 10464 Lansing St (between Albion and Ukiah Sts). 937.4120

26 WILLIAM ZIMMER GALLERY

Formerly **Gallery Fair**, this is the place for fine handcrafted jewelry, paintings, and superb handmade furniture created by local and other North American artisans. Everything here is very special—and rather costly. For those looking for the perfect rocking chair, designer Robert Erickson will make one to your measurements. ♦ Daily. 10481 Lansing St (at Ukiah St). 937.5121. www.williamzimmergallery.com

27 WHITEGATE INN

$$$ This elegant white Victorian gem in the heart of the village offers six guest rooms with private baths (some have claw-foot tubs and fireplaces). There's also a one-bedroom cottage with a fireplace, living room, full modern kitchen, and private yard and deck. Antique crystal chandeliers, feather beds, and lace-edged sheets add to the charm. Innkeepers Carol and George Bechtloff prepare a full country breakfast that might include caramel-apple French toast, muffins, fruit parfaits, juice, tea, and coffee; they also serve wine and hors d'oeuvres in the parlor in the evening. A perpetually full cookie jar and See's chocolates at bedtime are additional treats. ♦ 499 Howard St (at Ukiah St). 937.4892, 800/531.7282. www.whitegateinn.com

28 MENDOCINO VILLAGE INN & SWEETWATER GARDENS & SPA

Here's the spot for indulging in a hot tub and sauna (there's even a large tub and sauna for groups). Swedish/Esalen massage and deep-tissue bodywork are available by appointment. The best deal is the "Rub-a-Dub" special: On Monday, Wednesday, and Friday you get a free soak in the hot tub with your massage. ♦ Daily. 955 Ukiah St (between School and Howard Sts). 937.4140

CAFE BEAUJOLAIS

29 CAFE BEAUJOLAIS

★★★$$$ John Stroup runs the kitchen of this lovely Victorian home. The appetizers are tasty and colorful (try the grilled, marinated chanterelles and prosciutto-wrapped figs served on arugula) but you'll want to focus on the inventive entrées, such as the oven-steamed fresh salmon fillet with sauce vierge, the roasted free-range chicken with saffron-chanterelle sauce, or the broiled pork rib chop with ginger-plum sauce. The dessert menu is tantalizing too. If you have room, try the wild blackberry *clafoutis* (warm French custard cake) or the chocolate hazelnut *fragilité* (hazelnut meringue layered with praline ganache) with Frangelico whipped cream.

Restaurants/Clubs: Red | Hotels: Purple | Shops: Orange | Outdoors/Parks: Green | Sights/Culture: Blue

Tuesday through Thursday a fixed-price, three-course country dinner is also offered. The two-page wine list ranges from an excellent but expensive Caymus, Special Select, Napa to a more modestly priced Navarro Gewürztraminer from Anderson Valley, with plenty of others in between. The garden around the house, designed by Jaen Treesinger, is planted with drought-tolerant shrubs, edible and decorative flowers, lots of herbs, and long-blooming antique roses. Call in advance for a garden tour. ♦ Californian ♦ Daily, dinner. Reservations recommended. 961 Ukiah St (at Evergreen St). Reservations 937.5614; garden tour 937.0783

Within Cafe Beaujolais:

THE BRICKERY

The wood-fired oven was Christopher Kump's project, hand-built brick by brick and decorated with tiles he brought back from Provence after a visit to the French teacher and cookbook author Simone Beck. It sits in the middle of the garden and turns out wonderful breads. The breads change daily but often include a Mendocino sourdough leavened with wild yeasts; a sourdough rye with a touch of Red Seal Ale; olive-rosemary *fougasse*, a Provençale-style flat loaf in a distinctive tree shape; Beaujolais herb *stirato*, a moist, large-celled loaf flavored with blended herbs; and an Austrian sunflower bread. ♦ Daily, until the breads are sold out (usually about 1PM)

MacCALLUM HOUSE
RESTAURANT
Albion St., In the Heart of the village

30 MacCALLUM HOUSE INN

$$ This ornate 1882 Victorian was built as a honeymoon haven for Daisy Kelley (daughter of lumber magnate William Kelley) and her husband, Alexander MacCallum. The inn, comprising the main house, carriage house, greenhouse, barn, and water tower, features 19 guest rooms. Innkeepers Melanie and Joe Reding have recently made improvements to the property, and now all rooms have private bathrooms, some with spa tubs or claw-foot tubs for two. They are furnished with period décor, including treasured antiques. The former greenhouse is now a redwood cottage with skylights, a private bath, and a wood-burning stove, whereas the water tower offers one room on each of its three floors with ocean views, two queen-size beds, and private bath. Some of the loveliest accommodations are in the restored barn. ♦ 45020

Albion St (between Lansing and Kasten Sts). 937.0289, 800/609.0492

Within the MacCallum House:

MacCALLUM HOUSE RESTAURANT

★★$$$ Under the ownership of chef Alan Kantor, this cozy restaurant, with riverstone fireplaces, offers dinner in the formal dining room or in the more casual café and bar. The menu, which changes with the seasons, features fresh local North Coast seafood and organic meats and produce from nearby farms and ranches. If you'd like to start with an aperitif, try Alexander's Antidote (named for Alexander MacCallum), a blend of Scharffenberger's Brut and Bonnie Doone framboise, and follow it with field lettuce salad or a seasonal soup. Typical entrées that highlight the chef's innovative use of wines in sauces include peppered ahi tuna seared rare, sauced with Pinot Noir beurre rouge and served with wild mushroom hash, and pan-seared duck breast and leg confit with Mendocino wild-huckleberry–Petite Sirah sauce and chestnut spaetzle. The sumptuous apple gingerbread soufflé is an excellent finale. A fine selection of North Coast wines is available. The more casual café menu offers simpler fare—rosemary-olive pizzetta, and MacTwins (two cheese-topped burgers on sesame seed buns), to name a few. ♦ Californian ♦ Daily, dinner. Reservations recommended. 937.5763. www.maccallumhousedining.com

31 VILLAGE TOY STORE

An electric train chugs along on its tracks in this old-fashioned toy shop owned by Bill and Susie Carr. Shelves are stuffed with high-quality toys, books, and games, as well as a great selection of kites. Brio trains and Breyer horses are among the most popular items. ♦ Daily. 10450 Lansing St (at Albion St). 937.4633

31 COMMUNITY COOKIE COMPANY

This is the spot for very sweet, freshly baked cookies (including a dynamite double chocolate chip), scones, and muffins, plus espresso and coffee drinks to go. Fat-free goodies are available too. ♦ Daily. 10450 Lansing St (at Albion St). 937.4843

31 TOTE FÊTE

Choose from at least a dozen kinds of sandwiches, including homemade chicken salad, meat loaf, and turkey, avocado, and jack cheese at this take-out shop. They also have pizza by the slice, their own rosemary-and-garlic focaccia, and an array of salads. Try to get here a little before the lunch hour—the place is tiny and the line of people waiting often spills through the door into the street.

WINE-MAKING: FROM THE GRAPE TO THE BOTTLE

There are almost as many methods for making wine as there are winemakers. And different procedures can produce totally different wines—even when they're made from the same grapes. This basic chart outlines the major stages for making white and red wine.

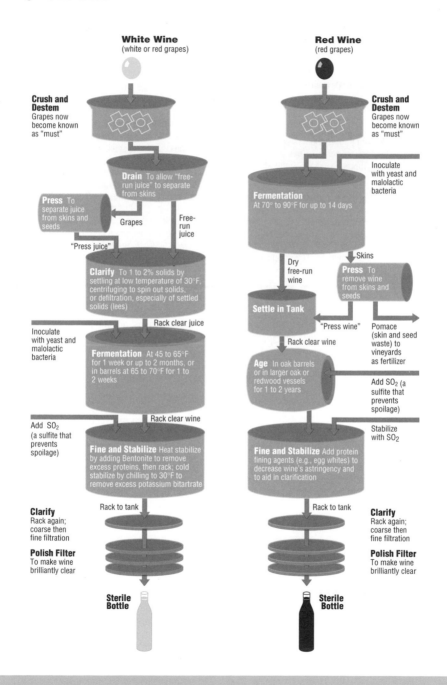

White Wine
(white or red grapes)

Red Wine
(red grapes)

Crush and Destem
Grapes now become known as "must"

Crush and Destem
Grapes now become known as "must"

Drain To allow "free-run juice" to separate from skins

Inoculate with yeast and malolactic bacteria

Press To separate juice from skins and seeds

Grapes

Free-run juice

Fermentation
At 70° to 90°F for up to 14 days

"Press juice"

Clarify To 1 to 2% solids by settling at low temperature of 30°F, centrifuging to spin out solids, or defiltration, especially of settled solids (lees)

Dry free-run wine

Skins

Press To remove wine from skins and seeds

Inoculate with yeast and malolactic bacteria

Rack clear juice

Settle in Tank

"Press wine"

Pomace (skin and seed waste) to vineyards as fertilizer

Rack clear wine

Fermentation At 45 to 65°F for 1 week or up to 2 months, or in barrels at 65 to 70°F for 1 to 2 weeks

Age In oak barrels or in larger oak or redwood vessels for 1 to 2 years

Add SO$_2$ (a sulfite that prevents spoilage)

Add SO$_2$ (a sulfite that prevents spoilage)

Rack clear wine

Stabilize with SO$_2$

Fine and Stabilize Heat stabilize by adding Bentonite to remove excess proteins, then rack; cold stabilize by chilling to 30°F to remove excess potassium bitartrate

Fine and Stabilize Add protein fining agents (e.g., egg whites) to decrease wine's astringency and to aid in clarification

Clarify
Rack again; coarse then fine filtration

Rack to tank

Rack to tank

Clarify
Rack again; coarse then fine filtration

Polish Filter
To make wine brilliantly clear

Polish Filter
To make wine brilliantly clear

Sterile Bottle

Sterile Bottle

THE BEST

Charles and Martha Barra

Owners, Redwood Valley Vineyards, and co-owners, with Bill and Janet Pauli, Redwood Valley Cellars

Going from winery to winery at the **Taste of Redwood Valley** event. Here you will find small-production, handcrafted wines from this unique wine appellation. Held Saturday and Sunday every Father's Day weekend. Food pairings, barrel sampling, entertainment.

Scones and coffee at **Schat's Courthouse Bakery Cafe/Deli** across from the courthouse in **Ukiah**. This place serves such good lunches that waiting lines are the norm.

Riding the **Skunk Train** through the redwoods from **Willits** to the **Mendocino Coast**. The train stops at Northspur for lunch. This is an activity for the whole family.

Wandering around the wharf in **Noyo Harbor** in **Ft. Bragg**. Visit with some of the old-time fishers and listen to their stories about whiskey-running out of the harbor, logging in the 1920s, and how the fishing industry has changed in the last few years. Walk down North Harbor Drive until you find the kiosk selling smoked salmon. Yum!

Pumpkinfest in October takes over the whole town of Ukiah. Streets are sectioned off to display the assemblage of competing scarecrows. Hometown bands play; food booths and entertainment are plentiful.

Strolling through the **Mendocino Coast Botanical Gardens** right on the coast in **Ft. Bragg**. A mile-long path leads you through acres of babbling streams, redwoods, rhododendrons, and seasonal show-stopping blossoms.

Dinner at **955 Ukiah** in the town of **Mendocino**. The wine list is excellent, and the food is delectable. Makes every day a special occasion. Good place to go for the evening following the hilarious **Fourth of July parade**. The diversity of **Mendocino County** really comes out in this small-town parade.

Taking our dinner, getting in the boat, and trolling out to fish for large-mouth bass on a summer's evening at **Lake Mendocino**.

Riding, or hiking, up Tomki Road, fording streams, looking for spawning salmon. If you're in a vehicle, you can eventually get to **Emandal**, a unique country resort on the Eel River 'way back in the woods.

Bread for the sandwiches comes fresh from the oven in the **Garden Bakery** (937.3140) around the corner on Albion Street, along with baked doughnuts, pastries, double chocolate cake by the slice, and other delectable treats. ♦ Takeout ♦ Daily; Su, till 4PM. 10450 Lansing St (at Albion St). 937.3383

31 OLD GOLD

Furnished with Oriental carpets, palms, and orchids, this elegant shop specializes in antique jewelry and wedding rings. The store has some top-notch pieces, such as a ruby-and-diamond Victorian bracelet and a 1940s floral diamond-cluster brooch by Cartier (both made of 18-karat gold), as well as an English Victorian opal-and-diamond ring. It also carries contemporary pieces and a large selection of wedding rings. ♦ Daily. Albion and Lansing Sts. 937.5005

32 MENDOCINO CAFÉ

★$$ Blue tables and bright paintings set the sunny mood in this charming little café serving fresh, healthy fare. Lunch offerings include a hot Thai salad with fresh greens, topped with beef, pork, chicken, or tofu, and a spicy lime dressing; a Thai burrito made with stir-fried vegetables, rice, and peanut sauce, with Thai chili sauce on the side; less

exotic burritos; and a range of sandwiches. For dinner, a good bet is the Delhi curry, or Thai firepot, to which you add rice or noodles, meat, shrimp, or tofu. Less spicy entrées include pastas, grilled fish, and house-smoked, free-range chicken. The desserts change often but almost always include a rich bread pudding and seasonal fruit crisps. They have a well-chosen list of beers and North Coast wines. In good weather, sit on the deck out back. ♦ Continental ♦ M-F, lunch and dinner; Sa, Su, brunch and dinner. 10451 Lansing St (at Albion St). 937.2422

33 MENDOCINO HOTEL & GARDEN SUITES

$$$ This 1878 false-front hotel sits on Main Street and has an unobstructed view of the sea. There are a number of buildings in back, including the 1852 **Heeser House**, and an acre of gardens. The accommodations here cover a wide range of prices, from simple European-style rooms with shared baths (the hotel provides bathrobes) and twin or double beds to rooms with private baths, queen-size beds, and wood-burning stoves to deluxe rooms and large suites. There are 51 units in all, most decorated with Victorian antiques and each differentiated by its décor, the view, or by

having a balcony or a garden. The most luxurious are the **Heeser Garden** suites, all with fireplaces, spacious modern bathrooms, and king- or queen-size beds, plus an extra sofa bed that's handy for families. ♦ 45080 Main St (between Lansing and Kasten Sts). 937.0511, 800/548.0513; fax 937.0513

Within the Mendocino Hotel & Garden Suites:

MENDOCINO HOTEL RESTAURANT

★$$$ The chef here is Colleen Murphy, formerly head chef at the **Little River Inn Restaurant** (see page 203). The hotel actually has two restaurants: Breakfast and lunch are served in the informal garden room filled with plants, whereas dinner is in the more formal Victorian dining room. Breakfast offers Belgian waffles with caramelized apple compote or olallieberries (a distant relative of the blackberry), four-grain porridge, omelettes, and other egg dishes. Lunch features moderately priced sandwiches, burgers, and salads. Dinner entrées include pasta dishes such as cappellini tossed with Portobello mushrooms, peppers, roasted garlic, and Gorgonzola spiked with balsamic vinegar; Pacific Coast ahi tuna with herbs; baked double pork chops with Roman Beauty–apple relish; or prime rib au jus. For dessert, try the deep-dish olallieberry pie, served with homemade vanilla ice cream. That same ice cream goes into the sinfully rich sundae, which is topped with melted chocolate truffles and honey-roasted pecans. ♦ American ♦ Daily, breakfast, lunch, and dinner

34 KELLEY HOUSE MUSEUM

The restored home of Mendocino pioneer William Kelley is now a museum that chronicles the cultural life and history of this seaside town. It is also the headquarters for Mendocino Historical Research, Inc., which operates the museum and has compiled impressive archives of historical photos and research material. The museum staff has done extensive work on the grounds, planting native California plants and old-fashioned flowers. ♦ Nominal admission. Daily, June-Sept; M, F-Su, Oct-May. 45007 Albion St (between Lansing and Kasten Sts). 937.5791

35 OCEAN QUILTS

This tiny shop is crammed with everything to do with quilting—embossed paper quilts, wrapping paper in quilt patterns, patchwork greeting cards, books on quilting, and a collection of antique and contemporary patchwork quilts. ♦ Daily. 45156 Main St (between Kasten and Woodward Sts). 937.4201

35 CREATIVE HANDS OF MENDOCINO

Handmade gifts and clothing from a group of local artisans are sold here. Don't overlook the imaginatively made stuffed animals from **That's Irrelephant** in Elk. ♦ Daily. 45170 Main St (between Kasten and Woodward Sts). 937.2914

35 ARTISTS CO-OP OF MENDOCINO

Eight local artists run this second-floor gallery that features landscape paintings. Their work covers a variety of media, including pastels, oils, watercolors, and acrylics. Every 2 months a well-known guest artist is showcased. ♦ Daily. 45270 Main St (between Kasten and Woodward Sts). 937.2217

35 MENDOCINO JAMS & PRESERVES

A small blue cottage at the very end of Main Street houses Robert and Shay Forest's wide variety of tasty toppings. You may even stop by and sample all the jams and preserves the Forests make. Most famous is their fudge rum sauce, but come back to sample the praline pecan sauce—it's so rich you'll have to diet for a month, but trust us, it's worth the penance. Other top sellers in the shop are rhubarb marmalade, olallieberry, sour cherry, and apricot. They will pack up your purchases and ship them for you. Mail order is available too. ♦ Daily, May-Jan; M, F-Su, Feb-Apr. 440 Main St (at Woodward St). 937.1037, 800/708.1196; fax 937.4039

36 OUT OF THIS WORLD

Big and little kids will have fun browsing through this space-age store, which features maps of the heavens and earth, star charts, and celestial music tapes. Several powerful telescopes are set up inside, so you can gaze out at the headlands and beyond. ♦ Daily. 45100 Main St (at Kasten St). 937.3335

37 MENDOCINO ICE CREAM COMPANY

★$ Winner of a gold medal at the California State Fair, this shop does a brisk business in ice cream cones, scooping out its more than

---

Restaurants/Clubs: Red | Hotels: Purple | Shops: Orange | Outdoors/Parks: Green | Sights/Culture: Blue

THE BEST

Gay Milliman

President, California Western Railroad

Riding the **Skunk Train** through the Redwoods, between **Ft. Bragg and Willits.**

Watch the seals from the end of the Boardwalk at **MacKerricher Beach State Park.**

Wine tasting in the **Anderson Valley.**

The **Fourth of July Salmon Barbecue** in Ft. Bragg.

The annual **Hand Car Races** in Willits.

Walking through the historic **Guest House Museum** in Ft. Bragg.

Enjoying the Pomo basket exhibit at the **Grace Hudson Museum and Sun House** in **Ukiah.**

A walk along the **Headlands** in **Mendocino.**

Lunch at the **Mendocino Hotel Restaurant.**

A walk on the beach at **Ten Mile River** or **Pudding Creek.**

Enjoying a salad garnished with locally made **Trillium Delights** dressing.

two dozen flavors of homemade ice creams into regular or waffle cones. Try the Black Forest (chocolate, bing cherries, and chocolate chips) or the black walnut. Sundaes and shakes are also available, along with low-calorie ice cream (try cappuccino chocolate chunk or chocolate raspberry truffle). Eat at one of the wooden booths inside or take your cone out to enjoy as you stroll along Main Street. ♦ Ice cream ♦ Daily. 45090 Main St (between Lansing and Kasten Sts). 937.5884

37 GOLDEN GOOSE

The opulent beds on display will tempt all weary shoppers to plop themselves down here. This is a good place to buy featherbeds, duvets, down pillows, fine Austrian linens, or even an antique bed or armoire. ♦ Daily. 45094 Main St (between Lansing and Kasten Sts). 937.4655

37 THE COURTYARD

Big blue bowls with high rims for mixing bread dough, as well as lovely pottery pie plates, are for sale here. There are also spices, country crafts, and cookware. ♦ Daily. 45098 Main St (between Lansing and Kasten Sts). 937.0917

37 GALLERY BOOKSHOP

This is where you can find the *New York Times*, the *San Francisco Chronicle*, and the *Wall Street Journal*, plus an intriguing mix of good reading (and not just the usual best-sellers). Founded in 1962, the bookstore is the oldest on the North Coast. The owners of this shop clearly love to read; they'll take special orders and are ready to advise on what's new or best in a number of subjects. There's a top-notch children's books section. You also can find a good collection of books on the history of Mendocino and Northern California. ♦ Daily. Main and Kasten Sts. 937.BOOK

38 BAY VIEW CAFÉ

★$$ Light, casual fare is served almost all day here. Breakfast includes omelettes, pancakes, and French toast, and for lunch there's a short menu of sandwiches, burgers, fish and chips, and salads. Dinner is only a bit fancier with pastas, steaks, and a few Mexican dishes added to the menu. The entrance is at the top of the water tower's stairs; the dining room has an outdoor deck and a great view of the ocean. ♦ American ♦ Daily, breakfast, lunch, and dinner. 45040 Main St (between Lansing and Kasten Sts). 937.4197

38 THE IRISH SHOP

A small house at the back of a brick walk features woolens and cottons from Ireland and Scotland. Look for natural cotton, crocheted or hand-knitted throws, and tweed sport coats and caps, along with teatime necessities such as shortbread, imported jams, and teas. ♦ Daily. 45050 Main St (between Lansing and Kasten Sts). 937.3133

38 HIGHLIGHT GALLERY

The works of local and regional artisans fill this large two-story gallery. Paintings, bronze and marble sculptures, ceramics, hand-turned and hand-covered wooden bowls made with exotic hardwoods, weaving, and other media are featured. Don't miss the beautiful jewelry boxes and the small collection of handcrafted furniture exhibited upstairs. ♦ Daily. 45052 Main St (between Lansing and Kasten Sts). 937.3132

39 RAINSONG

Toasty Patagonia coats, sweaters, and designer clothing for men and women are sold in this tastefully decorated shop. ♦ Daily. 45000 Main St (at Lansing St). 937.4165; fax 937.2531

40 MENDOCINO FARMERS' MARKET

Fill a basket with fresh fruit, vegetables, flowers, or the makings of a picnic supper or lunch at this farmers' market held on Fridays in a parking lot during the summer and early fall. ♦ F, noon-2PM, May-Oct. Howard and Main Sts. 937.2728

41 MENDOCINO HEADLANDS FORD HOUSE VISITORS' CENTER AND MUSEUM

This park, which encompasses the headlands in and around the town of Mendocino, uses a two-story 1857 residence, originally built for Bursley Ford, co-owner of one of the town's first sawmills, as a visitors' center. Stop here for information on Mendocino and for books on its history, nature, and wildlife, and on the sea. Tide tables, maps, field guides to tide pools and birds, and, of course, books on spotting whales are also available here. In fact, the house is a favorite observation point during the annual migration of the California gray whale. Pop in to see the large model of Mendocino circa 1890, created for the town's centennial by Leonard Peterson. A couple of rooms have exhibits on the logging and seafaring days of Mendocino. Outside, the park has picnic tables with views of the headlands. ♦ Daily. 735 Main St (west of Shoreline Hwy). 937.5397

LITTLE RIVER

Like many of the small cities up and down the coast, Little River was once a bustling logging and shipbuilding town. Now it's a quiet, charming hamlet dotted with quaint inns. It's certainly worth a visit, particularly for a stroll along the lush trails in Van Damme State Park and a boat ride through the Big River estuary.

42 RACHEL'S INN

$$ In the early 1980s Rachel Binah renovated an 1860s farmhouse and turned it into a pleasant bed-and-breakfast. Not only are all the rooms comfortable and quite private, but Binah turns out wonderful, generous breakfasts served family style in the dining room of the main house. The main house has five guest rooms: three upstairs, plus a parlor suite and a secluded garden room with its own entrance downstairs. A former textile artist who is now active in fighting against offshore oil drilling, Binah has furnished the rooms in quiet colors and has used some of her artwork. All rooms have queen-size beds and private baths; most feature views of the meadow and the

Mendocino headlands. A barn beside the house, blending contemporary and traditional design, has four large guest rooms and suites on three levels. They have most of the conveniences of a small, first-class hotel—all four have fireplaces, and the suites boast wet bars, refrigerators, private sitting rooms, and Murphy beds for extra guests and families. Two great walks await just outside the inn: one down to the beach in front of Van Damme State Park, the other a long hike through the headlands, among pines and meadows where deer and other wildlife abound. There is a log bench—a memorial with no connection to the inn—situated so visitors can sit and watch the seals and sea lions and coastal splendor below. ♦ 8200 N Hwy 1 (between Rte 128 and Comptche Ukiah Rd). 937.0088, 800/347.9252

43 VAN DAMME STATE PARK

This beautiful park covers 2,480 acres of dramatically diversified landscape. The visitors' center at the head of the park can give you trail maps and information; pick up some bird- or fern-finder guides to take on the hike along the lush Fern Canyon Trail, which is definitely worth a stroll and is also a great place for an early-morning jog. Another prime attraction is the Pygmy Forest, where the acidic, compacted soil has stunted cypresses and pines; some of the mature trees are only a foot tall. The Discovery Trail through the Pygmy Forest is accessible to those with disabilities via a redwood walkway. The park also has 74 very popular campsites suitable for tents or RVs; reserve ahead. Ten additional campsites can be reached only on foot. ♦ Fee per vehicle. Shoreline Hwy (between Rte 128 and Comptche Ukiah Rd). 937.5804; reservations 800/444.7275

43 STEVENSWOOD LODGE

$$ Tucked away on a private drive off Route 1 and bordered on three sides by Van Damme State Park, this distinctive inn is a great place to get away from it all without sacrificing comfort (there's even concierge service). All 10 of the guest rooms are equipped with private baths, wood-burning fireplaces, and honor bars (stocked with California wines, of course); nine also have separate sitting rooms. Modern furnishings and tasteful artwork add sophistication. The 26-seat breakfast-only dining room (at press time, the management had plans to add a dinner menu) is open to the public as well as to inn guests. Chef Lynn Derrick uses only organic ingredients in her roster of well-

THE BEST

Bill Zacha

Founder, Mendocino Art Center/Zacha's Bay Window Gallery

From **Cloverdale**, **Highway 128** follows the **Navarro River** to the ocean—through the **Anderson Valley**. In late September, **Boonville** hosts the **Apple Fair**. The wineries are at **Philo**. Try La Robera at **Husch Vineyards**, the champagne at **Pacific Echo Cellars**. The Navarro redwood grove continues to the sea.

In September, "A Great Day in Elk," 8 miles south of the river—wonderful!

Going north on the coast, stopping at the **Albion River Inn**. At **Little River**, visit **Heritage House** and **Little River Inn**. Next, **Mendocino** and its great **Art Center**. Fairs in August and Thanksgiving. Great wine tasting in March at the **Whale Festival**. Try the onion soup at **Mendocino Hotel Restaurant**. Many inns and gourmet dining, galleries and shops, theaters. On the first Friday in **Ft. Bragg** and second Saturday in **Mendocino**, openings at galleries and wine tastings by **Mendocino County** wineries.

In July, the **Music Festival** on the **Headlands**.

In August, **Winesong**, the wine-tasting event of the year.

Complete calendar monthly at Mendocino Art Center.

---

prepared omelettes and other egg dishes, waffles and assortment of breakfast breads, and fresh-squeezed juices and seasonal fruits. ♦ 8211 N Hwy 1 (between Rte 128 and Comptche Ukiah Rd). 937.2810, 800/421.2810

RESTAURANT AT STEVENSWOOD

★★★$$$ Chef Marc Dym, one of the rising stars on the coastal restaurant scene, knows how to create an exciting dining experience. His artistic presentations and savory fusion of Mediterranean and wine-country-inspired dishes stimulate the senses. The dining room off the lobby glows in candlelight and warmth from the fireplace: a comfortable place to settle in for the evening. The menu features fresh organic food and ranges freely among Asian, French, and Mediterranean influences. Appetizers may include green-lip mussels with wasabi-tobiko mayonnaise over chilled sesame noodle salad as well as potato gateaux with forest mushrooms, cognac truffle glacé, and cured foie gras. A favorite entrée is pine nut–crusted salmon fillet with basil oil, wilted escarole, and grilled Parmesan polenta. His steak entrées are a U.S.D.A. prime dry-aged New York steak and a prime fillet "Pacific Star" with prosciutto, Maytag blue cheese, mushroom risotto, and red wine reduction. These dishes call for Pacific Star Winery's Zinfandel. Other Mendocino wines to try are Steele Du Pratt Vineyard's Chardonnay or Pacific Star's Viognier. Dym creates special vegetarian entrées on request. Desserts also change seasonally from persimmon pudding to apple cobbler and fresh peach trifle. ♦ Th-Tu, dinner. Reservations recommended. 937.2810

43 GLENDEVEN INN

$$ Isaiah Stevens first settled this 2-acre property on the east side of Route 1 in 1867; he built the New England–style farmhouse the same year. The handsomely renovated farmhouse, the restored hay barn, and a newer building make up the inn. A grand piano and redbrick fireplace are focal points in the large, attractive living room of the main house; a picture window offers views of the **Glendeven** garden and beyond to the headlands and the ocean. There are 10 guest rooms and suites; some are larger than others, and they range in price from moderate to expensive. They're all furnished country style, with a mix of antique and contemporary pieces; all have private baths, and the four suites and four of the rooms also feature fireplaces. Innkeepers Jan and Janet deVries serve a continental breakfast (including juice, fruit, homemade pastries, and coffee or tea) that's delivered to your room. Wine in the evening is also included in the room rate. ♦ 8221 N Hwy 1 (between Rte 128 and Comptche Ukiah Rd). 937.0083, 800/822.4536; fax 937.6108. www.innaccess.littleriver.com/gdi

Within Glendeven Inn:

PARTNERS GALLERY

This gallery features fine arts and crafts created by local artisans, some of the best on the coast. ♦ M, W-Su. 937.3525

44 HERITAGE HOUSE

$$$ Dating from 1877, this New England-style lodge on a 37-acre estate is perhaps the best known on the Mendocino Coast, and it offers privacy and outstanding ocean views from many of the 66 rooms and cottages.

The inn includes a range of accommodations, from moderately priced rooms to large, costly suites and cottages. All are individually decorated with contemporary or antique furniture, and many have fireplaces. The cottages overlooking the cove are the most popular, and many are reserved several months in advance. ♦ Closed January through mid-February. 5200 N Hwy 1 (between Rte 128 and Comptche Ukiah Rd). 937.5885, 800/235.5885

Within Heritage House:

HERITAGE HOUSE RESTAURANT

★★$$$ Diners gather under the beautiful chandeliered ceiling to enjoy a meal prepared by chefs Jason Hayter and Gerry Dimma. The à la carte breakfast and dinner menus contain old standards as well as innovative new dishes. Breakfast offerings vary—eggs Benedict, steel-cut oats with brown sugar, apple pancakes with Chantilly cream, and a variety of omelettes are a few of the choices. Dinner entrées are equally appealing: our favorites include pan-seared salmon with spinach and wild mushrooms in a lemon–tarragon vinaigrette sauce; braised lamb shank with white beans, Swiss chard, and red pepper aioli; and grilled New York steak with Cabernet mashed potatoes, green beans, and roasted beet and blue cheese butter. You won't be able to resist the warm apple gratin with vanilla ice cream and nutmeg cream for dessert. No smoking is allowed. ♦ Continental ♦ Daily, breakfast and dinner. Reservations recommended

44 LITTLE RIVER MARKET

Here you'll find cheese, cold cuts, cold drinks, ice cream, and a collection of local wines, among other basic items. ♦ Daily. 7746 N Hwy 1 (between Rte 128 and Comptche Ukiah Rd). 937.5133

44 EDGE OF THE EARTH RESTAURANT

★★$$ This cozy spot adjoining the post office has a half-dozen tables and no view to speak of. The attraction is the vegetarian and seafood menu of fresh, local organic produce and sustainably harvested seafood. The dishes borrow from culinary traditions around the world, so you can globetrot from grilled Pacific swordfish with wasabi-garlic aioli to cioppino brimming with Mediterranean seafood. This is a menu without borders. There's an excellent Cajun petrale sole, coconut-vegetable polenta, and California sushi bowl. Salads include warm goat cheese in a hazelnut crust served on mixed organic greens with raspberry vinaigrette. The kitchen caters to special dietary needs, if you inform your server. Hours of operation change seasonally, so call to make sure they are open. ♦ Californian ♦ Th-Su, dinner. 7750 N Hwy 1 (between Rte 128 and Comptche Ukiah Rd), Little River. 937.1970. ♿ www.edgeoftheearth.biz

45 DENNEN'S VICTORIAN FARMHOUSE

$$ Gingerbread scrolls and curlicues adorn this Victorian bed-and-breakfast. Originally built in 1877 as a residence, it has 12 guest rooms and a cottage. All have queen- or king-size beds, private baths, and either ocean or forest views. In keeping with the inn's 19th-century style, rooms are furnished with period antiques, and some have fireplaces. In the morning breakfast is delivered and attractively set at a table in your room. ♦ 7001 N Hwy 1 (between Rte 128 and Comptche Ukiah Rd). 937.0697, 800/264.4723.
www.victorianfarmhouse.com

45 LITTLE RIVER INN

$$$ A white New England–style farmhouse that was built in the 1850s serves as the inn's office, whereas lodgings are spread out in bungalows and cottages scattered throughout the hillside grounds. All of the 64 units have private baths, TVs, and VCRs and are furnished with country pine antiques or modern oak, and most have balconies overlooking the sea; some also have fireplaces and Jacuzzis, and a few have views of the **Little River Golf & Tennis Club** (see page 204). ♦ 7751 N Hwy 1 (between Rte 128 and Comptche Ukiah Rd). 937.5942, 888/INN.LOVE. www.littleriverinn.com

At the Little River Inn:

LITTLE RIVER INN RESTAURANT

★$$ The tables by the windows offer a glimpse of the ocean as well as a garden view at this casual place for breakfast or dinner. Breakfast features hotcakes, egg omelettes, and other egg dishes, whereas the dinner menu offers a dozen regular entrées along with daily specials. Everything is served with freshly made soup or salad, vegetables, rice or potatoes, and warm biscuits. Choose from broiled swordfish marinated in tequila and lime juice, grilled prawns rolled in bread crumbs and chopped hazelnuts, or the inn's famous pepper steak. There's a champagne breakfast on the weekends that's well worth

---

Restaurants/Clubs: Red | **Hotels: Purple** | **Shops: Orange** | **Outdoors/Parks: Green** | **Sights/Culture: Blue**

getting up for. ♦ American/Californian ♦ Daily, breakfast and dinner

LITTLE RIVER GOLF & TENNIS CLUB AND SPA

This club features two championship tennis courts and a regulation nine-hole golf course with a driving range and putting green. Golf-cart rentals are available, and the pro shop can supply you with golf togs and equipment. ♦ Daily. 937.5667

46 LITTLE RIVER AIRPORT

This small airstrip accommodates private aircraft—and certainly a small plane is the fastest and most convenient way to get to Mendocino, if you can afford it. The airport also handles car rentals and chartered small planes. ♦ 43001 Little River Airport Rd (between Albion Little River Rd and Shoreline Hwy). 937.5129

ALBION

Homesick for Britain, Captain William A. Richardson, former port captain of San Francisco and a large land-holder on the Mendocino Coast, dubbed this coastal village Albion, the ancient name for Britain. Richardson also built the town's first sawmill in 1853, just where the **Albion River** meets the sea. Today, with clusters of wooden buildings clinging to the bluffs above the river, Albion is a charming seaside town popular with tourists. The section of town along **Route 1** is lined with several good bed-and-breakfasts.

47 ALBION RIVER INN

$$$ A series of contemporary cottages strung across a dramatic piece of real estate over-looking the ocean comprise this popular Mendocino retreat. Each of the 20 rooms (complete with a private bath and fireplace) has a knockout view through the large windows or from the deck. Six rooms have Jacuzzis, and eight feature bathtubs built for two. The décor has been kept plain, but the style is more condo than rustic cottage. The room rates include a full breakfast served in the restaurant (see below). ♦ 3790 N Hwy 1 (between Rte 128 and Comptche Ukiah Rd). 937.1919, 800/479.7944 (in northern CA); fax 937.2604

Within the Albion River Inn:

ALBION RIVER INN RESTAURANT

★$$$ At the very end of the row of cottages is the inn's restaurant, a large, simply tailored room that boasts a spectacular view (especially at sunset) of the headlands and the sea beyond. Chef Stephen Smith's menu often changes from day to day. If it is on the menu,

start with one of his hearty soups, or grilled prawns with tomato-tequila butter. Grilled New York steak with either pepper or Dijon mustard sauce, filet mignon with caramelized ginger sauce, or the penne pasta with roasted peppers and a tangy blue and Parmesan-cheese sauce are just some of the main courses frequently offered; specials might include grilled Canadian salmon with cucumber-dill sauce or roasted duck flavored with dried cherry cassis. The housemade ice cream and sorbets are superb. An extensive wine list includes hard-to-find producers such as **Dehlinger** and **Williams & Selyem**, and the bar also stocks 90 single-malt scotches. ♦ Continental ♦ Daily, dinner. Reservations recommended

48 FENSALDEN INN

$$ Right off Route 1 on Navarro Ridge Road, this bed-and-breakfast is set on 20 acres of land, with views of the ocean on the other side of the road. Originally serving as a stage-coach stop in the 1890s, the structure now houses four guest rooms and a two-room suite with a fireplace. The property's water tower has been converted into two guest rooms, and a separate bungalow has been added that sleeps four and has a full kitchen. All accommodations have private baths. Guests may gather in the living room around the fire or the grand piano. And in the morning, innkeeper Evelyn Hamby serves a full breakfast in the dining room. ♦ 33810 Navarro Ridge Rd (east of Shoreline Hwy). 937.4042, 800/959.3850. www.Fensalden.com

GUALALA

The local Indians used to call this area **Walali**, meaning "where the river meets [the sea]," until the Spanish started calling it Gualala. Nowadays, you might hear some of the locals call it "Walala" (a combination of the two names), but don't let that confuse you. Gualala is still the town's official name. Like most of the cities along this coast, Gualala was once a thriving lumber port where schooners were loaded with timber bound for San Francisco. With its river beaches and good fishing spots, Gualala is a haven for anglers and nature lovers. Travelers who want to spend time exploring the local beaches can find very reasonably priced lodging at the old-time **Gualala Hotel**. The town is also home to **St. Orres**, one of the best restaurants along the North Coast and definitely worth a detour.

49 ELK COVE INN & SPA

$$ The inn commands a Pacific vista envied by Mendocino innkeepers. L.E. White Lumber Co. built the Victorian mansion in 1883 for the private recreation of its executives. The property is set off the highway, settled by oak

trees along a creek, but open to the ocean. You can choose from 15 accommodations, located in the Victorian mansion or in cliffside oceanfront cottages. All the rooms have feather beds, down comforters, European bed linens, and silky robes, and most have fireplaces and full or partial ocean views. A generous basket with a split of wine, fresh fruit, and homemade oatmeal cookies welcome you on arrival, and chocolates and a decanter of port greet you at bedtime. The inn features a full-liquor bar in a gleaming, wood-paneled living room. Take a stroll in the moonlight out to the Victorian gingerbread gazebo with a glass of port or cognac. In the morning you won't want to sleep in—the dining room rolls out a full buffet breakfast, also included in the room rate. A new European-style day spa is also available for guests. ♦ 6300 S Coast Hwy 1 (at Philo Greenwood Rd). 877.3321, 800/275.2967. ♿ www.elkcoveinn.com

Within Elk Cove Inn & Spa:

Zebo Restaurant

★★$$ Named for the gazebo on the ocean bluff, this rustic yet chic dining room is transformed for evening with European table linens, porcelain dinnerware, and glowing candles. Chef Gary Robinette has created a healthful fine-dining experience using produce grown by local farmers or by himself at his family farm. Zebo is also known for its house-made pasta, free-range hormone-free beef, and locally baked artisan breads. Don't miss the salads. What could be more satisfying to the senses than greens and vegetables that spent that morning in the garden? A signature salad is organic greens tossed with fennel, blood oranges, oil-cured olives, and champagne vinaigrette. Another popular appetizer is the broiled oysters with chili-coriander pesto. Two highlights of this American bistro menu are a spicy wine-laced stew with red snapper, shrimp, and mussels; and tri-tip steak rubbed with spices, mesquite-grilled and served with fresh salsa and chipotle cream. Each of the Mendocino and Sonoma wines is offered by the glass. Save room for Gary's famous homemade shortcake with fresh strawberries and homemade vanilla ice cream. Call for days and hours December through March. ♦ American ♦ F-M, dinner. 877.3321, 800/275.2967 ♿

50 Whale Watch Inn by the Sea

$$$$ At this contemporary inn set on 2 acres at the edge of the sea, owners Jim and Kazuko Popplewell offer 18 luxurious guest rooms in five separate buildings, all with ocean views, private baths, and ocean-facing decks. Each features queen-size beds with down comforters; most have fireplaces, whirlpool baths or saunas, and skylights; some have kitchens. One of the most luxurious is **The Bath Suite**, which features hand-carved furniture, a fireplace, and a two-person whirlpool bath at the top of a spiral staircase with a view of the Pacific. A full breakfast is served in your room. ♦ 35100 S Hwy 1 (north of Collins Landing). 884.3667, 800/WHALE.42

51 St. Orres

$$ This is one of the few inns on the North Coast that combines appealing accommodations with a first-class restaurant. The building—with its Russian-influenced architecture marked by elaborately carved wooden balustrades, stained-glass windows, and ornate towers capped with copper domes—is owned by Ted and Eric Black and Rosemary Campiformio, the chef. The hotel, designed by Eric, was built in 1976. The eight guest rooms upstairs share three baths; two have ocean views and French doors opening onto the balcony, whereas the less expensive side rooms overlook the gardens or trees. Scattered over the large property are also 11 unique and secluded cottages, some along a creek and others at the edge of a redwood forest; all have private baths. One favorite is the modest **Wildflower**, a rustic cabin with a double bed nestled in a loft, a skylight, a sitting area with a wood burning stove, and an outdoor hot-water shower. The **Sequoia** cottage features a king-size bed, a fireplace, full bath with soaking tub, and an ocean view. The largest cottage, **Pine Haven**, is a mini-domed building with a stone fireplace, two redwood decks, and an ocean view. ♦ 36601 S Hwy 1 (north of Pacific Woods Rd). 884.3303, 884.3335. www.storres.com

Within St. Orres:

St. Orres Restaurant

★★★$$$ The inn's dramatic dining room is in one of the Russian-style towers and has a soaring three-story ceiling. Tables are set with

fresh flowers and handsome dinnerware, and the service is attentive. In the kitchen, chef Campiformio turns out inventive prix-fixe, three-course meals. Appetizers might include a sumptuous garlic flan with locally foraged wild mushrooms, Stilton baked in phyllo, or North Coast game pâté, a winning mixture of venison, pheasant, wild huckleberries, and pistachios. Campiformio's selection of appealing entrées leaves most diners struggling to decide what to order: Choices may vary from venison in a wild huckleberry and Zinfandel sauce served with sweet-potato waffles to grilled quail marinated in tequila and garlic served with yam and green-onion pancakes. For dessert, consider the chocolate decadence cake or an individual fruit pie crowned with house-made ice cream. There's a very good, mostly California wine list too. ♦ Continental ♦ Th-Tu, dinner. Reservations recommended

51 MAR VISTA COTTAGES

$ A dozen white-clapboard cottages are set at the edge of a redwood forest. Choose between one- or two-bedroom housekeeping cottages, each with a queen-size bed and a private bath, and some with additional double or twin-size beds. Several have fireplaces or outdoor decks. The 8-acre property also includes a picnic and barbecue area, a hot tub, and a path to the beach. ♦ 35101 S Hwy 1 (north of Collins Landing). 884.3522. www.marvistamendocino.com

52 CAFÉ LA LA

$ Stop at this local spot for homemade soup, specialty sandwiches, salads, and gourmet coffee. Choose a table with an ocean view or sit outdoors on the deck. Daily, breakfast and lunch. ♦ Across from the Sandpiper Restaurant in Cypress Village, on Ocean Drive. 884.1104

52 OCEANSONG

★★$$$ This restaurant's nautical theme and ocean view afford a delightful setting for chef Rene Fueg's culinary treats. Start with crisp wonton prawns, deep fried in Cajun-spiced wrappers and topped with a zesty wasabi cream sauce, or cornmeal chowder, fragrant with ginger and cilantro and rich with steamed clams in their shells. Entrées might include the chef's seafood mixed grill with medium-hot fruity curry sauce and jasmine Thai rice; there also are standards such as New York steak topped with sautéed shiitake mushrooms. There's a nice selection of wines by the glass, and a well-priced wine list, chosen to partner with the menu. ♦ Californian ♦ Daily, lunch and dinner. 39350 S Hwy 1 (just north of Gualala River). 884.1041

52 BREAKERS INN

$$ Perched on a bluff overlooking the mouth of the Gualala River and the Pacific Ocean, this luxury inn offers 27 individually decorated rooms. All rooms have fireplaces, two-person whirlpool baths, king-size beds, private baths, and private balconies, most with spectacular ocean views; garden rooms offer partial ocean or garden views. Each room is decorated in a national or regional theme, from the luxury oceanfront **Japan** room, with a spa tub made of warm Hinoki cypress wood, to the Early American–style **Connecticut** room, with a patchwork quilt on the four-poster bed. Continental breakfast is included in the rate. Innkeeper Heidi Price offers tips on wine tasting, whale watching, abalone diving, and other activities in the Gualala area. ♦ 39300 S Hwy 1 (just north of Gualala River). 884.3200; fax 884.3400

52 FOOD COMPANY

$$ Stop here for a made-to-order take-out picnic. Choices include salads, sandwiches, and pastries baked fresh daily, plus hot entrées. Patio seating is also available. ♦ American ♦ Daily, breakfast, lunch, and dinner. 38411 Robinson Reef (corner of S Hwy 1). 884.1800

53 GUALALA HOTEL

$ The year 1903 is proudly inscribed on the front of this historic two-story hotel that resembles something you'd expect to see on an Old West movie set. In fact, it was built to house lumbermill workers and stagecoach travelers. Most of the 19 rooms upstairs share a bath, just as they did at the turn of the 19th century (though the baths have been remodeled since then). Call ahead to reserve one of the five rooms with private baths and ocean views. The unfussy period décor throughout—patterned wallpaper, old-fashioned water basins, bouquets of fresh flowers—is charming. ♦ 39301 S Hwy 1 (just north of Gualala River). 884.3441

Within the Gualala Hotel:

GUALALA HOTEL RESTAURANT

★$$ Here at this gold-hued dining room, breakfast includes omelettes, French toast, and hotcakes; the lunch menu offers sandwiches, salads, and daily specials; and dinner entrées range from fresh salmon and deep-fried oysters or prawns to a variety of pastas, rib-eye steak, and pork chops. A children's menu is available, and Friday and Saturday are prime-rib nights. There's also a lively bar and what is said to be the widest

wine selection on the North Coast.
♦ Italian/American ♦ Daily, breakfast, lunch, and dinner. Reservations recommended on weekends

54 GUALALA POINT REGIONAL PARK

This park is another prime spot for winter whale watching, and for bird watching and wildlife spotting throughout the year. Look for great blue herons, pygmy owls, shorebirds, deer, jackrabbits, and gray foxes. Cormorants can be seen offshore on Gualala Point Island. The 75-acre park has river and ocean access and includes 19 campsites with picnic facilities and fire pits, available on a first-come, first-served basis. ♦ Park: daily. Visitors' center: M, F-Su. Rte 1 (between Annapolis Rd and Gualala River). 785.2377; fax 785.3741

ANDERSON VALLEY

For a tour of one of the most pleasurable wine roads in California, just north of Cloverdale in Sonoma County, take Mendocino County's **Route 128** toward **Boonville** and the Anderson Valley. Highway 128, between Cloverdale and the Mendocino Coast, passes through three viticulture areas: Yorkville Highlands, Anderson Valley, and Mendocino Ridge. There's no four-lane superhighway here to carve up the landscape, just a fairly narrow country road that dips and turns with the topography, more or less following the course of the **Navarro River** through this ravishing 25-mile-long valley and then through the towering redwoods to the **Mendocino Coast**. It's an unforgettable drive, meandering past apple orchards and weathered farmsteads and through the hamlets of **Yorkville** and **Boonville** and the town of **Philo**. Wineries along the highway include Yorkville, Handley, Esterlina, Husch, Brutocao, Christine Woods, Greenwood Ridge, Navarro, Souzao Cellars, Pacific Echo, and Roederer. Despite being next door to prestigous vineyards, local hamlets have retained a homespun character. Most of the wineries lie along the main route; a few are off **Route 128** and require further directions from the owners. There's no reason to hurry; these tasting rooms stay open until 5PM or later, and it takes only a half hour at most to drive from one end of the valley to the other unless you stop to taste. The best company for the road is Philo's **KZY** (90.7 FM), one of the smallest public radio stations in the country. It plays a mixed bag of great music: rock, jazz, classical, folk, and country.

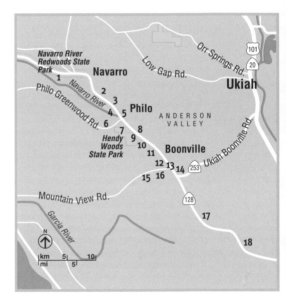

The towns are close by one another (an average drive of 10 minutes), with wineries the main attractions in and around Yorkville and Philo, and Boonville the place that offers lodging, restaurants, and shops. From 1880 to 1920, when few visitors came to Boonville, residents developed a language, Boontling, which is occasionally heard today. The locals laced their language with "nonch harpins," which means "objectionable talk." Roughly 15 percent of the nouns, verbs, and modifiers refer to sexual activity and bodily functions that were taboo decades ago. Horn of Zeese, the name of a local café, is Boontling for "cup of coffee." You can stay at the comfortable **Boonville Hotel** (which has one of the best restaurants in the region) and sample the Anderson Valley brew at the **Buckhorn Saloon**. The village also has several secluded bed-and-breakfast inns and a historical museum in the little red schoolhouse at the north end of town.

The wineries are renowned for crisp, dry whites, primarily Chardonnay, Riesling, and Gewürztraminer, all grapes that thrive in the cool growing conditions of the Anderson

Valley. Pinot Noir does well here too, but the valley is gaining world recognition for its sparkling wines, led by **Scharffenberger Cellars**, and **Roederer Estate**, owned by the prestigious French Champagne house **Louis Roederer**. All of this means that inviting wine tasting awaits you in this little valley. In fact, as you travel along the wine road sampling the local varieties, you may discover that you really *do* like dessert wines after all.

This valley was apple country long before vineyards ever appeared, and it remains a prime apple-growing region. Many of the farms have switched to commercial growing methods and added antique apple varieties to their repertoire. September and October yield the freshest prime apples, but you'll find apple juice and other apple products year-round. The **Apple Farm** in Philo is a great source for organic cider and chutneys. And just down the road is an excellent produce stand, **Gowan's Oak Tree**, where you can find all of summer's bounty.

When you've finished exploring Anderson Valley's vineyards, continue driving northwest along **Route 128**, through the **Navarro River Redwoods State Park** with its miles of stately redwoods and, finally, spectacular views of the ocean. At the coast, you can head north to **Albion, Little River**, and **Mendocino**.

PHILO

The tiny town of Philo is marked by just three or four buildings, with several wineries and other attractions set along the road north of it.

1 NAVARRO RIVER REDWOODS STATE PARK

As you drive from Philo past the last of the wineries and enter a thick redwood grove, you'll pass through this state park, an 11-mile corridor of redwoods extending from the river to a little north of the highway. In 1991 more than 600 acres of Navarro redwoods were added to the original 22-acre **Paul Dimmick State Park** to create this spacious recreation area, which offers visitors numerous activities, including swimming in the Navarro River, fishing for steelhead, hiking on many trails, and camping. The campground has 28 sites suitable for tents or RVs, available on a first-come, first-served basis. The one primitive campground has a flush toilet and water in the summer (only a pit toilet is available in the winter). ♦ Rte 128 (between Soda Creek Rd and Shoreline Hwy). 937.5804

2 ESTERLINA VINEYARDS

This winery has a smashing view across Anderson Valley clear over to the **Roederer** vineyards. The focus of the wine production, which totals about 1,000 cases, is mainly on Pinot Noir. They also make small lots of Chardonnay and Fumé Blanc. Part of the fun is getting to this winery up an unmarked,

unpaved road. ♦ Tasting by appointment. 1200 Holmes Ranch Rd (north of Rte 128, at Mile Marker 17.51). 895.2920

2 CHRISTINE WOODS WINERY

After spending 20 years as a home winemaker, Vernon Rose decided to take the plunge in 1980 and move from Walnut Creek, east of San Francisco, to the 40-acre property he bought as a vacation site in 1966. With classes in wine-making and viti-culture at the **University of California, Davis** under his belt, he made his first commercial Chardonnay in 1982, and it won a gold medal at the Mendocino County Fair. He also makes Pinot Noir. The name of the winery comes from an early settlement called Christine in honor of Christine Gschwend, child of Swiss immigrants who was the first white child born in the Anderson Valley. Remnants of the old road to the settlement can still be seen on the property. ♦ Daily, June-Sept; M, Th-Su, Oct-May. 3155 Hwy 128 (between Indian Creek and Flynn Creek Rds). 895.2115. www.christinewoods.com

2 HANDLEY CELLARS

Milla Handley, great-great granddaughter of beer brewer Henry Weinhard, studied enology at the **University of California, Davis** and worked at **Chateau St. Jean** before founding this winery in the basement of her home near Philo in 1982. (She and her husband, Rex McClellan, have since moved into these larger quarters.) A rich, complex, barrel-aged Chardonnay is her best-known wine, but she

Restaurants/Clubs: Red | Hotels: Purple | Shops: Orange | Outdoors/Parks: Green | Sights/Culture: Blue

also makes a fine Sauvignon Blanc from grapes grown on the Handley family's Dry Creek Valley vineyard in Sonoma, a spicy, off-dry Gewürztraminer, and a small amount of sparkling Brut, three parts Pinot Noir to one part Chardonnay, aged on the yeasts (*sur lie*) for 24 to 36 months. Her rosé, made from Pinot Noir grapes and a touch of Chardonnay, is an ideal picnic wine. Some wines, such as her Pinot Noir and late-harvest Riesling, are primarily available only at the winery. Sample them all at the sunny tasting room, filled with exotic art, or at the garden courtyard. ♦ Tasting and sales daily; tours by appointment only. 3151 Hwy 128 (between Indian Creek and Flynn Creek Rds). 895.3876, 895.2190; fax 895.2603; 800/733.3151. www.handleycellars.com

2 CLAUDIA SPRINGS WINERY

One of California's smallest wineries, it has won some prized awards in Mendocino County competitions for its Chardonnay, Zinfandel, and Pinot Noir, and it offers them at tastings in its barrel room. ♦ Tasting and sales, Sa, Su; by appointment only, M. 2160 Guntly Rd (east of Rte 128). 895.3926. Also at Redwood Valley Cellars, 7051 N State St, between Rte 20 and Hwy 101, Redwood Valley. 485.0322

3 ROEDERER ESTATE

When the prestigious 200-year-old Champagne firm Roederer (maker of Cristal and Brut Premier) decided to establish a California estate in the late 1970s, Jean-Claude Rouzaud spent more than 2 years researching sites before choosing the Anderson Valley. With its long, cool growing season, the climate in the valley is remarkably similar to that of Champagne. Local residents are very happy with the winery's low-key design, which fits unassumingly into the hillside—the large state-of-the-art structure is built partially underground to better maintain the cellars' cool temperature. The estate's French winemaker, Dr. Michel Salgues, worked for 7 years to develop the vineyards and hone his skills before releasing his first wine, the Anderson Valley Brut, in October 1988. Made from a blend of Pinot Noir and Chardonnay, it spends 20 to 24 months aging on the yeasts. Tours of this first-class operation give a good overview of the complicated process of making sparkling wines by the traditional *méthode champenoise*. The tasting room, which features an antique French bistro bar topped with zinc, is furnished with comfortable banquettes and iron-and-tile tables. The 200-year-old terra-cotta tiles on the floor come from a château in France. ♦ Tasting and sales daily; tours by appointment only. 4501 Hwy 128 (between Indian Creek and Flynn Creek Rds). 895.2288; fax 895.2120

4 LAZY CREEK

The road to this small winery is unpaved but well worth the drive to taste Johann and Theresia Kobler's wines. Their total production—5,000 cases a year—includes highly praised Gewürztraminer and Pinot Noir wines and an excellent Chardonnay. The 80-year-old wine cellar that burrows into the earth is redwood-lined. Serious tasters linger on the redwood deck overlooking Lazy Creek. Call the Koblers for directions. ♦ Tasting by appointment only. 4610 Hwy 128 (north of Philo Greenwood Rd). 895.3623

4 HUSCH VINEYARDS

Founded in 1971, this is the oldest winery in the Anderson Valley. In 1979 the Oswald family purchased it from the Husch family, and five generations of this third-generation farming family are involved in the winery. The tasting room is a rustic redwood shack covered with climbing roses, and it is hosted by one of the friendliest and most knowledgeable staffs around. More than six people at the bar is a tight fit, but you may take your glass of wine out to the sundeck. Nearby picnic tables are set up under a vine-covered arbor. The wines are all well made and offer some of the best values in Mendocino County. The whites range from a barrel-fermented, oak-aged Chardonnay and a dry Sauvignon Blanc to a dry, Alsatian-style Gewürztraminer and an off-dry Chenin Blanc. Reds include a good Pinot Noir and a firmly structured Cabernet. (Look for the Reserve wines.) The grapes for the Pinot Noir, Gewürztraminer, and Chardonnay come from the winery's vineyards in the Anderson Valley; the Sauvignon Blanc, Cabernet, and Chenin Blanc hail from its warmer Ukiah vineyards. After tasting the wines, guests are welcome to stroll through the vineyards. ♦ Tasting and sales daily. 4400 Hwy 128 (north of Philo Greenwood Rd). 895.3216; fax 895.2068; 800/55-HUSCH. www.huschvineyards.com

NAVARRO
Vineyards

5 NAVARRO VINEYARDS

This small, family-owned winery founded in 1974 specializes in premium white wines and Pinot Noir, made in both a traditional Burgundian style and a fresh, youthful style.

It is best known for its classic dry Gewürztraminer, among the best in the state, but also try the elegant and complex Chardonnay Première Reserve and the excellent dessert wines, including a late-harvest White Riesling. The winemaker is Jim Klein. The tasting room here is quite small and tours are infrequent, but it's hard to find a friendlier welcome. (Owner Ted Bennett and his wife, Deborah Cahn, can sometimes be found in the tasting room pouring wines.) The winery's vintages are sold only at the winery and at a few selected restaurants; most are sold by mail order. Also note the bottled grape juice that comes in a wine bottle with the vineyard's handsome label. Outside the small wooden building is a redwood deck with brightly colored umbrellas overlooking a landscape of vineyards and rolling hills—a peaceful spot for a picnic. A few more tables are sheltered under an arbor shaded with grapevine leaves. ♦ Tasting and sales daily. 5601 Hwy 128 (between Indian Creek and Flynn Creek Rds). 895.3686, 800/537.9463

5 GREENWOOD RIDGE VINEYARDS

The redwood building with a distinctive, tall roof (inside, it resembles a wooden tepee) is surrounded by a vineyard originally planted in 1972. The winery gets its moniker from a ridge that was named for the Caleb Greenwood family, who settled the area in the 1850s. By coincidence the current owner and winemaker is a graphic designer and wine aficionado named Allan Green, who came to the Anderson Valley in the early 1970s. He produces an off-dry (semisweet) White Riesling and a sweet late-harvest White Riesling, along with Chardonnay, Cabernet Sauvignon, Pinot Noir, Merlot, Sauvignon Blanc, and a Zinfandel from the **Scherrer Vineyard** (planted in 1919) near Healdsburg in the Russian River Valley. Several picnic tables are set up by the pond, and visitors may stretch out on the lawn. Since 1983, the annual **California Wine Tasting Championships** have been held here the last weekend in July. Food, wine, live music, and sunshine are the components of this spirited event, in which novice tasters and experienced professionals alike try to identify a series of wines by varietal type. ♦ Tasting and sales daily. 5501 Hwy 128 (between Indian Creek and Flynn Creek Rds). 895.2002

6 THE APPLE FARM

Karen Schmitt, her husband, Tim Bates, and their children live right in the midst of the organic apple orchard where they grow about a dozen varieties of antique and heirloom apples. At harvest time (August through November), they have apples galore, but year-round you may stop by for their subtle, organic apple-cider vinegar, jams, jellies, and chutneys. They also make lovely dried-apple wreaths, and the bundled apple twigs are terrific for barbecues. At the cooking school, you can sign up for single sessions, held on Thursday mornings; 3-day weekend sessions are hands on, each day culminating in meals eaten by participants. Call for a schedule of upcoming classes. ♦ Shoppers follow the Anderson Valley honor system at the produce stand. In the valley, farmers post a price list and put out a money jar. 18501 Philo Greenwood Rd (west of Rte 128). 895.2333; e-mail: applefarm@pacific.net

7 BRUTOCAO CELLARS TASTING ROOM

In addition to the one in Hopland where their winery is located, **Brutocao** has a tasting room here. The wide range of wines offered includes Chardonnay, Cabernet Sauvignon, Merlot, Pinot Noir, Sauvignon Blanc, Sémillon, and Zinfandel. The winery's homespun newsletter offers wine tips and recipes, and fun sketches of items for sale in the tasting room, especially helpful around the holidays. Ask to be put on their mailing list. ♦ Tasting and sales daily. 7000 Hwy 128 (between Mountain View and Philo Greenwood Rds). 895.2152

7 GOWAN'S OAK TREE

Since the 1930s, the Gowan family has been selling their homegrown produce at this white clapboard roadside stand, one of the Anderson Valley's main attractions. Stop here for fresh-pressed cider and apples from their own orchards, which you will see as you drive up. They have peaches, plums, apricots, and whatever else is in season, such as cucumbers, green beans, incredibly fresh sweet

---

Restaurants/Clubs: Red | Hotels: Purple | Shops: Orange | Outdoors/Parks: Green | Sights/Culture: Blue

corn, and vine-ripened tomatoes. In hot weather, they have apple and berry ice pops; in winter, hot spiced cider. And in a shady grove out back, there are picnic tables and a swing for kids, making this a great rest stop on the drive to the coast. ♦ Daily. 6600 Hwy 128 (just south of Philo Greenwood Rd). 895.3353, 895.3225

7 HENDY WOODS STATE PARK

From the highway, following a ridge to the south, a tall grove of enormous redwoods, so dark they almost look black against the sky, marks this 690-acre state park. **Gentle Giant Trail** leads visitors for a half mile through groves of redwoods harboring trees more than 1,000 years old and 270 feet tall. Bring a picnic to enjoy beside the Navarro River. There are several hiking paths and trails along the river, where visitors can also fish for steelhead in the fall, swim during the summer, and canoe or kayak in late winter and early spring. The park has 92 campsites suitable for tents, trailers, and RVs, as well as day-use facilities. ♦ Between mid-May and early October, campsites must be reserved; the rest of the year, they're available on a first-come, first-served basis. Philo Greenwood Rd (west of Rte 128). 937.5804; reservations 800/444.7275

8 PACIFIC ECHO CELLARS

Founded in 1981 by John Scharffenberger, this winery is now owned by the French Champagne house Champagne Pommery, with the new name of Pacific Echo Cellars. Scharffenberger was the Anderson Valley's pioneer in *méthode champenoise* wines (sparkling wines made in the traditional French way). Today winemaker Willis Tex Sawyer produces three cuvées: a toasty, beautifully balanced nonvintage Brut made from a blend of 37% Pinot Noir and 63% Chardonnay, a Brut Rosé made primarily from Pinot Noir, and a subtly effervescent nonvintage Crémant. They also produce an elegant vintage Blanc de Blancs made entirely from Chardonnay. The Crémant, made from a blend of grapes similar to that used in the nonvintage Brut, was created for a dinner hosted by President Ronald Reagan at the 1988 Moscow summit. Sample them all at the winery's tasting room in a remodeled farmhouse. The discreet winery building was designed by **Jacques Ullman** of Sausalito, who also designed the **Roederer Estate**. **Pacific Echo Cellars** runs periodic daylong culinary workshops featuring some of California's most renowned chefs. ♦ Tasting and sales, daily; tours by appointment only. 8501 Hwy 128 (north of Indian Creek Rd). 895.2065; fax 895.2758

9 PHILO POTTERY INN

$ Built entirely of heart redwood, this 1888 house, once an old stagecoach stop, makes a thoroughly appropriate and charming bed-and-breakfast inn. Innkeepers Sue and Barry Chiverton have four guest rooms in the main house (two with private baths, two with shared), although the little one-room cottage with a wood-burning stove, detached private bath, and its own back porch is everybody's favorite. For breakfast Chiverton might serve fresh melon, whole-wheat buttermilk pancakes, chicken-and-apple sausages, and fresh blackberry muffins (the blackberries are picked from the inn's own patch). The word *pottery* in the name of the inn comes from the original owners, who were potters and had a gallery on the premises. ♦ 8550 Hwy 128 (between Mountain View and Philo Greenwood Rds). 895.3069

10 INDIAN CREEK COUNTY PARK

This is an easily accessible, lovely spot for a picnic along the creek. There are also self-guided nature walks among the coast redwoods. ♦ Rte 128 (between Mountain View and Philo Greenwood Rds). 463.4267

10 INDIAN CREEK INN

$$ This charming Swiss chalet–style bed-and-breakfast, located on 17 acres bordered by the Navarro River and Indian Creek, is decorated throughout with original Swiss folk art and paintings. All of the armoires and some of the four-poster beds, chairs, and tables are hand-painted in the Swiss style. The walls and exposed beams in the five cozy rooms and suites are made of Canadian cedar, and each guest room has its own private bath. Innkeepers Lisabeth and Phillip Ashiku greet guests with wine, imported cheeses, cold meats, and fruits. And if their guests feel a snack attack at midnight—well, that's okay too. There's a fully stocked kitchen open 24 hours to satisfy hunger pangs. The bountiful breakfast is served buffet style. For guests' added enjoyment during their visit, there's a patio and garden, and nature hikes in Hendy Woods. ♦ 9050 Hwy 128 (between Mountain View and Philo Greenwood Rds). 895.3861

BOONVILLE

During the early years of the 20th century, the Anderson Valley was still fairly remote, and few travelers made their way along the narrow country road to the tiny community of Boonville. To amuse themselves and totally mystify the rare stranger who did show up, the folks here developed an elaborate language of their own that they called "Boontling." Much of it is bawdy stuff—or at least what would have passed for bawdiness in those days. It's been the subject of scholarly study (you can pick up books about Boontling in town), and you can still see a few signs of it around (such as the name of the **Horn of Zeese Coffee Shop**). **Lauren's**, the **Boonville Hotel**, and the **Buckhorn Saloon** across the street are the main places to eat; the hotel and several bed-and-breakfasts offer lodging. Be sure to pick up a copy of the *Anderson Valley Advertiser*, an eccentric local newspaper filled with passionate debate on a number of subjects.

11 ANDERSON CREEK INN BED AND BREAKFAST

$$ Set amid towering old oak trees off Route 128, this comfortable ranch-style inn has two creeks coursing through the 16-acre property. The owners' pets—two llamas, three Belgian draft horses, and a potbellied pig—are ensconced in their own private quarters. Innkeeper Jim Minton has five guest rooms, all with king-size beds, private baths, and a fresh, contemporary décor. All rooms have views of meadows and oaks and three have fireplaces. A full gourmet breakfast is served, including homemade breads and organic juices. There's a "treehouse" in the 300-year-old oak tree out back, with a two-person hammock; plus a hot tub and large pool on the grounds. Borrow a bike and make the easy ride into town down the frontage road, past apple orchards and blackberry fields. Or ask Rod Graham to book an old-fashioned horse-drawn carriage for your tour. ◆ 12050 Anderson Valley Way (just south of Rte 128). 895.3091, 800/552.6202

12 ANDERSON VALLEY HISTORICAL SOCIETY MUSEUM

One mile north of Boonville, look for the little red schoolhouse on the west side of the road. If the flag is flying out front, this homespun museum dedicated to the history of the valley is open. The one-room Conn Creek schoolhouse dates from 1891; the museum also includes a model sheep-shearing shed. Exhibits are set up to demonstrate different aspects of everyday life in the early days of the valley. Pieced together with donations from local families, the collection includes old farming tools, everyday objects, and furniture. The Pomo Indian baskets and stone tools on display were all found in or around the Anderson Valley. ◆ Donation requested. F-Su. Rte 128 (north of Mountain View Rd). 895.3207

13 MENDOCINO SPECIALTY VINEYARDS

Three small Mendocino County wineries— Claudia Springs, Eaglepoint Ranch, and Raye's Hill—share this tasting room across from the Boonville Hotel. Eaglepoint Ranch Winery, formerly Lonetree Winery, makes award-winning Syrah, using grapes from John Scharffenberger's Eaglepoint Ranch. The 1,800-foot elevation and shallow mountain topsoil produces a highly concentrated, lush Rhône-style red. Raye's Hill is known for its Anderson Valley Pinot Noir made from grapes grown 15 miles from the coast. Claudia Springs makes excellent Viognier and Zinfandel. The Boonville General Store (895.9477) is next door in case you want to nibble on some bread and cheese while you are tasting. ◆ Daily. 17810 Farrer La (on Hwy 128). 895.3993

14 LAUREN'S

★★$$ A host of fans crowd this funky, local hangout where chef-owner Lauren Keating's inventive menu offers something for every taste—pasta, Caribbean curry, chicken potpie, and a first-rate burger, to name a few dishes. Desserts change, but apple dumpling, fresh gingerbread, and cheesecake are frequently on the menu. If the tables are filled, you can eat at the bar. Some nights, the restaurant features musical events; on occasion, dinner theater; and often, after-dinner dancing. Families like it here too. ◆ American ◆ Dinner, Tu-Sa. 14211 Hwy 128 (just north of Ukiah Boonville Rd). 895.3869

14 BUCKHORN SALOON/ ANDERSON VALLEY BREWING COMPANY

★$ Pub grub with a California flair is served at this funky saloon and local hangout. Forget about wine here and order one of the eight kinds of beer and ale on tap, all brewed down the road at the brewing company. If you want to see how the company makes stout, ale, or porter, staff members give a brief tour in the late afternoon on request (providing someone is available to take you to the brewing company). ◆ California/pub ◆ Daily, lunch and dinner, Memorial Day weekend to Thanksgiving; M, Tu, Th-Su, Dec-Jan; M, Th-Su, mid-February–Memorial Day weekend; closed the first 2 weeks of February. 14081 Hwy 128 (north of Ukiah Boonville Rd). 895.3369; brewery, 895.2337

14 HORN OF ZEESE COFFEE SHOP

★★$ "Horn of zeese?" you might ask. That means "a cup of coffee" in the local Boonville lingo. And this is the place to get that quick caffeine fix. Eggs, biscuits and gravy, homemade soups, burgers, and sandwiches are served. Chicken potpie, vegetable lasagna, and barbecued baby-back pork ribs are among the choices for dinner. Note the sign over the booth outside: "buckey walter" (otherwise known as a phone booth). ♦ Diner ♦ Daily, breakfast and lunch; Th-Su, dinner. 14025 Hwy 128 (north of Ukiah Boonville Rd). 895.3525

14 BOONT BERRY FARM

Stop here for picnic fare (sandwiches, cold cuts, vegetarian dishes, etc.) and fresh baked goods, along with berries and other produce. ♦ Daily. 13981 Hwy 128 (north of Ukiah Boonville Rd). 895.3576

THE BOONVILLE HOTEL

15 BOONVILLE HOTEL

$$ The eight simple but wonderfully stylish guest rooms upstairs at this historic hotel are a real surprise. Designed by owner John Schmitt, the décor is Shakerlike in its simplicity and thoughtfulness. The rooms are filled with beautifully crafted details, such as the marble star set into the bathroom tile, the handcrafted steel shower-curtain rods, and the natural-wood Venetian blinds. One room even has hand-blown water glasses. When Schmitt took over the hotel in 1987, the upstairs was virtually gutted. Instead of going to furniture showrooms, he sought out a handful of local artisans, proposing that each create a bedroom set. One room has a geometric blond-wood and ebony bed and matching armoire. Another features a whimsical four-poster metal bed made by local artist Steven Derwinski, satiny wooden floors, and an extra-large oval tub. The most spacious are the two suites with tall French doors opening onto a broad, second-floor balcony. The smaller but equally comfortable room no. 4 gets the morning sun and has a queen-size bed and a shower. Additionally, the property's former workshop in the garden has been converted into two light and airy guest rooms, each with a porch; one is

Beer is mentioned in the Talmud, and some of the rabbinical scholars who assembled its ancient books were brewers. The six-pointed Star of David frequently appears on ancient engravings of breweries as a sign for alchemy.

equipped to be suitable for disabled persons. A buffet continental breakfast (freshly squeezed juices, fruit, and warm, crumbly scones served with sweet country butter and homemade jams) is served in the hotel's sunny dining room. Eat it there or take it onto the patio beside the garden. ♦ Closed the first 2 weeks in January. 14050 Hwy 128 (south of Mountain View Rd). 895.2210. www.boonville.com

At the Boonville Hotel:

BOONVILLE HOTEL RESTAURANT & BAR

★★$$$ John Schmitt learned to cook in his parents' popular Yountville restaurant, **The French Laundry** (which they have since sold). Here Schmitt focuses on the vibrant flavors of Southwestern cooking with a little Italian and American regional tastes thrown in for good measure. The restaurant is eminently cheerful and fun to boot. The dinner menu changes frequently—tasty beginnings include homemade soup, a small pizza (for two) topped with glazed onions, goat cheese, wilted spinach, and rosemary, or the kitchen's great Caesar salad. Grilled entrées, such as fresh ahi tuna with cilantro pesto on jasmine rice or rib-eye steak served on wilted greens with fresh horseradish cream, are excellent here. And desserts by Greg Barnes are equally appealing: Try the cappuccino or orange-ginger crème brûlée or the lemon curd tart with berry sauce. If you want to match wines to courses but don't want full bottles, there are fine by-the-glass selections to choose from. The wine-and-beer bar is lively in the evenings. Good music, terrific espresso, and a friendly staff make this local hangout the highlight of the Anderson Valley. ♦ Continental ♦ M, W-Su, dinner; W-Su, lunch. Closed the first 2 weeks of January. Reservations recommended

15 FAULKNER COUNTY PARK

🅿 This 40-acre park off twisting Mountain View Road offers a quarter-mile-long nature trail through wild azaleas and redwood groves, plus several picnic areas, a few with barbecue pits. ♦ Day-use only. Mountain View Rd (west of Rte 128). 463.4267

16 ROOKIE-TO GALLERY

This gallery, named after the Boontling term for quail, features pottery, jewelry, textiles, and sculpture—primarily the work of local craftspeople. ♦ Daily, June-Dec; M, W-Su, Jan-May. 14300 Hwy 128 (south of Mountain View Rd). 895.2204

YORKVILLE

Nestled in a peaceful landscape halfway between Cloverdale and Boonville on Route 128 is tiny Yorkville. Settled some 130 years ago by the York family from England, it is today a rural community of 25 people, with two visitor-friendly wineries and vineyards and the bonus of lovely views.

17 MAPLE CREEK VINEYARDS

You can taste estate-bottled wines including prizewinners Flora and Chardonnay, and a fine Merlot and Cabernet Sauvignon. The vineyard also produces a lovely Zinfandel from 80-year-old vines from Ukiah. Visitors can schmooze with the staff in the winery's cheerful garden tasting room, where the wines are sold. ◆ Tasting and sales daily. 20799 Hwy 128 (at Mile Marker 36.1). 895.3001

18 YORKVILLE CELLARS

Deborah and Edward Wallo started with a small vineyard in 1987; a decade later, their estate had grown to 30 acres, planted in Bordeaux-style grapes. Small lots of prize-winning Merlots and Sauvignon Blancs are the result. Winemaker Greg Graziano also turns out unique Meritages, like the classic Graves-style, Bordeaux-blend Eleanor of Aquitaine, made from Sauvignon Blanc and Sémillon grapes. The entrance drive through the vineyard is lined with Red Simplicity rosebushes. ◆ Tasting and sales daily. 25701 Hwy 128 (at Mile Marker 40.4). 894.9177

Restaurants/Clubs: Red | Hotels: Purple | Shops: Orange | Outdoors/Parks: Green | Sights/Culture: Blue

LAKE COUNTY

Due north of Napa County and east of Mendocino County, Lake County is dominated by **Clear Lake**, California's largest natural lake and the county's main tourist attraction. With no big cities and only a sprinkling of towns, most on the shores of the lake, this region offers the great outdoors in a wine-country setting. The feeling around here is small-town and rural, comfortable and unpretentious. Asking a question will spark a conversation—on wine, weather, or the state of the country. Even

more refreshing, you won't find busloads of tourists crowding you at the tasting bar or fanatical connoisseurs bent on putting yet another notch in their wine-tasting belts.

Dormant 4,200-foot Mount Konocti, which formed slowly in several eruptions from 100,000 to 10,000 years ago, looms above Clear Lake and its 100-mile shoreline. Clear Lake may be the oldest lake in North America, as scientific evidence has proven the lake to be at least 150,000 years old.

By 6,000 B.C., Clear Lake had become home to several immigrating groups of early Native Americans. The Pomo Indians hunted, fished, and collected plants on the shores of Clear Lake. The lake yielded an abundance of fish, as well as tule reeds from which they made clothing, boats, dwellings, and household items.

Tourism still centers around Clear Lake, where canoes, sailboats, fishing boats, speedboats, pontoon boats, and even oarless boats take advantage of this beautiful lake. It holds more fish per acre than any other US lake and is stocked with bass, trout, bluegill, and catfish. Winter bald eagles and Canadian geese spend the winter (from Alaska and Canada) at Anderson Marsh and Boggs Lake Preserve.

Surrounding the lake is rural countryside and an agricultural region devoted to growing Bartlett pears, walnuts, and grapes. Lake County's four wineries have earned more awards per acre than any other per-acre area in the world.

But there's plenty to do besides winery hopping. Winery visits in Lake County could fit easily into a day of golfing, boating, or hiking among the redwoods. Summer and early fall events in Lakeport include the **May Winemaker Dinners**, the **Lake County Rodeo** in July, and **Lake County Fair and Horse Show** on Labor Day weekend—all three at the fairgrounds. In nearby Kelseyville, famous for Bartlett pears, the annual Pear Festival takes place the last weekend in September. **Anderson Marsh**, a large wetlands nature preserve on the southernmost tip of Clear Lake, which is particularly rich in Indian history and wildlife habitats, is the site of the **Blackberry Festival** each August. And Clear Lake's great fishing (lots of bass, catfish, crappie, and bluegill) is one of the county's biggest draws. So catch those fish and pop that cork—this could be the life.

Though there are only a handful of wineries now, this is not a new region for

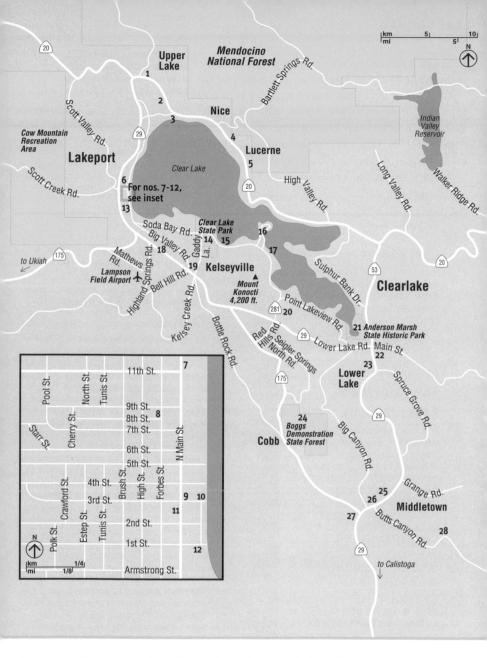

viniculture. Grapes were planted as early as the 1870s in Lake County, and just after the turn of the century, when people flocked to the lakeside resorts, the county boasted 36 wineries. Then, just like today in Napa Valley and Sonoma Valley, the rich and famous became involved in wine-making. The celebrated British actress Lillie Langtry bought an estate in **Guenoc Valley** in the 1880s and brought a winemaker over from Bordeaux to make her wines. Before things really got going, though, Prohibition closed the wineries, and farmers had to turn to other crops.

It's been only a few decades since the vineyards were replanted with grapevines, but in that short time, Lake County has reestablished itself as an up-and-coming wine region. Wine production has increased dramatically, with several new wineries and 150 vineyards. More than 60 wineries carry the Lake County appellation—especially the full-bodied Sauvignon Blanc, the county's signature grape. Its wines have been served at the White House and overseas on presidential trips.

One way to visit Lake County wineries is to make a day trip, starting from **Guenoc Winery** in Middletown and following the lake to Kelseyville and Lakeport. If you decide to stay overnight to take in the sights, resorts along the shores of Clear Lake offer a wide variety of lodgings, from the luxurious **Konocti Harbor Resort and Spa** to several moderate and inexpensive family resorts.

For information, call 1-800-LAKESIDE (525.3743) or go online at www .lakecounty.com.

1 UPPER LAKE

Upper Lake, whose Main Street was once a stagecoach road, is one of Lake County's oldest settlements. It still retains its Early American charm and makes an ideal stop for antiquing or just browsing. At the northern tip of Clear Lake, it is the gateway to Mendocino National Forest and Snow Mountain Wilderness.

Within Upper Lake:

FIRST AND MAIN ANTIQUES MALL

Take a peek at the eclectic collections displayed here by seven antiques dealers. There's an abundance of books, toys, Indian and cowboy photos, advertising art, and other memorabilia in a wide range of prices. **Gracious Ladies** sells handcrafted gifts created by local artisans. You'll find gourd and horseshoe art, pottery, jewelry, afghans, quilts, and children's items. ♦ Daily. 9495 Main St (at First St). 275.3124

2 ROBINSON RANCHERIA BINGO & CASINO

This 1950s-themed, Pomo-owned facility offers high-stakes gambling, 600 slot machines, the **Rancheria Grille**, a sports bar, a 48-room hotel, and a conference center. A concession stand serves sandwiches and light snacks. ♦ Daily, 24 hours. 1545 E Hwy 20 (between Nice–Lucerne Cutoff and Rte 29), Nice. 275.9000, 800/809.3636; fax 275.9100

Within the casino:

RED ROSE

You'll find a winning collection of Pomo arts and crafts in this minuscule store. Check out

In ancient Egypt, laborers were paid with jugs of beer.

the wonderful gourds made into vases. ♦ W-Sa, 11AM-7PM, or by appointment. 275.2963

3 FEATHERBED RAILROAD COMPANY

$$ In a parklike setting overlooking Clear Lake, Len and Lorraine Bassignani have converted nine vintage red cabooses into a luxuriously appointed bed-and-breakfast inn. Each caboose has a unique décor. **Lover's** has a romantic, lace-trimmed canopy bed; the **Easy Rider Room** is for Harley enthusiasts; and **Mint Julep** is decorated with white wicker furniture. All nine have feather beds and big bathrooms (six with Jacuzzis), heating and air conditioning, TVs, VCRs, and mini refrigerators. A full breakfast is served on the veranda of the 100-year-old ranch house; or, if guests prefer, breakfast trays are brought to their caboose. There's also a swimming pool and spa. ♦ 2870 Lakeshore Blvd (between Rte 20 and Nice–Lucerne Cutoff), Nice. 274.8378, 800/966.6322. www.featherbedrailroad.com

4 CEÀGO DEL LAGO

Jim Fetzer invested $10 million to build a pristine lakefront winery and farm that will someday be the state's first biodynamic resort. Already the 220 acres have been transformed. Much like an early California hacienda, the farm, winery, and other buildings face a walled courtyard. Fetzer has planted an organic garden and brought in sheep and chickens. He planted his first biodynamic organic garden at his family's Mendocino County winery estate, where he began making wine at age 16. His vineyards roll down to the shore, planted with Cabernet Sauvignon, Sauvignon Blanc, Merlot, and Syrah. Until the first release, the tasting room staff pours the Ceàgo Del Lago wines from Mendocino County. The winery is between Nice and Lucerne on the northeastern shore of Clear Lake. ♦ Daily, tasting and sales. Tours by appointment only. 5115 E Hwy 20, Nice. 274.1462. & www.ceago.com

5 LAKE COUNTY VISITORS' INFORMATION CENTER

The dynamic, interested staff has the lowdown on everything about Clear Lake and its surroundings. The center also has a great view of the lake from the parking lot. ◆ Daily. 6110 E Hwy 20, Lucerne. 274.5652; 800/525.3743. www.lakecounty.com

6 THE ARBOR HOUSE

$ This 1900 Victorian farmhouse features oak paneling in the main rooms. Each of the five guest bedrooms has a private bath, whirlpool tub, TV, refrigerator, and covered porch for private access. The **Courtyard Suite** features a fireplace, double spa tub, and wet bar. **Vintage** is furnished with antiques, and **Arbor** has rose-bordered walls and a king-size bed. A full breakfast is served either in the dining room or outdoors. Afternoon refreshments always include a glass of Lake County wine. There's a garden and a small pool. ◆ 150 Clear Lake Ave (between N Main and N Forbes Sts), Lakeport. 263.6444

7 SKYLARK MOTEL

$ Reserve early for this moderately priced lakefront motel with 45 comfortable, conventionally decorated units. Accommodations include poolside rooms, housekeeping cottages with one or two bedrooms (rented by the day, week, or month), and fancier suites (some with kitchens) in a one-story building with lake views and patios. It also has a boat-launching ramp and dock. ◆ 1120 N Main St (just south of Clear Lake Ave), Lakeport. 263.6151. www.skylarkshores.com

8 FORBESTOWN INN

$$ Just a block from the lake, this bed-and-breakfast dates from 1863, when Lakeport was still called Forbestown (in honor of early settler William Forbes). Furnished with oak antiques, the inn has just four guest rooms, and all but one share a bath. The largest is the **Bartlett Suite**, with a king-size bed and a private sitting area. The **Sayre Room** features a queen-size bed and a private bath; like the **Henry McGee Room**, it adjoins the library. The **Carriage House** has a king-size bed, dressing room, living room, and direct access to the hot-tub deck. There's a

secluded garden with a large pool. Innkeepers Jack and Nancy Dunne offer a full country breakfast. They also serve afternoon tea with desserts, wine, and cheese. Bicycles are available for guests who want to ride into town or along the lakeshore. ◆ 825 Forbes St (between Eighth and Ninth Sts), Lakeport. 263.7858; fax 263.7878. www.forbestowninn.com

9 BICYCLE RACK

This full-service shop sells and repairs bicycles. The owner is Nina Alumbaugh. No tours are available, but you can pick up road maps and off-road trail maps as well as information on the popular "Pedal the Puddle," a 100-mile annual bike race. ◆ M-Sa. 302 N Main St (at Third St), Lakeport. 263.1200

10 PARK PLACE

★★$ Partners Nancy Zabel and Barbara Morris had just the right idea when they put together this popular café. A garden at a friend's farm supplies the vegetables and herbs—all picked fresh every morning. The soups are prepared with homemade stocks; they also make their own pasta and top it with housemade sauces. There's always steak and fresh fish. For dessert, try carrot or chocolate cake. The café's lunch menu is mainly light fare—soups, salads, sandwiches, and pastas. The iced tea is fresh-brewed. Eat inside at a booth or take your food out onto the deck and enjoy the view of the lake. ◆ American ◆ Daily, lunch and dinner. 50 Third St (east of N Main St), Lakeport. 263.0444; fax 263.4837

10 ON THE WATERFRONT

Rentals of Jet Skis, pedal boats, ski boats, water skis, patio boats (which accommodate up to 14 people), and fishing boats are available here. ◆ Daily. 60 Third St (east of N Main St), Lakeport. 263.6789; fax 263.6353

11 LAKE COUNTY MUSEUM

Housed in the **Old Courthouse**, a stately 1870 Georgian building that was the county seat until 1958, this museum has a wonderful collection of local Indian artifacts, including intricate Pomo baskets, arrowheads, tools, and polychrome baskets adorned with feathers. Historical photos provide a glimpse of how the lake and town looked in the days of steamships and old spas. Upstairs the displays change and may include collections of old clocks, gems, and musical instruments. The museum also houses a research library and a genealogy library. ◆ Donation requested. W-Sa. 255 N

Restaurants/Clubs: Red | Hotels: Purple | Shops: Orange | Outdoors/Parks: Green | Sights/Culture: Blue

Main St (between Second and Third Sts), Lakeport. 263.4555

12 TNT's on the Lake

★$ The menu at this popular Mexican eatery is familiar enough—tacos, tostadas, enchiladas, guacamole dip, and a range of interesting burritos. The décor also has a south-of-the-border flavor—with tiny sombreros dotting the walls of the airy lakeside restaurant. Sitting outdoors on the deck sipping a margarita and nibbling TNT's assorted appetizers is especially pleasant at sundown. ◆ Mexican ◆ Daily, lunch and dinner. 1 First St (east of N Main St), Lakeport. 263.4TNT

13 Lakeport Chamber of Commerce

Staff members at this office will provide you with information on Lakeport and Lake County lodging, restaurants, activities, and events. ◆ M-F. 875 Lakeport Blvd (east of Hwy 29), Lakeport. 263.5092. www.lakeportchamber.com

14 Clear Lake State Park

Each year thousands of people visit this spectacular park at Soda Bay on the southwest shores of beautiful Clear Lake, the largest natural lake in California. The park covers a diverse terrain, from 1,400-foot elevations all the way down to lake level. There are four developed campgrounds, plus numerous picnic sites and several miles of hiking trails. The 3-mile **Dorn Trail**, rated moderately strenuous, winds through forests of oak and chapparal to emerge now and then in fields of wildflowers; the easy quarter-mile, self-guided **Indian Nature Trail** is designed to show visitors a sample of the local tribes' in-depth knowledge of native plants. The picnic area along the east side of Cole Creek has tables and barbecues, and, if you're lucky, you might catch a crappie, catfish, or largemouth bass to cook for lunch. Indigenous fish include blackfish, Sacramento perch, and tule perch. The park also has a fine swimming beach and a boat launch. Stop at the visitors' center (west of the boat-ramp parking lot) for more detailed information about lake resources and activities. A large aquarium will introduce you to some of the fish that live in Clear Lake. ◆ Fee per vehicle. 5300 Soda Bay Rd (east of Gaddy La), Kelseyville. 279.4293

Within Clear Lake State Park:

Campgrounds

These four developed campgrounds—**Cole Creek**, **Kelsey Creek**, **Lakeside Premium**, and **Lower and Upper Bayview**—have a total of 147 sites, most of which accommodate RVs as well as tents, plus two sites set aside

in one of the campgrounds for campers who arrive on foot or bicycle. **Kelsey Creek Campground** has two sites for people with disabilities. Be aware that campsites are popular and should be reserved 8 weeks in advance. Drinking water is available throughout all four campgrounds, and all but one have rest rooms with hot showers. ◆ For more information, contact Clear Lake State Park, 5300 Soda Bay Road, Kelsyville, CA 95451. 279.4293; reservations 800/444.7275

15 Clear Lake Queen

★★$$ Roberta and Harvey Weller's Mississippi-style paddle steamer, the elegant *Clear Lake Queen*, has a gingerbread-trimmed railing and plushy interiors. Three stories high, the boat holds 150 passengers and offers delightful dining for 96 on two decks—with a lake view from every table. Freshly prepared meals from the boat's galley are paired with Lake County wines. On the dinner cruise, entrées include prime rib, poached salmon, or chicken cordon bleu, all served with soup and salad. Pear Melba (pear topped with ice cream and raspberry sauce) is served for dessert. The lunch menu changes but often includes shaved beef on a French roll or grilled hamburger melt (melted cheese) with potato salad. If you'd like to cruise without dining, you may do so on the observation deck or at the bar overlooking the paddle wheel. There is a dinner dance once a month. The boat also may be rented for private parties. ◆ American ◆ W-Su, lunch and dinner, Apr-Dec. Departures: 11AM for lunch cruise; 6PM for dinner cruise. Boarding begins a half hour before departure. 6190 Soda Bay Rd (east of Gaddy La), Kelseyville. 994.5432. www.paddlewheel.com

16 Buckingham Golf and Country Club

This nine-hole golf course sits at the foot of the inactive volcano Mount Konocti. The golf course and clubhouse restaurant (see below) are open to the public. ◆ Daily. 2855 E Lake Dr (north of Crystal Dr), Kelseyville. 279.4863

Within the Buckingham Golf and Country Club:

The Tee Room Restaurant

★★★$$$ In this rather nondescript room, Lauretta Bonfiglio's food is anything but. The former chef-owner of the famous Lauretta's Mexican Kitchen in Aspen offers her own interesting variations on familiar Mexican and American dishes. Among the enticing appetizers are quesadillas with rock shrimp or traditional Chesapeake Bay–style crab cakes. Main courses might feature sautéed prawns or herb-rubbed rack of lamb. If you can't make up your mind about the pairing of food and wine, Lauretta offers excellent advice. For dessert, either berry cobbler with vanilla ice cream on flan is fine. ♦ Mexican/American ♦ Dinner, W-Su, May-Sept, and Th-Su, Oct-Apr. Reservations recommended. 279.1140

17 KONOCTI HARBOR RESORT & SPA

$$$ The fanciest place to stay in these parts is at the 252-room resort at the foot of Mount Konocti on the shores of Clear Lake. All the rooms, suites, apartments, and cottages come equipped with phones, cable TV, and air conditioning. Deluxe apartments feature king-size beds (or two double beds), a sofa bed in the living room, a kitchen, and a large balcony; every four units share a barbecue. The most secluded accommodations are the **Haven Apartments**, which are one-bedroom cabins with living room and a full kitchen. The **Lakeside Cottages**, set on a large lawn that leads down to the lake, are the most popular. The staff will arrange for fishing, boating, waterskiing, and other sports, or even services at the multimillion-dollar **Dancing Springs Health and Fitness Spa** (see opposite). The tennis complex (with eight regulation courts) overlooks the lake; two championship swimming pools ensure that it's never too crowded to swim. The resort also has two wading pools and a playground for children, a recreation center with a pool table and video games for teenagers, and miniature golf. There's a fully equipped marina with boat, pontoon, and Jet Ski rentals, 100 boat slips, launch ramp and hoist, dockside fuel, and the **Ski 'n Sport Shop**. Though there are no golf courses on the complex, the nine-hole **Buckingham** and the nine-hole **Clear Lake Riviera** are close by. Guests can easily get to the **Konocti Vista Casino** via the 24-hour complimentary shuttle. The resort sponsors concerts year-round (featuring headliners in everything from country music to classic rock and comedy) in a 1,000-seat indoor hall and 4,000-seat outdoor amphitheater (see opposite) and offers special room rates for concertgoers. It also hosts the rollicking **Lake County Summer Festival** 10 days prior to the end of summer featuring concerts, boat races, a celebrity golf tournament, wine tastings, and a fireworks finale. Every Sunday year-round,

an impressive champagne brunch buffet is offered between 10AM and 2PM in either the **Classic Concert Showroom** or the **Full Moon Cafe**. Reservations are a must. ♦ 8727 Soda Bay Rd (between Point Lakeview Rd and Crystal Dr), Kelseyville. 279.4281, 800/862.4930; fax 279.8575

At Konocti Harbor Resort:

DANCING SPRINGS HEALTH AND FITNESS SPA

This spa offers a number of half- and full-day packages at relatively affordable prices. You can sign up for massages, facials, or even an herbal body wrap, or just head straight for the steam room, sauna, and whirlpool. Day-use privileges include exercise classes, workouts in the fitness room, and use of the lap pool (a small fee is charged both for hotel guests and outsiders). You can also get your hair done and your legs waxed, and for true hedonists, the spa offers an almond-mint body scrub and a special honey-mango or seaweed bubble bath.♦ Daily. Reservations recommended for massages, facials, and spa packages

CLASSIC ROCK CAFÉ

★★$$$ The menu at this trendy café reads a lot like *The Hit Parade*. All of the offerings are for famous rock, pop, and country tunes. Order the Abbey Road Club at lunch and the waitperson will bring a croissant club sandwich with turkey, bacon, lettuce, and tomato; Whole Lot of Love will get you a ticket to the all-you-can-eat soup and salad bar. If you'd prefer the fettuccine Alfredo, ask for Thriller. Dinner fare is a little more mellow—the rock lobster and steak combo is called Love the One You're With; grilled chicken breast with corn salsa, Love Me Tender; and chicken or beef fajitas, Try a Little Tenderness. All manner of rich desserts, shakes, and sundaes are offered. The ambiance and décor are strictly music memorabilia. The usual breakfast fare is served here too. If you feel like dancing the evening away, head for the **Full Moon Saloon** in the resort's lounge area. ♦ American ♦ Daily, breakfast, lunch, and dinner

KONOCTI FIELD AMPHITHEATER AND CLASSIC CONCERT SHOWROOM

The resort boasts two state-of-the-art music halls: a 1,000-seat concert hall and an outdoor 4,000-seat amphitheater. Both theaters are considered top venues for headliner acts in everything from country to

---

Restaurants/Clubs: Red | Hotels: Purple | Shops: Orange | Outdoors/Parks: Green | Sights/Culture: Blue

classic rock and other top entertainers. Performers have included Ray Charles, Bill Cosby, Kenny Rogers, Tony Bennett, Chicago, Doobie Brothers, Willie Nelson, and a number of classic rhythm-and-blues groups. Dinner and brunch shows are offered indoors, buffets in the amphitheater. ♦ Indoors: year-round; outdoors: Apr-Nov. Reservations required

18 STEELE WINERY

The focus at this winery—set in an old walnut orchard a little north of Kelseyville—is strictly on the stylish wines of owner Jed Steele, one of the most respected vintners in these parts. Steele and his wife, Marie, bought the property (formerly **Konocti Winery**) in 1996. A winemaker at **Kendall Jackson** between 1982 and 1989, Steele is well known for creating distinctive wines for a number of top wineries, as well as for his own labels—Steele and Shooting Star. Here Steele concentrates on Chardonnay, Pinot Noir, and Zinfandel, but he also turns out small lots of well-made Sauvignon Blanc, Cabernet Franc, and Merlot, and plans to release Lake County's first Syrah. There's a large lawn and shaded picnic area, and a small demonstration vineyard. The winery stages a Harvest Festival the second weekend of October with grape stomping, wine tasting, food, crafts, and music. There's also a farmers' market on the winery grounds every Saturday morning from 8AM to noon. May through October. ♦ Tasting and sales: daily Memorial Day–last Sa in Oct; otherwise, by appointment. Rte 29 and Thomas Dr, Kelseyville. 279.9475; fax 279.9633

19 WILDHURST VINEYARDS

This historic structure, built in 1926 as an Odd Fellows Hall, retains its original character while serving as a sleek showcase for winemaker Marc Burch's carefully crafted Wildhurst wines. His was the only Lake County wine to make the *San Francisco Chronicle*'s Top 100 wines for 2004. The majority are made from grapes grown in Myron Holdenried's vineyard on a "hurst," or wooded hillside, overlooking Konocti Bay and crushed there. Wines include Sauvignon Blanc, Chardonnay, Reserve Chardonnay, Reserve Fumé Blanc, and Reserve Cabernet Sauvignon. The friendly and helpful tasting room staff is a plus for visitors. Call for winter hours. ♦ Daily. 3855 Main St (between First and Second Sts), Kelseyville. 279.4302; fax 279.4875

19 QUILTED TREASURES

This shop carries quilting supplies and offers quilting lessons as well. Fabric, books on quilting, sewing patterns, and other quilting paraphernalia are sold up front and classes in machine or hand quilting take place in the back of the store. Occasionally quilts and other quilted objects are for sale. ♦ M-Sa. 3925 Main St (between Second and Third Sts), Kelseyville. 279.0324; fax 279.4430

20 CLEAR LAKE RIVIERA GOLF COURSE

🅟 This is another nine-hole golf course at the base of Mount Konocti. It's also open to the public, and there's a pro shop and a restaurant here that serves dinner Thursday through Saturday; there's also a Sunday brunch. ♦ Daily. 10200 Fairway Dr (between Point Lakeview and Soda Bay Rds), Kelseyville. 277.7129

21 ANDERSON MARSH STATE HISTORIC PARK

🅟 A state park since 1983, this site is rich in Indian artifacts and wildlife. It was inhabited by Native Americans for more than 10,000 years. Located at the southern end of Clear Lake, the park includes more than 50% of the lake's remaining wetlands. A paradise for bird watchers, the marsh counts numerous American bald eagles among its feathered residents. More than 151 species of birds have been identified in the park, including herons, marsh wrens, mallard ducks, and great egrets. The best way to observe the marsh's wildlife is by boat, which you can rent nearby (call **Garner's Resort**, 994.6267, or **Shaw's Shady Acres**, 994.2236). You can also hike through the 170-acre **McVicar Preserve**, which is run by the **Redbud Audubon Society**. The Audubon Society hosts a nature walk on the first Saturday of every month at 9AM, but you can take the hike on your own and finish at the picnic tables at the end of the trail. ♦ Official schedule is W-Su, 10AM-5PM, year-round, but park is accessible all week. During off hours, park alongside the entrance road and walk in. Rte 53 (between Lower Lake Rd and Old Hwy 53), Clearlake. 994.0688, 800/525.3743. www.redbudaudubon.org

22 LOWER LAKE HISTORICAL SCHOOLHOUSE & MUSEUM

This Lake County museum opened in 1994 in the restored Lower Lake Grammar School, which was built in 1877 and is now a state historic site. Inside are a reconstructed classroom from the late 1800s to early 1900s, an extensive geological display donated by the Homestake Mining Company, a scale model of the dam on Cache Creek, and collections of memorabilia and other items from pioneer families. ♦ W-Sa. 16435 Main St (east of Rte 29), Lower Lake. 995.3565

LEARNING ABOUT THE NATIVE AMERICANS OF LAKE COUNTY

The earliest residents of Lake County were the Pomo Indians, a collective designation for some 70 different Northern California tribes speaking a total of seven different languages (of which only three now survive). What are now the four counties of the wine country were the Indians' winter home; they summered on the coast, especially around Bodega Bay, gathering clams, fishing, and hunting seal. There, in the first half of the 19th century, began a long and unhappy history of interaction with Europeans. Today Native Americans make up only an estimated 2% of the Lake County population—yet their culture survives.

Many Pomo Indians now living in Lake County share their heritage at colorful public events held throughout the year. These festivals feature traditional ceremonial dances and tool-making and crafts demonstrations. Check with the **Lake County Visitors' Information Center** (263.9544, 800/525.3743) for a schedule.

To learn more about the Pomo and the area's other Native American groups, visit one of the following exhibits:

Anderson Marsh State Historic Park in **Clearlake** includes an Indian village with tule houses and a dance house. The park's **Annual Native American Day**, held in late spring, features Pomo dancers, crafts, and cooking. ◆ Rte 53 (between Lower Lake Rd and Old Hwy 53). 994.0688, 800/525.3743

Clear Lake State Park in **Kelseyville** has an interpretative diorama of an Indian village in the visitor center. The park also has a self-guided **Indian Nature Trail** where hikers may see some of the plants the local Native Americans used as food (also see page 220). ◆ 5300 Soda Bay Rd (east of Gaddy La). 279.4293

Lake County Museum in **Lakeport** has a series of interesting displays highlighting Pomo weavings, jewelry, weapons, and baskets (also see page 219). ◆ 255 N Main St (between Second and Third Sts). 263.4555

The best place to buy local Native American handicrafts is **Red Rose**, a tiny shop hidden away at the **Robinson Rancheria Bingo & Casino** in **Nice** (1545 E Hwy 20, between Nice–Lucerne Cutoff and Rte 29; 275.2963). It carries wonderful Pomo gourd vases, weaving, and baskets (see page 218).

With more than 100 miles of shoreline, Lake County's Clear Lake is the largest natural clear-water lake in California.

23 PLOYEZ WINERY

New owners of the old **Stuermer Winery**, Gerald and Shirley Ployez have put a sparkle in Lake County. Gerald was born in the Champagne region of France and produces the same highly regarded *méthode champenoise* Champagne for which three generations of the Ployez family are renowned in France. His Lake County winery produces Cabernet Sauvignon, Chardonnay, Gamay, Merlot, and Red Zinfandel. ◆ Tasting, sales, and tours daily. 11171 Hwy 29 (just north of Spruce Grove Rd), Lower Lake. 994.2106; fax 994.6514

24 BOGGS DEMONSTRATION STATE FOREST

The purpose of this park is to demonstrate forest-management practices; ask the forest manager for a tour if you're interested. Otherwise, just enjoy the groves of pine and fir trees on this ridgetop site on Boggs Mountain. The forest has miles of trails for hiking, horseback riding, and mountain biking. There are 14 primitive campsites (which are currently in poor condition) with tables and fire rings; you can park near the campsites. The campground is operated on a first-come, first-served basis. ◆ Rte 175 (between Bottle Rock and Loch Lomond Rds), Cobb. 928.4378

25 CRAZY CREEK GLIDERS AND SKYDIVERS

With its 4,200-foot grass airfield, the **Middletown Glider Port**, this is the place where you can soar with experienced glider pilots on a

Restaurants/Clubs: Red | Hotels: Purple | Shops: Orange | Outdoors/Parks: Green | Sights/Culture: Blue

ride high above the Mayacamas Mountains and Lake County landscape or take gliding lessons. The fleet of gliders include the DG-505. For those who own their own gliders, they'll tow your plane aloft. And for the particularly adventurous (or insane!), there's also the **Crazy Creek Skydiving School**. ♦ Daily. Rte 29 (between Grange Rd and Wardlaw St), Middletown. 987.9112; fax 987.2494. www.crazycreekgliders.com

26 BOAR'S BREATH RESTAURANT & BAR

★★$$ The historic stone building on Middletown's three-block-long main drag was waiting for good people to bring it back to life. Frank and Suzie Stephenson created a large, attractive dining room with flowers and white table linens, leaving the handsome stone walls exposed. They also put in a brick oven for Frank's thin-crust pizzas and gourmet toppings. His signature dish is grilled pork loin served with apple, pancetta, and dried-plum sauce. The California wine country menu also features oven-roasted chicken, salmon, and grilled New York steak. Don't miss the onion soup and house-made dessert. Reservations recommended. ♦ Californian ♦ Tu-Sa, dinner. 21148 Calistoga St (at Hwy 29), Middletown. 987.9491 ♿

27 MOUNT ST. HELENA BREWING COMPANY

★★$$ This is a welcome addition to Lake County for beer lovers—or wine tasters looking for a change of pace. Brewmaster

Greg Gabriel produces six ales at his 20-barrel brewhouse in downtown Middletown: Palisades Pale Ale, Honey Wheat, Brown Ale, Imperial Stout, and two seasonal ales, all available for tasting. It's a cheerful place with a full menu of pub grub plus an array of pizzas and more solid fare—steaks, chicken, fish, and pork. Nice deck too. ♦ American ♦ Daily. 21167 Calistoga St (between Douglas and Main Sts), Middletown. 987.2106

28 GUENOC VINEYARDS ESTATE AND WINERY

Six miles east of downtown Middletown lies this large estate, once owned by British actress Lillie Langtry, who bought the property in the 1880s as a country retreat. She thought she'd try her hand at running a vineyard and imported a winemaker from Bordeaux to help her, but Prohibition intervened before they could get the experiment off the ground. When the current owners, Bob and Orville Magoon, bought the 23,000-acre property in 1982, they decided to feature Lillie's portrait on their wine labels. There's a view of the vineyards and Langtry's Victorian house from the winery and tasting room. Winemaker Malcolm Siebly also produces Sauvignon Blanc, three Chardonnays, two Meritage reds, a Meritage white, and a Petite Sirah. ♦ Tasting, sales, and tours daily. 21000 Butts Canyon Rd (east of Rte 29), Middletown. 987.2385. www.guenoc.com

Within Guenoc Vineyards Estate and Winery:

LODGING AT GUENOC

$$ The hospitality of this vineyard estate is a rare pleasure. And Lillie Langtry's Victorian mansion offers a rare opportunity to sleep in the actress's upstairs bedroom. The mansion has two other rooms, and there are also rooms in the lodge. During hunting and fishing season, outdoors folks fill the four rustic rooms in the Fred Gebhard hunting lodge (named for Lillie's boyfriend). Ducks and wild boar are plentiful on the Magoons' 22,000-acre property and bass and bluegill fill the estate's nine lakes. Gamekeeper Jim Bolander takes care of the hunters and the winemaker hosts the evening gourmet dinner, pouring Guenoc's premium wines and enlivening the evening with stories. Orville, who is now retired, acquired the property in a land swap with the University of Hawaii: 10 acres for 23,000 acres!

The name for Mount Konocti, the huge mountain that towers over Clear Lake, comes from the Pomo Indian word *Knoktai—Kno* for "mountain" and *hatai* for "woman." The 4,200-foot volcanic peak first erupted 600,000 years ago, and recent scientific investigations say it last erupted a few thousand years ago.

HISTORY

Native American tribes lived in this fertile California paradise for thousands of years, thriving off the bounty of the land by hunting, fishing, and gathering. Many tribes shared the area, including the Miwok, Wappo, Pomo, Yuki, and Wintun.

1542   After repeated attempts by Spaniards Hernán Cortés and Viceroy Antonio de Mendoza to explore the coast north of Mexico, Juan Rodríguez Cabrillo first sights Alta (upper) California.

1579   Englishman Sir Francis Drake and his ship, the *Golden Hind*, find safe harbor at Drake's Bay near Point Reyes in Marin County.

1603   Mexican explorer Sebastián Vizcaíno sets off from Acapulco to explore the coast of Northern California and changes many of California's old Spanish place-names along the coast.

1775   Spanish explorer Juan Francisco de la Bodega y Cuadro discovers the bay that now bears his name (**Bodega Bay**, about 1.5 hours north of San Francisco).

1776   The **San Francisco Mission and Presidio** is founded.

1808   Russian fur traders explore Bodega Bay.

1811   The Russians build **Fort Ross** on the coast just north of the **Russian River** and hunt for sea otters.

1821   California becomes a far-flung province of independent Mexico.

1822   The Russians build the **Fort Ross Chapel** with hand-hewn redwood.

1823   The first recorded expedition into **Napa County** is made when Padre José Altimira scouts sites for his northernmost California missions. He selects **Sonoma** and founds **Mission San Francisco Solano de Sonoma**, bringing Mission grapes with him to plant in the fertile valley.

1834   General Mariano Guadalupe Vallejo secularizes the mission and establishes a presidio in Sonoma; 1 year later, he surveys the site of the Sonoma plaza.

1836   George C. Yount, a pioneer from North Carolina, receives the **Rancho Caymus** land grant: 12,000 acres in the heart of what is now **Napa Valley** and the town of **Yountville**.

1841   Cyrus Alexander is given a 120-acre land holding in the Russian River region that is eventually named after him (**Alexander Valley**).

1843   The impoverished English surgeon Edward Turner Bale marries General Vallejo's niece and receives the **Rancho Carne Humana** land grant, encompassing the whole northern Napa Valley.

1846   The Bear Flag Revolt in Sonoma. General Vallejo is imprisoned and an independent California Republic is proclaimed; 25 days later, the US steps in to halt the rebellion, and the American flag flies over Sonoma.

1847   While tracking bear, hunter William B. Hackett discovers geysers in the **Russian River Valley** and describes his find as "the gates of the inferno."

1848   Gold is discovered at Sutter's Mill in the foothills of the Sierra Nevada, heralding the Gold Rush.

1850   California gains its statehood.

1852   German immigrant William Kasten, lone survivor of a shipwreck off the Pacific coast, is washed ashore and builds a cabin in the area now known as **Mendocino**.

1857   After tasting General Vallejo's wines, Agoston Haraszthy realizes the potential of winemaking in the region and soon founds **Buena Vista**, California's oldest winery.

1857   Lieutenant Horatio Gates Gibson is ordered to establish a military post on the Mendocino Indian reservation; the site of that military post is now the city of **Ft. Bragg**.

1858   Millionaire Samuel Brannan purchases a tract of land in Napa Valley to establish a hot-springs resort and plant a vineyard. Ten years later he establishes the town of **Calistoga**.

1861   Governor Downey commissions

Agoston Haraszthy to go to Europe and bring back cuttings of European grape varieties. Haraszthy returns from his venture with 100,000 cuttings of 300 varieties.

1864   The first formal vintage celebration in California history is held at Agoston Haraszthy's Pompeian-style villa near Sonoma; the guests of honor are General and Mrs. Mariano Guadalupe Vallejo.

1869   The transcontinental railroad is completed and California wines are shipped to the Midwest and the East Coast.

1871   Prospector Charles Evans excavates the **Petrified Forest** near Calistoga and is thereafter known as "Petrified Charlie."

1874   A destructive root louse called phylloxera begins to attack Sonoma vineyards planted with European vines and eventually destroys much of California's vineyards before it is discovered that vines can be grafted onto native American rootstock resistant to the pest.

1876   Frederick Beringer establishes the **Beringer** winery in **St. Helena**.

1878   Luther Burbank moves from Massachusetts and begins his horticultural experiments in **Santa Rosa**.

1880   Robert Louis Stevenson and his bride, Fanny, spend their honeymoon in a deserted miner's cabin on the slopes of **Mount St. Helena**, an experience the author memorializes in his book *The Silverado Squatters*.

1888   British actress Lillie Langtry purchases an estate in the **Guenoc Valley** and hires a winemaker from Bordeaux to start a winery.

1895   Samuele Sebastiani arrives in the US from Tuscany and makes his first wine, a Zinfandel, a few years later.

1906   The Great San Francisco Earthquake hits; the epicenter is near Santa Rosa.

1909   Author Jack London settles permanently at his **Glen Ellen** estate, **Beauty Ranch**.

1919   National Prohibition is voted into law and hundreds of wineries close throughout California.

1933   Prohibition is repealed, but only a handful of wineries that produce sacramental wines or wines for medicinal uses are still in operation.

1935   The **University of California, Berkeley** Department of Viticulture and Enology, the leading research and training institute in winemaking and viticulture, moves to the **University of California, Davis**.

1937   The completion of the Golden Gate Bridge opens a new era of business and travel between San Francisco and the North Coast.

1938   André Tchelistcheff, wine consultant extraordinaire, arrives in California from Europe.

1943   Newspaperman Frank Bartholomew buys and reopens the old **Buena Vista Winery**, which had closed after the 1906 earthquake.

1950s   A handful of abandoned wineries are acquired, mostly by outsiders moving to the wine country from San Francisco.

1956   James D. Zellerbach, former owner of **Hanzell Vineyards** in Sonoma, decides to try aging his wines in *barriques* (French oak barrels from Burgundy), creating a trend among local vintners.

1964   Jack and Jamie Davies buy the **Schramsberg** winery near Calistoga.

1966   Robert Mondavi builds his winery in **Oakville**, ushering in a new wine-making era in Napa Valley.

1968   Americans now drink more dry table wine than dessert wine.

1975   The French Champagne house of **Moët-Chandon** builds its Napa Valley winery, **Domaine Chandon**.

1976   The famous Paris tasting, organized by Paris wine merchant Steven Spurrier, changes the world's preconceptions that California produces inferior wines; a blind tasting of Chardonnay and Cabernet Sauvignon is conducted with an expert panel of French tasters and results in top honors for two Napa Valley wines: the 1973 Château Montelena Chardonnay and the 1973 Stag's Leap Wine Cellars Cabernet Sauvignon.

1979   The first vintage of **Opus One** is launched. The brainchild of Robert Mondavi and Baron Philippe de Rothschild of **Mouton-Rothschild**, Opus One becomes the inspiration for a number of Bordeaux-style wines to come.

1980s   Foreign investment in the California wine country increases. Producers from Europe enter into joint ventures with American vintners or establish their own California-based wineries.

1991   Attempting to balance the state's budget, California legislators increase the excise tax on wine production from 1 to 20 cents per gallon (still lower than the US average of 70 cents). For the consumer, this equals about a 10-cent increase per bottle.

1995   One of the worst winter rainstorms of the century hits Napa, **Sonoma**, **Mendocino**, and **Lake Counties** in late March. The deluge of rain floods hundreds of acres of vineyards and pounds the delicate leaf buds on many grapevines. However, because the vines are not yet in bloom, the damage is not extensive.

1997   Sales of California table wine hit a new record—369 million gallons—with shipments to all markets, including overseas, up 8% over 1996.

1998   California bans smoking in bars. El Niño–related storms flood hundreds of acres of vineyards. However, vines escape damage because they were dormant at the time of the deluge.

2001   The long-awaited Copia: the American Center for Wine, Food and the Arts opens in November in Napa.

2002   The **Charles M. Schulz Museum** opens in Santa Rosa.

2004   Since its inception in 1981, the annual **Napa Valley Wine Auction** has raised more than $52 million, making it the world's most successful charity wine event.

WINE GLOSSARY

acidity: Refers to a wine's tartness. Acidity comes from a grape's natural acids and keeps wine from spoiling during the fermentation and aging processes.

aerate: To allow a wine to breathe (come in contact with air) by decanting. You can also aerate a wine by swirling it around in a glass, which releases aroma.

ageworthy: Describes a wine that has the potential to age. Not all wines are suited for aging. What determines ageworthiness is the varietal, the vintage, the style of vinification, and the balance of tannins, acids, and fruit in the wine.

aging cellar: Where wines in a cask or bottle are aged. Traditionally, the cellar or cave was underground or tunneled into a hillside, where a steady, cool temperature was naturally maintained. Today it can be any structure that is dark and has temperature control that's suitable for aging wine.

appellation: The geographic region a wine's grapes are grown in. For a wine to be classified by state, such as California, 100% of the grapes used for the wine must come from that state. For a county designation, such as Sonoma County, a minimum of 75% of the grapes must come from that area. And for a more specific American Viticultural Area (AVA) designation, such as Guenoc Valley or Anderson Valley, at least 85% is required.

aroma: The fragrance of a wine (it's redolent of the grape from which it was made). It can be sensed through smelling and tasting.

Balthazar: Holds the equivalent of 16 standard bottles of wine.

barrel fermented: When wine has been fermented in small oak barrels, instead of the usual stainless-steel tanks. The technique requires more wine-making skill but results in a wine with a more complex flavor.

barrique: The name for a type of wooden barrel used in the Bordeaux region of France. Made of oak, the small barrel holds 225 gallons of wine and is widely used by California winemakers, particularly for aging Chardonnay, Cabernet Sauvignon, Merlot, and Pinot Noir.

biodynamic farming: Viticulturists are experimenting with biodynamic techniques to improve fruit quality and strengthen the vines. They may replenish the soil by burying cow horns in the vineyards and spray the vines with homeopathic "teas" (silica, chamomile, oak bark, stinging nettle, valerian, and other herbs). Other methods include picking fruit at night.

Blanc de Blancs: White wine, particularly a sparkling wine, made from white grapes. The term originated in the Champagne region of France to distinguish more delicate Champagnes from those made with both white and red grapes.

Blanc de Noirs: White wine made from "black" or dark grapes (i.e., red grapes). In Champagne, France, where the term originated, it refers almost exclusively to Pinot Noir. The color of the grapes resides in the skins; if the juice is separated immediately from the skins, the juice will remain clear. In California, Blanc de Noirs also refers to so-called blush wines, such as White Zinfandel or White Cabernet, which are tinged with color.

blend: A wine created from several grape varietals (e.g., a Cabernet Sauvignon and Merlot blend or a Sémillon and Sauvignon Blanc blend). A wine can also be a blend of wines from different vintages.

blind tasting: When a group of wine "tasters" meets to compare a selection of wines. The participants know which wines are featured in the tasting, but they don't know in what order the wines are being poured into their glasses. In a **double-blind tasting**, the wines as well as the order of the pouring are unknown. In both situations, the wines are usually disguised in plain brown paper bags until their identities are revealed at the end. This is done so the tasters' ratings and comments will not be influenced by the label or by any previous knowledge of the wine producer.

blush wine: The term used in California to describe the pale rose-colored wines made from red grape varieties including Zinfandel, Cabernet Sauvignon, or Pinot Noir. (See **Blanc de Noirs**.)

body: The way a wine feels on your tongue. Body may range from thin and light to full and heavy. Heaviness results from a wine's solids (sugars, glycerine, and pigments).

Bordeaux-style: See **Meritage**.

botrytis or ***Botrytis cinerea:*** A beneficial mold known as noble rot (or, in French, ***pourriture noble***) that creates tiny pinpricks on the grapeskin. As the liquid content of the grape evaporates, the sugar content becomes increasingly concentrated, so much so that when the grapes are crushed and the wine is fermented, not all of the sugar is transformed into alcohol. A certain amount of residual sugar remains, creating a dessert wine, such as late-harvest Riesling.

bottle: The typical American wine bottle holds 750 milliliters.

bouquet: The fragrance or scent of a wine that develops from the aging process. It tastes and smells more pronounced in a bottle of mature wine.

Brut: This French term for very dry Champagne is widely used in classifying sparkling wines throughout the world. Champagnes range from sweet to very dry.

cask: A large wooden container, usually oak, built much like an oversize barrel with oval or round heads joined by curved staves. Casks are generally used to age or store wines. Sometimes the face of the barrel is ornately carved.

cave: The French word for "cellar." Also refers to the tunnels hollowed out of hillsides used as aging cellars.

cellar: Where wines are made, stored, and aged. It may also refer to the act of storing wine while it ages.

crush: The period immediately after the harvest when the grapes are shipped to the winery, crushed, and made into wine; it's also another term for the grape harvest itself.

current release: The most recent vintage on the market. For white wines it is usually the previous year, but for red it can be 2 or more years earlier, depending on how long a producer ages each wine before releasing it to the marketplace.

cuvée: A French term that denotes a particular lot or blend of wine. It can be wine from a special barrel, such as **Stag's Leap Wine Cellars'** famous Cask 23 Cabernet Sauvignon, or a special blend that has a higher proportion of grapes from an especially good vineyard or from a particular variety.

decanting: The process of pouring wine from the bottle into another container. This is necessary only if the wine has sediment on the bottom.

dessert wine: Sweet wines, such as a late-harvest Riesling or Gewürztraminer, that are served with dessert or as dessert.

double magnum (or Jeroboam)**:** Holds the equivalent of four standard bottles of wine.

dry wine: Wines that lack sweetness; generally those with less than 0.5% residual sugar.

enology: The art and science of wine production. This field covers every aspect of producing wine, from the harvest and pressing of the grapes to the fermentation, aging, and bottling of the wine. An enologist is professionally trained in this science.

estate wines: Wines made from grapes grown by or supervised by the winery estate instead of grapes bought by the estate on the open market. The idea is that if the winemaker has control over the quality of the grapes and all goes well, the quality of the wine should be consistent from year to year.

fermentation: The segment of wine production in which the sugar in grape juice is turned into alcohol by the enzymes in yeast.

fining: The process of clarifying wine by adding such ingredients as clay, raw egg whites, or gelatin. These products drag the wine's suspended particles to the bottom of the tank.

French oak: When a winery boasts that a particular wine has been aged in French oak, this refers to the barrels (or **barriques**) and the wood they are made from. Currently, a French oak barrel costs more than $600; the barrel imparts an oaky flavor to the wine for only a few years, so it can be quite an investment. After a few years have passed, the barrels are called neutral.

generic wines: These wines do not come from one specific grape variety. The wine's name, such as Chablis or Burgundy, reflects that it's a general type of wine. A generic wine is different from a **varietal** or **proprietary** wine.

horizontal tasting: A tasting in which all the wines come from the same year or vintage. Participants rank the wines and try to distinguish the characteristics of the wines of that particular year.

Imperial (or **Methusaleh**)**:** Holds the equivalent of eight standard bottles of wine.

jug wine: Inexpensive wines that are typically sold in jugs; they are of a lower quality than bottled wines. They are usually generic, but sometimes they may be a varietal wine.

late-harvest: Wines made from extremely ripe grapes and/or grapes affected with **Botrytis cinerea**.

lees: The sediment young wines develop in a barrel or tank as a result of fermentation or aging. When the wine is transferred to another container, or racked, which happens several times before it is bottled, the lees remain behind. Sometimes a wine is deliberately left "on the lees" for a period of time to develop a more complex flavor.

library wines: Wines that come from the winery's "library" of older vintages. These are sometimes offered for tasting, so that visitors can get a sense of how wines evolve as they age, and many are sold only at the winery.

magnum: A large bottle that holds the equivalent of two regular bottles of wine. Often preferred by connoisseurs because the wine ages more slowly in the larger bottle, resulting in the development of more complex flavors.

Meritage: The name used for Bordeaux-style blends of California wines in which the predominant grape is below the 75% minimum required to bear a varietal label, yet the quality of the wine is such that calling it mere "table wine" would be a disservice. To honor these top-notch blends of Cabernet Sauvignon, Merlot, Cabernet Franc, and other varieties for reds, or Sauvignon Blanc and Sémillon for whites, the term *Meritage,* combining the words *merit* and *heritage,* was coined. (The word was chosen in a national contest that attracted more than 6,000 participants and was won by Neil Edgar of Newark, California.)

méthode champenoise: The traditional method of making sparkling wine in the Champagne area of France in which a special cuvée (or blend) is bottled, and a precise amount of sugar and yeast is added to induce a second fermentation inside the bottle, thereby trapping the bubbles that are a by-product of the fermentation process.

microclimate: Refers to a vineyard's particular combination of soil, angle of exposure to the sun, slope, altitude, weather, temperature, and other factors, all of which influence the quality of the grapes.

Nebuchadnezzar: Holds the equivalent of 20 standard bottles of wine.

nonvintage: Describes a wine that bears no particular vintage date. For example, many Brut Champagnes or sparkling wines are nonvintage, because they are actually a blend of wines from more than one year. The fact that a wine has no vintage does not necessarily mean that it is of inferior quality.

nose: The scent of a wine as determined by smelling alone. This is different from *aroma* and *bouquet*, which can still be sensed after tasting.

old vines: Grapevines that are typically more than 50 years old and are prized for the quality of grapes they produce. Old vines are less vigorous and produce fewer grapes, but they have a more concentrated flavor.

phylloxera: The plant louse that ravaged the world's vineyards in the late 19th century. The pesky insect actually comes from America's East Coast (where the native grapevines were resistant to its attack) and was accidentally introduced to Europe in 1860 when it arrived in the roots of vine cuttings exported for experimental purposes. It was not until most of the vineyards of Europe and later Russia, South Africa, Australia, New Zealand, and California (where European varietals had been planted) had been destroyed that scientists came up with a solution: grafting European grape varieties onto disease-resistant American rootstock. This is still the practice today, although it doesn't completely eliminate the

problem. In the early 1990s, many California vineyards were faced with yet another phylloxera threat, forcing some Napa and Sonoma wineries to replant their vineyards.

press: The wine-making apparatus that recovers the juice after the grapes have been crushed and later recovers the wine after the fermented must (pulp, seeds, and skins) has been discarded.

prise de mousse: The French term describing the effervescence created in the sparkling wine bottle during the second fermentation. Also called "the birth of the champagne."

proprietary: A winery's exclusive right to the brand name created for its own use. Examples include Trefethen's **Eschol Red** and **Opus One**, created by the **Mouton-Rothschild** and **Robert Mondavi** collaboration.

rack: The process of clarifying wine by transferring it from one storage container to another.

Rehoboam: Holds the equivalent of six standard bottles of wine.

reserve or **private reserve:** This term has no legal definition in California and is often used to denote a producer's top-flight wines. A reserve may be a special blend or may come from a special vineyard; in some cases the term is used to designate wines that are aged longer than a regular bottling before release.

residual sugar: The grape sugar that is unfermented in a wine.

rootstock: The stem and root of a non–fruit-producing grapevine to which wine-grape varieties are grafted. Growers choose a rootstock according to its level of pest-resistance (see **phylloxera**) as well as other qualities that will benefit the grafted grapevine.

Salmanazar: Holds the equivalent of 12 standard bottles of wine.

second or **secondary label:** In addition to a premium line, many wineries produce a second line of wines under a different label. These may be less expensive wines or wines made in a different style.

single vineyard: Designates a wine made from grapes grown in one particular plot.

sparkling wine: A wine that has gone through a second fermentation, resulting in bubbles.

split (half bottle): Holds 375 milliliters (half the quantity of a standard wine bottle).

sweet wine: Wine that generally has at least 1% residual sugar. Sweetness becomes noticeable at about 0.5% residual sugar.

tannin: This compound is what makes your mouth pucker when tasting a red wine and is the cause of a wine's astringency. Tannins come from grape skins, seeds, and stems.

varietal: A wine called by the name of the specific grape used to make it, such as Cabernet Sauvignon or Chardonnay. In California, a varietal must include at least 75% of the named grape.

vertical tasting: Tasters compare different vintages from one estate to understand how the wines age and how consistently the estate performs under varying conditions.

vinification: The conversion of fruit juice into wine through the fermentation process.

vintage: The year the grapes were picked and the wine was produced. Champagne and sparkling wines are often nonvintage wines that is, they are made from a blend of wines from different years.

vintner: One who takes part in the process of making wine.

viticulture: The cultivation of grapes for wine production.

winemaker: See **vintner**.

INDEX

RESTAURANTS

Only restaurants with star ratings are listed below. All restaurants are listed alphabetically in the main (preceding) index. Always call in advance to ensure a restaurant has not closed, changed its hours, or booked its tables for a private party. The restaurant price ratings are based on the average cost of an entrée for one person, excluding tax and tip.

★★★★ An Extraordinary Experience
★★★ Excellent
★★ Very Good
★ Good

$$$$ Big Bucks ($28 and up)
$$$ Expensive ($15–$28)
$$ Reasonable ($10–$15)
$ The Price Is Right (less than $10)

★★★★

★★★

★★

★

HOTELS

The hotels listed below are grouped according to their price ratings; they are also listed in the main index. The hotel price ratings reflect the base price of a standard room for two people for one night during the peak season.

$$$$ Big Bucks ($300 and up)
$$$ Expensive ($200–$300)
$$ Reasonable ($100–$200)
$ The Price Is Right (less than $100)

$$$$

$$$

$$